AF598926

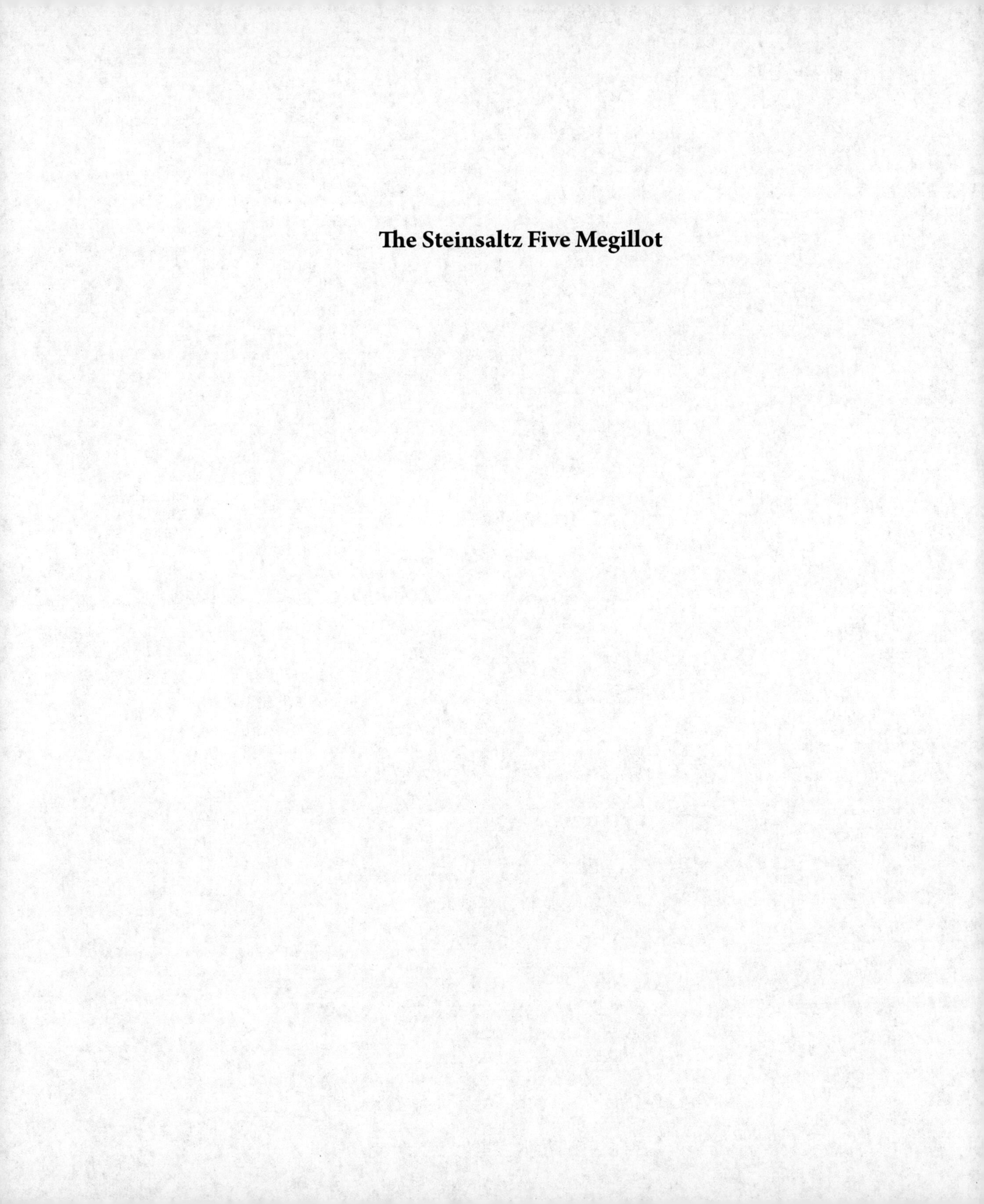

The Steinsaltz Five Megillot

The Steinsaltz Five Megillot

Megillot Translation and Commentary

Commentary by

Rabbi Adin Even-Israel Steinsaltz

Koren Publishers Jerusalem

The Steinsaltz Five Megillot

Commentary by
Rabbi Adin Even-Israel Steinsaltz
First Hebrew/English edition 2019

Koren Publishers Jerusalem Ltd.
POB 4044, Jerusalem 91040, ISRAEL
POB 8531, New Milford, CT 06776, USA

www.korenpub.com

Steinsaltz Center is the parent organization
of institutions established by Rabbi Adin Even-Israel Steinsaltz
POB 45187, Jerusalem 91450 ISRAEL
Telephone: +972 2 646 0900, Fax +972 2 624 9454
www.steinsaltz-center.org

ISBN 978-965-7760-41-3
Printed in PRC

Supported by the Matanel Foundation
Second printing, 2023

Executive Director, Steinsaltz Center
Rabbi Meni Even-Israel

Executive Editors
Rabbi Joshua Schreier
Rabbi Dr. Joshua Amaru

Editors
Rabbi Ayal Geffon, Senior Content Editor
Rabbi Yaakov Blinder, Senior Editor
Rabbi Yehoshua Duker, Senior Editor
Rabbi Avi Grossman, Senior Editor
Rabbi Yedidya Naveh, Senior Editor
Rabbi Michael Siev, Senior Editor
Rabbi Aryeh Sklar, Content Curator
Rabbi Alan Haber
Yisrael Kalker
Elisha Loewenstern
Rabbi Eli Ozarowski
Avi Steinhart
Rabbi David Strauss

Hebrew Edition Editors
Sara Friedland Ben Arza
Rabbi Yossi Ben Arza
Rabbi Meir Klein
Rabbi Daniel Eliav

Technical Staff
Tani Bednarsh
Adena Frazer
Shaltiel Shmidman

Editor in Chief
Rabbi Jason Rappoport

Copy Editors
Caryn Meltz, Manager
Aliza Israel, Consultant
Debbie Ismailoff, Senior Copy Editor
Ita Olesker, Senior Copy Editor
Chava Boylan
Suri Brand
Ilana Brown
Carolyn Budow Ben-David
Rachelle Emanuel
Charmaine Gruber
Deborah Meghnagi Bailey
Deena Nataf
Dvora Rhein
Elisheva Ruffer
Ilana Sobel

Maps Editors
Ilana Sobel, Map Curator
Rabbi Dr. Joshua Amaru, Senior Map Editor
Rabbi Alan Haber
Rabbi Aryeh Sklar

Language Experts
Dr. Stéphanie E. Binder, Greek & Latin
Rabbi Yaakov Hoffman, Arabic
Dr. Shai Secunda, Persian
Shira Shmidman, Aramaic

Design & Typesetting
Avishai Magence, Production Manager
Eliyahu Misgav, Art Director
Estie Dishon, Design & Typesetting
Bentzi Binder, Design

This volume
pays tribute to the memory of

Mr. Sami Rohr ז״ל

ר׳ שמואל ב״ר יהושע אליהו ז״ל

who served his Maker with joy,
and whose far-reaching vision, warm open hand, love of Torah,
and love for every Jew were catalysts for revival and growth of
vibrant Jewish life in the former Soviet Union
and in countless communities the world over,

and to the memory of his beloved wife

Mrs. Charlotte Rohr *(née Kastner)* ע״ה

שרה בת ר׳ יקותיאל יהודה ע״ה

who survived the flames of the Shoah to become
the elegant and gracious matriarch,
first in Colombia and later in the United States,
of three generations of a family
nurtured by her love and unstinting devotion.
She found grace in the eyes of all those whose lives she touched.

Together they merited to see all their children
build lives enriched by faithful commitment
to the spreading of Torah and *Ahavat Yisrael.*

Dedicated with love by

The Rohr Family

NEW YORK, USA

THE SONG OF SONGS

Dedicated in honor of
my beautiful wife,

Tatiana

whose wisdom, humor, warmth,

and love makes our family.

Michael G. Reiff

RUTH

פיה פתחה בחכמה ותורת חסד על לשונה.... קמו בניה ויאשרוה בעלה ויהללה. (משלי לא:כו–כח)

She opens her mouth with wisdom, and the Torah of kindness is on her tongue....
Her children arise and laud her; her husband, and he praises her. (Proverbs 31:26–28)

ישלם יהוה פעלך ותהי משכרתך שלמה מעם יהוה אלהי ישראל אשר ברת לחסות תחת כנפיו. (רות ב:יב)

May the Lord reward your conduct, and may your payment be complete from the Lord,
God of Israel, under whose wings you came to find refuge. (Ruth 2:12)

In loving memory of our wife, mother and grandmother,

Geneviève רות *Werthenschlag*

on the 30th anniversary of her passing.

She epitomized the Woman of Valor and
strengthened and comforted many
with her kindness and faith.

We, her family,
continue to sing her praise
and while we long for her every day,
we carry her example of *reut, tzedakah,*
ḥesed, and *ahavat yisrael* in our minds and deeds.

May her *neshama* have an *aliya*.

LAMENTATIONS

"Where are you?"

This question goes unanswered in Eicha.

Rabbi Steinsaltz,

your work challenges us to take up this question.
You have unlocked our texts so that we may seek the answer.
We are honored to join you in your sacred and restorative mission:
"Let My People Know"

Thank you for inspiring and educating us.

We dedicate this commentary
on the book of Kohelet
to our parents and grandparents
who believed in Jewish destiny
even in the darkest hours
of Soviet oppression.

Polina and Michael Liberman

ESTHER

דור לדור ישבח מעשיך

In honor of our grandchildren

Rena Ayelet, Tova Aliza, Ora Adina

Andrew Jeremy, Benjamin Zachary, Jonathan Meir

Aliza Ruth, Sophia Bella, Ayala Tamima, Samuel Issachar

Ella Orianna, Lily Claire, Ruby Jacqueline

Dedicated by

Monique and Mordecai Katz

Table of Contents

Introduction to The Steinsaltz Megillot

Scholars and lay readers alike are aware that writing a new commentary on the Bible requires assistance and blessings from Above, as well as substantial effort from below. Two fundamental challenges stand before one who seeks to write a commentary on the Bible: First, the aspiration to relate to the loftiest and holiest text and to explain it faithfully risks hubris. Second, a huge number of commentaries on the Bible have been composed over the course of the past three thousand years by the greatest people in our history. Who has the audacity to attempt to join this holy assembly or even grasp its coattails?

Sanction for undertaking this daunting task can be found in Rashi's statement to his grandson Rashbam, himself the author of an important commentary on the Torah. Rashbam reports Rashi to have said that if he had had the strength, he would have written another commentary in accordance with the "plain meanings that are renewed every day" (Rashbam, Genesis 37:2).

In every generation and on each passing day, fresh light can be shed on the verses of the Bible and new perspectives can be found. Not only are new answers offered to old questions, but in every era additional questions are raised by students of the Bible, due to both the diversity of the personalities, and the differing interests and perspectives, of each era. Throughout the ages, the great commentaries have discussed a wide range of different issues. To this day, thank God, there are many scholars and students of the Bible raising unique questions and challenges that require attention, analysis, and investigation. All these illuminate the eternal words of the Torah through a range of viewpoints and give rise to "plain meanings that are renewed every day."

This commentary seeks to offer the reader the plain meaning of the text, the *peshat*. Ostensibly, this is the simplest level of interpretation, but the elucidation of the plain meaning is actually the most difficult type of interpretation. Other kinds of interpretation, based on allusion [*remez*], midrashic hermeneutics [*derash*], or esoteric, mystical traditions [*sod*], are free to forge links between the text and the sources from which they draw and are not constrained by the language and concepts of the Bible. In contrast, discovering the plain meaning of the text requires the interpreter to adhere closely to the literal meaning of the words while paying attention to syntax and context.

Although this commentary includes references to many other commentaries, it is not an anthology. It was not intended to provide a comprehensive array of interpretations from across the generations. The aim of the references is to show that a suggested interpretation is based on earlier sources or discusses a similar question. Moreover, this work does not aspire to be revolutionary or novel. Rather, it aims to present what might be called a "transparent" commentary, one whose explanations should go almost unnoticed and serve only to give the reader and student the sense that there is no barrier between him or her and the text. The aim is to let the Torah speak for itself, to allow the prophets to prophesy and the wise men to impart their wisdom. In order to enable the "voice" of the verses to be heard, the annotations are brief, serving as a thin, barely perceptible screen rather than a heavy, concealing coat of armor.

At Mount Sinai, the entire Jewish people heard "a great voice" (Deuteronomy 5:18), which the Sages interpret to mean a voice that has never ceased (*Targum Onkelos*; *Sanhedrin* 17a). It is my hope that this project will help people hear the voice of the Torah even in our busy, noisy world.

Rabbi Adin Even-Israel Steinsaltz

Introduction by the Hebrew Editors

The purpose of this commentary is to assist the contemporary reader by bridging the gaps in language, outlook, and culture between us and the world of the Bible. As far as possible, it seeks to clarify ambiguities, elucidate problematic passages, and remove obstacles to understanding while dealing with both explicit and implicit difficulties.

The commentary consists of several parts, which complement but are independent of one another. The literal translation of the verses appears in boldface. Woven into the biblical text in non-bold typeface are brief explanatory comments and elaborations. Below the text are notes that offer more elaborate discussion of topics that appear in the verses as well as insights into the general context and scientific and historical realia that surround the biblical text.

The biblical text is divided into units based on subject matter, which do not always accord with the standard division into chapters. Each unit is prefaced by a heading and a short introduction. This structure should not be viewed as a definitive partition of the biblical text but as a suggestion, part of the commentary, for the reader's convenience and orientation.

The commentary seeks to concisely clarify the language and context at the most basic level so as not to encumber the reader. Consequently, it is not committed to a particular exegetical method and does not systematically defer to any particular commentator. In cases where there are differing explanations of a passage, alternative explanations may be cited. In cases where the halakhic tradition expounds a verse in a manner not consistent with the plain meaning, this will be noted and explained briefly in the annotations themselves or by means of a reference, allowing the plain meaning of the text to be preserved while not disregarding the interpretation of the Oral Law.

It must be stated that even when written without qualification, the interpretations offered are not meant to be seen as authoritative. They are no more than suggestions, occasionally novel ones, which are compatible with the simple meaning of the text and which speak to the average reader. There are no systematic exegetical considerations behind the decision to adopt any particular interpretation.

Much thought and labor have been invested to ensure that the design of this work is as aesthetically pleasing and convenient for the user as possible. This design is the fruit of an ongoing collaboration between the team at the Institute for Talmudic Publications and Koren Publishers. Our thanks to Rabbi Meir Hanegbi, whose wisdom, conviviality, and efficiency contributed greatly to the success of the project. Rabbi Hanokh Ben Arza, may his memory be for a blessing, was the father of the two editors in chief of the Hebrew edition; his spirit and respect for the written word inspired them in their work.

The Editors

Introduction by the Translators

ON THE TRANSLATION OF THE MEGILLOT

The English translation of *The Steinsaltz Megillot* includes a completely new translation of the Bible based on Rabbi Adin Even-Israel Steinsaltz's Hebrew commentary. Translation is necessarily an act of interpretation. In general, we have done our best, at Rabbi Steinsaltz's behest, to stay as close as possible to the original Hebrew verses so that the English reader will encounter the complexities of the text directly. In the course of translating, we have consulted other English translations, as well as relying heavily upon Onkelos' Aramaic translation and the classic medieval Jewish commentaries of the Torah: Rav Se'adya Gaon, Rashi, Ibn Ezra, Ramban, and Rashbam. Our goal throughout has been to produce a translation that is true to the original Hebrew text and commentary, yet at the same time is readable and accessible to a broad range of readers, from those who are familiar with Hebrew and seek to deepen their understanding of the Torah to those who will gain access to the text only by reading it in English. The commentary and notes are written in modern American English. In the spirit of the Hebrew edition, we have tried to preserve the lofty register of the biblical text while providing a commentary that is relevant and inspiring to our own generation. We hope that the Author of the Torah has aided us in achieving this goal.

THE LAYOUT OF THIS EDITION

On the left-hand side of each set of facing pages is the Hebrew text of the Bible with the traditional cantillation marks, meticulously edited over decades by the team at Koren Publishers, Jerusalem. On the facing page, the Steinsaltz translation of the Bible appears in boldface with the commentary interspersed between the words of the text in non-bold typeface. This enables the reader to easily follow either the direct translation alone or the translation augmented by the elucidated text.

The notes at the foot of the page are divided into two categories. Discussion notes provide background material, internal biblical parallels, alternative explanations, and a wealth of midrashic and philosophical ideas from Jewish commentaries over the generations. Background notes provide linguistic, historical, archaeological, and scientific information that is relevant to places, nations, flora and fauna, and other realia mentioned in the verses. Integrated into both the commentary and the notes are pictures, maps, and other graphics to aid the reader in grasping the biblical text.

References and sources for the commentary appear as endnotes, while the references and sources for the notes are interspersed throughout the notes themselves in parentheses. These references and sources, compiled by the Hebrew editors, include citations of other verses in the Bible, commentary elsewhere in the Bible, insights of the rabbinic Sages in the Talmud and *midrashim*, interpretations of the classical biblical commentaries, and citations of philosophical works and responsa by the early authorities [*rishonim*].

The translation of the verses of the Megillot was undertaken by Rabbi Joshua Schreier and reviewed meticulously by Rabbi Dr. Joshua Amaru. Many talented editors and translators participated in the translation of the commentary and notes as listed in the credits. We thank Matthew Miller, Avishai Magence, and the devoted and gifted team at Koren Publishers. We are grateful to Rabbi Meni Even-Israel, Executive Director of the Steinsaltz Center, whose wisdom and guidance have made this publication possible. We also thank Rabbi Dr. Natan Slifkin of the Biblical Museum of Natural History in Beit Shemesh for his help in identifying some animals and providing suitable images.

TRANSLITERATION

In general, we have tried to keep transliteration to a minimum and have relied upon it only for proper nouns and in places where a point of commentary relates to a Hebrew term. In the case of proper nouns, we have sought a middle ground between a rigorous adherence to Hebrew phonology and the use of anglicized versions of names taken from earlier translations of the Bible. For familiar names of both places and people, where encountering a transliteration would be jarring to many readers, we have used the well-known anglicized versions, such as Canaan, Egypt, Abraham, and Moses. Otherwise, proper nouns are transliterated according to the rules listed below. These transliterations offer the English reader an experience that is closer to that of the Hebrew reader.

Of course, determining which names count as familiar and which are not is not an exact science; the policy has been to use the anglicized names of familiar figures such as the names of prophets and books of the Bible, and some other well-known characters and place-names. The transliteration scheme generally follows modern Israeli Hebrew pronunciation, but note the following points:

- For proper nouns no special characters are used to designate sounds that do not exist in English. For example, the name אֲחִיעֶזֶר will not be rendered Aḥiezer (with a diacritic for the letter *ḥet* that is used for the transliteration of Hebrew terms that are not proper nouns) but rather Ahiezer. Consequently, the letter ח is rendered as *h* (like the letter ה).
- The letter *h*, representing the Hebrew letter ה, has been omitted at the end of a word unless its omission could lead to mispronunciation. For example, שלה is written Shela, while נינוה is written Nineveh.
- The soft letter כ is rendered as *kh*.
- No distinction has been made between a letter containing a *dagesh ḥazak* (elsewhere represented by a double consonant) and one without. For example, it is Hukat as opposed to Hukkat.
- Apostrophes indicating glottal stops are employed only where a name could be mispronounced without them. For example, it is Se'ir as opposed to Seir.
- We have maintained a more technical transliteration scheme for citations, including the diacritic *ḥ* and consonant doubling for cases of a *dagesh*. For example, in the citation *Tanḥuma, Korah* 5, *Tanḥuma* retains the diacritic *ḥ*, whereas *Korah* does not.

On behalf of the team of inspired and dedicated translators, editors, and copy editors with whom it has been a great privilege to work, I express my hope that the decisions we have made have produced a translation that is faithful to the Hebrew, readable, accessible, and useful to the reader.

Jason Rappoport
Editor in Chief

Cantillation Marks (*Trop*)

שמות הטעמים וסימניהם

אשכנזים:

מֵרְכָ֥א טִפְּחָ֖א מֻנַּ֣ח אֶתְנַחְתָּ֑א מֵרְכָ֥א טִפְּחָ֖א סוֹף־פָּסֽוּק

מַהְפַּ֤ךְ פַּשְׁטָא֙ מֻנַּ֣ח זָקֵף־קָטָ֔ן זָקֵף־גָּד֕וֹל מֻנַּ֣ח ׀ מֻנַּ֣ח רְבִ֗יעַ

קַדְמָ֨א דַּרְגָּ֧א תְּבִ֛יר מֻנַּ֣ח זַרְקָא֮ מֻנַּ֣ח סֶגּוֹל֒ תְּ֠לִישָׁא־גְדוֹלָה

תְּלִישָׁא־קְטַנָּה֩ קַדְמָ֨א וְאַזְלָ֨א אַזְלָא־גֵ֜רֵשׁ גֵּרְשַׁ֞יִם פָּזֵ֡ר

יְ֚תִיב שַׁלְשֶׁ֓לֶת גַּלְגַּ֪ל קַרְנֵי־פָרָ֟ה מֵרְכָא־כְּפוּלָ֦ה

לְגַרְמֵ֣הּ ׀ סוֹף־פָּסֽוּק׃

ספרדים:

זַרְקָא֮ מַקַּף־שׁוֹפָר־הוֹלֵ֣ךְ סְגוֹלְתָּא֒ פָּזֵר־גָּד֡וֹל

תְּ֠לְשָׁא תִּילְשָׁא֩ אַזְלָא־גֵּ֜רִישׁ פָּסֵק׀ רָבִ֗יעַ שְׁנֵי־גֵּרְשִׁ֞ין

דַּרְגָּ֧א תְּבִ֛יר מַאֲרִ֥יךְ טַרְחָ֖א אַתְנָ֑ח שׁוֹפָר־מְהֻפָּ֤ךְ

קַדְמָ֨א תְּרֵי־קַדְמִ֨ין זָקֵף־קָטָ֔ן זָקֵף־גָּד֕וֹל שַׁלְשֶׁ֓לֶת

גַּלְגַּ֪ל קַרְנֵי־פָרָ֟ה תְּרֵי־טַעֲמֵ֨י יְ֚תִיב סוֹף־פָּסֽוּק׃

Chronology of the Megillot

Megilla	Author according to the Sages	Period	Event	Date BCE
Ruth	Samuel	Judges		13th–11th century
Song of Songs; Ecclesiastes	Solomon	Kings	Reign of Solomon	969–930
Lamentations	Jeremiah	Babylonian Empire	Destruction of the First Temple	586
Esther	The Men of the Great Assembly	Persian Empire	Reign of Ahashverosh	486–465

The Song of Songs

The Song of Songs

INTRODUCTION TO THE SONG OF SONGS

The Song of Songs is a collection of love poetry. Despite the literary unity of the book and its themes, it is hard to discern a coherent narrative running through it all. Between the obscure starting point of the book and its conclusion, which could point toward marriage, there are elusive circles of mutual courtship and pursuit. Nevertheless, there is an overall harmony to the poems, and despite the peaks and troughs in the relationship between the lovers who are the poems' focus, there is no open conflict between them. They occasionally become distanced from one another, but soon return and become close once again.

Other characters apart from the two lovers make brief appearances, but they do not participate in the main events, and are marginal figures, who sometimes serve to provide a different perspective on the relationship between the principal couple.

The encounters depicted here are more intimate than the accepted manners of courtship in the ancient Jewish world. It is certainly possible that the poems do not tell of real face-to-face meetings, but rather represent the lovers' tender fantasies. The dreamlike vagueness of the narrative throughout the book supports this suggestion.

The love between man and woman, which is the focus of the entire book, has been understood throughout the generations as an allegory for the relationship between the people of Israel as a whole and the Holy One.[1] The Song of Songs evokes a relationship of intense longing and intimacy using very specific imagery. This representation of the love between God and His people through metaphors of sexual love is far from unique in the Bible, and not at all foreign to Jewish tradition. In the Bible this characterization is especially prevalent in the Prophets. Some of the prophets evoke a marital relationship, both as the ideal of the covenant and as the model for the betrayal and jealousy felt by God when Israel sins.[2] This imagery is often highly physical and even erotic. Nevertheless, the tone of The Song of Songs differs from these metaphors.

Allegorical love poems that express religious devotion and a believer's feeling for his god were not unusual in the ancient Middle East. For example, ancient Sumerian poems have been discovered that are broadly similar in their themes to The Song of Songs, and some of them were expressly designed for use in ritual ceremonies of worship. This fact serves to undermine the oft-heard suggestion that the allegorical reading of The Song of Songs offered by the Sages is the anachronistic reaction of a prudish culture shocked by its explicitness. It is rather an instance of an ancient and well-established phenomenon.

Notwithstanding the similarities between The Song of Songs and similar poems from other cultures, The Song of Songs is neither generic nor universal. The images are well defined, detailed, and local. They refer to the Land of Israel, its scenery and ways of life, with especial attention paid to Jerusalem and its environs. Although there is a certain continuity in the setting of the characters and events described, the book does not provide a well-articulated representation of the characters and their relationship as one finds typically in ancient Greek literature. Every so often, the characters shift and display different aspects of themselves, and thus another feature of the poem is revealed, inviting more and more exegetical interpretations and further investigations into hidden levels of meaning. Each detail remains vital and sensuous, and yet at the same time symbolic and fundamental. Over the generations, The Song of Songs has become a timeless recounting of the love between the nation of Israel and God.

It has been the custom since the Middle Ages to recite The Song of Songs on the festival of Passover, which always occurs in the spring. This is the season of the events described in the book, and Passover also represents the springtime of Israel as a nation.[3]

Many communities also have the custom of reading The Song of Songs every week, just before the start of Shabbat.

The Song of Songs

Song of the Young Woman to Her Beloved

THE SONG OF SONGS 1:1

At the simplest level, The Song of Songs is the poetic expression of the passion of two young lovers. It has always been understood as referring also to other sorts of love relationships. Beyond the allegorical reading of the Sages, in which The Song of Songs depicts the love between the Jewish people and God, the entire book can be read as the portrayal of the love of an individual soul for its Creator. Each level of interpretation, that of the collective Jewish people's relationship with God and that of the individual's relationship with God, makes use of different symbols.

1 1 **The song of songs,**[D] the most special of poems, **which is Solomon's.**[D] Solomon king of Israel is said to have composed a great number of poems.[4]

The Opening Poem

THE SONG OF SONGS 1:2–4

The first poem expresses the intensity of new love, while hinting at other dimensions of the love relationship.

2 The poem opens without identifying its speaker, but its grammatical context, which addresses a male beloved, leaves no doubt that these are the words of a young woman: **May he kiss me with the kisses of his mouth, as your love**[B] **is better than wine.** Alternatively: The wetness of your mouth is better than wine.[5] The speaker's transition from employing third person pronouns to directly addressing her subject likely alludes to a process in which passionate fantasies feel more and more real, eventually giving the impression that the beloved is present even if he is not.

3 The woman continues to praise her beloved: **By the fragrance of your good oils,** even **your name is** pleasant **like poured oil** [***shemen turak***],[B] and **therefore, the young women love you.** The young woman speaks not only of love for her partner and a yearning for personal closeness to him, but also of her admiration for him, noting that he is loved by all.

4 **Draw me; after you we will run** together. The verse portrays a budding romance: The young man woos the young woman, and she takes hold of his hand and runs with him. However, they do not run aimlessly: **The king brought me to his** private **chambers.** At this point, another layer is added to the poem, as the woman discovers that her beloved is no ordinary man but the king himself. Although the beloved will sometimes be described as a shepherd, perhaps the king prefers to appear as a simple man rather than a ruler when courting his loved one. However, when they finally run together, the king takes her specifically to his palace chambers. Alternatively, in the eyes of the woman, her beloved shepherd is a king, and she feels like a queen whose groom, the king, is leading her to his home.[6] This motif does not seem typical of a love poem. It reveals another layer of meaning: The soul, which until now has wandered in the familiar outside world, finds itself inside the chamber of the beloved king. There **let us exult and rejoice in you. We will recount your love,** which is sweeter and **more** intoxicating **than wine. Rightly** [***meisharim***] **do they love you,** or upright individuals love you.

An Address to the Daughters of Jerusalem

THE SONG OF SONGS 1:5–6

In the following few verses, the woman speaks to other figures, real or metaphorical.

5 The woman declares: **I am black but lovely,**[BD] **daughters of Jerusalem.** The city of Jerusalem serves as the backdrop for the poem. I am black **like the tents of** the tribes of **Kedar.**[B] These tents were made from the wool of the local goats, which were typically black, **like the curtains of Solomon,**[B] which were most splendid, and perhaps also black. The woman's black and beautiful appearance is illustrated by a pair of contrasting images: coarse wool and royal drapes.

Tents in the wilderness

שיר השירים

א ב שִׁ֥יר הַשִּׁירִ֖ים אֲשֶׁ֥ר לִשְׁלֹמֹֽה׃ יִשָּׁקֵ֙נִי֙ מִנְּשִׁיק֣וֹת פִּ֔יהוּ כִּֽי־טוֹבִ֥ים דֹּדֶ֖יךָ מִיָּֽיִן׃
ג ד לְרֵ֙יחַ֙ שְׁמָנֶ֣יךָ טוֹבִ֔ים שֶׁ֖מֶן תּוּרַ֣ק שְׁמֶ֑ךָ עַל־כֵּ֖ן עֲלָמ֥וֹת אֲהֵבֽוּךָ׃ מָשְׁכֵ֖נִי אַחֲרֶ֣יךָ
נָּר֑וּצָה הֱבִיאַ֨נִי הַמֶּ֜לֶךְ חֲדָרָ֗יו נָגִ֤ילָה וְנִשְׂמְחָה֙ בָּ֔ךְ נַזְכִּ֤ירָה דֹדֶ֙יךָ֙ מִיַּ֔יִן מֵישָׁרִ֖ים
ה אֲהֵבֽוּךָ׃ שְׁחוֹרָ֤ה אֲנִי֙ וְֽנָאוָ֔ה בְּנ֖וֹת יְרוּשָׁלִָ֑ם כְּאָהֳלֵ֣י קֵדָ֔ר כִּירִיע֖וֹת

BACKGROUND

1:2| **Your love [*dodekha*]:** This word has two meanings: First, it is the plural form of *dod*, "beloved," as in the verse "This is my beloved [*dodi*], and this is my companion" (5:16). Second, it denotes lovemaking, based on a similar Akkadian term, and this is the meaning of *dodekha* in this verse (see also verse 4, 4:10, 7:13; Proverbs 7:18).

1:3| **Poured oil [*shemen turak*]:** The word *turak* means poured or emptied. Alternatively, it is related to *tamruk*, cosmetics (see Vilna Gaon). According to this interpretation, *shemen turak* is perfumed oil. A similar term in Akkadian means a perfume or spice.

1:5| **I am black, but lovely [*nava*]:** In Akkadian, *nawru* means sparkling, shiny, and colorful. Indeed, a woman whose skin was darkened as a result of guarding vineyards (see verse 6) might stand out among her friends. It is worth noting the statement in the Mishna (*Nega'im* 2:1) concerning the typical complexion of the Jewish people in ancient times: "Rabbi Yishmael says: The children of Israel, may I be an atonement for them! They are like the box tree, neither black nor white, but in between." The color of the box tree, of the genus *Buxus*, is somewhere between ivory and light brown.

Kedar: In the Torah, Kedar is listed as Ishmael's second son (Genesis 25:13), and in the Prophets it refers to a nomadic tribe, or group of tribes, that raised cattle and camels and engaged in commerce (see Isaiah 42:11, 60:7; Jeremiah 49:28; Ezekiel 27:21). Assyrian records refer to the leaders of Kedar and their wanderings in the region of the Syrian-Arabian desert. Pliny the Elder lists them together with the Nabateans as migrants and settlers in Babylonia, present-day Jordan, and the Sinai Peninsula.

Like the tents of Kedar, like the curtains of Solomon: The root *kuf-dalet-reish* means dark or black. The tribes of Kedar were known by this name due to their dark clothing and tents. Against the background of the desert rocks and light sands, the dark tents of Kedar could be seen from a great distance. The comparison of a woman to Solomon's colorful woven curtains can be understood by noting that royal tents, as well as the Tent of Meeting in the wilderness, had two layers: an outer one of a uniform color, made of goats' wool, and an inner, multicolored one.

DISCUSSION

1:1| **The Song of songs:** The Sages teach: All the Writings, or in a different version, all the poems, are holy, but The Song of Songs is the holy of holies (Mishna *Yadayim* 3:5; see *Shir HaShirim Rabba* 1:11). From a grammatical perspective, the phrase "song of songs" can be considered an expression of emphasis, like "slave of slaves" (Genesis 9:25, and Ibn Ezra ad loc.). The title of the book also reflects its dual nature: The Song of Songs is simultaneously a single prose poem or story and a compilation of individual poems each relating its own partial narrative. Indeed, the transitions from one section to another are not always smooth and are likely to leave the reader seeking clarification.

Which is Solomon's: Solomon makes several appearances in The Song of Songs, not only as its author but also as a character, albeit with a somewhat obscure role. He is sometimes portrayed as a third party independent of the lovers, sometimes as a kind of custodian of the young woman, whom he presents to others. At other times, Solomon appears in the role of the beloved himself, although several other verses indicate that the beloved is not a king but a shepherd. According to the allegory, the figure of King Solomon in The Song of Songs represents God (see, e.g., *Shevuot* 38b). But even without resorting to the allegory, it is clear that the figure of Solomon is an amalgamation of a historical person and a symbol. This is one of the many fluid and enigmatic aspects of the book.

1:5| **I am black, but lovely:** This expression has been understood in an apologetic light: Although I am dark or tanned, and I do not perfectly match your image of ideal beauty, I am nevertheless beautiful. The perception of beauty expressed in the verse is typical of the ancient Middle East, where the inhabitants, particularly the poorer ones who worked outside, were usually of a dark complexion, while paler skin tones were associated with the elites and were considered more beautiful.

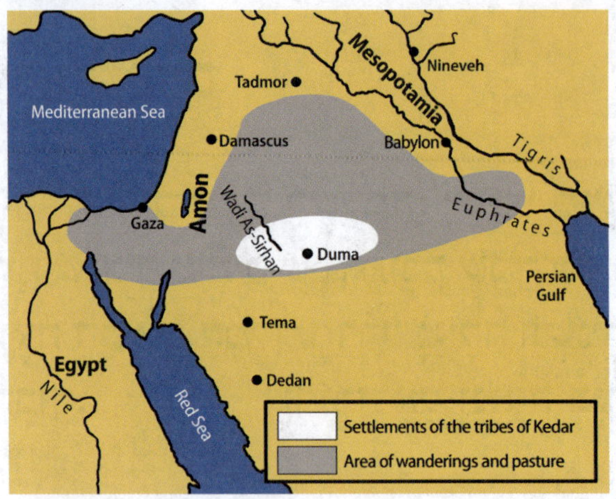

Wanderings of the tribes of Kedar

6 **Do not gaze at me** disrespectfully,[7] seeing **that I am dark, for**
this is not my natural color; rather, **the sun has tanned me.**[8]

The woman now addresses how a fair and modest daughter of Jerusalem faced such exposure to the sun: **The sons of my mother were incensed at me; they placed me as guard of the** family **vineyards,**[B] to chase away any animals that attempted to infiltrate. However, because of the task imposed upon me, **my own vineyard I did not guard.** I too have a vineyard of my own, but the members of my family who quarreled with me cared only for their vineyards, while mine was left abandoned. This verse can be understood as the personal struggle of a woman who wishes to extricate herself from the plight of her perceived external ugliness, and to reveal her hidden beauty. However, the verse can also be interpreted metaphorically as a declaration by the Jewish people: Admittedly we are not clean and pure as snow, but the blackness of our sins is not a natural blemish, nor was it caused by circumstances of our own choosing. As a nation, we have been forced to wander frequently. Because of the other nations, we were forced to fulfill various roles for the benefit of the world, to preserve their vineyards. Therefore, we were left without the time or opportunity to protect our own vineyard.

The Young Woman's Declaration and the Beloved's Response

THE SONG OF SONGS 1:7–2:7

The woman now turns to her beloved, who presumably was not present during her conversation with the daughters of Jerusalem. Perhaps this is not a real exchange, but an expression of a secret wish.

7 **Tell me,** you **whom my soul loves, where do you herd**[D] your
flock? **Where do you rest your flock at noon?**[B] **Why should I be as one bound to the flocks of your colleagues?** Alternatively: Why should I wrap myself up or veil myself for reasons of modesty, in following the flocks of other shepherds? If you tell me where to find you, I will not be forced to wander in the company of strangers.

Flock of sheep

8 For the first time, the lover's response is heard: **If you do not**
know where I am, you, **the fairest among women, go out in the footsteps of the sheep and herd your kids.** Apparently, in addition to being a keeper of vineyards, the woman is also a shepherdess. A young shepherdess would generally be given a small flock of kids, while the larger flocks were shepherded by men. The matriarch Rachel likely shepherded such a small flock.[9] You must seek me **by the tents of the shepherds.** The beloved is unable to give the young woman an address where she can find him. Rather, she must go out to seek him. Similarly, the final destination of the soul's great journey, like that of Israel's travels in the wilderness, lies beyond the horizon.

9 The lover briefly expresses his love for the woman, even more
emphatically than her expressions of affection for him: **To a mare in Pharaoh's chariots I have likened you, my love.** Horses are generally considered beautiful creatures. A horse harnessed to one of Pharaoh's chariots would be perfect and adorned with decorations.[10]

Horse pulling Pharaoh's chariot, fresco, Abu Simbel, southern Egypt, thirteenth century BCE

ו שְׁלֹמֹה: אַל־תִּרְאוּנִי שֶׁאֲנִי שְׁחַרְחֹרֶת שֶׁשֱּׁזָפַתְנִי הַשָּׁמֶשׁ בְּנֵי אִמִּי נִחֲרוּ־בִי שָׂמֻנִי
ז נֹטֵרָה אֶת־הַכְּרָמִים כַּרְמִי שֶׁלִּי לֹא נָטָרְתִּי: הַגִּידָה לִּי שֶׁאָהֲבָה נַפְשִׁי אֵיכָה
ח תִרְעֶה אֵיכָה תַּרְבִּיץ בַּצָּהֳרָיִם שַׁלָּמָה אֶהְיֶה כְּעֹטְיָה עַל עֶדְרֵי חֲבֵרֶיךָ: אִם־לֹא
תֵדְעִי לָךְ הַיָּפָה בַּנָּשִׁים צְאִי־לָךְ בְּעִקְבֵי הַצֹּאן וּרְעִי אֶת־גְּדִיֹּתַיִךְ עַל מִשְׁכְּנוֹת
ט י הָרֹעִים: לְסֻסָתִי בְּרִכְבֵי פַרְעֹה דִּמִּיתִיךְ רַעְיָתִי: נָאווּ לְחָיַיִךְ בַּתֹּרִים
יא יב צַוָּארֵךְ בַּחֲרוּזִים: תּוֹרֵי זָהָב נַעֲשֶׂה־לָּךְ עִם נְקֻדּוֹת הַכָּסֶף: עַד־שֶׁהַמֶּלֶךְ בִּמְסִבּוֹ

10 Like the horse in Pharaoh's chariot, **your cheeks are lovely** and decorated **with rings,** apparently large earrings that rest on the cheeks; **your neck** is decorated **with beads.**

11 You are worthy of even grander jewelry: **We will make you golden rings with studs**[11] **of silver.**[B] Silver studs stand out prominently on a golden background, like white spots on dark fur. Allegorically, the chariots of Pharaoh recall Israel's exodus from Egypt, while the various ornaments are reminiscent of the great wealth taken from there by the children of Israel. This combination of gold and silver has been given many other interpretations, some of them mystical.

12 The young woman's response again expresses her desire to be close to her

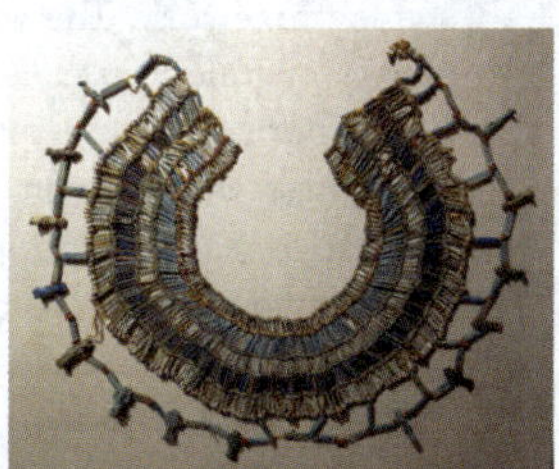
Necklace, Egypt, seventh century BCE

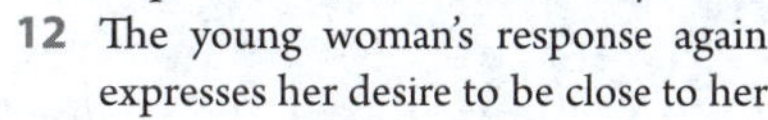

Gold earring, Italy, fourth century BCE

BACKGROUND

1:6 | **Guard of the vineyards:** The main work in a vineyard, namely the harvesting and storage of grapes, and the production of wine and raisins from the fruit, is performed over the course of a three- to five-month period. During this time, the vineyard is vulnerable to animals and to thieves who might take grapes without permission. To protect against these threats, vineyard owners and their families would guard their vineyards. In many cases, round, tall structures suitable as lookouts were built to house the guards. These structures were typically constructed from stones gathered from a clearing, with a booth erected at the top of each of them.

1:7 | **Rest your flock at noon:** A day of shepherding is generally divided into three stages: In the morning hours, the sheep graze in the fields; during the noon hours, the flock rests in the shade and chews its cud; in the afternoon, the flock grazes again until close to sunset, before returning to its pen or shelter for the night.

1:11 | **We will make you golden rings with studs of silver:** It is possible that these silver studs are to be integrated between golden spherules, in order to enhance the visual effect. The combination of gold and silver is a motif in other sources as well (see Proverbs 25:11; Mishna *Pesaḥim* 5:5).

DISCUSSION

1:7 | **Where do you herd:** This question is left unanswered. The only response the woman receives is that she should continue looking. This constant searching is an attribute of the soul and can also be metaphorically ascribed to the heavenly bodies that are constantly orbiting. This idea is echoed by the question attributed to the angels, in which they ask repeatedly: Where is the place of His glory? (*Musaf* prayer for Shabbat and festivals; see *Ḥagiga* 13b; *Pirkei deRabbi Eliezer* 4). This question appears in a different form as a request by Moses: "If I have found favor now in Your eyes, inform me, please, of Your ways.… Show me, please, Your glory" (Exodus 33:13–18). As with the request of the young woman, Moses appeals to God: If You love me, then allow me to approach You and to know You.

beloved: **While the king was at his feast, my lavender**[B] **emitted its fragrance.** Among all the fragrances at the king's feast, the scent of my lavender is the most pronounced.[12]

Lavender

13 **A bundle of myrrh**[B] **is my beloved to me, lying between my breasts.** The young woman dreams: If only my beloved were like a bundle of myrrh hanging from my neck and resting in my bosom.

Pendant with receptacle for fragrant herbs, Egypt, first century BCE

Trees from which myrrh is extracted

14 **A cluster of henna,**[B] a fragrant plant whose fruit grows in clusters, **my beloved is to me, in the vineyards of Ein Gedi,** where henna apparently grew. Perhaps the woman anticipates meeting her lover there.

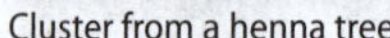
Cluster from a henna tree

Date flowers

15 As the pace of the exchange between the beloved and his lover increases, the beloved speaks again: **Behold, you are fair, my love; behold, you are fair; your eyes are like doves.** Doves are a symbol of beauty and grace; the comparison of the woman's eyes to doves is also indicative of perfection and tranquility, which arouse the man's love.[13]

16 The young woman responds: **Behold, you are fair, my beloved,** your company is **pleasant too; indeed our bed is fresh.** She fantasizes of a shared home and bed.

17 **The beams of our houses are** made of **cedars,**[B] **and our rafters are junipers.**[B] Two aspects of the lovers' relationship are intertwined in this passage. Alongside passionate love, there is a motif of calm and the stability of home. When the woman calls to her lover, "Draw me; after you we will run" (verse 4), the intention is not to run and play aimlessly, as the same verse concludes: "The king brought me to his chambers." The blossoming love between them, which is expressed by the fresh bed of the previous verse, is followed by the dream of sharing a home. Their relationship must eventually be brought into a stable framework. The young man and woman, though completely engulfed in a passionate love, still set as their goal a shared home, symbolizing the nation of Israel in Egypt or in the wilderness who, caught up in their romance with God, still yearned to reach their homeland.

Greek juniper

2 1 The young woman continues: **I am** as beautiful as **a daffodil of the Sharon,**[B] **a lily of the valleys.**[B]

Sea daffodil

2 Her beloved confirms: Indeed, **like a lily among the thorns, so is my love among the girls.** You stand out among all the other girls, and you are different from them. Furthermore, just as one can enjoy the conspicuous beauty of a lily, but it is difficult to approach the flower due to the thorns, so too you are not easily accessible. This depiction alludes to the simultaneous intimacy and distance present in their relationship, which can be understood at all levels of interpretation.

Madonna lily

3 The young woman praises her beloved: **Like an apple tree,**[B] with its distinct aroma,[14] **among the** plain **trees of the forest, so is my beloved among the boys.** In addition to its scent, the apple tree possesses other advantages: **In its shade I delighted and I sat, and its fruit was sweet to my palate.**

Apple tree

נִרְדִּי נָתַן רֵיחוֹ׃ צְרוֹר הַמֹּר ׀ דּוֹדִי לִי בֵּין שָׁדַי יָלִין׃ אֶשְׁכֹּל הַכֹּפֶר ׀ דּוֹדִי לִי בְּכַרְמֵי יג יד
עֵין גֶּדִי׃ הִנָּךְ יָפָה רַעְיָתִי הִנָּךְ יָפָה עֵינַיִךְ יוֹנִים׃ הִנְּךָ יָפֶה דוֹדִי אַף טו טז
נָעִים אַף־עַרְשֵׂנוּ רַעֲנָנָה׃ קֹרוֹת בָּתֵּינוּ אֲרָזִים רחיטנו בְּרוֹתִים׃ אֲנִי חֲבַצֶּלֶת רָהִיטֵנוּ יז א
הַשָּׁרוֹן שׁוֹשַׁנַּת הָעֲמָקִים׃ כְּשׁוֹשַׁנָּה בֵּין הַחוֹחִים כֵּן רַעְיָתִי בֵּין הַבָּנוֹת׃ כְּתַפּוּחַ ב ג

BACKGROUND

1:12| **Lavender [*nerd*]:** Later in The Song of Songs (4:14), *nerd* appears in a list of fragrant plants. As to its identity, there are two main suggestions. The first identifies it as lavender, *Lavandula angustifolia*, that grows wild throughout the Middle East and is a common feature of modern Israel's landscape. Its flowers emit a familiar scent, and are arranged like stalks [*shibbolet*] on their twigs, leading the Sages to refer to it as *shibbolet nerd* (see *Karetot* 6a). In Ancient Greek, lavender is known as *nardus*.

The second suggested identification is spikenard, *Nardostachys jatamansi*, a plant that grows in the Himalayan mountains. The leaves and root of the spikenard are the source of a valuable fragrant oil whose aroma is similar to musk, and whose scent is agreeable to some more than others. According to this interpretation, the term *shibbolet nerd* refers to hairs that cover the underside of the spikenard's stalk.

The Aramaic translations of the Bible, as well as some researchers, suggest other identifications for *nerd*, such as turmeric, the rose, or *Moringa peregrine*, which is found in desert oases in Israel.

1:13| **Myrrh [*mor*]:** One of the most important spices in the ancient world, myrrh was extracted from the resin of trees of the genus *Commiphora*, native to Africa, southern Arabia, and eastern India. Myrrh is mentioned in inscriptions and manuscripts from the ancient Orient and was used in cosmetics until modern times. Alternatively, *mor* has been identified with *anpakinon*, oil extracted from unripe olives (*Shabbat* 80b), used as a depilatory. According to the Rambam, *mor* is extracted from the glands of musk deer (see Ramban, Exodus 30:23).

1:14| **Henna [*kofer*]:** Most researchers identify the *kofer* plant with the henna tree, *Lawsonia inermis*, which stands 1–6 m tall. Requiring a warm climate, it once grew on the terraces of the oasis of Ein Gedi. Its clusters of flowers are fragrant, and the natural henna dye is extracted from its roots. Other possible identifications of the *kofer* include date palm flowers, known as *kufra* in the Talmud; cloves and the camphor tree, neither of which grows in Israel; the cypress, and early ripening grapes, which could conceivably have been grown in Ein Gedi.

1:17| **Cedars:** The cedar, genus *Cedrus*, is a large and beautiful conifer tree. The tree, which can reach a height of 40 m, grows in elevated and cold regions, and is common in Lebanon. Due to its strength and flexibility, cedar wood was particularly useful in the construction of public structures and palaces.

According to Egyptian and Assyrian records from the first and second millennia BCE, the forests of Lebanon were a main source of building materials for large buildings and ships as well as ritual boats, furniture, and coffins. Cedars were imported from Lebanon for the construction of both the First Temple (I Kings 5:20) and the Second Temple (Ezra 3:7).

Junipers [*berotim*]: *Berotim*, or *beroshim*, usually appear in the Bible alongside cedars, and this tree also grows in the mountains of Lebanon (see II Kings 19:23; Ezekiel 27:5). The term *berotim* does not refer to the genus *Cupressus*, known in modern Hebrew as the *berosh*, but rather to the Greek juniper, *Juniperus excelsa*. This tree is common in Lebanon and reaches a height of 30 m.

2:1| **Daffodil [*ḥavatzelet*] of the Sharon:** The Sharon is the coastal plain of Israel immediately north of what is now the Tel Aviv area. An inscription on the sarcophagus of Eshmunazar II, a Phoenician king of Sidon, as well as ancient Egyptian sources, refer to the region by this name. On the beaches of this region one can find the sea daffodil, *Pancratium maritimum*, from the Amaryllidaceae family. Its attractive flowers are white and fragrant. The petals have a diameter of roughly 10 cm, and it grows to a height of 60 cm. The mature flower has a great deal of nectar and emits a strong, pleasant aroma. The *ḥavatzelet* of the Sharon has been previously identified as the Madonna lily, the narcissus, or even the saffron crocus, but none of these flowers is typically found in the Sharon.

Lily [*shoshana*] of the valleys: There are numerous opinions with regard to the identity of the *shoshana*. Based on a similar Akkadian term, the *shoshana* is the flower known as the Madonna lily, *Lilium candidum*. Alternatively, it is the water lily, or the blue lotus, *Nymphaea caerulea*. The identification of the *shoshana* as the Madonna lily fits the next verse, "a lily [*shoshana*] among the thorns," since thorn bushes are sometimes found near this plant. Nevertheless, it is not a wild plant that grows in the valleys. By contrast, the water lily flourishes in freshwater pools, or in marshes in lowlands or valleys. However, thorns do not grow around it.

Another possible identification of the *shoshana* is *Rosa phoenicia*, a prickly shrub with beautiful and fragrant white flowers that grows in Israel on the banks of valley streams, which fits both characterizations in the verses. It is also possible that the *shoshana* of the valleys and the *shoshana* among the thorns are different species. If so, then one may identify the *shoshana* of the valleys as the lotus, which grows in the valleys, and the *shoshana* among the thorns as the Madonna lily.

Yet another possibility is that *shoshana* is a general term for beautiful multi-petaled flowers. If so, the date palm could also be referred to as a *shoshana* of the valleys due to the terrain in which it grows, its resemblance to a flower with splendid petals, and the fact that just above the ground it is surrounded with prickly shoots. This identification is also supported by the proto-Ionic capital design found on columns in the area, which were called *timorot*, comparable to *tamar*, the date (see I Kings 7:19, and commentary ad loc.).

4 **He brought me to the wine house,** a kind of tavern where men would drink. It is not clear whether such a tavern would serve women as well. Consequently, it seems that this phrase is an expression of the young woman's wish that her lover would allow her to accompany him wherever he goes. It is also possible that this wine house was the equivalent of a modern-day café. Alternatively, this term refers to a vineyard. **And his gaze [*diglo*] upon me is love.** *Diglu* in Akkadian indicates seeing or gazing. Alternatively, our love is his banner [*degel*]; he takes pride in displaying to others the love that radiates from us.[15]

5 **Support me with raisin cakes,**[16] **cushion me with** a bed of **apples, for I am lovesick.** In her weakness, the woman requests to be surrounded by fruit so as to create an aromatic, pleasant environment.[17] It is possible that she mentions raisin cakes [*ashishot*] because of the reinforcement [*ishush*] that she requires. They were known by this name because they were considered to give strength to those who ate them. The raisin cakes and apples literarily parallel the wine house and the apple tree mentioned in the previous two verses.

6 **His left** arm **is under my head and his right embraces me.** In pining for her beloved, she imagines that she is lying close to him.

7 **I administer an oath to you, daughters of Jerusalem,** who are not active participants in the story but background characters surrounding the woman, **by the gazelles,**[B] **and by the deer of the field,**[B] **that you not awaken and not rouse love, until it desires** to awaken by itself. Do not stir the love from the outside; let it develop naturally. Since this oath involves matters of the heart, the woman invokes animals that symbolize beauty and love. This obscure language, which is repeated elsewhere in The Song of Songs (3:5, 8:4), indicates that the young woman is confident that her relationship with her beloved will ultimately blossom, and so she requests that her love be allowed to advance at the appropriate pace. Her fantasies of constant and public companionship, represented by the wine house, do not need to come to fruition immediately; on the contrary, she is worried that they might materialize prematurely. Still, she yearns for her beloved to reveal their mutual love before all at the appropriate time. Allegorically understood, the nation of Israel wishes for God to reveal Himself and display before all the nations His love and closeness to Israel.

It is noteworthy that one does not ordinarily take an oath by gazelles or deer. In choosing these images, the woman evokes different names of God. In Hebrew, the word "gazelles" [*tzeva'ot*] alludes to one of God's names: Lord of Hosts [*Adonai Tzeva'ot*], while the term "deer of the field" [*ayalot hasadeh*] resembles another: God Almighty [*El Shadai*].

Gazelles

Roe deer

Entreaties and Rejections

THE SONG OF SONGS 2:8–3:5

Alongside declarations of mutual love and desire, the poem emphasizes the fluctuations of the developing connection between the lovers. The need for patience with regard to matters of the heart is stressed as well.

8 **The sound of** the footsteps of **my beloved, behold he approaches, leaping on the mountains, bounding on the hills** toward me.

9 **My beloved is like a gazelle or a fawn,** skipping speedily over the hills, in all its splendor; **behold, he is** already **standing behind our wall.** I can hear him behind the wall, and I can sense his presence,[18] **watching from the windows, peering** at me **through the cracks.** Like the events of national redemption, an individual's relationship with God is neither linear nor orderly. The gazelle racing over the mountains is alternately visible and hidden, as is the woman's beloved as he stands behind the wall, only visible through a crack in the structure. The metaphor of the wall expresses varying stages of revelation and concealment.

10 Drawing near, **my beloved** turned to me and **spoke up, and he said to me: Get up, my love, my fair one, and go** by yourself. Alternatively, come with me. The time has arrived for you to venture forth on a journey and to progress to a higher plane.

11 **For, behold, the winter [*setav*],** the rainy season, **has passed; the rain is over and gone.** Although in modern Hebrew *setav* means autumn, in this verse it refers to winter, and this is also its meaning in Aramaic.[19] In fact, it is questionable whether the Land of Israel has an autumn season at all, since its two principal seasons are a hot, dry summer and a rainy winter.[20]

Almond blossom

12 **The blossoms have been seen in the land, the time of the nightingale**[B] **has arrived, and the** characteristic **sound of the turtledove**[B] **is**

ד בַּעֲצֵי הַיַּעַר כֵּן דּוֹדִי בֵּין הַבָּנִים בְּצִלּוֹ חִמַּדְתִּי וְיָשַׁבְתִּי וּפִרְיוֹ מָתוֹק לְחִכִּי׃ הֱבִיאַנִי

ה אֶל־בֵּית הַיָּיִן וְדִגְלוֹ עָלַי אַהֲבָה׃ סַמְּכוּנִי בָּאֲשִׁישׁוֹת רַפְּדוּנִי בַּתַּפּוּחִים כִּי־חוֹלַת

ו ז אַהֲבָה אָנִי׃ שְׂמֹאלוֹ תַּחַת לְרֹאשִׁי וִימִינוֹ תְּחַבְּקֵנִי׃ הִשְׁבַּעְתִּי אֶתְכֶם בְּנוֹת

יְרוּשָׁלִַם בִּצְבָאוֹת אוֹ בְּאַיְלוֹת הַשָּׂדֶה אִם־תָּעִירוּ ׀ וְאִם־תְּעוֹרְרוּ אֶת־הָאַהֲבָה

ח עַד שֶׁתֶּחְפָּץ׃ קוֹל דּוֹדִי הִנֵּה־זֶה בָּא מְדַלֵּג עַל־הֶהָרִים מְקַפֵּץ עַל־

ט הַגְּבָעוֹת׃ דּוֹמֶה דוֹדִי לִצְבִי אוֹ לְעֹפֶר הָאַיָּלִים הִנֵּה־זֶה עוֹמֵד אַחַר כָּתְלֵנוּ מַשְׁגִּיחַ

י מִן־הַחַלֹּנוֹת מֵצִיץ מִן־הַחֲרַכִּים׃ עָנָה דוֹדִי וְאָמַר לִי קוּמִי לָךְ רַעְיָתִי יָפָתִי וּלְכִי־

יא יב לָךְ׃ כִּי־הִנֵּה הַסְּתָו עָבָר הַגֶּשֶׁם חָלַף הָלַךְ לוֹ׃ הַנִּצָּנִים נִרְאוּ בָאָרֶץ עֵת הַזָּמִיר

BACKGROUND

2:3| **Apple tree** [***tapuaḥ***]**:** The verse is almost certainly referring to one of the ancestors of the modern-day apple tree, *Malus domestica*, a species of deciduous fruit trees from the Rosaceae family. The wild apple, *Malus sieversii*, with its multicolored peel, grows in Kazakhstan. The yellow and fragrant European crab apple, *Malus sylvestris*, grows throughout Europe. The oriental apple, *Malus orientalis*, a hybrid produced from wild and crab apple strains, grows in Turkey. All naturally occurring apple trees grow in forests or on the outskirts of forests, and produce beautiful, fragrant, whitish-pink flowers. Some of them are also prickly. According to the *Targum*, the *tapuaḥ* is actually the *etrog* (see *Tosafot*, *Shabbat* 88a). The apple tree appears later in The Song of Songs as a shady, aromatic location suitable for a lovers' rendezvous (see 7:9, 8:5).

2:7| **Gazelles:** The mountain gazelle, *Gazella gazella*, is a swift, long-legged antelope of the family Bovidae. Gazelles generally live in groups and herds, and their activity can be best viewed at night, in the light of a full moon. They are gentle, cautious creatures and, like all antelope, are kosher, since they both chew the cud and have cloven hoofs. The coat of the gazelle is light brown in color, while its belly and rump are white, making its short, black tail conspicuous. Both males and females have straight horns that grow throughout their lifetime. As part of their mating ritual, the male chases the female for long distances until the latter accedes; hence the phrase "until it desires" (see also 3:5).

Deer of the field: These are generally identified as the roe deer, *Capreolus capreolus*, and a member of the family Cervidae. Like all deer, roe deer are kosher, since they chew the cud and have cloven hoofs. Originally indigenous to the Land of Israel, this breed of deer disappeared from the area in the early twentieth century. Attempts have been made in recent years to restore the breed to its natural habitat on Mount Carmel.

The roe deer grows to a length of 95–135 cm and a height of approximately 75 cm, weighing on average 15–30 kg. As opposed to gazelles, only the male roe deer have antlers, which regrow annually. During mating season, the males seek out the females, who attract them to their territories.

2:12| **Nightingale** [***zamir***]**:** This refers to the common nightingale, *Luscinia megarhynchos*, a brown bird with a reddish tail. The nightingale measures roughly 15 cm in length and passes through Israel on its migratory flight to Europe from Africa, mainly during the Hebrew month of Nisan, at the beginning of spring. Some remain in Israel throughout the summer. The nightingale is named, in both Hebrew and English, for its loud, sweet song [*zemer*], which is especially noticeable at night.

Turtledove [***tor***]**:** This is the European turtledove, *Streptopelia turtur*, a migratory bird from the Columbidae family that flocks to Israel from Africa during the spring. During their migration, some of these birds continue northward, while others remain until the autumn migratory season when they return south. The turtledove varies in color, ranging from gray to chestnut. It has bright patches on its neck, and its body is approximately 28 cm long. During mating season, the male turtledove emits a characteristic cooing sound, which is the origin of its name in Hebrew and Arabic, as well as in a number of European languages.

heard in our land. These migratory birds pass through Israel during the spring, and are therefore a sign of winter's end.

Common nightingale

Turtledove

13 **The fig tree formed its unripe figs.** Unripe figs begin to form in early spring. **And the** blossoming **vines** have formed their **budding,** and **emitted** their pleasant **fragrance.** These buds appear as clusters of small white flowers. **Get up, my love, my fair one, and go.** Spring is the best time for walking in nature.

"The fig tree formed its unripe figs"

14 **My dove,** my love, who hides **in the clefts of the rock, in the covert of the terrace:** Come out, and **show me your appearance, let me hear your voice, for your voice is pleasant, and your appearance is lovely.** The time has come for you to reveal yourself. This can be understood as a call to the individual soul or the nation of Israel to take action, as the time of redemption has arrived. According to the Sages' allegorical reading, these verses allude to Israel's exodus from Egypt, which took place in the spring. According to the allegory of the individual soul's yearning for God, these verses describe how the periods of cold and darkness during which the soul was in hibernation are over, and have been replaced with light and life; it is therefore time to rise and venture forth.

Dove in the cleft of a rock

15 However, the path ahead is neither straight nor smooth: **Catch for us** the **foxes,** those **little foxes that ruin the vineyards,**[B] **as our vineyards are** already **in bud,** and the damage caused by the foxes can be significant. The little foxes symbolize the troubles of both the individual and the collective. Although they are not dangerous to humans, they can cause significant damage to vineyards as the grapes begin to grow. Likewise, even when the lovers' romance begins to blossom, other troubles lie ahead.

Jackal

Fox

16 Although there are obstacles to our coming together, this is not due to emotional distance: **My beloved is mine, and I am his, who herds among the lilies.** Although my beloved shepherds among the lilies, as I gather from his pleasant scent,[21] he always remembers me, and I him; so the love between us will last. Even when I must chase away the foxes that ruin the vineyard, and he is occupied with important matters in his own world, there can be no doubting our bond.

17 We cannot see each other **until the day is great,** until the sun shines fully, or until the wind blows,[22] **and the shadows flee.** In the meantime, **turn** around, **my beloved, and be like a gazelle or a young hart on the cleft mountains,** mountains that are scored by ravines and valleys. Alongside the yearning for closeness, the partners give each other space. This point is often lost between lovers. Not all times are ripe for intense passion, and it is sometimes preferable to allow one's beloved to tend to his or her own matters. Here the young woman is confident in the strength of their bond; she is certain that her beloved will return. Whether this verse refers to historical events in the process of national redemption or to the experiences of the individual's soul, there are times of passion, revelation, and intimacy, and there are also times of calm, concealment, and distance. In these moments of distance, the couple is not truly separated from one another. Rather, their connection is toned down, demanding less of each of them. Love requires moments of respite so that its intensity does not become overwhelming.

"Cleft mountain." Mount Arbel

3 1 While the woman's beloved runs over the hills, she remains at home, yearning for him: **On my bed during the nights I sought the one whom my soul loves.** In light of verse 4 below, it seems her sleeping chambers are not in her parents' house. **I sought him, but I did not find him.** He was not close by. One of the symbolic interpretations of this description is that the soul seeks God at times of loneliness and difficulty, only to find Him distant.

2 She takes action: **I will rise now, and go about the city, in the streets and in the squares. I will seek the one whom my soul loves;** perhaps he can be found in the city streets. However, again, **I sought him, but I did not find him.**

יג הִגִּיעַ וְקוֹל הַתּוֹר נִשְׁמַע בְּאַרְצֵנוּ: הַתְּאֵנָה חָנְטָה פַגֶּיהָ וְהַגְּפָנִים ׀ סְמָדַר נָתְנוּ
יד רֵיחַ קוּמִי לכי רַעְיָתִי יָפָתִי וּלְכִי־לָךְ: יוֹנָתִי בְּחַגְוֵי הַסֶּלַע בְּסֵתֶר לָךְ
הַמַּדְרֵגָה הַרְאִינִי אֶת־מַרְאַיִךְ הַשְׁמִיעִינִי אֶת־קוֹלֵךְ כִּי־קוֹלֵךְ עָרֵב וּמַרְאֵיךְ
טו נָאוֶה: אֶחֱזוּ־לָנוּ שׁוּעָלִים שֻׁעָלִים קְטַנִּים מְחַבְּלִים כְּרָמִים וּכְרָמֵינוּ
טז יז סְמָדַר: דּוֹדִי לִי וַאֲנִי לוֹ הָרֹעֶה בַּשּׁוֹשַׁנִּים: עַד שֶׁיָּפוּחַ הַיּוֹם וְנָסוּ הַצְּלָלִים סֹב
א דְּמֵה־לְךָ דוֹדִי לִצְבִי אוֹ לְעֹפֶר הָאַיָּלִים עַל־הָרֵי בָתֶר: עַל־
ב מִשְׁכָּבִי בַּלֵּילוֹת בִּקַּשְׁתִּי אֵת שֶׁאָהֲבָה נַפְשִׁי בִּקַּשְׁתִּיו וְלֹא מְצָאתִיו: אָקוּמָה
נָּא וַאֲסוֹבְבָה בָעִיר בַּשְּׁוָקִים וּבָרְחֹבוֹת אֲבַקְשָׁה אֵת שֶׁאָהֲבָה נַפְשִׁי בִּקַּשְׁתִּיו
ג וְלֹא מְצָאתִיו: מְצָאוּנִי הַשֹּׁמְרִים הַסֹּבְבִים בָּעִיר אֵת שֶׁאָהֲבָה נַפְשִׁי רְאִיתֶם:
ד כִּמְעַט שֶׁעָבַרְתִּי מֵהֶם עַד שֶׁמָּצָאתִי אֵת שֶׁאָהֲבָה נַפְשִׁי אֲחַזְתִּיו וְלֹא אַרְפֶּנּוּ
ה עַד־שֶׁהֲבֵיאתִיו אֶל־בֵּית אִמִּי וְאֶל־חֶדֶר הוֹרָתִי: הִשְׁבַּעְתִּי אֶתְכֶם בְּנוֹת יְרוּשָׁלִַם

3 **The watchmen who patrol the city found me,** and I asked them: **Have you seen the one whom my soul loves?** It appears that they too had not seen her beloved. The appearance of watchmen indicates that this takes place in an established city, probably Jerusalem, which contains not only marketplaces and streets but also a patrol.

4 Since the watchmen offer no help, she turns elsewhere. **I had almost passed them, when I found the one whom my soul loves.** After three desperate attempts to find her beloved, first at home, then in the streets, and finally after asking others, she finds him. **I grasped him and I would not release him until I brought him to my mother's house, and to the chamber of the one who conceived me.** Unlike in other parts of the text, where the house and bed represent erotic love (e.g., 1:4, 16), in this verse the home symbolizes emotional closeness and family. In terms of the soul's experience, the soul seeks the object of its love in order to return to the emotional relationships of its childhood. One's parents' house is the place of his initial development. Therefore, the relationship must be built there. Symbolically, returning to the mother's home represents the Jewish people returning to their national homeland from their exile among the gentile nations, and in a spiritual sense, returning to God. The people of Israel implore God: Let us return to our original state.

5 Once again, the woman issues her warning: **I administer an oath to you, daughters of Jerusalem, by the gazelles, or by the deer of the field, that you not awaken and not rouse love, until it desires** to awaken by itself. As mentioned above (2:7), love has a natural course of development, and it must be allowed to intensify on its own at the appropriate pace. Elsewhere, the poem contains expressions of great passion, but this verse speaks of a contrasting idea: Let love develop on its own terms; do not fan its flames prematurely.

BACKGROUND

2:15| **Little foxes [*shu'alim*] that ruin the vineyards:** The term *shu'al* likely refers to the red fox, *Vulpes vulpes*, which can be found in Israel and whose diet includes fruit. It can also refer to the golden jackal, *Canis aureus*. The jackal is often found near populated areas, where it takes advantage of the local agricultural supply for food in the spring and summer. In the ancient world, the hills of Jerusalem and Hebron were terraced mostly with vineyards. When these blossomed in the spring, and when the grapes ripened in the summer, jackals searching for food would be attracted to them (see commentary on 1:6; Judges 15:4).

The Young Woman's Appearance and Solomon's Splendor

THE SONG OF SONGS 3:6–11

This section opens with praise for the woman, envisioned coming out of the wilderness, perhaps to meet her groom. It then moves on to a description of the magnificent canopy and crown of King Solomon. There is no definitive explanation as to why King Solomon appears at this point. Perhaps the mysterious beloved is none other than Solomon himself, who until now has been anonymously walking through the streets of Jerusalem, courting a young woman unaware of his identity. Alternatively, King Solomon's appearance is meant only to provide background imagery for the story. In order to highlight the simplicity of the love between the Jerusalemite woman and her beloved and their modest lives, the poem portrays Solomon as reigning majestically over the city, surrounded by guards. According to the Sages, the name Solomon in The Song of Songs refers to the highest king, God Himself, who is constantly present in the backdrop of the narrative.

6 **Who is this coming up from the wilderness like columns of smoke,** which are visible in the desert from afar? This is not regular smoke, but **perfumed with myrrh and frankincense,**[B] fragrant spices, **and with all the powders of the merchant.** Merchants used to travel from place to place peddling cosmetics and jewelry to women.

Frankincense

"Like columns of smoke." Smoke from incense altar

7 At this point, the story turns in a new direction. King Solomon, who until now was mentioned only in the opening verse of the book, appears as a character in the story, as a king among his people: **Behold the bed of Solomon: There are sixty valiant men**[D] forming one or several perimeters **around it,**[B] **from the valiant of Israel.**

8 **All** these valiant men are **armed with a sword, trained in war; each man, a sword on his thigh, from fear in the nights.** There are fears that prey even on great rulers such as Solomon, and the guards therefore surround his bed. Although they primarily served as a guard of honor, these valiant men also protect Solomon from sudden attack in the night.

King in palanquin with canopy, illustration based on fresco, Ancient Egypt

9 **King Solomon made himself a** grand **canopy,** or perhaps a canopied bed, **from the wood of Lebanon.**

10 **He made its pillars of silver, its cushioning of gold,** and **its seat of** valuable **purple wool.**[B] Solomon's guards protect his canopy against strangers approaching from the outside, but **its interior is inlaid with love, from the daughters of Jerusalem** who came to King Solomon's bed. This could refer to Solomon's many wives and concubines (see 6:8).

11 **Emerge, daughters of Zion,** who represent the surrounding public, **and gaze at King Solomon,**[D] **at the crown with which his mother crowned him on the day of his wedding,**[D] **and on the day of the rejoicing of his heart.**[B]

Gold garland crown, Greece, 320–300 BCE

DISCUSSION

3:7 | **Sixty valiant men:** The number sixty has symbolic significance. It appears later in the book as the number of queens, also apparently of King Solomon (6:8; Rashbam). The Sages offer various allegorical explanations for this number. For example, the queens have been said to symbolize the sixty tractates of the Talmud (see *Shir HaShirim Rabba* 6:8), while the sixty valiant men have been interpreted as an allusion to the sixty letters in the priestly blessings (see *Shir HaShirim Rabba* 3:7).

בִּצְבָאוֹת אוֹ בְּאַיְלוֹת הַשָּׂדֶה אִם־תָּעִירוּ ׀ וְאִם־תְּעוֹרְרוּ אֶת־הָאַהֲבָה עַד
ו שֶׁתֶּחְפָּץ׃ מִי זֹאת עֹלָה מִן־הַמִּדְבָּר כְּתִימֲרוֹת עָשָׁן מְקֻטֶּרֶת
ז מֹר וּלְבוֹנָה מִכֹּל אַבְקַת רוֹכֵל׃ הִנֵּה מִטָּתוֹ שֶׁלִּשְׁלֹמֹה שִׁשִּׁים גִּבֹּרִים סָבִיב לָהּ
ח מִגִּבֹּרֵי יִשְׂרָאֵל׃ כֻּלָּם אֲחֻזֵי חֶרֶב מְלֻמְּדֵי מִלְחָמָה אִישׁ חַרְבּוֹ עַל־יְרֵכוֹ מִפַּחַד
ט בַּלֵּילוֹת׃ אַפִּרְיוֹן עָשָׂה לוֹ הַמֶּלֶךְ שְׁלֹמֹה מֵעֲצֵי הַלְּבָנוֹן׃ עַמּוּדָיו
עָשָׂה כֶסֶף רְפִידָתוֹ זָהָב מֶרְכָּבוֹ אַרְגָּמָן תּוֹכוֹ רָצוּף אַהֲבָה מִבְּנוֹת יְרוּשָׁלִָם׃
יא צְאֶינָה ׀ וּרְאֶינָה בְּנוֹת צִיּוֹן בַּמֶּלֶךְ שְׁלֹמֹה בָּעֲטָרָה שֶׁעִטְּרָה־לּוֹ אִמּוֹ בְּיוֹם חֲתֻנָּתוֹ

BACKGROUND

3:6| **Perfumed with myrrh and frankincense [*levona*]:** Frankincense is a fragrant, whitish-yellow resin derived from *Boswellia sacra* trees. Its name in Hebrew, *levona*, is probably due to its whitish [*lavan*] color. Frankincense grows in the southern part of the Arabian Peninsula, as well as in Somalia and Ethiopia. In King Solomon's time, it was probably grown in the Jordan Valley. Frankincense, which produces a fragrant smoke when burned, was used as part of the meal offerings in the Tabernacle in the wilderness, and in the Temple in Jerusalem (see Leviticus 2:1, and commentary ad loc.). With regard to myrrh, see commentary on 1:13.

3:7| **The bed of Solomon: There are sixty valiant men around it:** In ancient times the royal guard served both to guard a monarch or ruler in case of rebellion, and as a symbol of his importance. It seems that King David also had a special guard, comprising two groups of thirty soldiers each (see I Chronicles 11, and *Da'at Mikra* ad loc.). During the tranquil period of Solomon's reign, these "valiant men" served primarily as an honor guard. Even today, it is still customary for kings and rulers to maintain such an honor guard, such as the Household Division of the British monarch.

3:10| **Purple wool [*argaman*]:** *Argaman* is a general name for a reddish-purple dye produced from the spiny dye-murex, *Murex brandaris*, a snail that lives in the Mediterranean Sea. The liquid used for preparing this dye was extracted from a secretion of the snail found in minute quantities in its hypobranchial gland. Thus, many thousands of snails were required to dye a fabric. Ancient documents attest that wool dyed with this substance was forty times more expensive than wool dyed with other colors (see, e.g., Daniel 5:7). Consequently, *argaman* was used mainly for priests, kings, and ministers. Due to its importance and high price, its production was controlled, and at times, free trade of the dye was prohibited.

3:11| **At the crown with which his mother crowned him on the day of his wedding, and on the day of the rejoicing of his heart:** In ancient times, it was customary in many cultures to adorn the heads of bridegrooms and brides with crowns. The crowns of bridegrooms were generally made from expensive metals such as silver and gold, but there were also wreaths of flowers and reeds.

DISCUSSION

3:11| **King Solomon [*Shelomo*]:** If this is a reference to God, who is described as the One for whom peace [*shalom*] is His, then this entire portrayal relates to Him. The Sages explain that "the day of his wedding" refers to the giving of the Torah, and "the day of the rejoicing of his heart" refers to the building of the Temple. Solomon is of course the king who oversaw the construction of the Temple (Mishna *Ta'anit* 4:8; see I Kings 6). The canopy is reminiscent of the Holy of Holies, the innermost and most intimate chamber in the Sanctuary (see *Shir HaShirim Rabba*). This canopy is constructed from extremely valuable materials, and it is filled with the love of the daughters of Jerusalem, which represents the connection between man below and God above. According to this interpretation, these verses depict the appearance of the King in His glory over the course of history as a Savior, and as the One who holds the future in His hand.

At the crown with which his mother crowned him on the day of his wedding: The Talmud states that crowns were placed on the heads of the children of Israel in honor of the giving of the Torah (*Shabbat* 88a). It was customary to place a crown on the heads of bridegrooms on their wedding day, but this practice was suspended after the destruction of the Temple (see Mishna *Sota* 9:14). In certain places there developed a custom to place the crown of the Torah scroll on the head of the groom, and the authorities discuss the appropriateness of this custom. See *Shulḥan Arukh*, *Oraḥ Ḥayyim* 154:10, where the ruling is that this custom should not be practiced.

The First Song of the Beloved to the Young Woman

THE SONG OF SONGS 4:1–7

The beloved now uses imagery from various landscapes to praise the beauty of his love. However, toward the end of the passage he announces a temporary separation.

4 1 The beloved's praise for the young woman's beauty is not superficial; it first focuses on those parts of the body through which the personality finds expression: **Behold, you are fair, my love; behold, you are fair; your eyes are** graceful and calming as a pair of **doves;**[B] they peer out from **behind your braid,** which rests partly on your face. In the context of God's song to Israel, these dovelike eyes have been interpreted as an allusion to the willingness to accept a burden without complaint, and to go wherever one is sent. **Your hair is like a flock of goats that stream down from the highlands of Gilad,**[B] an area of pasture. The goats in this imagery are black, and more active than sheep, evoking the way a young woman's curly black locks flow down her head.

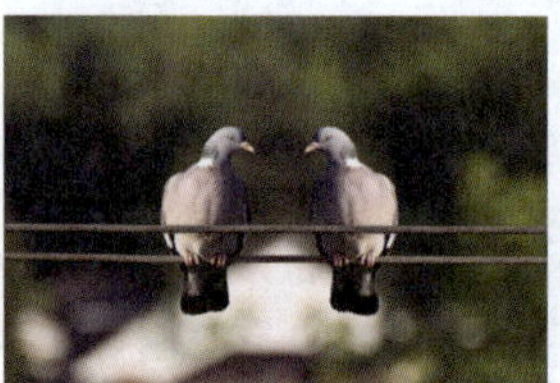
Pair of doves

Flock of goats moving down a mountain

2 **Your teeth are like a flock of ordered ewes that have come up from being washed,** when they are extremely white and clean. As the ewes emerge simultaneously from the water, the entire herd is lined up like white teeth, **that are all paired, and there is none missing among them.**

3 **Your lips are like a scarlet**[B] **thread, and your speech is lovely.** Some people have beautiful mouths but as soon as they open them to speak, their charm fades. In your case, however, your speech complements your physical beauty. **Your temple [*rakkatekh*] is like a pomegranate slice** which is exposed **behind your braid.** The Sages expound *rakkatekh* based on the word *reik*, empty. Even the emptiest or most depraved member of Israel is like a pomegranate slice containing numerous seeds, which represent good deeds.

Pomegranate slices

4 **Your neck is like the tower of David,** long and upright, **built magnificently [*talpiyot*].** This tower of David is not the construction known by that name today, but another tall tower in ancient Jerusalem that no longer stands. Here, the beloved praises the posture of the bride, the nation of Israel. The Sages explain this verse as a reference to the Temple, which stood on the hill [*tel*] to which all mouths [*piyot*] turn in prayer. **One thousand bucklers are hung upon it, all the shields of the mighty.**[B] The mighty men in the fortress would hang their shields on the tower as a show of strength. This tower on which a thousand shields hung resembled the woman's upright neck decorated with many ornaments.

Pendant necklace in the shape of warriors' shields, Iran, first millennium BCE

5 **Your two breasts are like two fawns, twins of a gazelle.**[B] The birth of twins is not a particularly common phenomenon among gazelles or deer. When twin fawns stand together, their black noses stand out, **which** is especially striking when they **graze among the** white **lilies.**

Two fawns

6 In the meantime, **until the day is great,** or until the hot wind blows, that is, until noon, **and the shadows flee, I will go to the mountain of myrrh,** the mountain where myrrh grows, **and to the hill of frankincense,** where the air is fragrant and pleasant. The beloved, who grazes his flock among the lilies and wanders in the mountains, tells his love that he is leaving for a short while and will return home when the sun is at full strength.

7 The beloved concludes his poem with a verse that echoes its beginning: **All of you is fair, my love, and there is no blemish in you;** you are perfect. When one is in love, one sees no flaw in the object of one's love. Even if certain blemishes or problems appear, one considers them no more than temporary stains and passing shadows, and the overall picture remains perfect. This holds true even with regard to divine love.

א וּבְיוֹם שִׂמְחַת לִבּוֹ׃ הִנָּךְ יָפָה רַעְיָתִי הִנָּךְ יָפָה עֵינַיִךְ יוֹנִים מִבַּעַד
ב לְצַמָּתֵךְ שַׂעְרֵךְ כְּעֵדֶר הָעִזִּים שֶׁגָּלְשׁוּ מֵהַר גִּלְעָד׃ שִׁנַּיִךְ כְּעֵדֶר הַקְּצוּבוֹת שֶׁעָלוּ
ג מִן־הָרַחְצָה שֶׁכֻּלָּם מַתְאִימוֹת וְשַׁכֻּלָה אֵין בָּהֶם׃ כְּחוּט הַשָּׁנִי שִׂפְתוֹתַיִךְ וּמִדְבָּרֵךְ
ד נָאוֶה כְּפֶלַח הָרִמּוֹן רַקָּתֵךְ מִבַּעַד לְצַמָּתֵךְ׃ כְּמִגְדַּל דָּוִיד צַוָּארֵךְ בָּנוּי לְתַלְפִּיּוֹת
ה אֶלֶף הַמָּגֵן תָּלוּי עָלָיו כֹּל שִׁלְטֵי הַגִּבֹּרִים׃ שְׁנֵי שָׁדַיִךְ כִּשְׁנֵי עֳפָרִים תְּאוֹמֵי צְבִיָּה
ו הָרֹעִים בַּשּׁוֹשַׁנִּים׃ עַד שֶׁיָּפוּחַ הַיּוֹם וְנָסוּ הַצְּלָלִים אֵלֶךְ לִי אֶל־הַר הַמּוֹר וְאֶל־
ז ח גִּבְעַת הַלְּבוֹנָה׃ כֻּלָּךְ יָפָה רַעְיָתִי וּמוּם אֵין בָּךְ׃ אִתִּי מִלְּבָנוֹן

The Beloved's Second Poem

THE SONG OF SONGS 4:8–11

In the second love poem, the beloved expresses deepening emotions. The young woman, who was previously called his love, is now referred to as his bride, and he addresses her with increasing frequency.

8 **With me from** Mount **Lebanon, my bride, with me from Lebanon, come.** Let us wander together in Lebanon and return. Perhaps the beloved is approaching from northern Israel. **Look from the peak of Amana,**[B] **from the peak of Senir and Hermon.** Senir is another name for Mount Hermon, perhaps a specific side of the mountain. Look out **from the dens of**

BACKGROUND

4:1| **Your eyes are doves:** The rock dove, *Columba livia,* which is common in Israel, nests in terraced fields, near human residences, or in rocky areas in the hills. Doves are monogamous birds; they change mates only after the death of their partner. The male and female are practically identical in appearance, predominantly gray with black stripes. The verse may be alluding to the color of the girl's eyes. The domestic pigeon is a domesticated subspecies of the rock dove, and it resembles the latter in both behavior and appearance. Domestic pigeons are also monogamous.

A flock of goats that stream down from the highlands of Gilad: The region known as Gilad extends from the Sea of Galilee to the Dead Sea on the eastern side of the Jordan River. It is a hilly region, rich in water sources and vegetation, and suitable for pasture (see Numbers 32:1). However, it is relatively unsuitable for farming. The woman's hair is compared to the sight of black goats streaming down a hill, black lines against the bright background of the highlands of Gilad.

4:3| **Scarlet [*shani*]:** A dye of bright red, produced from a scale insect known as a kermes. The dye is extracted from the creatures by drying them, crushing them, and then cooking them. Besides its use in dying expensive fabrics, this substance was used in the ritual for the purification of lepers (Leviticus 14:4, 49) and of people who had come in contact with a dead body (Numbers 19:6). In the description of the building of the Temple (II Chronicles 2:6, 13), the term *karmil* appears instead of *shani*, *karmil* being the Hebrew name for the kermes insect (Rav Se'adya Gaon; Rashi; Radak).

4:4| **All the shields of the mighty:** Early necklaces were made from long, colorful beads that were threaded in rows. These would rest upon the neck like shields hanging from a wall or tower.

4:5| **Twins of a gazelle:** There are two types of gazelle in Israel: the mountain gazelle, also known as the Levantine mountain gazelle, and the dorcas gazelle. It is possible that the verse is referring to another type of gazelle that lived in this region, the black-tailed gazelle, *Gazella subgutturosa*, which currently inhabits an area spanning from the Arabian Peninsula to central Asia, and was once very common in Jordan and Syria. Between the ages of three and eight, when a female black-tailed gazelle is at her most fertile, she can bear twins (Azarya Alon, ed., *Plants and Animals of the Land of Israel*: *An Illustrated Encyclopedia*. Ministry of Defense/Society for the Protection of Nature, 1983–1990 [Hebrew]).

4:8| **From the peak of Amana:** Since Amana is listed alongside Senir and Hermon, which are in the southern Anti-Lebanon Mountains, it appears that Amana is a peak in the same range, near the source of the Amana River, which is mentioned as one of the rivers of Damascus. This river is generally identified with the Barada River, which cuts through the city. In Sumerian documents, Amana is mentioned as Amanum, and until the Roman era there was a waystation of this name. Amana has been identified with Mount Zabadani, which is northwest of Damascus and reaches a height of 1800 m. Amana's forests and rocky cliffs are features of its impressive landscape. The Amana of this verse should not be confused with the Amanos Mountains in southeastern Turkey.

lions, from the mountains of leopards.[B] These forested areas were largely uncultivated expanses in which lions and leopards roamed. The wild regions of Lebanon, with their array of predators, serve as a contrasting background to the gentle bride, the Jewish people, or the soul.

Mount Hermon

Lebanon

9 **You have charmed me, my sister,**[D] my love, **my bride; you have charmed me with** my seeing even just **one of your eyes, with** even **one bead of your necklace.** Even the smallest glimpse of you moves me.
10 **How fair is your loving,** or the moistness of your mouth, **my sister, my bride. How much better is your loving than wine, and the fragrance of your oils,** even the simplest of them, is more delightful **than all spices.**
11 **Your lips drip nectar, my bride, honey and milk are under your tongue,** your taste is sweet and pleasant, **and the scent of your garments is like the scent of Lebanon,** a rainy, fertile, and forested region.

The Third Poem and the Bride's Invitation to Her Beloved

THE SONG OF SONGS 4:12–5:1

In his third poem, the beloved praises the bride's qualities of modesty and loyalty, and concludes with a wish. After the poem, the text briefly hints at unification between the lovers.

12 **A locked garden is my sister, my bride; a locked fountainhead,**[23] **a sealed spring.** Although your beauty is arresting, it is not in the public domain; it is designated for one man only.
13 **Your branches,**[24] your external appearance, your garments and coverings, **are** like the pleasant sight of **an orchard of pomegranates, with delicious fruit,** and they are scented like **hennas with lavenders,** perfumes (see 1:12, 14). You radiate beauty from every angle.
14 Your garments are scented like **lavender and saffron,**[B] **lemongrass and cinnamon,**[B] **with all trees of frankincense; myrrh and aloes,**[B] **with all the finest spices.**[25] Of the eleven spices blended into the incense used in the Temple, only four are specified by name in the Torah. Almost all of the rest are taken from this list.
15 The singer returns to the image of the bride as a spring in a locked garden: She is a source of life, **a garden spring, a well of spring water, and flowing streams from Lebanon.** The spring's source is in the distant and fertile mountain peaks.[26]

Sealed spring

"Orchard of pomegranates"

Saffron crocus

Cinnamon

Frankincense tree

Indian aloe tree

16 **Awake, north wind, and come, south wind; blow upon my garden,** my bride, and **its perfume will spread,** or: The sap of its perfumed trees will flow. Unlike many places in the Bible that mention the covenant between God and Israel and its ensuing obligations, this passage expresses the romantic aspect of the covenant. This poem of love and praise is reminiscent of Jeremiah's invocation of the nuptial love between God and Israel in the wilderness.[27] At the starting point in their shared journey, there was a sense of confidence and mutual commitment regarding the future, a faith that all would be well. The groom is moved by the perfect beauty and loyalty of the bride, and he waits for her lovely scent to spread across great distances.

כַּלָּה אִתִּי מִלְּבָנוֹן תָּבוֹאִי תָּשׁוּרִי ׀ מֵרֹאשׁ אֲמָנָה מֵרֹאשׁ שְׂנִיר וְחֶרְמוֹן מִמְּעֹנוֹת
ט אֲרָיוֹת מֵהַרְרֵי נְמֵרִים׃ לִבַּבְתִּנִי אֲחֹתִי כַלָּה לִבַּבְתִּינִי באחד מֵעֵינַיִךְ בְּאַחַד עֲנָק
י מִצַּוְּרֹנָיִךְ׃ מַה־יָּפוּ דֹדַיִךְ אֲחֹתִי כַלָּה מַה־טֹּבוּ דֹדַיִךְ מִיַּיִן וְרֵיחַ שְׁמָנַיִךְ מִכָּל־
יא בְּשָׂמִים׃ נֹפֶת תִּטֹּפְנָה שִׂפְתוֹתַיִךְ כַּלָּה דְּבַשׁ וְחָלָב תַּחַת לְשׁוֹנֵךְ וְרֵיחַ שַׂלְמֹתַיִךְ
יב יג כְּרֵיחַ לְבָנוֹן׃ גַּן ׀ נָעוּל אֲחֹתִי כַלָּה גַּל נָעוּל מַעְיָן חָתוּם׃ שְׁלָחַיִךְ
יד פַּרְדֵּס רִמּוֹנִים עִם פְּרִי מְגָדִים כְּפָרִים עִם־נְרָדִים׃ נֵרְדְּ ׀ וְכַרְכֹּם קָנֶה וְקִנָּמוֹן עִם
טו כָּל־עֲצֵי לְבוֹנָה מֹר וַאֲהָלוֹת עִם כָּל־רָאשֵׁי בְשָׂמִים׃ מַעְיַן גַּנִּים בְּאֵר מַיִם חַיִּים
טז וְנֹזְלִים מִן־לְבָנוֹן׃ עוּרִי צָפוֹן וּבוֹאִי תֵימָן הָפִיחִי גַנִּי יִזְּלוּ בְשָׂמָיו יָבֹא דוֹדִי לְגַנּוֹ

BACKGROUND

From the mountains of leopards: This refers to the Arabian leopard, *Panthera pardus nimr*, one of the smallest leopards in the world. The Arabian leopard is a solitary predator, weighing 20–30 kg. It can be found in the mountains of the Judean Desert, and in the Negev in the region of Mitzpe Ramon.

4:14| **Saffron:** Since ancient times, saffron has been obtained from the *Crocus sativus* flower. It is used mainly as a seasoning and coloring agent in food and is still one of the world's most expensive spices.

Lemongrass and cinnamon [*kaneh vekinnamon*]: Some consider *kaneh vekinnamon* the name of a single spice (Septuagint). Perhaps this spice was cinnamon extracted from the inner bark of the tropical cinnamon tree, of the genus *Cinnamomum*, which grows in the Far East. This hypothesis is supported by the verse: "And the good cane [*kaneh*] from a distant land" (Jeremiah 6:20). The bark of this tree curls up when dried and looks like a stick, the literal meaning of the word *kaneh*. Others identify *kaneh* with a plant from the lemongrass genus, *Cymbopogon*, whose leaves contain aromatic oils. Yet another opinion identifies *kaneh* as *Acorus calamus*, also called sweet flag, a plant of the Acoraceae family with fragrant roots (Zohar Amar, *Flora of the Bible*. Jerusalem: Rubin Mass Ltd., 2012 [Hebrew], p. 181).

Aloes [*ahalot*]: *Ahal* is generally identified with one of the species of the tropical Indian aloe tree, genus *Aquilaria*, from whose bark a potent and expensive perfume is extracted.

DISCUSSION

4:9| **My sister:** This term for a lover has been in use from ancient times and can be found also in modern Hebrew poetry. Although the title is sometimes used in a literal sense, as when Abraham said of Sarah that she was his sister (Genesis 20:2), it can also be indicative of a relationship that is not familial. In various monarchies in the ancient Orient, the queen was sometimes called the king's sister, whether or not she was actually his sister, although on more than one occasion this was indeed the case.

After all this praise by the beloved, the bride responds with a brief, modest invitation: **Let my beloved come to his garden and eat his delicious fruits.** The garden is not locked to you; the fountain is open before you.

5 1 After the bride's invitation, the beloved describes the satisfaction he found in his perfect bride: **I came to my garden,** filled with all types of goodness, **my sister, my bride; I gathered my myrrh with my perfume; I ate my honeycomb with my honey; I drank my wine with my milk. Eat, friends; drink, and make love.** The image is of a romantic lovers' tryst.

Honeycomb

The Longing of the Young Woman

THE SONG OF SONGS 5:2–6:3

Now the woman relates her experiences. She opens with a story, perhaps only a dream,[28] of a missed opportunity in which she failed to meet her beloved because of her hesitation to open her door to him. Now, she is regretful and lonely, and she yearns for him.

2 **I am sleeping, but my heart is awake.** In this semiconscious state, something inside me alerted me: **The sound of my beloved is knocking.**[D] Despite my drowsiness, some part of me was alert, eagerly listening for him. I could hear him calling out to me: **Open for me, my sister, my love, my faultless dove,** my perfect beauty. There is a tone of familiarity and closeness in these expressions of affection by the male protagonist. He continues: Open for me, **for my head is filled with dew** from waiting outside at night; **my locks** are filled with the **drops of night,** dew. I am wet, it is uncomfortable outdoors, and I seek shelter.

Dew

3 The woman says to herself: **I have** already **taken off my tunic; how can I don it** now? **I have washed my feet** before bed; **how can I soil them** by walking on the floor to open the door? She does not answer her beloved's call.

4 **My beloved extended his hand through the hole**[D] in the door.[29] When he did so, my love welled up **and my core** [*me'ay*] **was moved for him,** my insides turned over from excitement. Although in modern Hebrew the term *me'ayim* refers specifically to the intestines, in the Bible it refers to the internal cavity of one's body, and by extension, to the heart and soul.[30]

5 Despite my hesitations, when I realized that my beloved was almost inside I could no longer restrain myself: **I arose to open for my beloved; my** perfumed **hands were dripping with** liquid **myrrh, and my fingers with myrrh passing onto the handles of the latch.** The scent of myrrh reached outside.

Bolt on a door

6 **I opened for my beloved; but** while I had hesitated, **my beloved had slipped away, was gone. My soul had departed with his speaking.** When he turned to me before, my heart stopped due to my profound love and longing. Now he was nowhere to be found. **I sought him, but I did not find him; I called him, but he did not answer me.** The verse possibly describes not an actual event, but a lover's troubled dream brought on by anxiety over a potential missed opportunity. Allegorically, this episode refers to real missed opportunities for redemption, on both a national and a personal level. Historically and personally, complacency and other obstacles to salvation prevent the long-sought union with God from taking place.

7 After searching for my beloved near the house to no avail, I went out into the streets. There **the sentries patrolling in the city found me,** and when they saw that I was wandering alone at night **they struck me, they wounded me;** apparently, they considered me a loiterer deserving of punishment. **The guards of the walls took my shawl from upon me.** The guards of the walls are not necessarily her enemies. Since they are charged with preserving the public order, they punish the woman for what they perceive as inappropriate behavior. Similarly, the individual's soul or the nation as a whole can react to a missed opportunity counterproductively. Plagued with visions of what might have been, it can attempt to seize the moment after it has passed, and in the process transgress boundaries. Such transgression always incurs punishment.

8 Here, it seems, the dream comes to an end. Now the woman addresses her friends: **I administer an oath to you, daughters of Jerusalem;** now, come to my aid: **If you find my beloved, what should you tell him?** Tell him **that I am lovesick.** Previously she bid the daughters of Jerusalem to promise that they would let the love awaken by itself (2:7, 3:5). Now, after the nocturnal episode, whether real or imagined, she no longer has the strength to hide her feelings or to keep up appearances. She entreats the daughters of Jerusalem to reveal her powerful love to her beloved.

וַיֹאכַל פְּרִי מְגָדָיו׃ בָּאתִי לְגַנִּי אֲחֹתִי כַלָּה אָרִיתִי מוֹרִי עִם־בְּשָׂמִי אָכַלְתִּי יַעְרִי א
עִם־דִּבְשִׁי שָׁתִיתִי יֵינִי עִם־חֲלָבִי אִכְלוּ רֵעִים שְׁתוּ וְשִׁכְרוּ דּוֹדִים׃ אֲנִי ב
יְשֵׁנָה וְלִבִּי עֵר קוֹל ׀ דּוֹדִי דוֹפֵק פִּתְחִי־לִי אֲחֹתִי רַעְיָתִי יוֹנָתִי תַמָּתִי שֶׁרֹּאשִׁי
נִמְלָא־טָל קְוֻצּוֹתַי רְסִיסֵי לָיְלָה׃ פָּשַׁטְתִּי אֶת־כֻּתָּנְתִּי אֵיכָכָה אֶלְבָּשֶׁנָּה רָחַצְתִּי ג
אֶת־רַגְלַי אֵיכָכָה אֲטַנְּפֵם׃ דּוֹדִי שָׁלַח יָדוֹ מִן־הַחוֹר וּמֵעַי הָמוּ עָלָיו׃ קַמְתִּי אֲנִי ד ה
לִפְתֹּחַ לְדוֹדִי וְיָדַי נָטְפוּ־מוֹר וְאֶצְבְּעֹתַי מוֹר עֹבֵר עַל כַּפּוֹת הַמַּנְעוּל׃ פָּתַחְתִּי ו
אֲנִי לְדוֹדִי וְדוֹדִי חָמַק עָבָר נַפְשִׁי יָצְאָה בְדַבְּרוֹ בִּקַּשְׁתִּיהוּ וְלֹא מְצָאתִיהוּ
קְרָאתִיו וְלֹא עָנָנִי׃ מְצָאֻנִי הַשֹּׁמְרִים הַסֹּבְבִים בָּעִיר הִכּוּנִי פְצָעוּנִי נָשְׂאוּ אֶת־ ז
רְדִידִי מֵעָלַי שֹׁמְרֵי הַחֹמוֹת׃ הִשְׁבַּעְתִּי אֶתְכֶם בְּנוֹת יְרוּשָׁלִָם אִם־תִּמְצְאוּ אֶת־ ח
דּוֹדִי מַה־תַּגִּידוּ לוֹ שֶׁחוֹלַת אַהֲבָה אָנִי׃ מַה־דּוֹדֵךְ מִדּוֹד הַיָּפָה בַּנָּשִׁים מַה־דּוֹדֵךְ ט
מִדּוֹד שֶׁכָּכָה הִשְׁבַּעְתָּנוּ׃ דּוֹדִי צַח וְאָדוֹם דָּגוּל מֵרְבָבָה׃ רֹאשׁוֹ כֶּתֶם פָּז קְוֻצּוֹתָיו י יא

9 The women ask her: **How is your beloved more than another beloved, O fairest of women?** Who is your beloved? How can we recognize him? **How is your beloved more** special **than another beloved, that you administer an oath to us so?** Notably, in The Song of Songs, the beloved is unknown. He appears intermittently and then vanishes, and no one can identify or locate him. In the background of the text hovers the question of how real the beloved actually is. For the time being, he has no formal relationship with the woman. They rarely meet, and at this stage of the story they are never seen together in public. Allegorically understood, the mysterious nature of the beloved represents the mysterious nature of God.

10 The young woman responds: The face of **my beloved is clear and ruddy,** his skin is clean and white, and his cheeks are red like a beautiful youth.[31] This mixture of red and white is consistent with the image of an apple to which the beloved was previously compared (2:3). My beloved is **more eminent** [***dagul***] **than ten thousand.** Like a flag [*degel*], my beloved stands out from the masses, unique.

11 **His head is** impressively shaped as a work of **the finest gold;**[32]

DISCUSSION

5:2 | **I am sleeping…My beloved is knocking:** On more than one occasion in history, the people of Israel were given a chance to redeem themselves, but they slumbered, failing to seize the moment. On the most fundamental level, and in the depths of the nation's heart, it is true that "I am my beloved's, and my beloved is mine" (6:3; see also 2:16), I desire redemption and a connection to God. But alas, I am lazy and slow to act. Throughout these love poems, with all their ups and downs, the lovers constantly desire one another, but external circumstances do not allow them to unite easily and they are frequently left alone with their longings. The beloved's knocking awakens her love, but she is too slow to act, and by the time she rises he has passed. In the wake of this vision, the woman is left with strengthened passion and will, but an opportunity has been missed.

5:4 | **My beloved extended his hand through the hole:** Locking a door from the inside was performed in biblical times by means of a vertical or horizontal bolt, which was wedged into the doorpost, the lintel, or the doorstep, thus preventing the door from being opened from the outside. The hole mentioned here probably served as means of grasping the door in order to open or close it when unlocked. Although in the ancient world there were locking mechanisms, which required the insertion of a key through a hole from the outside, such mechanisms have been found in the Land of Israel only from the Roman period.

his locks are curls, black as a raven. In ancient times, the hair color of Israelites was typically black.[33]

12 **His eyes are** perfect, radiating beauty and calm, **like doves beside streams of water.** This is a pastoral image of grace and tranquility. A dove drinks by sucking water[34] into its beak and directly into its throat, making no swallowing movement of its head. A pair of doves drinking thus appears to be in synchrony, as they change neither their stance nor their movements. His dark eyes are set against the backdrop of his light skin as if **they are bathed in milk, well set** like precious stones, neither protruding nor sunken.[35]

Dove beside water

13 **His cheeks are like a bed of fragrant plants, growths of spice mixtures.** An Israelite of the time would not be clean-shaven, and as the beloved is young, his beard is likely to be short, like small herbs growing in their beds. **His lips are** colored,[36] or velvety and fragrant[37] like **lilies;**[B] **dripping with flowing,** fragrant **myrrh.**

14 **His hands are** built as **rods of gold set with beryl [*tarshish*];**[B] **his belly is** like **a** solid **slab of ivory covered with sapphires.**[B]

15 **His calves are pillars of marble, set on bases of fine gold.** The beloved is compared to a work of art. **His appearance is like** the forested region of **Lebanon,** fertile and teeming with life, **choice like** the tall, impressive **cedars** that grow there.

16 **His palate is sweet and all of him is delightful. This is my beloved, and this is my companion, daughters of Jerusalem.** The bride lovingly depicts her beloved as the epitome of beauty. In her eyes, all of his features are wonderful and perfect. Her descriptions do not provide her listeners with practical details that might help them locate her beloved, but they illustrate her feelings for him. Many allegorical interpretations have been offered for these descriptions. The question: "How is your beloved more than another beloved"? (verse 9) has been posed to the nation of Israel for over two thousand years. The answer to this question is: You may not be able to see Him until He reveals Himself, but we can see that He is perfect, and we can do nothing other than seek Him everywhere.

Aquamarine

"Slab of ivory"

Peridot

Sapphire

6 1 The daughters of Jerusalem respond in unison: **Where did your beloved go, fairest of women? Where did your beloved turn? We will seek him with you.**

2 The woman responds: **My beloved descended to his garden, to the beds of fragrant plants.** She does not provide an exact location, but she knows that he is supposed to be in a place of beauty and fragrance, **to herd** his flock **in the gardens, and to gather lilies** for himself.

"Beds of fragrant plants"

3 She concludes: **I am my beloved's, and my beloved is mine.** It is he **who herds among the lilies.** Though he is not currently with me, this does not mean he is avoiding me. I am certain that our love is real. For now, however, my beloved has descended to his garden. Perhaps he will return to me with flowers.

The Beloved and His Love Grow Closer

THE SONG OF SONGS 6:4–7:14

The exchanges between the beloved and his love intensify in their passion with the rising intensity depicted by increasingly overt and bold imagery. The couple stand in wonder at their mutual love. Although it has not been fully consummated, they have full faith in its reality, despite temporary separations, sudden disappearances, and delays.

4 The beloved himself speaks, though the object of his love is likely not present. **You are fair, my love, like Tirtza,**[B] a small city in the portion of Manasseh, which at one point served as the capital of the Kingdom of Israel.[38] It is possible that its beauty played a role in its being chosen as the capital. You are **lovely like Jerusalem**[39] and you are **formidable like banners [*nidgalot*].** You stand out as a banner on display as it flutters

יב תַּלְתַּלִּים שְׁחֹרוֹת כָּעוֹרֵב: עֵינָיו כְּיוֹנִים עַל־אֲפִיקֵי מָיִם רֹחֲצוֹת בֶּחָלָב יֹשְׁבוֹת
יג עַל־מִלֵּאת: לְחָיָו כַּעֲרוּגַת הַבֹּשֶׂם מִגְדְּלוֹת מֶרְקָחִים שִׂפְתוֹתָיו שׁוֹשַׁנִּים נֹטְפוֹת
יד מוֹר עֹבֵר: יָדָיו גְּלִילֵי זָהָב מְמֻלָּאִים בַּתַּרְשִׁישׁ מֵעָיו עֶשֶׁת שֵׁן מְעֻלֶּפֶת סַפִּירִים:
טו טז שׁוֹקָיו עַמּוּדֵי שֵׁשׁ מְיֻסָּדִים עַל־אַדְנֵי־פָז מַרְאֵהוּ כַּלְּבָנוֹן בָּחוּר כָּאֲרָזִים: חִכּוֹ
א מַמְתַקִּים וְכֻלּוֹ מַחֲמַדִּים זֶה דוֹדִי וְזֶה רֵעִי בְּנוֹת יְרוּשָׁלִָם: אָנָה הָלַךְ דּוֹדֵךְ הַיָּפָה
ב בַּנָּשִׁים אָנָה פָּנָה דוֹדֵךְ וּנְבַקְשֶׁנּוּ עִמָּךְ: דּוֹדִי יָרַד לְגַנּוֹ לַעֲרֻגוֹת הַבֹּשֶׂם לִרְעוֹת
ג בַּגַּנִּים וְלִלְקֹט שׁוֹשַׁנִּים: אֲנִי לְדוֹדִי וְדוֹדִי לִי הָרֹעֶה בַּשּׁוֹשַׁנִּים:
ד ה יָפָה אַתְּ רַעְיָתִי כְּתִרְצָה נָאוָה כִּירוּשָׁלִָם אֲיֻמָּה כַּנִּדְגָּלוֹת: הָסֵבִּי עֵינַיִךְ מִנֶּגְדִּי
ו שֶׁהֵם הִרְהִיבֻנִי שַׂעְרֵךְ כְּעֵדֶר הָעִזִּים שֶׁגָּלְשׁוּ מִן־הַגִּלְעָד: שִׁנַּיִךְ כְּעֵדֶר הָרְחֵלִים
ז שֶׁעָלוּ מִן־הָרַחְצָה שֶׁכֻּלָּם מַתְאִימוֹת וְשַׁכֻּלָה אֵין בָּהֶם: כְּפֶלַח הָרִמּוֹן רַקָּתֵךְ

high above. Alternatively, *nidgalot* refers to arrays of decorated soldiers.[40]

5 **Avert your eyes from me, as they excite my arrogance,** or passion,[41] when they gaze upon me. **Your** black, curly **hair,** flowing down your back, **is like a flock of goats that has streamed down from the Gilad.**

Tirtza Ravine

6 **Your teeth are like a flock of ewes that have come up from being washed, that are all paired, and there is none missing among them.** Your teeth are perfect and beautiful.

7 **Your temple is like a pomegranate slice,** round and beautiful, **behind your braid,** or lock of hair, falling over your face and sides.

BACKGROUND

5:13| **His lips are lilies [*shoshanim*]:** The identity of the *shoshana* is unclear (see commentary on 2:1). If this description refers to the color of his lips, then the *shoshana* must be red (see Alsheikh). If so, it likely refers to the rose and not the white Madonna lily. However, it is possible that the verse intends to describe the shape or feel of the beloved's lips, rather than their color, in which case the *shoshana* can still be identified as the Madonna lily.

5:14| **Beryl [*tarshish*]:** *Tarshish* is one of the precious stones set into the breast piece of the High Priest (Exodus 28:20). Various opinions are offered in rabbinic literature and the Aramaic translations regarding the identity and color of *tarshish*. Nowadays, it is commonly accepted to identify *tarshish* with peridot or with the bluish-green variety of beryl known as aquamarine. Some have noted a similarity between the word *tarshish* and the Akkadian word for red, *rususu*.

Sapphire: A blue variety of the extremely hard mineral corundum, the sapphire is valued as a precious stone for jewelry. Corundum can also appear in other colors. The red variety is called ruby.

6:4| **Tirtza:** Tirtza was an important city in the territory of the tribe of Manasseh, identified with Tel el-Far'a, approximately 10 km northeast of Shekhem. This city controlled the roads leading from Shekhem to the crossings of the Jordan River near Adam and to Beit She'an. Archaeological discoveries in the area reflect the biblical accounts of Tirtza. Nearby, there is a large spring, Ein el-Far'a.

The city was protected by ravines on three sides. The beautiful, green, and water-rich environment surrounding Tirtza, along with its strategic location, justified its choice as the capital city of the Kingdom of Israel. During a rebellion it was destroyed, and the more fortified city of Samaria was selected in its stead.

8 **They are sixty queens,** wives of King Solomon, **and eighty concubines, and** around him there are also **young women without number.** Perhaps this is a poem composed about or by King Solomon, presumably in his youth.[42]

9 Despite Solomon's many women, **unique is my faultless dove;** she stands above them all. **Unique to her mother,** there is no woman like her; she is **pure to the one who bore her. Girls see her and laud her, queens and concubines** see her **and praise her.**

10 The beloved continues to praise his bride: **Who is she who appears** in the distance, glowing **like** the **dawn, fair like the moon, pure** and shining **like the sun?** The initial light of dawn is very gentle; the light of the moon is not strong, but it is pleasant and clear; the sun that eventually shines forth is the brightest of all.[43] She is **formidable like banners.**

Dawn

11 Here the narrator could be either the beloved or his love, but it is probably the latter:[44] **I have gone down to the nut garden to look at the budding** [*ibbei*] **of the vale,**[45] the fresh fruits or plants of the valley. Perhaps the word *aviv*, spring, is derived from *ibbei*, as spring is the season of regrowth and vitality.[46] I have gone **to see whether the vine has blossomed and the pomegranates are in bloom.** This takes place in spring, when people generally venture down to gardens and streams to see the blossoming plants. Many commentaries explain this image of initial growth as representing the exodus from Egypt.

Unripe nuts

Unripe dates

"Pomegranates are in bloom"

12 I am utterly amazed by the experience, as if **I do not know my own soul** in this surreal state that resembles a dream. **It has set me,** I feel as though I have been set **on chariots of my noble** [*nadiv*] **people,** as if he has taken me upon his chariot among his soldiers. Some suggest that the phrase *ami nadiv*, my noble people, is an allusion to Aminadav father of Nahshon, the prince of Judah.

7 **1** This part of the song evokes the dancing young women, calling to the most beautiful among them: **Return, return,** turn around, or rejoin our dancing, **the Shulamite.** This is probably not a person's name, but an appellation for a perfect [*mushlemet*], beautiful girl, the bride of the beloved. **Return, return, and we will gaze upon you.** And a response: **Why will you gaze at the Shulamite like a dance of two companies** of dancers? Why do you look at the Shulamite in this circle of dancers? Although the Shulamite appears together with all the other girls, she stands out. Allegorically understood, the Shulamite could be a metaphor for Israel among the nations or for the soul that shines out from the body.

2 The Shulamite's beauty is now described in detail, from her toes to her head: **How fair are your steps,**[47] or your feet,[48] **in sandals, daughter of a nobleman. Your rounded thighs are like ornaments, the handiwork of a master craftsman,**[B] perfect as a work of art.

Necklace of gold links, Egypt, Roman period

3 **Your navel is a moon-shaped goblet,** or bowl. **May it not lack mixed wine. Your belly is** round, smooth, and symmetrical, like **a pile of wheat** in a granary, **hedged with lilies.** This last expression is an image of carefully guarded beauty.[49]

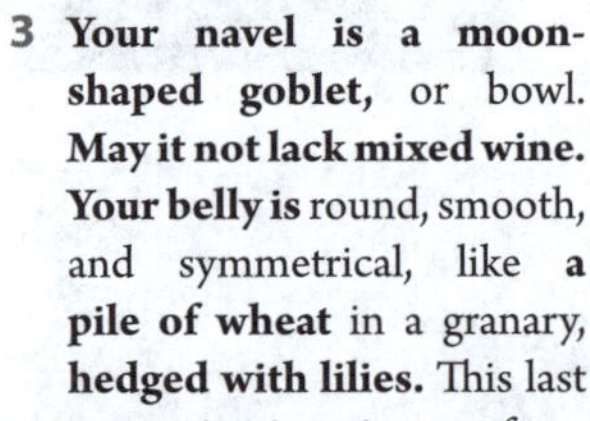

Pile of threshed wheat

4 **Your two breasts are like two fawns, twins of a gazelle.** This simile relies on both the fawns' physical shape and their aesthetic beauty.

5 **Your neck is** upright, white, and beautiful, **like an ivory tower; your eyes are** like the **pools in Heshbon,**[B] **by the gate of Bat Rabim.** Heshbon was an ancient city located on the eastern side of the Jordan River that served as a political and commercial center even before Israel entered the land of Canaan. It is possible that Heshbon boasted two large pools near its city gates, perhaps in a public square where many people [*rabim*] would gather.[50] The imagery evokes large, deep, and tranquil eyes. **Your nose,**[D] or your forehead, **is like the tower of Lebanon overlooking Damascus** in the distance.[51]

ח מִבַּעַד לְצַמָּתֵךְ: שִׁשִּׁים הֵמָּה מְלָכוֹת וּשְׁמֹנִים פִּילַגְשִׁים וַעֲלָמוֹת אֵין מִסְפָּר:
ט אַחַת הִיא יוֹנָתִי תַמָּתִי אַחַת הִיא לְאִמָּהּ בָּרָה הִיא לְיוֹלַדְתָּהּ רָאוּהָ בָנוֹת
י וַיְאַשְּׁרוּהָ מְלָכוֹת וּפִילַגְשִׁים וַיְהַלְלוּהָ: מִי־זֹאת הַנִּשְׁקָפָה כְּמוֹ־שָׁחַר
יא יָפָה כַלְּבָנָה בָּרָה כַּחַמָּה אֲיֻמָּה כַּנִּדְגָּלוֹת: אֶל־גִּנַּת אֱגוֹז יָרַדְתִּי לִרְאוֹת בְּאִבֵּי
יב הַנָּחַל לִרְאוֹת הֲפָרְחָה הַגֶּפֶן הֵנֵצוּ הָרִמֹּנִים: לֹא יָדַעְתִּי נַפְשִׁי שָׂמַתְנִי מַרְכְּבוֹת
א עַמִּי נָדִיב: שׁוּבִי שׁוּבִי הַשּׁוּלַמִּית שׁוּבִי שׁוּבִי וְנֶחֱזֶה־בָּךְ מַה־תֶּחֱזוּ בַּשּׁוּלַמִּית
ב כִּמְחֹלַת הַמַּחֲנָיִם: מַה־יָּפוּ פְעָמַיִךְ בַּנְּעָלִים בַּת־נָדִיב חַמּוּקֵי יְרֵכַיִךְ כְּמוֹ חֲלָאִים
ג מַעֲשֵׂה יְדֵי אָמָּן: שָׁרְרֵךְ אַגַּן הַסַּהַר אַל־יֶחְסַר הַמָּזֶג בִּטְנֵךְ עֲרֵמַת חִטִּים סוּגָה
ד ה בַּשּׁוֹשַׁנִּים: שְׁנֵי שָׁדַיִךְ כִּשְׁנֵי עֳפָרִים תָּאֳמֵי צְבִיָּה: צַוָּארֵךְ כְּמִגְדַּל הַשֵּׁן עֵינַיִךְ
בְּרֵכוֹת בְּחֶשְׁבּוֹן עַל־שַׁעַר בַּת־רַבִּים אַפֵּךְ כְּמִגְדַּל הַלְּבָנוֹן צוֹפֶה פְּנֵי דַמָּשֶׂק:

BACKGROUND

7:2 | **Your rounded thighs are like ornaments [*ḥala'im*], the handiwork of a master craftsman:** The word *ḥelya*, or *ḥali*, apparently refers to a round ornament. The *ḥali* is also mentioned alongside earrings in the book of Proverbs (25:2). Some associate this term with the word *ḥuliya*, a term used by the Sages to denote a link in a chain or bead (Rashi). Alternatively, *ḥali* may be related to a similar Akkadian word that means loins. If so, the beloved is praising the figure of his love as suitable for birthing children.

7:5 | **Heshbon:** Heshbon was an important city located on the border between the territories of Gad and Reuben (Joshua 13:17). It is generally identified with Tel Hesban, which is located on the ancient King's Highway, on the highlands above the Madaba Plains, about 20 km southwest of Rabat Amon, or present-day Amman. According to Josephus, control of Heshbon changed hands during various wars, and was under Jewish control during the Hasmonean period. It can be inferred from this verse that the people of Israel were familiar with this city (see also Ramban, Numbers 32:38). Although the surrounding region was fertile, the city was located on the edge of the desert. It was therefore necessary to channel the water that flowed through nearby ravines in the winter, and to store it in pools.

DISCUSSION

7:5 | **Your nose [*apekh*]:** Rashi notes that a large nose is not considered a sign of beauty, and he therefore maintains that the word *apekh* here refers to the forehead, since the face as a whole can be referred to as *apayim*. Others maintain that *apekh* indeed refers to her nose, as in verse 9 that follows, and explain that the comparison between the young woman's nose and the tower of Lebanon refers to its renowned beauty and straightness, not its size (see Ibn Ezra; Rav Yosef Kara; Rav Yeshaya of Trani).

6 **Your head is** elegantly set **upon you like the Carmel.** This could also be a reference to the woman's curly hair, since Mount Carmel has lush vegetation. **And the locks of your head are** carefully arranged **like** soft strands of **purple wool,** displayed in magnificent arrangements due to the wool's rarity and price.[52] **A king,** the beloved, is **bound in the tresses.**[BD]

Mount Carmel

"King bound in the tresses." Tasseled headdress, Troy, Bronze Age

7 The previous description of the bride, which was the most intimate so far, is now followed by expressions of the mutual adoration between the lovers: **How fair you are and how pleasant you are, love in its delights.** Love waxes and wanes, and includes, alongside dreams and aspirations, also heartache. However, love in its delights is consummated love, in which joy is fully realized.

8 The beloved's poem of intimacy: **This, your stature, is likened to a** tall, beautiful **date palm, and your breasts** are likened **to** round **clusters** of dates that hang at its sides.

9 The image of the date palm continues: **I said** to myself: **I will ascend the date palm, I will grasp its branches;**[53] **and please may your breasts be like clusters of the vine, and the fragrance of your nose** pleasant **like apples.**

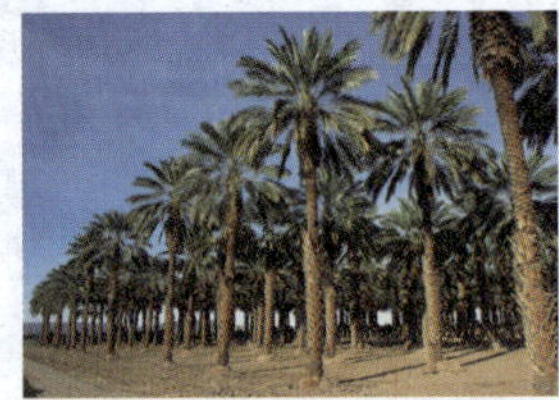
Date palms

Date palm branches

"Clusters of the vine"

10 **Your palate,** the taste of your kisses, **is like fine wine that goes pleasantly with my lovemaking** [*dodi*], or that goes pleasantly into my mouth.[54] Another possible interpretation is that the word *dodi* here means "my beloved," a reference to the male lover. If so, this phrase is recited by the bride. However, since the first phrase, "Your palate is like fine wine," is addressed to the female lover, then this latter phrase must be an interjection as the young woman completes her beloved's sentence. The man continues: Your palate is like fine wine, **moving the lips of the sleeping** so that they speak.[55]

11 The woman responds: **I am my beloved's,** or I yearn for my beloved, **and his desire is toward me.**

12 **Come, my beloved, let us go out** alone **to the field; let us stay the night in the villages.** These are not necessarily actual plans. They may simply be fantasies that convey the depth of her emotion and passion.

13 **Let us arise early to the vineyards; let us see whether the vine has blossomed, the grape bud has sprouted.**[56] Let us see whether **the pomegranates have bloomed.**[B] This scene takes place during the spring, when the flowers of the pomegranate tree appear, undoubtedly a beautiful sight. **There,** in the tranquil and beautiful vineyard, **I will give my love to you.** These descriptions of springtime can also be understood as an allusion to the exodus from Egypt, as Passover is always in the spring. There is a special obligation to remember the exodus, which was itself the springtime blossoming of Israel into a nation, during the month in which all of nature blossoms and the promise of the future beckons.

"The grape bud has sprouted." Tiny grapes visible between stamens

14 After a while, **the mandrakes have emitted fragrance.**[B] Mandrakes do not emit their pleasant fragrance in the spring. Rather, they ripen approximately one and a half months later, at the time of the wheat harvest. Therefore, a considerable time must have passed since the invitation of the previous verse. **And at our entrance are** the scents of **all types of delicacies,** both **new,** which have sprouted recently, **and old.** All of this sweetness, new and old, **I have hidden them away for you, my beloved.** At this point, the courtship that has been developing throughout the entire story reaches its conclusion. The love between the beloved and his bride is depicted here at its apex, when the beloved describes his love as utterly beautiful and graceful, and she responds by noting that all of nature is ripe for the consummation of their love, and that she waits only for him.

Mandrakes

ו ז רֹאשֵׁךְ עָלַיִךְ כַּכַּרְמֶל וְדַלַּת רֹאשֵׁךְ כָּאַרְגָּמָן מֶלֶךְ אָסוּר בָּרְהָטִים: מַה־יָּפִית
ח וּמַה־נָּעַמְתְּ אַהֲבָה בַּתַּעֲנוּגִים: זֹאת קוֹמָתֵךְ דָּמְתָה לְתָמָר וְשָׁדַיִךְ לְאַשְׁכֹּלוֹת:
ט אָמַרְתִּי אֶעֱלֶה בְתָמָר אֹחֲזָה בְּסַנְסִנָּיו וְיִהְיוּ־נָא שָׁדַיִךְ כְּאֶשְׁכְּלוֹת הַגֶּפֶן וְרֵיחַ
י יא אַפֵּךְ כַּתַּפּוּחִים: וְחִכֵּךְ כְּיֵין הַטּוֹב הוֹלֵךְ לְדוֹדִי לְמֵישָׁרִים דּוֹבֵב שִׂפְתֵי יְשֵׁנִים: אֲנִי
יב יג לְדוֹדִי וְעָלַי תְּשׁוּקָתוֹ: לְכָה דוֹדִי נֵצֵא הַשָּׂדֶה נָלִינָה בַּכְּפָרִים: נַשְׁכִּימָה לַכְּרָמִים
נִרְאֶה אִם־פָּרְחָה הַגֶּפֶן פִּתַּח הַסְּמָדַר הֵנֵצוּ הָרִמּוֹנִים שָׁם אֶתֵּן אֶת־דֹּדַי לָךְ:
יד הַדּוּדָאִים נָתְנוּ־רֵיחַ וְעַל־פְּתָחֵינוּ כָּל־מְגָדִים חֲדָשִׁים גַּם־יְשָׁנִים דּוֹדִי צָפַנְתִּי
א לָךְ: מִי יִתֶּנְךָ כְּאָח לִי יוֹנֵק שְׁדֵי אִמִּי אֶמְצָאֲךָ בַחוּץ אֶשָּׁקְךָ גַּם לֹא־יָבֻזוּ לִי:

Toward a Permanent Covenant

THE SONG OF SONGS 8:1–14

In this last section, though the poem remains the same poem and the love the same love, one can discern a new element. At the conclusion of The Song of Songs the reader finds premonitions of significant changes in the relationship between the beloved and his love. The previous descriptions of a vague, open-ended love gradually transition to a more functional, almost legal form. This section also includes certain insights on the nature of love, and the accompanying emotion of jealousy.

8 1 Until this point, the poem described a love bounded neither by space nor by time, with the lovers seemingly everywhere and nowhere at once. In the following verses, the woman expresses her desire to strengthen and stabilize her bond with her beloved: **If only you were like a brother to me, who sucked the breasts of my mother. I would find you outside; I would kiss you, yet they would not despise me.** Kissing a brother in public is not considered an undignified act. The young woman yearns to openly display her love for her beloved in such a natural manner.

BACKGROUND

7:6 | **A king [*melekh*] bound in the tresses [*barehatim*]:** Some suggest that the word *melekh* in this context does not mean king at all but is derived from the Akkadian term *malu*, which means an uncombed lock of hair. A similar Greek word, *mallu*, refers to a curl of wool or hair. If this is correct, then the word *rehatim* should be understood as the beams of a loom, such that the entire phrase means: Her hair is naturally arranged like weaving on the beams of a loom.

7:13 | **The vine has blossomed, the grape bud has sprouted, the pomegranates have bloomed:** After the start of the spring season, when the flowers of the field bloom, and the nightingale and turtledove have appeared (see 2:12), springtime reaches its peak, culminating in the blossoming of the vine and pomegranate. At this stage, one can observe the shedding of the joined, closed petals of the grape bud, as the stamen and pistils are released for pollination.

7:14 | **The mandrakes have emitted fragrance:** The mandrake, *Mandragora autumnalis*, which grows in Israel, ripens during the wheat harvest. It possesses a bright orange color and emits a pungent fragrance. The mandrake grows throughout the winter surrounded by purple flowers in a rosette of leaves close to the ground. The fruit is edible; however, its leaves, roots, and seeds are poisonous. In folklore, the mandrake is considered to have medicinal properties, and to be a remedy for infertility.

DISCUSSION

7:6 | **King bound in the tresses [*melekh asur barehatim*]:** Despite his power, wealth, and freedom, the king is captivated by her hair (see Ibn Ezra). Some explain that the tresses, *rehatim*, are not the bride's hair but the ribbons and fine chains decorating it, which were now tied around the king's head, according to the ancient custom for a bridegroom to tie his bride's hair decorations around his own head. It is also possible to translate the verse as follows: And the locks of your head are like purple wool of the king, bound in ribbons.

2 **I would lead you** unabashedly, I **would bring you to my mother's house, who teaches me;**[57] there **I would give you from the spiced wine to drink, from the juice of my pomegranate.**

3 Another fantasy: **His left** arm **is under my head, and his right embraces me** intimately.

4 Nevertheless, **I administer an oath to you, daughters of Jerusalem: For what do you awaken and for what do you rouse love, until it desires**[D] to awaken by itself? Let the love develop at its own pace.

5 This verse is spoken by a third party, depicting the relationship from a more stable, objective perspective: **Who is that coming up from the wilderness, leaning upon her beloved?**[58] Is it not the woman, who says to her beloved: **Under the apple tree** I met you and **I roused you** from your slumber; or, I roused your love for me. **There your mother conceived you; there she who bore you conceived.** The word *ḥibela*, translated here as "conceived," could also mean "suffered birth pangs." The shade of the apple tree is the beloved's place of origin, and it is there that he now encounters his love. Previously, the woman sought to bring her beloved into her mother's house; now, she arrives from an unknown wilderness, drawn to the place where her beloved was formed. Though she does not meet his parents, she makes reference to them. Understood allegorically, this verse refers to the soul's quest to rise above the mundane, and to find God in its own source and origin.

Apple tree

6 The woman asks of her beloved: **Set me as a seal upon your heart, as a seal upon your arm.**[B] Let me be like your seal, a personal item unique to you. This is another symbol of the increasing permanence of their bond. So powerful is the woman's devotion that she wishes to relinquish her independent existence altogether, preferring to attach herself to her beloved as a seal. There is, however, another side to this, **as love is as intense as death.** Alongside the delights of love, there is also a dark side. Just as death swallows everything and cannot be deferred, so too the feelings of love are so overpowering as to be inescapable. Furthermore, **jealousy is as cruel as the grave.** This refers to the demand for exclusive possession of the object of one's love. Such jealousy is a profound emotion that is difficult to bear. Understood allegorically, the jealousy that is built into love for God, who demands complete devotion, is very difficult for other peoples to comprehend. To the nation of Israel, the relationship with God is not only its most important bond, but the only thing in the world that matters. This feeling is as harsh, absolute, and uncompromising as the grave. **Its sparks,** the sparks of love, **are the sparks of fire,** which can burn and even destroy a person. Love is **a great conflagration.**

7 If love is true, **much water cannot extinguish** the fire of that **love, and rivers cannot wash it away;** even **if a man were to give all the wealth of his house for** the purchase of **love, he would be scorned.**[D] By means of gestures, gifts, and displays of emotion, one can acquire a certain level of friendship, but not love.

8 Now, relatives of the lovers begin to openly discuss their relationship. The brothers of the young woman speak first: **We have a little sister, and she has no breasts,** she is too young and insufficiently developed. Therefore, **what shall we do for our sister on the day that she will be spoken for** concerning marriage? Since she is not yet ready for marriage, what shall we do when the proposal arrives? How long can we delay it?

9 As long as the little sister was simply playing outside, singing and dancing, the brothers did not take much notice of her behavior. Now, however, they begin to appraise her character: **If she is a wall,** guarded and modest, **we will build upon her a silver parapet,**[B] we will decorate her with conspicuous jewelry. **And if she is a door,** which can be open and unguarded, **we will affix on her cedar panels** to protect her.[59]

Headdress with parapet on statuette, Rome, second century CE

10 The young woman responds: First, **I am a wall,** not a door, **and** second, **my breasts** are **like the towers.** I have breasts; you have merely failed to notice how much I have grown. **Then,** in this state, **I was in his eyes,** the eyes of the beloved, who is perhaps not immediately present, **as one who finds peace.** My beloved already knows that I have found my peace with my choice of him. You should have no misgivings

"I am a wall"

ב ג אֶנְהָגֲךָ אֲבִיאֲךָ אֶל־בֵּית אִמִּי תְּלַמְּדֵנִי אַשְׁקְךָ מִיַּיִן הָרֶקַח מֵעֲסִיס רִמֹּנִי׃ שְׂמֹאלוֹ
ד תַּחַת רֹאשִׁי וִימִינוֹ תְּחַבְּקֵנִי׃ הִשְׁבַּעְתִּי אֶתְכֶם בְּנוֹת יְרוּשָׁלָ͏ִם מַה־תָּעִירוּ ׀ וּמַה־
ה תְּעֹרְרוּ אֶת־הָאַהֲבָה עַד שֶׁתֶּחְפָּץ׃ מִי זֹאת עֹלָה מִן־הַמִּדְבָּר
מִתְרַפֶּקֶת עַל־דּוֹדָהּ תַּחַת הַתַּפּוּחַ עוֹרַרְתִּיךָ שָׁמָּה חִבְּלַתְךָ אִמֶּךָ שָׁמָּה חִבְּלָה
ו יְלָדַתְךָ׃ שִׂימֵנִי כַחוֹתָם עַל־לִבֶּךָ כַּחוֹתָם עַל־זְרוֹעֶךָ כִּי־עַזָּה כַמָּוֶת אַהֲבָה
ז קָשָׁה כִשְׁאוֹל קִנְאָה רְשָׁפֶיהָ רִשְׁפֵּי אֵשׁ שַׁלְהֶבֶתְיָה׃ מַיִם רַבִּים לֹא יוּכְלוּ לְכַבּוֹת
אֶת־הָאַהֲבָה וּנְהָרוֹת לֹא יִשְׁטְפוּהָ אִם־יִתֵּן אִישׁ אֶת־כָּל־הוֹן בֵּיתוֹ בָּאַהֲבָה בּוֹז
ח יָבוּזוּ לוֹ׃ אָחוֹת לָנוּ קְטַנָּה וְשָׁדַיִם אֵין לָהּ מַה־נַּעֲשֶׂה לַאֲחוֹתֵנוּ
ט בַּיּוֹם שֶׁיְּדֻבַּר־בָּהּ׃ אִם־חוֹמָה הִיא נִבְנֶה עָלֶיהָ טִירַת כָּסֶף וְאִם־דֶּלֶת הִיא נָצוּר
י עָלֶיהָ לוּחַ אָרֶז׃ אֲנִי חוֹמָה וְשָׁדַי כַּמִּגְדָּלוֹת אָז הָיִיתִי בְעֵינָיו כְּמוֹצְאֵת שָׁלוֹם׃

BACKGROUND

8:6| **Set me as a seal upon your heart, as a seal upon your arm:** The seal was a valuable personal accessory, used mainly for signing and confirming contracts or statutes. It was used primarily by men, and was framed within a ring that was worn on one's finger, or hung around one's neck. The seal would be sunk and rolled in a soft substance, such as wax or clay, which would later harden, retaining the design that was imprinted on it.

8:9| **Silver parapet [*tira*]:** In both the Bible and the Mishna, a *tira* refers to a low fence or parapet that surrounds a defined area (see Genesis 25:16; Ezekiel 46:23; Mishna *Kelim* 3:5). Later, the word *tira* came to mean a palace and fortress, as in modern Hebrew. It is possible that this silver *tira* is actually a crown-like ornament, like the "city of gold" mentioned in the Mishna (*Shabbat* 6:1; *Eduyyot* 2:7; *Kelim* 11:8).

DISCUSSION

8:4| **For what do you rouse love, until it desires:** This phrase is repeated throughout the book. Even when the love is mutual and clear, it cannot be enhanced by artificial means, by external displays, or through the participation of gossiping strangers. To goad emotion from the outside can even disturb or delay the fruition of love. Furthermore, the request to not rouse love prematurely displays a confidence that the love is real and strong, and not to be anxious or fretted about. Therefore, the daughters of Jerusalem are told not to involve themselves in the situation, which is solely between the woman and her beloved.

8:7| **If a man were to give all the wealth of his house for love, he would be scorned:** Sometimes it seems that anything can be bought, so long as one finds the right price. However, no matter how great one's fortune, love cannot be purchased. When it appears that a person has succeeded in buying love, in practice he has acquired no more than a person's body. Furthermore, love cannot be relinquished or sold.

about my relationship. I am ready physically, emotionally, and morally to be married.

11 An anonymous third party provides background for the continuation of the woman's speech: King **Solomon had a vineyard at Baal Hamon.**[B] **He gave the vineyard to the guards,** to take care of it. **Each would bring,** earn in exchange **for its fruit, a** sizable income of one **thousand** pieces **of silver.** The vineyard symbolizes a woman, specifically the female protagonist of the poem, and Solomon is her guardian, the closest thing to a paternal figure, who has appointed the brothers to look after their sister. These guards of the vineyard receive a handsome payment for fruits of the vineyard. Allegorically, the nation of Israel is the vineyard. When it fulfills its divine purpose, its profits are distributed among the nations, if they only know to appreciate the vineyard and show responsibility for it.

Vineyard

12 Now, the young woman, who considers herself mature, decides for herself the fate of her vineyard: **My vineyard is before me,** and I intend to give it to my beloved; I intend to marry him. As part of the arrangement, the profits from the vineyard will be distributed: **The thousand is for you, Solomon,** the custodian, **and two hundred** will be given **for those who guard its fruit.** Now, when the couple wishes to establish their bond in marriage, they erect boundaries. Allegorically speaking, the bride is the individual soul or the Jewish people that yearns and seeks to be married to God. In this context, the Sages expound that "the day of his wedding" (3:11) refers to the giving of the Torah, and "the day of the rejoicing of his heart" refers to the building of the Temple (see commentary on 3:11). Of course, there was love between God and Israel before these events, but their relationship was not cemented in a formal covenant. The giving of the Torah was the wedding of Israel to God, as it was at that moment that a binding relationship was established. Likewise, when God dwelled among the nation of Israel with the building of the Temple, it was as if the bride and groom had created a new, shared household. On every level of interpretation, the same questions are posed: Who is the bride? Is she worthy? Is she ready for marriage or must she wait a few more years? And on every level of interpretation, a permanent relationship consists of agreements and commitments, and carries with it a price. The great King Solomon clearly does not require more money. Still, in order to finalize the agreement, the bride must relinquish part of her inheritance and give her vineyard as a dowry.

13 Throughout this dialogue, the beloved was not present. Now, he addresses his bride-to-be: You, **the one who dwells in the gardens,** whose **companions listen to your voice,** as you proved when you spoke to the brothers: **Let me hear it.** I wish to meet you and listen to your sweet voice myself.

14 She responds: Indeed, the consummation of our relationship is nearer than ever, but its time has not yet arrived. In the meantime, **flee, my beloved, and be like a gazelle or a young deer on the mountains of spices.** You are assured of my love; I am yours. Now leap on the hills and enjoy their fragrance, for I know that you will return.

BACKGROUND

8:11 | **Baal Hamon:** No place of this name has been identified. Perhaps Baal Hamon is not the name of a place, but a phrase referring to the work by a contractor for the owner [*baal*] of a fortune [*hamon*] (see Ecclesiastes 5:9). Some suggest that this is Baal Hermon, located on the slopes of the Hermon (see Judges 3:3). This is a fertile and well-watered area, and it produces quality vines even today. According to the *Targum* and Rashi, Baal Hamon is Jerusalem, where masses [*hamon*] of people gathered, especially on Passover, the spring festival.

יא כֶּ֣רֶם הָיָ֤ה לִשְׁלֹמֹה֙ בְּבַ֣עַל הָמ֔וֹן נָתַ֥ן אֶת־הַכֶּ֖רֶם לַנֹּטְרִ֑ים אִ֛ישׁ יָבִ֥א בְּפִרְי֖וֹ אֶ֥לֶף

יב יג כָּֽסֶף׃ כַּרְמִ֥י שֶׁלִּ֖י לְפָנָ֑י הָאֶ֤לֶף לְךָ֙ שְׁלֹמֹ֔ה וּמָאתַ֖יִם לְנֹטְרִ֥ים אֶת־פִּרְיֽוֹ׃ הַיּוֹשֶׁ֣בֶת

יד בַּגַּנִּ֗ים חֲבֵרִ֛ים מַקְשִׁיבִ֥ים לְקוֹלֵ֖ךְ הַשְׁמִיעִֽנִי׃ בְּרַ֣ח ׀ דּוֹדִ֗י וּֽדְמֵה־לְךָ֤ לִצְבִי֙ א֛וֹ

לְעֹ֥פֶר הָֽאַיָּלִ֖ים עַ֥ל הָרֵ֥י בְשָׂמִֽים׃

Ruth

Ruth

INTRODUCTION TO RUTH

The story of the book of Ruth can be described as a kind of idyll. It unfolds in a quiet Judean community during the era of the judges, in Israel's early history. No earth-shattering miracles occur in this book, nor any events of historical import. While there is a certain amount of conflict in the story, a sense of calmness and harmony infuses the narrative. The book's main characters are memorable not for their fastidiously correct behavior, but for their personal decisions to conduct themselves with kindness and generosity toward one another.

The central focus of this book is the personal story of a daughter-in-law and her mother-in-law who are left to wander through the world destitute, before they eventually achieve security. Only the final verses, which relate how the eponymous heroine, Ruth, becomes the mother of the royal dynasty of Israel, transform the plot from a personal, human story to one of national significance. The conclusion also shows how God guides events in the world, as He nurtures a person on the margins of society, a female Moavite convert, until she becomes the ancestor of King David himself. One of David's psalms contains a verse that aptly describes the plot of this book: "The stone that the builders rejected became the cornerstone."[1]

Ruth

Elimelekh and His Family in Moav

RUTH 1:1–5

The story of Ruth begins with a famine in the Land of Israel, which causes Elimelekh's family to relocate from Bethlehem to Moav. This move is not as strange as it might first seem, as the Moavite nation shared common roots with the Jewish people. The founding ancestor of the nation Moav was a son of Lot, the nephew of Abraham our patriarch. Ancient inscriptions indicate that the Moavite language was very similar to Hebrew. Accordingly, Elimelekh's family remains within the same broad cultural context, despite the numerous differences between the nations. While residing in Moav, the exiled family is struck by a series of tragedies, and only Naomi survives.

1 1 **It was in the days when the judges judged;**[D] **there was a famine in the land** due to a drought. **And a** wealthy, prominent **man**[2] **from Bethlehem,** which was in the territory **of Judah,**[B] near Jerusalem, **went to reside** temporarily **in the fields of Moav,** where conditions were better, **he, his wife, and his two sons.** The verse specifies Bethlehem in Judah in order to distinguish this place from the town of Bethlehem located in the Galilee.[3]

Bethlehem, illustration, 1894

2 **The name of the man was Elimelekh, the name of his wife was Naomi, and the names of his two sons were Mahlon and Kilyon.**[D] **They were Efratites from Bethlehem of Judah.** The region near Bethlehem was named after their family of Efrat,[4] who was a descendant of Hur.[5] **They came to the fields of Moav and were there** for some time.

Mountains of Moav, view from Eretz Yisrael to the east

Bethlehem of Judah and the fields of Moav

3 **Elimelekh, Naomi's husband, died** while they were living in Moav, **and she and her two sons remained** in the fields of Moav.

4 **They,** Naomi's two sons, **married** local **Moavite women: The name of the one was Orpa, and the name of the second Ruth;**[D] **they lived there approximately ten years.**

5 **Also both of them, Mahlon and Kilyon, died** childless; **and the woman,** Naomi, **remained of her two children and her husband.**

רות

א וַיְהִ֗י בִּימֵי֙ שְׁפֹ֣ט הַשֹּׁפְטִ֔ים וַיְהִ֥י רָעָ֖ב בָּאָ֑רֶץ וַיֵּ֨לֶךְ אִ֜ישׁ מִבֵּ֧ית לֶ֣חֶם יְהוּדָ֗ה לָגוּר֙
ב בִּשְׂדֵ֣י מוֹאָ֔ב ה֥וּא וְאִשְׁתּ֖וֹ וּשְׁנֵ֥י בָנָֽיו׃ וְשֵׁ֣ם הָאִ֣ישׁ אֱלִימֶ֡לֶךְ וְשֵׁם֩ אִשְׁתּ֨וֹ נָעֳמִ֜י
וְשֵׁ֥ם שְׁנֵֽי־בָנָ֣יו ׀ מַחְל֤וֹן וְכִלְיוֹן֙ אֶפְרָתִ֔ים מִבֵּ֥ית לֶ֖חֶם יְהוּדָ֑ה וַיָּבֹ֥אוּ שְׂדֵי־מוֹאָ֖ב
ג ד וַיִּֽהְיוּ־שָֽׁם׃ וַיָּ֥מָת אֱלִימֶ֖לֶךְ אִ֣ישׁ נָעֳמִ֑י וַתִּשָּׁאֵ֥ר הִ֖יא וּשְׁנֵ֥י בָנֶֽיהָ׃ וַיִּשְׂא֣וּ לָהֶ֗ם
נָשִׁים֙ מֹֽאֲבִיּ֔וֹת שֵׁ֤ם הָֽאַחַת֙ עָרְפָּ֔ה וְשֵׁ֥ם הַשֵּׁנִ֖ית ר֑וּת וַיֵּ֥שְׁבוּ שָׁ֖ם כְּעֶ֥שֶׂר שָׁנִֽים׃
ה ו וַיָּמ֥וּתוּ גַם־שְׁנֵיהֶ֖ם מַחְל֣וֹן וְכִלְי֑וֹן וַתִּשָּׁאֵר֙ הָֽאִשָּׁ֔ה מִשְּׁנֵ֥י יְלָדֶ֖יהָ וּמֵאִישָֽׁהּ׃ וַתָּ֤קָם
הִיא֙ וְכַלֹּתֶ֔יהָ וַתָּ֖שָׁב מִשְּׂדֵ֣י מוֹאָ֑ב כִּ֤י שָֽׁמְעָה֙ בִּשְׂדֵ֣ה מוֹאָ֔ב כִּֽי־פָקַ֤ד יהוה֙ אֶת־עַמּ֔וֹ

The Return from Moav to Judah

RUTH 1:6–22

Naomi, the sole survivor of the family that had traveled to Moav, returns to the land of Judah in a miserable state. As Naomi is an impressive individual, her daughters-in-law seek to come with her to the Land of Israel, and it is clear from the text that there is an especially warm relationship between this mother-in-law and her daughters-in-law. After Naomi urges them to remain in their land, Ruth alone insists on accompanying her, and Ruth arrives with Naomi in Bethlehem of Judah.

6 **She and her daughters-in-law rose, and returned from the fields of Moav,** not only because Naomi had lost her husband and sons, but also **because she had heard in the fields of Moav that the Lord had remembered His people to give**

BACKGROUND

1:1 | **Bethlehem of Judah:** This has been identified with the hill that extends eastward from the center of the modern city of Bethlehem, approximately 9 km south of Jerusalem, and 1.5 km east of the ancient road along the central ridge of the highlands of the Land of Israel known as the Way of the Patriarchs. It is possible that the city was named for the fertile plains on its eastern side, where wheat and barley were grown. Bethlehem is also referred to as Efrat, according to the verse "Efrata, the father of Bethlehem" (I Chronicles 4:4).

DISCUSSION

1:1 | **In the days when the judges judged:** During this period, the setting for the book of Judges, tribes and families were the most important social units in Israel, although the people were still one nation. There were periodic skirmishes with enemies, but Israel did not engage in any major wars. The Torah and its commandments were generally observed in accordance with the tradition that the people had received. Nevertheless, the stories related in the Judges that span this lengthy period depict Israel as a people with a warped ethical sensibility, along with a corrupt religious and national consciousness.

1:2 | **Mahlon and Kilyon:** There is a possible allusion to the story of Elimelekh's family in I Chronicles (4:22), although the names that appear there differ from the ones mentioned here. If that verse indeed refers to the same story, Mahlon and Kilyon might not have been their real names, but pseudonyms given to them following their deaths at a young age. While the name Mahlon seems to connote sickness (*maḥala*), it can also be interpreted in a positive sense, similar to Mahli (Exodus 6:19) and Ahlai (I Chronicles 2:31), which mean jewelry (see, e.g., Proverbs 25:12). It could also be related to sweetness, as indicated by the root in Arabic, from which the name for the modern sesame snack halva is derived. However, the name Kilyon, literally "annihilation" (see Isaiah 10:22), bears an unambiguously negative connotation (see Ibn Ezra; *Bava Batra* 91b; *Ruth Rabba* 2:5). Appropriately, as evident from the continuation of the narrative, Kilyon did not merit a lasting remembrance, whereas Mahlon's name was perpetuated and glorified by his widow, Ruth.

1:4 | **Orpa and Ruth:** The text does not reveal anything about the identity of these two women. According to Jewish tradition, Ruth descended from the royal line of Moav, while Orpa apparently came from an upper-class

them bread. In the meantime, the famine had ended and normal life had resumed in the land of Judah.

7 **She departed from the place where she was, and her two daughters-in-law were with her,** as they were her only surviving family members; **they went on the way to return to the land of Judah.**

8 **Naomi said to her two daughters-in-law:** I am returning to my home and my people, but as for you, **go, each return to her mother's house** and family. She added with great affection: **May the Lord deal kindly with you** and assist you, **as you have dealt with the dead and with me.**

9 **May the Lord grant you that you find repose, each in the house of her husband.** I bless each of you that you should both remarry and live in peace with new husbands. Since nothing remains from our family relationship, there is no reason for you to accompany me. Naomi wished to treat these two women fairly, as they were apparently relatively young, having married a mere few years earlier. She therefore encouraged them to resume their lives elsewhere. **She,** Naomi, **kissed them** a farewell kiss; **and they,** possibly all three of them, **raised their voices and wept.** This shared weeping is indicative of the profound ties between them, despite the fact that the pair were not Naomi's biological daughters.

10 **They said to her: No, for we will return with you to your people** and live among your nation. We are one family, and we will continue to remain a family.

11 **Naomi said: Return, my daughters; why would you go with me?** There is no reason for you to do so. **Do I have more sons in my womb**[6] **who will be husbands for you?** Is there any chance that I will give birth to boys who might later marry you and produce offspring?[7]

12 Accordingly, **return, my daughters; go, as I am too old to** remarry and **have a** second **husband.** Even **if I were to** entertain an utterly unrealistic idea and **say: I have hope, then even if I had a husband tonight, and even if I were to bear sons,**

13 **would you wait for them,** these imaginary sons, **until they grow up? For them, would you constrain yourselves** and stop your lives, **to not have a husband? No, my daughters, for I am embittered on your account** that I am unable to assist you or provide you with anything, **for the hand of the Lord has been extended against me.** I am left wretched and hopeless. Apparently, any property or possessions the family had once owned had been lost over the years.

14 **They raised their voices and wept more; Orpa kissed her mother-in-law** farewell, as she had been convinced by Naomi's argument and decided to return home, **but Ruth clung to her** and would not consent to any separation.

15 **She,** Naomi, **said** to Ruth: **Behold, your sister-in-law returned to her people and to her god;**[D] **return after your sister-in-law.**

16 **Ruth said: Do not implore me to leave you,**[8] **to return from following you,** to abandon you. **For wherever you will go, I will go; and wherever you lodge, I will lodge;** moreover, **your people is my people, and your God my God.**[D] You said that Orpa should return to her nation and her gods, but Moav is no longer my nation, and the gods of Moav are no longer my gods. My ties to your family and way of life are not an accident, and I no longer feel any connection to the Moavite nation and its faith;

17 **wherever you die, I will die, and there I will be buried.** I will remain alongside you until death, and I will be buried together with you. I swear that **so may the Lord do to me, and so may He continue, for death will separate between me and you.** Note that Ruth takes an oath in the name of the God of Israel.

18 **She,** Naomi, **saw that she was resolute to go with her,** despite her best efforts to convince Ruth that she should return home, **and she ceased speaking with her** and urging her to return.

19 **The two of them walked until they arrived in Bethlehem.** Since Bethlehem was not far from Moav, they presumably walked for only a few days. **It was, upon their arriving in Bethlehem, that the whole city was in a tumult over them; the women said: Is that Naomi?** No one was familiar with Ruth, but everyone in the small city knew the distinguished Naomi. At this stage, however, she had not only aged physically, but her dress and her appearance had changed, as the vicissitudes of life had left their scars.[9]

20 **She said to them: Do not call me Naomi,** meaning pleasant [*no'am*], as I have not had any pleasantness in my life; rather, **call me Bitterness [*Mara*].**[10] This name is more appropriate, **as the Almighty has greatly embittered me** and brought much bitterness and suffering upon me.

DISCUSSION

family as well. The prominent status of these women is consistent with the supposition that Elimelekh and his family did not come to Moav as beggars, but rather as distinguished individuals, and that they traveled there in order to live in an honorable fashion (see Rashi, verse 2; *Targum*; *Ruth Rabba* 2; *Nazir* 23b).

1:15 | **Returned to her people and to her god:** The marriage of Orpa and Ruth to men from Judah would likely have included their acceptance of the commandments of the Torah. Although it is unknown whether any sort of ceremony was performed to mark the occasion, foreign women who married into an Israelite household accepted upon themselves

ז לָתֵת לָהֶם לָחֶם׃ וַתֵּצֵא מִן־הַמָּקוֹם אֲשֶׁר הָיְתָה־שָּׁמָּה וּשְׁתֵּי כַלֹּתֶיהָ עִמָּהּ
ח וַתֵּלַכְנָה בַדֶּרֶךְ לָשׁוּב אֶל־אֶרֶץ יְהוּדָה׃ וַתֹּאמֶר נָעֳמִי לִשְׁתֵּי כַלֹּתֶיהָ לֵכְנָה שֹּׁבְנָה
אִשָּׁה לְבֵית אִמָּהּ יַעֲשֶׂה יְהוָה עִמָּכֶם חֶסֶד כַּאֲשֶׁר עֲשִׂיתֶם עִם־הַמֵּתִים וְעִמָּדִי׃ יעש
ט יִתֵּן יְהוָה לָכֶם וּמְצֶאןָ מְנוּחָה אִשָּׁה בֵּית אִישָׁהּ וַתִּשַּׁק לָהֶן וַתִּשֶּׂאנָה קוֹלָן
י יא וַתִּבְכֶּינָה׃ וַתֹּאמַרְנָה־לָּהּ כִּי־אִתָּךְ נָשׁוּב לְעַמֵּךְ׃ וַתֹּאמֶר נָעֳמִי שֹׁבְנָה בְנֹתַי לָמָּה
יב תֵלַכְנָה עִמִּי הַעוֹד־לִי בָנִים בְּמֵעַי וְהָיוּ לָכֶם לַאֲנָשִׁים׃ שֹׁבְנָה בְנֹתַי לֵּכְןָ כִּי זָקַנְתִּי
מִהְיוֹת לְאִישׁ כִּי אָמַרְתִּי יֶשׁ־לִי תִקְוָה גַּם הָיִיתִי הַלַּיְלָה לְאִישׁ וְגַם יָלַדְתִּי בָנִים׃
יג הֲלָהֵן ׀ תְּשַׂבֵּרְנָה עַד אֲשֶׁר יִגְדָּלוּ הֲלָהֵן תֵּעָגֵנָה לְבִלְתִּי הֱיוֹת לְאִישׁ אַל בְּנֹתַי
יד כִּי־מַר־לִי מְאֹד מִכֶּם כִּי־יָצְאָה בִי יַד־יְהוָה׃ וַתִּשֶּׂנָה קוֹלָן וַתִּבְכֶּינָה עוֹד וַתִּשַּׁק
טו עָרְפָּה לַחֲמוֹתָהּ וְרוּת דָּבְקָה בָּהּ׃ וַתֹּאמֶר הִנֵּה שָׁבָה יְבִמְתֵּךְ אֶל־עַמָּהּ וְאֶל־
טז אֱלֹהֶיהָ שׁוּבִי אַחֲרֵי יְבִמְתֵּךְ׃ וַתֹּאמֶר רוּת אַל־תִּפְגְּעִי־בִי לְעָזְבֵךְ לָשׁוּב מֵאַחֲרָיִךְ
יז כִּי אֶל־אֲשֶׁר תֵּלְכִי אֵלֵךְ וּבַאֲשֶׁר תָּלִינִי אָלִין עַמֵּךְ עַמִּי וֵאלֹהַיִךְ אֱלֹהָי׃ בַּאֲשֶׁר
תָּמוּתִי אָמוּת וְשָׁם אֶקָּבֵר כֹּה יַעֲשֶׂה יְהוָה לִי וְכֹה יֹסִיף כִּי הַמָּוֶת יַפְרִיד בֵּינִי
יח יט וּבֵינֵךְ׃ וַתֵּרֶא כִּי־מִתְאַמֶּצֶת הִיא לָלֶכֶת אִתָּהּ וַתֶּחְדַּל לְדַבֵּר אֵלֶיהָ׃ וַתֵּלַכְנָה
שְׁתֵּיהֶם עַד־בֹּאָנָה בֵּית לָחֶם וַיְהִי כְּבֹאָנָה בֵּית לֶחֶם וַתֵּהֹם כָּל־הָעִיר עֲלֵיהֶן
כ וַתֹּאמַרְנָה הֲזֹאת נָעֳמִי׃ וַתֹּאמֶר אֲלֵיהֶן אַל־תִּקְרֶאנָה לִי נָעֳמִי קְרֶאןָ לִי מָרָא

DISCUSSION

the service of God. Even though the process of conversion is ordinarily administered by the court, it is possible that a would-be convert who fulfills the Torah in its entirety may be considered Jewish even without explicit action by a court (see *Yevamot* 45b). With regard to Orpa, although she had joined the Israelite nation to a limited extent, when her connection was terminated against her will by the death of her husband, she returned home and once again resumed the status of a Moavite who worshipped the Moavite gods (see Alsheikh; *Ruth Rabba* 2:21; Rambam, *Hilkhot Issurei Bia* 13:15–17).

1:16| **Your people is my people, and your God my God:** The relationship between Ruth and Naomi began with Ruth's marriage to Mahlon, but over the years Ruth had fully adopted her new family's way of life. For this reason, she serves as a model convert for future generations. Her attachment to God, the Israelite people, and its ways of life has become a symbol of the experience of a true convert. He or she must feel that the conversion is not temporary, and that it does not depend on location or convenience. Rather, the change of status must be due to total identification with Israel. The transformation that Ruth underwent led her to deny any further connection to her homeland and her past. As far as she was concerned, she had been born anew as a daughter to Naomi. Although there was no longer any formal familial relationship between them, the two remained extremely close.

21 **I went**[11] **full,** with a husband, children, and possessions, **and the Lord returned me empty,** with nothing; **why would you call me Naomi, and the Lord has testified against me**[12] and rebuked me for my sins; alternatively, He has warned me **and the Almighty has harmed me?**

22 **Naomi returned, and Ruth the Moavite, her daughter-in-law, was with her, who returned from the fields of Moav; they came to Bethlehem at the beginning of the barley harvest,** the period after the festival of Passover, when barley is first reaped. Thus, it was relatively easy to find food during this time of the year.

Beginning of the barley harvest

Ruth's First Visit to the Field of Boaz

RUTH 2:1–23

Several gestures of kindness figure prominently in this section: Ruth, a foreigner, volunteers to go out and glean in the harvested fields for herself and her mother-in-law, while Boaz, the owner of the field where she finds herself, takes steps to ease Ruth's difficult task. Indeed, the overall context is one of kindness, as the residents of Bethlehem are presented as fulfilling the Torah's command to leave any fallen or forgotten stalks in the field for the needy.

2 1 **Naomi had an acquaintance**[13] **of her husband,** who was **a mighty man of valor,** prominent in stature, **from the family of Elimelekh, and his name was Boaz.**[D]

2 **Ruth the Moavite said to Naomi: Let me now go to the field, and glean among the stalks of grain,**[D] in accordance with the common practice of the poor, which Ruth had apparently noticed, **following anyone in whose eyes I find favor.** I will go to the field of someone in whose eyes I find favor and who will allow me to glean there.[14] Although the Torah requires the owner of a field to leave gleanings of his harvest for the destitute, in practice not every landowner welcomed the poor graciously. Some were concerned that the poor might distract the reapers from their work, while others suspected them of dishonesty, and there might even have been some individuals who did not wish to interact with or assist others at all. **She,** Naomi, **said to her: Go, my daughter.**

3 **She went, and came, and gleaned** the stalks that had fallen or had not been harvested **in the field after the reapers; it happened for her that it was the tract of land belonging to Boaz, who was from the family of Elimelekh,** without prior knowledge of the landowner's identity.

4 **Behold,** at that time **Boaz came from Bethlehem** to his field outside the city, presumably in order to supervise the harvest. **And** Boaz **said to the reapers** a greeting in the form of a blessing: **The Lord be with you** and assist you. **They said to him: The Lord bless you.**[D]

5 **Boaz said to his lad set over the reapers** to ensure that the harvest was performed properly: **Whose young woman is this?** With whom is she associated? Bethlehem was not a large city, and Boaz, one of the long-standing residents of the city, was surprised to see a young woman whom he did not recognize.

Harvest, illustration based on fresco, Egypt

Reapers

כא כִּי־הֵמַר שַׁדַּי לִי מְאֹד׃ אֲנִי מְלֵאָה הָלַכְתִּי וְרֵיקָם הֱשִׁיבַנִי יְהוָה לָמָּה תִקְרֶאנָה
כב לִי נָעֳמִי וַיהוָה עָנָה בִי וְשַׁדַּי הֵרַע־לִי׃ וַתָּשָׁב נָעֳמִי וְרוּת הַמּוֹאֲבִיָּה כַלָּתָהּ עִמָּהּ
א הַשָּׁבָה מִשְּׂדֵי מוֹאָב וְהֵמָּה בָּאוּ בֵּית לֶחֶם בִּתְחִלַּת קְצִיר שְׂעֹרִים׃ וּלְנָעֳמִי מידע מוֹדַע
ב לְאִישָׁהּ אִישׁ גִּבּוֹר חַיִל מִמִּשְׁפַּחַת אֱלִימֶלֶךְ וּשְׁמוֹ בֹּעַז׃ וַתֹּאמֶר רוּת הַמּוֹאֲבִיָּה
אֶל־נָעֳמִי אֵלְכָה־נָּא הַשָּׂדֶה וַאֲלַקֳטָה בַשִּׁבֳּלִים אַחַר אֲשֶׁר אֶמְצָא־חֵן בְּעֵינָיו
ג וַתֹּאמֶר לָהּ לְכִי בִתִּי׃ וַתֵּלֶךְ וַתָּבוֹא וַתְּלַקֵּט בַּשָּׂדֶה אַחֲרֵי הַקֹּצְרִים וַיִּקֶר מִקְרֶהָ
ד חֶלְקַת הַשָּׂדֶה לְבֹעַז אֲשֶׁר מִמִּשְׁפַּחַת אֱלִימֶלֶךְ׃ וְהִנֵּה־בֹעַז בָּא מִבֵּית לֶחֶם
ה וַיֹּאמֶר לַקּוֹצְרִים יְהוָה עִמָּכֶם וַיֹּאמְרוּ לוֹ יְבָרֶכְךָ יְהוָה׃ וַיֹּאמֶר בֹּעַז לְנַעֲרוֹ הַנִּצָּב
ו עַל־הַקּוֹצְרִים לְמִי הַנַּעֲרָה הַזֹּאת׃ וַיַּעַן הַנַּעַר הַנִּצָּב עַל־הַקּוֹצְרִים וַיֹּאמַר נַעֲרָה
ז מוֹאֲבִיָּה הִיא הַשָּׁבָה עִם־נָעֳמִי מִשְּׂדֵי מוֹאָב׃ וַתֹּאמֶר אֲלַקֳטָה־נָּא וְאָסַפְתִּי
בָעֳמָרִים אַחֲרֵי הַקּוֹצְרִים וַתָּבוֹא וַתַּעֲמוֹד מֵאָז הַבֹּקֶר וְעַד־עַתָּה זֶה שִׁבְתָּהּ
ח הַבַּיִת מְעָט׃ וַיֹּאמֶר בֹּעַז אֶל־רוּת הֲלוֹא שָׁמַעַתְּ בִּתִּי אַל־תֵּלְכִי לִלְקֹט בְּשָׂדֶה

6 **The lad set over the reapers answered and said: She is a young Moavite woman who returned with Naomi from the fields of Moav.**

7 **She said,** asked of us:[15] **Please let me glean and gather among the sheaves, following the reapers. She came and has been standing** in the field **from the morning until now; she sat in the house only a bit.** She went to a nearby house to rest for a short time, before returning to the field.[16]

8 **Boaz said to Ruth: Hear truly, my daughter; do not go to glean in a different field; also do not pass on from here** to another field, as my field is sufficiently large, **but** rather **attach**

Sheaves in the field

DISCUSSION

2:1| **Boaz:** Little is related about Boaz in the book of Ruth itself, although his high social status is evident from the narrative, and his noble lineage appears at the conclusion of the book. Some Sages identify him with the judge Ivtzan of Bethlehem (see *Bava Batra* 91a; *Ruth Rabba* 3:6; Judges 12:8–10, and Radak ad loc.). Furthermore, the book later indicates that he was one of the judges of the city, perhaps even the most senior of them (see 4:1–2, and Ralbag ad loc.).

2:2| **And glean among the stalks of grain:** The Torah commands the owner of land to give gifts to the poor from his field: "When you reap the harvest of your land, you shall not finish reaping the corner of your field, and the gleanings of your harvest you shall not gather. Your vineyard you shall not harvest completely, and the fallen fruit of your vineyard you shall not gather; for the poor and for the stranger you shall leave them" (Leviticus 19:9–10; see also Leviticus 23:22). According to this commandment, the farmer and his workers must leave the stalks that fall during the time of harvest for the poor. Furthermore, the commandment of forgotten produce (Deuteronomy 24:19) requires a harvester who forgot grain or other crops in the field, whether harvested or not harvested, to leave them there for the needy, rather than returning and taking them for himself. Although there was no centrally organized government in the period of the judges to enforce the Torah, many of the commandments of the Torah were transmitted by tradition and observed. The book of Ruth teaches that at that time the poor did in fact benefit from these philanthropic commandments.

2:4| **The Lord be with you.... The Lord bless you:** Boaz likely did not create this formulation; rather, it was already an accepted greeting, as it appears elsewhere as well (see Judges 6:12; *Berakhot* 63a).

yourself to my young women. Keep close to my maidservants and go with them.
9 **Let your eyes be on the field that they reap, and follow them,** the other maidservants. **Haven't I commanded the lads not to touch you,** and bother you, but rather treat you with respect? Moreover, as you are outside in the heat, **when you become thirsty, go to the vessels** that contain water for the reapers, **and drink from that which the lads have drawn.** I permit you to drink from their water, so that you can continue to reap here in comfort.[17]
10 **She fell on her face and prostrated herself to the ground; she said to him: Why have I found favor in your eyes, that you should acknowledge me** and treat me in such a friendly manner, **and I am a foreigner?** I am not from the house of Israel, and I am a stranger to this area.
11 **Boaz answered and said to her:** Although I have not seen you until now, **everything that you did for your mother-in-law after the death of your husband was told to me; you left your father and your mother, and the land of your birth, and you went to a people that you did not know previously.**
12 **May the Lord reward your conduct, and may your payment be complete from the Lord, God of Israel, under whose wings you came to find refuge.** Boaz understood that Ruth had not converted for merely social or financial reasons, and that she did not come to the Land of Israel just in order to accompany her mother-in-law. Rather, she wished to be close to God.
13 **She said: May I find favor in your eyes, my lord.** I am grateful that I have found favor in your eyes;[18] **for you have comforted me, for you have spoken to the heart of your maidservant.** You have encouraged me and treated me in a special manner, **though I am not** worthy **even** of a status **as one of your maidservants.**[19]
14 **Boaz said to her** sometime later, **at mealtime,** when the reapers gathered to sit and eat: **Come over here, and eat from the bread** shared by the reapers, **and dip your piece in the vinegar**[B] that is used as a sauce for the bread. **She sat beside the reapers,** not mingling with them, **and he,** Boaz, **handed her** kernels of **roasted** fresh **grain.** Some of the starch inside of these kernels is converted to sugar when heated, and the slightly sweet roasted kernels were considered a delicacy. **And she ate and was satisfied, and left over.** Boaz had given her a sizable portion, which was more than enough to satisfy her.

To the left: fresh wheat kernels; to the right: dry wheat kernels

15 **She rose to glean, and Boaz commanded his lads, saying:** She is permitted to glean in the field not only after you have removed the bound-together sheaves of harvested grain, but **let her glean among the sheaves as well, and do not shame her.** You must allow her to glean without voicing any objections;[20]
16 **also pull some for her from the bundles.** You are to forget, or intentionally remove,[21] some stalks from those that are tied together ready to be harvested with the sickle, **and leave them, and let her glean, and do not rebuke her.**

Bundle of grain

17 **She gleaned in the field until evening.** Since Ruth had been given a comfortable place to rest, perhaps in the shade near the reapers, and provided with food and drink, she did not need to return home in the middle of the day. **And she beat out that which she had gleaned,** in order to separate the kernels of grain from the stalks, **and it was approximately an ephah of barley,** a sizable dry measure equivalent to roughly 24 L.

Beating kernels with a stick

18 **She took it up,** the barley, **and came to the city, and her mother-in-law saw that which she had gleaned,** a larger quantity than Naomi had expected;[22] **she took out and gave to her that which she had left over from her fill.** As stated, Ruth did not eat all of what Boaz had given her. She brought her mother-in-law roasted grain in addition to the barley.
19 **Her mother-in-law said to her: Where did you glean today and where did you work? Blessed be he who acknowledged you,** who assisted you, and who treated you with exceptional generosity. **She told her mother-in-law** the identity of the man **with whom she worked, and said: The name of the man,** the owner of the field, **with whom I worked today is Boaz.**
20 **Naomi said to her daughter-in-law: Blessed be he to the Lord, who has not forsaken His kindness to the living and to the dead.** Boaz had maintained close ties with the family when Naomi's husband and sons were still alive, and he was now honoring their memory by helping Naomi and Ruth.[23] **Naomi said to her:** I am familiar with him not only as a resident of this city,

ט אחר וגם לא תעבורי מזה וכה תדבקין עם־נערתי: עיניך בשדה אשר־יקצרון
והלכת אחריהן הלוא צויתי את־הנערים לבלתי נגעך וצמת והלכת אל־
י הכלים ושתית מאשר ישאבון הנערים: ותפל על־פניה ותשתחו ארצה ותאמר
יא אליו מדוע מצאתי חן בעיניך להכירני ואנכי נכריה: ויען בעז ויאמר לה הגד
הגד לי כל אשר־עשית את־חמותך אחרי מות אישך ותעזבי אביך ואמך
יב וארץ מולדתך ותלכי אל־עם אשר לא־ידעת תמול שלשום: ישלם יהוה
פעלך ותהי משכרתך שלמה מעם יהוה אלהי ישראל אשר־באת לחסות
יג תחת־כנפיו: ותאמר אמצא־חן בעיניך אדני כי נחמתני וכי דברת על־לב
יד שפחתך ואנכי לא אהיה כאחת שפחתך: ויאמר לה בעז לעת האכל גשי
הלם ואכלת מן־הלחם וטבלת פתך בחמץ ותשב מצד הקצרים ויצבט־לה
טו קלי ותאכל ותשבע ותתר: ותקם ללקט ויצו בעז את־נעריו לאמר גם בין
טז העמרים תלקט ולא תכלימוה: וגם של־תשלו לה מן־הצבתים ועזבתם
יז ולקטה ולא תגערו־בה: ותלקט בשדה עד־הערב ותחבט את אשר־לקטה
יח ויהי כאיפה שערים: ותשא ותבוא העיר ותרא חמותה את אשר־לקטה
יט ותוצא ותתן־לה את אשר־הותרה משבעה: ותאמר לה חמותה איפה לקטת
היום ואנה עשית יהי מכירך ברוך ותגד לחמותה את אשר־עשתה עמו
כ ותאמר שם האיש אשר עשיתי עמו היום בעז: ותאמר נעמי לכלתה ברוך
הוא ליהוה אשר לא־עזב חסדו את־החיים ואת־המתים ותאמר לה נעמי

but **the man is** also **related to us, he is among our redeemers** [***go'aleinu***]. When someone becomes poor and is forced to sell his field, a relative may redeem the field from the buyer if he can afford to do so.[24] Although some Sages maintain that it is obligatory for such a relative to do so, the *halakha* is that it is optional.[25] This purchase is called the redemption [*ge'ula*] of the field, and every relative is considered a potential redeemer [*go'el*].

BACKGROUND

2:14| **In the vinegar:** In ancient times, vinegar was considered to have cooling features, and it would be used on hot days. This notion appears both in ancient scientific documents, such as Pliny's encyclopedia, *Natural History* (first century CE), and in statements of the Sages in reference to this verse: It is derived from here that vinegar is beneficial in hot weather (*Shabbat* 113b; *Pesikta Zutreta*, *Ruth* 2:14).

21 In keeping with Naomi's excitement and the praises she had bestowed upon Boaz, **Ruth the Moavite said** in the same vein: **Indeed, he said to me: You shall attach yourself to my lads** and continue gleaning with them, **until they complete my entire harvest.**

22 **Naomi said to Ruth, her daughter-in-law:** Since Boaz is treating you so well, **my daughter, it is better that you go out with his young women** and remain in his field, **that you not be accosted in another field.**

23 **She attached herself to Boaz's young women to glean until the end of barley harvest and wheat harvest.** The barley harvest begins in the spring and lasts for some seven weeks. It is followed by the wheat harvest, which generally starts at around the time of Shavuot, which is called the Festival of the First Fruits of the wheat harvest.[26] This harvest concludes approximately three months after the start of the barley harvest.[27] **And she lived with her mother-in-law.** During that entire period, Ruth would glean in the field and bring the grain home to her mother-in-law.

Wheat

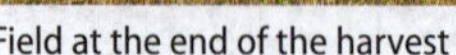

Field at the end of the harvest

Barley

Ruth's Descent to the Threshing Floor

RUTH 3:1–18

In this section, Ruth meets Boaz under different circumstances and for a very different purpose. In contrast to her daily, public visits to his field during the harvest season, this encounter occurs at night when Ruth comes alone to the threshing floor. Whereas Ruth arrived in the field to glean in order to provide for herself and her mother-in-law, she now goes, at Naomi's initiative, to the threshing floor in order to find a permanent solution for their plight. Naomi's motive for this stems not only from her role as mother-in-law but also as Ruth's teacher and mentor, and from her sense of responsibility for Ruth's future.

3 **1** **Naomi, her mother-in-law, said to her: My daughter, do I not seek repose for you, so that it may be well for you?** You are currently living in a temporary manner; I wish to find a more permanent arrangement for you. Naomi had expressed a similar wish while they were still in Moav (see 1:9).

2 **Now, isn't Boaz our acquaintance** and friend, **that you were with his young women? Behold, he is winnowing**[B] **the barley threshing floor**[B] **tonight.** Boaz was not married at that time; some maintain that he was a widower.[28] Naomi sought to arrange a match between him and Ruth.

Winnowing on a threshing floor

3 **Bathe, anoint yourself** with oil in order to enhance your appearance, **place your** most attractive **garment upon**[29] **you,**[D] **and descend to the threshing floor; do not make yourself known to the man.** Hide in the threshing floor so that Boaz will not discover you **until he finishes eating and drinking.**

4 **It shall be that when he lies down** to sleep on the threshing floor that night, in order to guard the grain, or perhaps because he wishes to resume work early in the morning, **you shall know the place where he lies, and you shall come and uncover his feet.** Even in the summer the evenings in the Judean hills are not particularly hot, and therefore Boaz's feet would be covered. **And lie down** near his feet. **He will tell you what you shall do.** Allow him to proceed in whatever manner he sees fit. Through this unusual act, which is direct and authentic, but at the same time discreet and non-binding, Ruth will issue an unconventional proposition: A request for Boaz's full protection, which means that in essence she is asking him to marry her.[30]

DISCUSSION

3:3 | **Place your garment upon you:** The Sages explain that this is referring to the fine garments that are worn on the Sabbath (*Ruth Rabba* 5:12).

כא קרוב לנו האיש מגאלנו הוא: ותאמר רות המואביה גם | כי־אמר אלי עם־
כב הנערים אשר־לי תדבקין עד אם־כלו את כל־הקציר אשר־לי: ותאמר נעמי
אל־רות כלתה טוב בתי כי תצאי עם־נערותיו ולא יפגעו־בך בשדה אחר:
כג ותדבק בנערות בעז ללקט עד־כלות קציר־השערים וקציר החטים ותשב
א את־חמותה: ותאמר לה נעמי חמותה בתי הלא אבקש־לך מנוח אשר ייטב־
ב לך: ועתה הלא בעז מדעתנו אשר היית את־נערותיו הנה־הוא זרה את־גרן
ג השערים הלילה: ורחצת | וסכת ושמת שמלתך עליך וירדתי הגרן אל־תודעי
ד לאיש עד כלתו לאכל ולשתות: ויהי בשכבו וידעת את־המקום אשר ישכב־
ה שם ובאת וגלית מרגלתיו ושכבתי והוא יגיד לך את אשר תעשין: ותאמר
ו אליה כל אשר־תאמרי אעשה: ותרד הגרן ותעש ככל אשר־צותה חמותה:
ז ויאכל בעז וישת וייטב לבו ויבא לשכב בקצה הערמה ותבא בלט ותגל

שמלתיך
וירדת

ושכבת
אלי

5 She, Ruth, **said to her: Everything that you say to me, I will do.** Ruth could have hesitated to follow such a strange suggestion, which was not in keeping with conventional norms of decency and modesty. Nevertheless, she accepted her mother-in-law's plan without hesitation.

6 She went down to the threshing floor, and acted in accordance with everything that her mother-in-law had commanded her.

7 When the workday was concluded, **Boaz ate and drank** wine, **and his heart was merry, and he came to lie at the end of the pile of grain,** the mound of grain stalks, where there is grain on the ground that is comfortable to lie on and where he could also watch over the harvested grain. **She came surreptitiously, and she uncovered his feet, and she lay down** at his feet, per Naomi's instruction.

"At the end of the pile of grain"

BACKGROUND

3:2| **Winnowing:** After barley was gathered in the threshing floor, it was threshed in order to separate the kernels from the stalks, either by beating it with flails or by having an animal tread on it on a hard surface. The kernels were then winnowed in order to separate the grain from the husks by tossing it in the air with a shovel or a fork when there is a wind. The heavier grain fell back down while the husks, called chaff, blew away. Winnowing was usually performed in the late afternoon, evening, or early morning hours, when there is often a breeze in many parts of Israel.

The threshing floor: This was a public area that was exposed to the air and the wind, where the harvested grain was threshed and winnowed.

8 **It was midnight, and the man was startled and recoiled** in confusion,[31] as he had gone to sleep alone, and now he suddenly discerned the presence of another person;[32] **behold, a woman was lying at his feet.**

9 **He said** in complete surprise: **Who are you? She said: I am Ruth, your maidservant,** whom you know; **spread the corner of your garment,** your patronage, **over your maidservant,** and take me as your wife, **for you are a redeemer.** Owing to your familial ties to Naomi, you are also related to me, as I am her son's widow. Naomi had presumably explained to Ruth the significance of this type of redemption as practiced among the Israelites.

10 **He said: Blessed be you to the Lord, my daughter; your latter kindness,** when you chose to marry a relative of your deceased husband, **is greater than the former,**[D] when you left your land and accompanied your mother-in-law,[33] **in not going after the lads, whether poor or rich.** Had you sought to marry merely in order to reestablish your own life, you would have chosen a young man, closer in age to yourself. By selecting me, a man who is far older than you, because of my formal status as a redeemer, you have revealed the purity of your intentions.[34]

11 **Now, my daughter, do not fear, everything that you say I will do for you, for everyone** who is found **at the gate of my people,** the important men of the city,[35] **knows that you are a woman of valor [*eshet ḥayil*],** an unusual personality and an exceptional person. The term *eshet ḥayil* here parallels the phrase "mighty man of valor" [*gibbor ḥayil*] that appeared earlier in reference to Boaz (2:1). It also features as a general expression of praise in the book of Proverbs, which was written by King Solomon, a descendant of Ruth and Boaz.[36]

12 **Now it is true that I am a redeemer,** as I am part of the family; **however, there is a redeemer who is closer than I,** and the proper order must be maintained with regard to these matters.[37]

13 Therefore, **stay** here **tonight, and when it is morning, if he,** the redeemer who has a closer relationship to you, **redeems you,** then it is **good [*tov*], he will redeem,** as he has the right.[38] Alternatively, the word *tov* is the name of the redeemer.[39] According to this interpretation, the verse reads: And when it is morning, if Tov performs his role as redeemer, then let him do so. **But if he does not wish to redeem you, I will redeem you,**[D] as I will then be the next in line to redeem you. I swear **as the Lord lives; lie** down **until the morning** and rest; I will not touch you.[40]

14 **She lay at his feet until the morning, and rose before one could discern another. He,** Boaz, **said: Let it not be known that the woman came to the threshing floor.** Since he did not want her to be identified or her actions publicized, she departed before the light of day.[41]

15 **He,** Boaz, **said** to Ruth: **Hand me the** large **kerchief that is upon you, and hold it out; and she held it out. He measured six measures of barley,**[42] a sizable amount, **and placed it,** the full kerchief, **on her; and he** too **entered the city,** to take care of his business.

16 **She came to her mother-in-law,** when it was still quite early in the morning, and therefore she was unable to identify Ruth immediately.[43] **And she,** Naomi, **said: Who are you, my daughter? She told her everything that the man had done for her.**

17 **She,** Ruth, **said: These six measures of barley he gave me, as he said to me: Do not go empty-**handed **to your mother-in-law.** This is not a payment of any sort, but a gift to bring to your mother-in-law.[44]

18 **She said: Sit** and wait, **my daughter, until you know how the matter will develop; for the man will not rest until he completes the matter today.** I know that he is a determined man, and I am certain that he will not delay.

The Redemption of the Field and the Redemption of Ruth

RUTH 4:1–12

Boaz wants to marry Ruth, but he first has to deal with a formal limitation: According to the laws of inheritance and monetary rights, there is another individual who has a closer familial relationship to Elimelekh. Consequently, the right to redeem Naomi's field and to marry Ruth as a wife belongs to him. For this reason Ruth has not yet received a definite answer from Boaz with regard to her future. The response has to be given the next day in public, after a conversation with the other potential redeemer. The section concludes with the confirmation of the legal action, and with a blessing from the elders and the residents of the city to Boaz on the occasion of his marriage to Ruth.

4 1 Boaz did not postpone the matter of the redemption. **Boaz went up to the gate,**[B] the place of judgment, where the dignitaries of the city were present, **and sat there, and behold, the redeemer of whom Boaz had spoken was passing. He,** Boaz, **said: Turn aside** from wherever you are going and enter, **sit here, So-and-So. He turned aside and he sat.** The redeemer's name is not stated here, either because it is not known, or because he acted inappropriately by refusing the redemption.[45]

2 **He,** Boaz, **took ten men of the elders of the city, and said: Sit here** to serve as judges; **and they sat** down.

ח מַרְגְּלֹתָיו וַתִּשְׁכַּב׃ וַיְהִי בַּחֲצִי הַלַּיְלָה וַיֶּחֱרַד הָאִישׁ וַיִּלָּפֵת וְהִנֵּה אִשָּׁה שֹׁכֶבֶת
ט מַרְגְּלֹתָיו׃ וַיֹּאמֶר מִי־אָתְּ וַתֹּאמֶר אָנֹכִי רוּת אֲמָתֶךָ וּפָרַשְׂתָּ כְנָפֶךָ עַל־אֲמָתְךָ
י כִּי גֹאֵל אָתָּה׃ וַיֹּאמֶר בְּרוּכָה אַתְּ לַיהוָה בִּתִּי הֵיטַבְתְּ חַסְדֵּךְ הָאַחֲרוֹן מִן־הָרִאשׁוֹן
יא לְבִלְתִּי־לֶכֶת אַחֲרֵי הַבַּחוּרִים אִם־דַּל וְאִם־עָשִׁיר׃ וְעַתָּה בִּתִּי אַל־תִּירְאִי כֹּל
יב אֲשֶׁר־תֹּאמְרִי אֶעֱשֶׂה־לָּךְ כִּי יוֹדֵעַ כָּל־שַׁעַר עַמִּי כִּי אֵשֶׁת חַיִל אָתְּ׃ וְעַתָּה כִּי
יג אָמְנָם כִּי אם גֹאֵל אָנֹכִי וְגַם יֵשׁ גֹּאֵל קָרוֹב מִמֶּנִּי׃ לִינִי ׀ הַלַּיְלָה וְהָיָה בַבֹּקֶר
אִם־יִגְאָלֵךְ טוֹב יִגְאָל וְאִם־לֹא יַחְפֹּץ לְגָאֳלֵךְ וּגְאַלְתִּיךְ אָנֹכִי חַי־יְהוָה שִׁכְבִי
יד עַד־הַבֹּקֶר׃ וַתִּשְׁכַּב מַרְגְּלוֹתָו עַד־הַבֹּקֶר וַתָּקָם בטרום יַכִּיר אִישׁ אֶת־רֵעֵהוּ בְּטֶרֶם
טו וַיֹּאמֶר אַל־יִוָּדַע כִּי־בָאָה הָאִשָּׁה הַגֹּרֶן׃ וַיֹּאמֶר הָבִי הַמִּטְפַּחַת אֲשֶׁר־עָלַיִךְ
טז וְאֶחֳזִי־בָהּ וַתֹּאחֶז בָּהּ וַיָּמָד שֵׁשׁ־שְׂעֹרִים וַיָּשֶׁת עָלֶיהָ וַיָּבֹא הָעִיר׃ וַתָּבוֹא אֶל־
יז חֲמוֹתָהּ וַתֹּאמֶר מִי־אַתְּ בִּתִּי וַתַּגֶּד־לָהּ אֵת כָּל־אֲשֶׁר עָשָׂה־לָהּ הָאִישׁ׃ וַתֹּאמֶר
יח שֵׁשׁ־הַשְּׂעֹרִים הָאֵלֶּה נָתַן לִי כִּי אָמַר אַל־תָּבוֹאִי רֵיקָם אֶל־חֲמוֹתֵךְ׃ וַתֹּאמֶר אֵלַי
שְׁבִי בִתִּי עַד אֲשֶׁר תֵּדְעִין אֵיךְ יִפֹּל דָּבָר כִּי לֹא יִשְׁקֹט הָאִישׁ כִּי־אִם־כִּלָּה הַדָּבָר
א הַיּוֹם׃ וּבֹעַז עָלָה הַשַּׁעַר וַיֵּשֶׁב שָׁם וְהִנֵּה הַגֹּאֵל עֹבֵר אֲשֶׁר דִּבֶּר־בֹּעַז וַיֹּאמֶר
ב סוּרָה שְׁבָה־פֹּה פְּלֹנִי אַלְמֹנִי וַיָּסַר וַיֵּשֵׁב׃ וַיִּקַּח עֲשָׂרָה אֲנָשִׁים מִזִּקְנֵי הָעִיר וַיֹּאמֶר

DISCUSSION

3:10 | **Your latter kindness is greater than the former:** The biblical commandment of levirate marriage applies to the brother of a married man who died childless. The Torah commands that the living brother should marry the widow, so that the children who will be born to them will continue the name of the deceased (see Deuteronomy 25:5). This chapter is not referring to a standard levirate marriage, as neither Boaz nor the anonymous man discussed below (verse 12) were Ruth's brothers-in-law. Rather, it is speaking of an analogous type of redemption based on a more distant relationship.

3:13 | **But if he does not wish to redeem you, I will redeem you:** Some claim that Elimelekh, Boaz's father, and the redeemer, whose name might have been Tov, and who is also referred to below as *Ploni Almoni*, So-and-So (4:1), were all brothers (see 4:3; *Ruth Rabba* 6:3; *Bava Batra* 91a; *Midrash Tanḥuma*, *Behar* 3). However, this was not necessarily the case, as in any event this was not an ordinary levirate marriage. If the redeemer and Boaz were brothers, then the anonymous redeemer was the older brother. If they were not brothers, then he was a closer relative to Elimelekh than Boaz.

BACKGROUND

4:1 | **The gate:** The city gate was the center of communal life. Archaeological evidence and various passages from the Bible indicate that the actual structure of the gate, as well as the adjacent area, was used for legal trials (see Genesis 23:10; Deuteronomy 21:19, 22:24; Joshua 20:4; Amos 5:15). In addition, the gate was a place for the sacrificial rites of the shrines, sometimes called "high places," which were eventually prohibited (II Kings 23:8), as well as economic transactions, announcements, public rebukes (Jeremiah 17:19, 19:2; Amos 5:10), and special gatherings of the people (Nehemiah 8:1). In several ancient cities that have been subject to archaeological research, communal structures unearthed close to the gate might also have been part of this complex. Due to the centrality of the gate, the expression "the gate of the city" sometimes refers to the entire city (see, e.g., Exodus 20:10; Deuteronomy 15:7, 23:17; I Kings 8:37).

3 **He said to the redeemer:** Regarding **the tract of land that belonged to our brother, to Elimelekh, Naomi, who has returned from the fields of Moav, is selling,** that is, she has put up the land for sale.[46] Naomi and Ruth could not work the field alone, and the money from the sale would help sustain them financially.
4 **I said: I will inform you, saying: Acquire before those who are sitting here, and before the elders of my people.** If you have not heard about it, I hereby inform you that the field is for sale, and you may purchase it officially in a public manner before all those who sit here. **If you would redeem, redeem,** as you have the first right to do so. **But if you will not redeem, tell me, and I will know. For there is no one besides you to redeem, and I am after you.** According to the laws of redemption, there is no other potential redeemer in the family apart from myself. If you refuse to redeem it, I will purchase it instead. **He,** the man, **said: I will redeem** it, by purchasing it.
5 The anonymous redeemer agreed to purchase the field belonging to the family of his relatives, but he did not realize that whoever redeems the field must also marry the young surviving widow, and thereby preserve the family by having more children. This is not a biblical obligation, as according to Torah law the redemption of an inheritance of a relative is not automatically accompanied by the obligation to marry his widow. Nevertheless, the practice was that anyone who takes over the inheritance of a relative must also marry his wife, similar to levirate marriage.[47] **Boaz said: On the day of your acquisition of the field from the hand of Naomi, and from Ruth the Moavite,**[D] **you acquire the wife of the dead;** the practice of redemption includes marrying her in order **to perpetuate the name of the dead upon his inheritance.** By marrying the widow of the deceased childless husband and fathering children with her, the name of the deceased will be perpetuated.
6 **The redeemer said: I cannot redeem for myself, lest I ruin my inheritance,** harm my family; **you redeem my redemption** in my place, **as I cannot redeem** it. Apparently, he did not want to marry Ruth because she was a foreign woman, and worse, a Moavite.[48] Alternatively, he was wary of bringing a younger wife into his home as a rival to his current wife, a move that would cause marital strife.[49]
7 **This was the tradition in Israel,** in the ancient past, **concerning redemption** of fields **and concerning exchange** of goods, in order **to validate any matter: A man removed his shoe,**

Shoe used in *ḥalitza* ceremony abrogating levirate marriage, New York, twentieth century

and he gave it to another; that action of removing one's shoe **was the testament in Israel.** It was a symbolic expression of the completion of a transaction.[50]
8 **The redeemer said to Boaz: Acquire it for yourself;** I waive my right to the purchase; **and he removed his shoe,** to indicate that he was prepared to validate the arrangement.
9 **Boaz said to the elders and to all the people: You are witnesses this day that I have acquired everything that was Elimelekh's and everything that was Kilyon's and Mahlon's from the hand of Naomi.**
10 **And Ruth the Moavite, wife of Mahlon, I have acquired as my wife,** similar to the levirate marriage discussed in the Torah.[51] Here too my intention is **to perpetuate the name of the dead upon his inheritance,** both by buying his field as well as through the descendants of his widow, **and** thus **the name of the dead will not be eliminated from among his brethren and from the gate of his place.** Any children from the match will be named after the deceased, and in this manner his existence will be continued in this world in a certain sense.[52] **You are witnesses today.** Boaz thereby invited the elders and the people to validate the proceedings.
11 **All the people who were at the gate, and the elders, said: We are witnesses,** and we all affirm your statement. Since Boaz intended to marry Ruth, they also blessed him: **May the Lord grant that the woman who is coming into your house be like Rachel and like Leah, both of whom built the house of Israel. Prosper in Efrat, and proclaim a name in Bethlehem.** Some explain that the last phrase means that you should merit

DISCUSSION

4:5 | **The Moavite:** The Torah prohibits marriage with converts from Moav: "An Amonite or a Moavite shall not enter into the assembly of the Lord; even the tenth generation shall not enter into the assembly of the Lord forever, because they did not greet you with bread and with water on the way upon your exodus from Egypt, and because he hired against you Bilam son of Beor, from Petor, Aram Naharayim, to

ג שְׁבוּ־פֹה וַיֵּשֵׁבוּ: וַיֹּאמֶר לַגֹּאֵל חֶלְקַת הַשָּׂדֶה אֲשֶׁר לְאָחִינוּ לֶאֱלִימֶלֶךְ מָכְרָה
ד נָעֳמִי הַשָּׁבָה מִשְּׂדֵה מוֹאָב: וַאֲנִי אָמַרְתִּי אֶגְלֶה אָזְנְךָ לֵאמֹר קְנֵה נֶגֶד הַיֹּשְׁבִים
וְנֶגֶד זִקְנֵי עַמִּי אִם־תִּגְאַל גְּאָל וְאִם־לֹא יִגְאַל הַגִּידָה לִּי וְאֵדַע כִּי אֵין זוּלָתְךָ
ה לִגְאוֹל וְאָנֹכִי אַחֲרֶיךָ וַיֹּאמֶר אָנֹכִי אֶגְאָל: וַיֹּאמֶר בֹּעַז בְּיוֹם־קְנוֹתְךָ הַשָּׂדֶה מִיַּד
נָעֳמִי וּמֵאֵת רוּת הַמּוֹאֲבִיָּה אֵשֶׁת־הַמֵּת קניתי לְהָקִים שֵׁם־הַמֵּת עַל־נַחֲלָתוֹ: קָנִיתָה
ו וַיֹּאמֶר הַגֹּאֵל לֹא אוּכַל לגאול־לִי פֶּן־אַשְׁחִית אֶת־נַחֲלָתִי גְּאַל־לְךָ אַתָּה אֶת־ לִגְאָל־
ז גְּאֻלָּתִי כִּי לֹא־אוּכַל לִגְאֹל: וְזֹאת לְפָנִים בְּיִשְׂרָאֵל עַל־הַגְּאוּלָּה וְעַל־הַתְּמוּרָה
ח לְקַיֵּם כָּל־דָּבָר שָׁלַף אִישׁ נַעֲלוֹ וְנָתַן לְרֵעֵהוּ וְזֹאת הַתְּעוּדָה בְּיִשְׂרָאֵל: וַיֹּאמֶר
ט הַגֹּאֵל לְבֹעַז קְנֵה־לָךְ וַיִּשְׁלֹף נַעֲלוֹ: וַיֹּאמֶר בֹּעַז לַזְּקֵנִים וְכָל־הָעָם עֵדִים אַתֶּם
הַיּוֹם כִּי קָנִיתִי אֶת־כָּל־אֲשֶׁר לֶאֱלִימֶלֶךְ וְאֵת כָּל־אֲשֶׁר לְכִלְיוֹן וּמַחְלוֹן מִיַּד
י נָעֳמִי: וְגַם אֶת־רוּת הַמֹּאֲבִיָּה אֵשֶׁת מַחְלוֹן קָנִיתִי לִי לְאִשָּׁה לְהָקִים שֵׁם־הַמֵּת
עַל־נַחֲלָתוֹ וְלֹא־יִכָּרֵת שֵׁם־הַמֵּת מֵעִם אֶחָיו וּמִשַּׁעַר מְקוֹמוֹ עֵדִים אַתֶּם הַיּוֹם:
יא וַיֹּאמְרוּ כָּל־הָעָם אֲשֶׁר־בַּשַּׁעַר וְהַזְּקֵנִים עֵדִים יִתֵּן יְהוָה אֶת־הָאִשָּׁה הַבָּאָה
אֶל־בֵּיתֶךָ כְּרָחֵל ׀ וּכְלֵאָה אֲשֶׁר בָּנוּ שְׁתֵּיהֶם אֶת־בֵּית יִשְׂרָאֵל וַעֲשֵׂה־חַיִל
יב בְּאֶפְרָתָה וּקְרָא־שֵׁם בְּבֵית לָחֶם: וִיהִי בֵיתְךָ כְּבֵית פֶּרֶץ אֲשֶׁר־יָלְדָה תָמָר

offspring from this marriage in Bethlehem,[53] which was near Efrata, or the very same place (see 1:2).

12 May your house be like the house of Peretz, your ancestor,[54] **whom Tamar bore to Judah,**[D] **from the descendants that the Lord will give you from this young woman.**

DISCUSSION

curse you" (Deuteronomy 23:4–5). The Oral Law teaches that this prohibition applies only to Moavite men, not women. This *halakha* was not well known at the time, and was not accepted in practice on a regular basis (see *Yevamot* 77a). The redeemer's refusal to marry Ruth may have been out of his misunderstanding of this law (see *Ruth Rabba* 7:10).

4:12 | **Like the house of Peretz whom Tamar bore to Judah:** Although Peretz was not Judah's firstborn, the sons of Tamar continued the legacy of Judah, and the leaders of the tribe of Judah came from this lineage for many generations. The mention of Tamar and Judah in the people's blessing highlights the similarity between the match of Ruth and Boaz and that story. Just as the marriage of Boaz to Ruth did not involve a simple case of levirate marriage, Judah and Tamar's relationship was also not a standard levirate marriage, as Judah was the father, not the brother, of the deceased.

There are other dimensions to this comparison to Judah and Tamar. In both stories, pure God-fearing women are placed in difficult circumstances, and they must devise unusual plans of action that breach the standard norms in order to maintain their ties to the family of Judah. Ultimately, both Tamar and Ruth successfully build the future royal family of David (see Alsheikh; Malbim).

Ruth's Marriage and the Birth of Her Son

RUTH 4:13–17

The hopes that have been placed upon Ruth and Boaz and the blessings bestowed upon them indeed come to pass. Naomi is not abandoned either, as the son born to Ruth is considered a redeemer for her as well. His birth preserves the name of her deceased son, and in her old age she helps to raise the child and serves as a kind of mother and nurse for him.

13 **Boaz took Ruth, and she became his wife; and he consort-**
ed with her, and the Lord granted her pregnancy, and she
bore[D] **a son.**[D]
14 Following the birth of a son to Ruth, **the women said to**
Naomi: Blessed be the Lord, who did not leave you today
without a redeemer. He is considered the heir of your deceased son, as he preserves his memory and existence in this
world, like the child born from a levirate marriage. In this manner, he redeems you, as though you had given birth to an additional son. **And let his name be called in Israel.** Now your
family lineage will be continued.
15 Furthermore, **may he be for you a restorer of life** merely by
virtue of his existence, **and one to sustain your old age.** When
he grows up and you grow old, you can rely upon him to care
for you. **For your daughter-in-law, who loves you, who is**
better for you than seven sons, bore him.
16 **Naomi took the child, and she placed him in her bosom,**
despite the lack of any direct blood relationship between her
and the boy, **and was a nurse for him.** She felt an unusual af-
finity to this boy for two reasons: First, he carried her deceased
son's legacy, and in a certain sense, his very existence. Second,
he was the son of Ruth, who was like a daughter to her, and
perhaps even closer than that, as Naomi considered Ruth her
successor.[55]
17 In fact, Naomi was treated as the mother of the child by those
in her immediate surroundings. **The women neighbors called**
him a name, saying: A son is born to Naomi.[56] **They called**
his name Oved; he is the father of Yishai, who was **the father**
of David.

The Lineage of the House of David

RUTH 4:18–22

Since the previous passage concluded with the list of generations from Boaz to King David, the book ends with the broader family lineage, starting with Peretz, who was the son of Judah, the father of the tribe. The purpose of this family lineage is to trace the roots of King David, whose remarkable deeds and accomplishments justify all of the difficulties and suffering described in the book of Ruth.

18 **These are the generations of** the family of **Peretz: Peretz be-**
got Hetzron;
19 **and Hetzron begot Ram, and Ram begot Aminadav;**
20 **and Aminadav begot Nahshon,** the prince of the tribe of
Judah at the time of the exodus from Egypt,[57] **and Nahshon**
begot Salmon;
21 **and Salmon begot Boaz, and Boaz begot Oved;**
22 **and Oved begot Yishai, and Yishai begot David.**[D]

Supposed graves of Yishai and Ruth, Hebron

יג לְיהוּדָ֑ה מִן־הַזֶּ֗רַע אֲשֶׁ֨ר יִתֵּ֤ן יְהוָה֙ לְךָ֔ מִן־הַֽנַּעֲרָ֖ה הַזֹּֽאת׃ וַיִּקַּ֨ח בֹּ֤עַז אֶת־רוּת֙
יד וַתְּהִי־ל֣וֹ לְאִשָּׁ֔ה וַיָּבֹ֖א אֵלֶ֑יהָ וַיִּתֵּ֨ן יְהוָ֥ה לָ֛הּ הֵרָי֖וֹן וַתֵּ֥לֶד בֵּֽן׃ וַתֹּאמַ֤רְנָה הַנָּשִׁים֙
אֶֽל־נָעֳמִ֔י בָּר֣וּךְ יְהוָ֔ה אֲשֶׁ֨ר לֹ֣א הִשְׁבִּ֥ית לָ֛ךְ גֹּאֵ֖ל הַיּ֑וֹם וְיִקָּרֵ֥א שְׁמ֖וֹ בְּיִשְׂרָאֵֽל׃
טו וְהָ֤יָה לָךְ֙ לְמֵשִׁ֣יב נֶ֔פֶשׁ וּלְכַלְכֵּ֖ל אֶת־שֵׂיבָתֵ֑ךְ כִּ֣י כַלָּתֵ֤ךְ אֲשֶׁר־אֲהֵבַ֙תֶךְ֙ יְלָדַ֔תּוּ
טז אֲשֶׁר־הִיא֙ ט֣וֹבָה לָ֔ךְ מִשִּׁבְעָ֖ה בָּנִֽים׃ וַתִּקַּ֨ח נָעֳמִ֤י אֶת־הַיֶּ֙לֶד֙ וַתְּשִׁתֵ֣הוּ בְחֵיקָ֔הּ
יז וַתְּהִי־ל֖וֹ לְאֹמֶֽנֶת׃ וַתִּקְרֶאנָה֩ ל֨וֹ הַשְּׁכֵנ֥וֹת שֵׁם֙ לֵאמֹ֔ר יֻלַּ֥ד־בֵּ֖ן לְנָעֳמִ֑י וַתִּקְרֶ֤אנָה
שְׁמוֹ֙ עוֹבֵ֔ד ה֥וּא אֲבִי־יִשַׁ֖י אֲבִ֥י דָוִֽד׃
יח יט וְאֵ֙לֶּה֙ תּוֹלְד֣וֹת פָּ֔רֶץ פֶּ֖רֶץ הוֹלִ֥יד אֶת־חֶצְרֽוֹן׃ וְחֶצְרוֹן֙ הוֹלִ֣יד אֶת־רָ֔ם וְרָ֖ם הוֹלִ֥יד
כ כא אֶת־עַמִּֽינָדָֽב׃ וְעַמִּֽינָדָב֙ הוֹלִ֣יד אֶת־נַחְשׁ֔וֹן וְנַחְשׁ֖וֹן הוֹלִ֥יד אֶת־שַׂלְמָֽה׃ וְשַׂלְמוֹן֙
כב הוֹלִ֣יד אֶת־בֹּ֔עַז וּבֹ֖עַז הוֹלִ֥יד אֶת־עוֹבֵֽד׃ וְעֹבֵד֙ הוֹלִ֣יד אֶת־יִשָׁ֔י וְיִשַׁ֖י הוֹלִ֥יד אֶת־
דָּוִֽד׃

DISCUSSION

4:13 | **And the Lord granted her pregnancy, and she bore:** This conception occurred with divine assistance. After all, Ruth was previously married to a man younger than Boaz, yet did not bear him any children. According to the Sages, this event was especially miraculous, as they state that Boaz passed away on the night after Ruth became pregnant (see Alsheikh; Malbim; *Midrash Ruth Zuta* 4).

And she bore a son: The narrative involving Ruth concludes here. Nothing is stated about the remainder of her life. However, the Sages say that she lived to a very old age, and merited to see not only King David, her grandson, but also his son, King Solomon (*Bava Batra* 91b).

4:22 | **And Yishai begot David:** It is unclear whether this is a complete family lineage covering every generation, as many years separate the generation of Peretz from that of David. If this is in fact a full list, each of the individuals mentioned here must have lived to a very old age and fathered children very late in life (see Ibn Ezra; *Yalkut Shimoni*; *Bereshit Rabba* 96:4; Ramban, Genesis 46:15). It is more plausible that certain individuals of lesser importance were omitted from this list (see Ibn Ezra; *Yalkut Shimoni*; commentary on I Chronicles 2:51).

Lamentations

Lamentations

INTRODUCTION TO LAMENTATIONS

According to tradition, the book of Lamentations was authored by the prophet Jeremiah.[1] However, the Sages explain that in fact it was Barukh ben Neriya the scribe, Jeremiah's friend, who wrote the book, based on the words of Jeremiah.[2] This book does not contain a running narrative or description of events, but rather consists of lamentations over the downfall of Israel: the killings, famine, exile, and sufferings of the Jewish people.

These lamentations are usually understood as specifically addressing the destruction of the Temple, but this interpretation is not absolute. Although they are lamentations for the downfall of an entire kingdom and describe the departure of the nation into exile, they are actually missing an explicit and detailed description of the destruction of the Temple. It is therefore possible that a large portion of these lamentations were written prior to the destruction of the Temple. Support for this suggestion can be found in a verse elsewhere in the Bible that describes the aftermath of the death of King Yoshiya, decades before the destruction of Jerusalem: "And Jeremiah lamented Yoshiya, and all the male and female singers spoke of Yoshiya in their lamentations until this day, and they made them a statute over Israel, and behold, they are written in the lamentations."[3] This indicates that many years before the destruction of the Temple, a collection of lamentations was compiled in which those of Jeremiah over the death of Yoshiya appeared. It would seem, therefore, that the earlier compilation of lamentations is in fact the book of Lamentations. The downfall of Yoshiya is especially fitting as the subject of the third lamentation, which is unique with regard to its length and structure.[4]

The death of King Yoshiya signified the conclusion of an era. This was understood by those with foresight who lived at the time, despite the fact that, in practice, Yoshiya's three sons as well as his grandson reigned in Judah after his death. During the reigns of Yoshiya's successors, Jerusalem was conquered twice, once by the Egyptians, who exiled the king of Judah, and later by the Babylonians, who after an extended siege took another king captive. Repeated attempts to rebel against Babylonian rule did not succeed. It is therefore certainly possible that the military defeat at Megiddo in which Yoshiya was killed was already perceived as the beginning of the end of the kingdom of Judah.

The lamentations in this book do not describe an absolute destruction or the final end of the Jewish people. Rather, alongside mourning, themes of hope for consolation in the future are also present. Nevertheless, the catastrophic nature of the downfall is not in doubt, and the lamenter does not anticipate the kingdom's revival in the near future. Consolation is only for the distant future. It is therefore understandable that these lamentations were written down for future generations, and it is logical that their recitation has become a permanent custom among the Jewish people.

Most of the lamentations were written according to an alphabetical acrostic arrangement, with some minor departures. Only the final chapter does not use this acrostic method; even so, it consists of twenty-two verses, just like all the others. This highly stylized method of writing attests to the fact that the contents of the book were composed deliberately, rather than being a spontaneous emotional outpouring. Their form may also indicate an awareness that they would be read on a regular basis. Even one in the midst of mourning, who has difficulty finding the appropriate words to articulate his or her pain, will be able to find an appropriate expression of his emotions within this book.

Lamentations

Jerusalem

LAMENTATIONS 1:1–22

This lamentation depicts the miserable condition of Jerusalem in its destroyed state in comparison with its past eminence. The lamenter describes the loneliness, siege, famine, killing, robbery, captivity, and exile of the inhabitants of the city, as well as the degradation of the city itself. Three times the lamenter pauses in his harsh descriptions and cries out to God, that He should see what He has done. The lamenter is not complaining or accusing God; on the contrary, toward the end of the lamentation he justifies the divine sentence that was passed against Jerusalem due to the sins of its inhabitants. Still, in his cries to Heaven, he expresses his bewilderment at the harshness of the punishment. The lamentation ends with a plea for revenge against Judah's enemies.

1 1 **How does the** once **greatly crowded city** of Jerusalem now **sit alone? She has become** without support, **like a widow.**[D] **Great** and important **among the nations,**[5] **a princess,** ruler, and minister **among the states: She has become a vassal,** subservient to others! Jerusalem, which was the seat of a great and glorious kingdom, has completely lost its prestige.

2 **She,** the helpless widow, Jerusalem, **weeps at night,** as she is ashamed to weep in the daytime when people can see her, **and her tears are on her cheeks.** She attempts to hide her tears from the eyes of strangers. **Of all her lovers,** or political allies, **she has no one to comfort her. All her allies have betrayed her; they have become her enemies;** all the countries that had friendly relationships with her abandoned her after her downfall.

3 **Judah has been exiled in affliction and in great enslavement. She has settled among the nations, finding no rest,** because **all her pursuers,** her perpetual enemies, who had borne animosity toward her for generations, **have overtaken her.** They seized the opportunity to take revenge against her while she was pressed **within the straits,** narrow areas with no escape routes.[6]

Men and women going into exile on a wagon, Lakhish reliefs, Nineveh, 701 BCE

4 In normal times, the roads to Jerusalem were busy, particularly during the pilgrimage festivals when all of Israel would travel there. But now, **the ways,** the roads, **of Zion mourn,** they are desolate, **without pilgrims to the festival; all her gates are desolate; her priests sigh,** as the city is destroyed and the Temple is deserted.[7] **Her young women are melancholy, and she is embittered.**

5 **Her besiegers are ascendant, her enemies are tranquil, for the Lord has tormented her for her abundant transgressions; her infants are led into captivity before the besieger,** at the time of Yehoyakhin's exile to Babylonia.

6 **All her splendor has gone out of the daughter of Zion. Her** free and esteemed **princes are** hungry and lost, **like deer that have not found pasture.**[8] **They went powerless before the pursuer;** they were led into captivity by their new masters.

Hunting deer, relief at the Palace of Ashurbanipal, Nineveh, 645–635 BCE

7 **In the days of her affliction and her wretchedness,** her suffering,[9] **Jerusalem recalled all her delights that were from the days of old.** At the moment of her downfall, Jerusalem remembers the good days of yesteryear. **With the fall of her people into the hand of the besieger, with no one to help her, the besiegers saw her; they mocked her deficiencies.** Even those who did not actively participate in her destruction took pleasure in her downtrodden state.

איכה

א אֵיכָה ׀ יָשְׁבָה בָדָד הָעִיר רַבָּתִי עָם הָיְתָה כְּאַלְמָנָה רַבָּתִי בַגּוֹיִם שָׂרָתִי בַּמְּדִינוֹת
ב הָיְתָה לָמַס׃ בָּכוֹ תִבְכֶּה בַּלַּיְלָה וְדִמְעָתָהּ עַל לֶחֱיָהּ אֵין־לָהּ מְנַחֵם מִכָּל־אֹהֲבֶיהָ
ג כָּל־רֵעֶיהָ בָּגְדוּ בָהּ הָיוּ לָהּ לְאֹיְבִים׃ גָּלְתָה יְהוּדָה מֵעֹנִי וּמֵרֹב עֲבֹדָה הִיא יָשְׁבָה
ד בַגּוֹיִם לֹא מָצְאָה מָנוֹחַ כָּל־רֹדְפֶיהָ הִשִּׂיגוּהָ בֵּין הַמְּצָרִים׃ דַּרְכֵי צִיּוֹן אֲבֵלוֹת
מִבְּלִי בָּאֵי מוֹעֵד כָּל־שְׁעָרֶיהָ שׁוֹמֵמִין כֹּהֲנֶיהָ נֶאֱנָחִים בְּתוּלֹתֶיהָ נּוּגוֹת וְהִיא
ה מַר־לָהּ׃ הָיוּ צָרֶיהָ לְרֹאשׁ אֹיְבֶיהָ שָׁלוּ כִּי־יְהוָה הוֹגָהּ עַל־רֹב פְּשָׁעֶיהָ עוֹלָלֶיהָ
ו הָלְכוּ שְׁבִי לִפְנֵי־צָר׃ וַיֵּצֵא מִן בַּת־צִיּוֹן כָּל־הֲדָרָהּ הָיוּ שָׂרֶיהָ כְּאַיָּלִים לֹא־מָצְאוּ מִבַּת־
ז מִרְעֶה וַיֵּלְכוּ בְלֹא־כֹחַ לִפְנֵי רוֹדֵף׃ זָכְרָה יְרוּשָׁלִַם יְמֵי עָנְיָהּ וּמְרוּדֶיהָ כֹּל מַחֲמֻדֶיהָ
אֲשֶׁר הָיוּ מִימֵי קֶדֶם בִּנְפֹל עַמָּהּ בְּיַד־צָר וְאֵין עוֹזֵר לָהּ רָאוּהָ צָרִים שָׂחֲקוּ עַל־
ח מִשְׁבַּתֶּהָ׃ חֵטְא חָטְאָה יְרוּשָׁלִַם עַל־כֵּן לְנִידָה הָיָתָה כָּל־מְכַבְּדֶיהָ הִזִּילוּהָ
ט כִּי־רָאוּ עֶרְוָתָהּ גַּם־הִיא נֶאֶנְחָה וַתָּשָׁב אָחוֹר׃ טֻמְאָתָהּ בְּשׁוּלֶיהָ לֹא זָכְרָה

8 **A sin has Jerusalem sinned; therefore she has become a pariah.**[D] **All who honored her have demeaned her, because they saw her nakedness;** her shortcomings and agonies have been exposed to all.[10] **Even she** herself **sighs and has regressed.** She has become weak and therefore does not actively respond; instead, she sighs and resigns herself to her misery and desolation.

9 **Her impurity,** the blood of her menstruation, **is** perceptible **on the edges of her skirts,** the hems of her garment; in other words, her sins are obvious. **She had not considered** the fact

DISCUSSION

1:1| **She has become like a widow:** In its simple sense, the verse is declaring Jerusalem akin to a widow simply because she is devoid of protection and her status has become low. But there is also a sense that the city's "husband," God, has abandoned her. A similar expression is found in the last lamentation (5:3): "We have become orphans, fatherless; our mothers are like widows." This verse can be read literally, but it can also be seen as an allegory of the sense of orphanhood felt by the people of the city toward their Father in Heaven; the subjective feeling of Jerusalem, or the people of Israel, that they have been abandoned forever (Rashi; *Targum Yonatan*; *Eikha Rabba* 1:3; *Targum Yonatan* and *Pesikta Zutreta* on 5:3; see also Isaiah 54:4–5).

1:8| **She has become a pariah** [*nidda*]: The Hebrew word *nidda* denotes something kept at a distance or shunned. It is also used to refer to a menstruating woman. Presumably, this usage arose due to the observance of the laws of ritual purity in Temple times. In order to avoid becoming impure, pure individuals would often avoid menstruating women and others who were ritually impure (see, e.g., Jerusalem Talmud, *Shekalim* 8:1). The imagery used here and in the next verse is of Jerusalem as a shunned menstruating woman. According to the Talmud (*Ta'anit* 20a), this metaphor was chosen to provide a sense of hope for the future: "Just as a menstruating woman will become permitted, so too Jerusalem will be restored."

that this would be **her end.**[11] **She has declined extraordinarily,** far beyond expectations;[12] **there is no one to comfort her.** Consequently, the lamenter pleads: **See, Lord, my affliction, for the enemy has expanded** his power; he acts in Jerusalem as he pleases.

10 **The besieger spread his hand over all her delights,** i.e., he has taken them, **as she saw the nations entering her Sanctuary,** those nations **whom You had commanded that they should not enter Your assembly.** This is referring to the Amonites and the Moavites, whom the Torah denies even the possibility of conversion to Judaism.[13] The entry of such banned and inferior nations into the Temple is therefore doubly insulting.[14]

"The besieger spread his hand over all her delights." Romans carrying away the Temple vessels in their victory march, stone relief, Arch of Titus, Rome, 82 CE

11 **All her people are sighing, seeking bread** during the siege; **they have given** all **their delights,** their most valuable items, **for food to sustain**[15] **life.** Again the lamenter requests that God look at him, but now his request is in the name of Jerusalem: **See, Lord, and look, for I have become abject.**[16] Alternatively, the lamenter is saying that the reason people are starving for bread is that in the past the city was full of gluttony.[17]

12 Desolate Jerusalem now turns to the people who pass through it unheedingly, and expresses its wishes for them: **May it not befall you, all wayfarers.** Let troubles like mine never befall you.[18] **Behold and see: Is there any pain like my pain, which has been done to me,**[19] **with which the Lord has tormented me on the day of His enflamed wrath?**

13 **From on high He sent fire into my bones, and He crushed them,** flattened and destroyed them. **He spread a net for my feet,** and once I was caught in it, **He set me back. He rendered me desolate, suffering,** ill and in pain, or, distanced like a menstruating woman,[20] **all day.**

14 **The yoke of my transgressions is preserved**[21] **in His hand;** the transgressions are **becoming entangled, coming upon my neck** like a yoke, **sapping my strength. The Lord delivered me into the hands of those against whom I cannot stand.**

15 **The Lord trampled**[22] **all my mighty in my midst; He proclaimed a festival** of many enemies **against me** in order **to break my young men; the Lord has trodden the virgin daughter of Judah,** a moniker for the tribe of Judah or the residents of Jerusalem, **in a winepress.** We have all been trampled like grapes by the enemy, and our blood has been spilled like wine in a winepress.[23]

Treading in a winepress

16 **For these I weep; my eye, my eye sheds water,** tears, **for a comforter,** a king or other savior, **restorer of my soul, has grown distant from me. My children have become desolate,** with no guide or supporter, **because the enemy has prevailed.**

17 **Zion spread her hands** as a sign of surrender, defeat, and despair;[24] **there was no comforter for her. The Lord has commanded for Jacob that his besiegers surround him** from all sides.[25] **Jerusalem has become like a pariah among them,** even more distanced and disgraced.[26]

18 The lamentation is composed with the mindset of acceptance of God's sentence: **The Lord,** who has done all this to us, **is righteous;** His judgment is correct, **for I have defied,** transgressed, **His word. Hear now all you peoples,** what God has done to us, **and see my pain: My young women and young men have gone into captivity.**

19 **I called to my lovers,** those who had presented themselves as my friends and allies,[27] but **they deceived me.** Meanwhile, **my priests and my elders,** who are usually sustained by public funds (see 4:16), **perished in the city, while they sought food for themselves,** as the public did not have the means to support them during the siege; they tried **to restore their lives** and sustain themselves, but to no avail.

"My young women and young men have gone into captivity." Jews exiled from Lakhish, above left: men, above right: women; Lakhish reliefs, Nineveh, 701 BCE

י אַחֲרִיתָהּ וַתֵּרֶד פְּלָאִים אֵין מְנַחֵם לָהּ רְאֵה יְהוָה אֶת־עָנְיִי כִּי הִגְדִּיל אוֹיֵב: יָדוֹ
פָּרַשׂ צָר עַל כָּל־מַחֲמַדֶּיהָ כִּי־רָאֲתָה גוֹיִם בָּאוּ מִקְדָּשָׁהּ אֲשֶׁר צִוִּיתָה לֹא־יָבֹאוּ
יא בַקָּהָל לָךְ: כָּל־עַמָּהּ נֶאֱנָחִים מְבַקְּשִׁים לֶחֶם נָתְנוּ מחמודיהם בְּאֹכֶל לְהָשִׁיב מַחֲמַדֵּיהֶם
יב נָפֶשׁ רְאֵה יְהוָה וְהַבִּיטָה כִּי הָיִיתִי זוֹלֵלָה: לוֹא אֲלֵיכֶם כָּל־עֹבְרֵי דֶרֶךְ הַבִּיטוּ
וּרְאוּ אִם־יֵשׁ מַכְאוֹב כְּמַכְאֹבִי אֲשֶׁר עוֹלַל לִי אֲשֶׁר הוֹגָה יְהוָה בְּיוֹם חֲרוֹן אַפּוֹ:
יג מִמָּרוֹם שָׁלַח־אֵשׁ בְּעַצְמֹתַי וַיִּרְדֶּנָּה פָּרַשׂ רֶשֶׁת לְרַגְלַי הֱשִׁיבַנִי אָחוֹר נְתָנַנִי
יד שֹׁמֵמָה כָּל־הַיּוֹם דָּוָה: נִשְׂקַד עֹל פְּשָׁעַי בְּיָדוֹ יִשְׂתָּרְגוּ עָלוּ עַל־צַוָּארִי הִכְשִׁיל
טו כֹּחִי נְתָנַנִי אֲדֹנָי בִּידֵי לֹא־אוּכַל קוּם: סִלָּה כָל־אַבִּירַי | אֲדֹנָי בְּקִרְבִּי קָרָא עָלַי
טז מוֹעֵד לִשְׁבֹּר בַּחוּרָי גַּת דָּרַךְ אֲדֹנָי לִבְתוּלַת בַּת־יְהוּדָה: עַל־אֵלֶּה | אֲנִי בוֹכִיָּה
עֵינִי | עֵינִי יֹרְדָה מַּיִם כִּי־רָחַק מִמֶּנִּי מְנַחֵם מֵשִׁיב נַפְשִׁי הָיוּ בָנַי שׁוֹמֵמִים כִּי גָבַר
יז אוֹיֵב: פֵּרְשָׂה צִיּוֹן בְּיָדֶיהָ אֵין מְנַחֵם לָהּ צִוָּה יְהוָה לְיַעֲקֹב סְבִיבָיו צָרָיו הָיְתָה
יח יְרוּשָׁלַםִ לְנִדָּה בֵּינֵיהֶם: צַדִּיק הוּא יְהוָה כִּי פִיהוּ מָרִיתִי שִׁמְעוּ־נָא כָל־עַמִּים הָעַמִּים
יט וּרְאוּ מַכְאֹבִי בְּתוּלֹתַי וּבַחוּרַי הָלְכוּ בַשֶּׁבִי: קָרָאתִי לַמְאַהֲבַי הֵמָּה רִמּוּנִי כֹּהֲנַי
כ וּזְקֵנַי בָּעִיר גָּוָעוּ כִּי־בִקְשׁוּ אֹכֶל לָמוֹ וְיָשִׁיבוּ אֶת־נַפְשָׁם: רְאֵה יְהוָה כִּי־צַר־לִי
מֵעַי חֳמַרְמָרוּ נֶהְפַּךְ לִבִּי בְּקִרְבִּי כִּי מָרוֹ מָרִיתִי מִחוּץ שִׁכְּלָה־חֶרֶב בַּבַּיִת כַּמָּוֶת:
כא שָׁמְעוּ כִּי נֶאֱנָחָה אָנִי אֵין מְנַחֵם לִי כָּל־אֹיְבַי שָׁמְעוּ רָעָתִי שָׂשׂוּ כִּי אַתָּה עָשִׂיתָ
כב הֵבֵאתָ יוֹם־קָרָאתָ וְיִהְיוּ כָמוֹנִי: תָּבֹא כָל־רָעָתָם לְפָנֶיךָ וְעוֹלֵל לָמוֹ כַּאֲשֶׁר עוֹלַלְתָּ
לִי עַל כָּל־פְּשָׁעָי כִּי־רַבּוֹת אַנְחֹתַי וְלִבִּי דַוָּי:

20 The lamenter again turns to God, and this time he is apparently representing both himself and Jerusalem as one: **See, Lord, for I am in distress, my innards burn;**[28] my entire body hurts, including my innards. I feel as if **my heart is overturned within me, for I have rebelled,** transgressed the word of God. **Outside, the sword bereaves; in the house, it is like death.** Outside the house, people are being killed, but even inside the house, the terror of death is found.

21 **They heard that I sigh; there is no comforter for me; all my enemies heard of my misfortune, were glad** at my misfortune, **because You acted.** The lamenter now begs:[29] Please, **may You bring the day that You proclaimed, and** punish them so that **they will be like me,** with similar suffering to mine.

22 **Let all their wickedness,** of those who pretended to be my friends and allies, **come before You, and do to them as You did to me for all my transgressions, for my sighs are many and my heart is suffering,** suffering from pain.

God's Treatment of the Daughter of Zion

LAMENTATIONS 2:1–22

Whereas the previous lamentation emphasized the enemy whom God sent to torment Jerusalem for her sins, this one opens by stressing the lamenter's astonishment at God's affliction of "the daughter of Zion," "the daughter of Jerusalem," and "the daughter of Judah." The word "daughter" appears eleven times in this lamentation. Here, it is God who degrades Israel and its leaders and destroys their homes and fortresses. God appears as an enemy Himself, not only as He who sent the enemy.

The lamenter subsequently accuses the false prophets of Jerusalem of having prevented the inhabitants of Jerusalem from confronting their sins and changing their ways by soothing them with false prophecies. Now, there are no longer any prophecies, and the sounds of rejoicing of those who would come for the pilgrimage festivals no longer emanate from the city. Instead, the sounds that are heard in Jerusalem are those of babies crying for food and drink; the shouts and cries of its defeated inhabitants; expressions of astonishment and sorrow, as well as eulogies, by those who pass through the ruined city; and the voices of enemies rejoicing over Israel's misfortune.

2 1 **How the Lord has clouded** over **the daughter of Zion in His wrath. He cast the splendor of Israel from the heavens to the earth and did not remember His footstool,** a flowery metaphor for the Temple,[30] **on the day of His wrath.**

2 **The Lord has demolished and has had no compassion for all the** pleasant **habitations of Jacob; He destroyed, in His ire, the strongholds of the daughter of Judah. He brought them to the ground;**[31] **He profaned,** disgraced, and eliminated **a kingdom and its princes.**

"He destroyed, in His ire, the strongholds of the daughter of Judah." The siege of Lakhish and the stronghold under attack, illustration based on Lakhish reliefs, Nineveh,

3 **He severed in enflamed wrath all the grandeur of Israel.** In normal times, God protects His nation and does not allow the enemy to do as it wishes toward it; but now, **He retracted His right hand,** which prevents the enemy from harming Israel, **from being before the enemy,** allowing the enemy to act unrestrained,[32] **who burned Jacob like flaming fire, consuming all around.**

4 **He,** God himself, **drew His bow** against us **as an enemy.** Not only did God withhold His hand from restraining the enemy, but **His right hand stood** against us **as a besieger, and He killed all delights of the eye. In the tent of the daughter of Zion, He poured His fury like fire.**

Arrows stretched for firing, relief at the Palace of Ashurbanipal, Nineveh, 645–635 BCE

"He poured His fury like fire." Burnt room, City of David, Jerusalem, sixth century BCE

5 **The Lord was like an enemy; He demolished Israel, demolished all its palaces, destroyed its strongholds, and multiplied** sounds of **mourning and moaning in the daughter of Judah.**[33]

6 **He stripped His shrine,** His dwelling place,[34] picking all its fruits, **like a garden;**[35] **He destroyed His place of assembly,** or the place where He attended.[36] **The Lord caused festival and Sabbath to be forgotten in Zion.** The times have become so bitter and hard that the festivals, and even the Sabbaths, are no longer discernable. The routine of life has become poor, dull, and sad. **And He,** God, **scorned,** cursed and harmed, **king and priest** of Israel **in His furious wrath.**

7 **The Lord forsook His altar, cursed** and ceased to protect **His Temple. He gave into the hand of the enemy the walls of her palaces.** Since the whole city has been delivered to the control of foreigners, **they made** a loud **noise in the House of the Lord, like a day of festival.** The sounds of the massacre and battle in the Temple brought back memories of voices raised in song and thanks that would emanate from those celebrating the festivals in previous years.[37]

8 **The Lord resolved to destroy the wall of the daughter of Zion; He drew,** marked **a line** in preparation of His plan of action, and **did not withdraw His hand from demolishing,** but implemented His plan. **He caused rampart and wall to mourn, together they languish.**

9 **Her gates sank into the ground;** essentially, they have disappeared, because people have stopped using them and therefore they no longer serve any purpose. **He eradicated and broke her bars,** which would have been used to close the gates. **Her king and her princes are** exiled **among the nations** and cannot help. **There is no Torah; her prophets, too, could not find a vision from the Lord.** All is hidden and unknown. The leaders have gone into exile, and those who are left offer no comfort.

10 **The elders of the daughter of Zion sit on the ground, are silent.**[38] **They have placed dust on their heads, have girded themselves with sackcloth. The young women of Jerusalem have lowered their heads to the ground.** Both the young and the old mourn.

א אֵיכָה יָעִיב בְּאַפּוֹ ׀ אֲדֹנָי אֶת־בַּת־צִיּוֹן הִשְׁלִיךְ מִשָּׁמַיִם אֶרֶץ תִּפְאֶרֶת יִשְׂרָאֵל
ב וְלֹא־זָכַר הֲדֹם־רַגְלָיו בְּיוֹם אַפּוֹ׃ בִּלַּע אֲדֹנָי לא חָמַל אֵת כָּל־נְאוֹת יַעֲקֹב הָרַס וְלֹא
ג בְּעֶבְרָתוֹ מִבְצְרֵי בַת־יְהוּדָה הִגִּיעַ לָאָרֶץ חִלֵּל מַמְלָכָה וְשָׂרֶיהָ׃ גָּדַע בָּחֳרִי־אַף
כֹּל קֶרֶן יִשְׂרָאֵל הֵשִׁיב אָחוֹר יְמִינוֹ מִפְּנֵי אוֹיֵב וַיִּבְעַר בְּיַעֲקֹב כְּאֵשׁ לֶהָבָה אָכְלָה
ד סָבִיב׃ דָּרַךְ קַשְׁתּוֹ כְּאוֹיֵב נִצָּב יְמִינוֹ כְּצָר וַיַּהֲרֹג כֹּל מַחֲמַדֵּי־עָיִן בְּאֹהֶל בַּת־צִיּוֹן
ה שָׁפַךְ כָּאֵשׁ חֲמָתוֹ׃ הָיָה אֲדֹנָי ׀ כְּאוֹיֵב בִּלַּע יִשְׂרָאֵל בִּלַּע כָּל־אַרְמְנוֹתֶיהָ שִׁחֵת
ו מִבְצָרָיו וַיֶּרֶב בְּבַת־יְהוּדָה תַּאֲנִיָּה וַאֲנִיָּה׃ וַיַּחְמֹס כַּגַּן שֻׂכּוֹ שִׁחֵת מֹעֲדוֹ שִׁכַּח
ז יהוה ׀ בְּצִיּוֹן מוֹעֵד וְשַׁבָּת וַיִּנְאַץ בְּזַעַם־אַפּוֹ מֶלֶךְ וְכֹהֵן׃ זָנַח אֲדֹנָי ׀ מִזְבְּחוֹ נִאֵר
מִקְדָּשׁוֹ הִסְגִּיר בְּיַד־אוֹיֵב חוֹמֹת אַרְמְנוֹתֶיהָ קוֹל נָתְנוּ בְּבֵית־יהוה כְּיוֹם מוֹעֵד׃
ח חָשַׁב יהוה ׀ לְהַשְׁחִית חוֹמַת בַּת־צִיּוֹן נָטָה קָו לֹא־הֵשִׁיב יָדוֹ מִבַּלֵּעַ וַיַּאֲבֶל־חֵל
ט וְחוֹמָה יַחְדָּו אֻמְלָלוּ׃ טָבְעוּ בָאָרֶץ שְׁעָרֶיהָ אִבַּד וְשִׁבַּר בְּרִיחֶיהָ מַלְכָּהּ וְשָׂרֶיהָ
י בַגּוֹיִם אֵין תּוֹרָה גַּם־נְבִיאֶיהָ לֹא־מָצְאוּ חָזוֹן מֵיהוה׃ יֵשְׁבוּ לָאָרֶץ יִדְּמוּ זִקְנֵי בַת־
צִיּוֹן הֶעֱלוּ עָפָר עַל־רֹאשָׁם חָגְרוּ שַׂקִּים הוֹרִידוּ לָאָרֶץ רֹאשָׁן בְּתוּלֹת יְרוּשָׁלָםִ׃
יא כָּלוּ בַדְּמָעוֹת עֵינַי חֳמַרְמְרוּ מֵעַי נִשְׁפַּךְ לָאָרֶץ כְּבֵדִי עַל־שֶׁבֶר בַּת־עַמִּי בֵּעָטֵף
יב עוֹלֵל וְיוֹנֵק בִּרְחֹבוֹת קִרְיָה׃ לְאִמֹּתָם יֹאמְרוּ אַיֵּה דָּגָן וָיָיִן בְּהִתְעַטְּפָם כֶּחָלָל
יג בִּרְחֹבוֹת עִיר בְּהִשְׁתַּפֵּךְ נַפְשָׁם אֶל־חֵיק אִמֹּתָם׃ מָה־אעודך מָה אֲדַמֶּה־לָּךְ אֲעִידֵךְ
הַבַּת יְרוּשָׁלִַם מָה אַשְׁוֶה־לָּךְ וַאֲנַחֲמֵךְ בְּתוּלַת בַּת־צִיּוֹן כִּי־גָדוֹל כַּיָּם שִׁבְרֵךְ

11 The lamenter's distress at the sight of his eyes is so great that he feels as though it physically harms him: **My eyes fail from** the many **tears; my innards burn.**[39] I am overcome with a terrible stomachache; **my liver is poured on the earth over the disaster of the daughter of my people, as the infants and the suckling babes faint in the city squares.**

12 **To their mothers they,** the young children, **say: Where is grain and** if there is no bread, where is there **wine** to refresh our souls? **while fainting like the wounded,** as lifeless corpses **in the city squares, while their souls are poured into their mothers' bosoms.**

13 **What shall I attest to you?** What similar case can I cite in order to comfort you?[40] **To what shall I liken you,** what metaphors can I use in order to explain your situation, **daughter of Jerusalem? To what shall I equate you,** with what can I compare your suffering, **and** thereby **comfort you, virgin daughter of Zion? For your disaster is as vast as the sea; who can heal you?** No one can.

14 **Your prophets,** who were not true prophets of God, **envisioned** and delivered prophecies of **futility and foolishness for you,** as they had no substance, **and did not reveal your iniquity to bring about your rehabilitation,** to return you to your previous state. They betrayed their mission, which was to castigate you for your sins and inspire you to repent. Instead, **they** allowed you to deteriorate and **envisioned for you prophecies of futility and deviance,** or incitement, which incited you to abandon the correct path.[41] Instead of telling you the hard truth, which would have convinced you to change your ways and repent, your prophets affirmed your behavior, enabling you to continue your evil ways unimpeded.

15 **All wayfarers clapped their hands at you; they whistled and shook their heads,** expressions of grief, **at the daughter of Jerusalem.** At the sight of your ruin, they wonder: **Is this the city that was said to be perfect beauty, the joy of the entire earth?**

16 **All your enemies opened their mouths wide,** jeering **against you; they whistled and gnashed** their **teeth,** expressions of anger or animosity. **They said: We have demolished** her; **indeed, this is the day for which we hoped,** the day of Jerusalem's downfall; now **we found** it, **we saw** it.

17 **The Lord accomplished that which He devised;**[D] **He implemented His statement that He commanded from the days of old.** He had warned you in His Torah of defeat and destruction, starvation and war, and now His retribution for your sins has come to pass.[42] **He destroyed and had no compassion. He caused the enemy to rejoice over you, raised the horn of your antagonists.** He has empowered them in their own eyes.

18 **Their hearts,** the hearts of the city's inhabitants, **cried to the Lord. Wall of the daughter of Zion, let tears fall like a stream, day and night; do not give yourself respite; let the apple of your eye not cease.** Do not allow yourself to stop weeping.[43]

19 The lamenter now turns to Israel: **Arise, cry out** while eulogizing **at night,**[44] **at the beginning of the watches.** For watchmen, the night is divided into shifts, and the time at the beginning of each shift is opportune for prayer.[45] **Pour out your heart like water,** sob uncontrollably during these hours of the night **before the face of the Lord** over your situation. **Lift up your hands to Him** in prayer **for the life of your infants, who are faint with hunger at the head of every street.** Not only the adults are starving to death; even the young children have nothing to eat.

20 Like the previous lamentation, this one also concludes with a call to God to see how lowly Jerusalem has become, and once again the lamenter personally identifies with Jerusalem: **See, Lord, and behold to whom You have done this. Shall women eat their fruit, the infants of their nurturing?** Was it Your intention that the starvation should be so terrible as to cause this to happen? **Shall the priest and the prophet be slain in the Temple of the Lord,** which is supposed to be a place of refuge? Was that Your intent?

21 **Lad and elder lay on the ground in the streets; my young women and my young men fell by the sword. You killed on the day of Your wrath; You slaughtered, had no compassion.** You have harmed us mercilessly.

22 **You have called,** invited, **as on an appointed day, my fears** to come **from all around, and there was no survivor or remnant on the day of the Lord's wrath.** All the houses, gardens, books, public works, and **those** children **whom I nurtured and reared, my enemy annihilated;** I remain alone in the world.

The Man Who Views the Suffering of His Nation

LAMENTATIONS 3:1–66

The third lamentation is distinct from the others in structure, style, and content.

As opposed to the other lamentations, whose verses are long and composed of several parts, the verses here are short. Most of the other lamentations feature one verse beginning with each letter of the Hebrew alphabet, forming an alphabetic acrostic; here, while the alphabetic acrostic structure is maintained, there are three verses for each letter.

Stylistically, the broad use of first person singular is conspicuous. Although throughout the book of Lamentations there are verses where the prophet speaks of his own personal anguish and pain upon observing the destruction, nevertheless Jerusalem is generally referred to in the third person, sometimes assuming the persona of a woman. This lamentation, by contrast, is recited by a man who considers himself an example and a symbol for the entire nation, and therefore his personal experience is emphasized.

There are further differences between this lamentation and the others that relate to the content: Whereas in the other lamentations the prophet describes the historical context for his feelings, including references to starvation and murder, the physical destruction of Jerusalem, and the enemies inflicting this destruction and rejoicing in it, this lamentation does not present any such descriptions. Instead, it focuses on the lamenter's personal suffering; his wavering between hope and despair; and his fluctuation between surrender and acceptance of the situation on the one hand, and his pain, cries, and struggling on the other. There is no question of "how [*eikha*] this can have happened," as is found in the other lamentations, only a description of the current situation.

The lamentation ends with a prayer that God deliver appropriate retribution to the enemy for mocking and inflicting destruction on the Jewish people.

3 1 **I am the man who has seen** and suffered **affliction by the rod of His fury.**[46]

2 **He,** God, **conducted and led me in darkness and not in light.**

יד מִי יִרְפָּא־לָךְ׃ נְבִיאַיִךְ חָזוּ לָךְ שָׁוְא וְתָפֵל וְלֹא־גִלּוּ עַל־עֲוֺנֵךְ לְהָשִׁיב שביתך שְׁבוּתֵךְ
טו וַיֶּחֱזוּ לָךְ מַשְׂאוֹת שָׁוְא וּמַדּוּחִים׃ סָפְקוּ עָלַיִךְ כַּפַּיִם כָּל־עֹבְרֵי דֶרֶךְ שָׁרְקוּ וַיָּנִעוּ
רֹאשָׁם עַל־בַּת יְרוּשָׁלָם הֲזֹאת הָעִיר שֶׁיֹּאמְרוּ כְּלִילַת יֹפִי מָשׂוֹשׂ לְכָל־הָאָרֶץ׃
טז פָּצוּ עָלַיִךְ פִּיהֶם כָּל־אֹיְבַיִךְ שָׁרְקוּ וַיַּחַרְקוּ־שֵׁן אָמְרוּ בִּלָּעְנוּ אַךְ זֶה הַיּוֹם שֶׁקִּוִּינֻהוּ
יז מָצָאנוּ רָאִינוּ׃ עָשָׂה יהוה אֲשֶׁר זָמָם בִּצַּע אֶמְרָתוֹ אֲשֶׁר צִוָּה מִימֵי־קֶדֶם הָרַס
יח וְלֹא חָמָל וַיְשַׂמַּח עָלַיִךְ אוֹיֵב הֵרִים קֶרֶן צָרָיִךְ׃ צָעַק לִבָּם אֶל־אֲדֹנָי חוֹמַת בַּת־
צִיּוֹן הוֹרִידִי כַנַּחַל דִּמְעָה יוֹמָם וָלַיְלָה אַל־תִּתְּנִי פוּגַת לָךְ אַל־תִּדֹּם בַּת־עֵינֵךְ׃
יט קוּמִי ׀ רֹנִּי בַלַּיִל לְרֹאשׁ אַשְׁמֻרוֹת שִׁפְכִי כַמַּיִם לִבֵּךְ נֹכַח פְּנֵי אֲדֹנָי שְׂאִי אֵלָיו
כ כַּפַּיִךְ עַל־נֶפֶשׁ עוֹלָלַיִךְ הָעֲטוּפִים בְּרָעָב בְּרֹאשׁ כָּל־חוּצוֹת׃ רְאֵה יהוה וְהַבִּיטָה
לְמִי עוֹלַלְתָּ כֹּה אִם־תֹּאכַלְנָה נָשִׁים פִּרְיָם עֹלְלֵי טִפֻּחִים אִם־יֵהָרֵג בְּמִקְדַּשׁ אֲדֹנָי
כא כֹּהֵן וְנָבִיא׃ שָׁכְבוּ לָאָרֶץ חוּצוֹת נַעַר וְזָקֵן בְּתוּלֹתַי וּבַחוּרַי נָפְלוּ בֶחָרֶב הָרַגְתָּ
כב בְּיוֹם אַפֶּךָ טָבַחְתָּ לֹא חָמָלְתָּ׃ תִּקְרָא כְיוֹם מוֹעֵד מְגוּרַי מִסָּבִיב וְלֹא הָיָה בְּיוֹם
אַף־יהוה פָּלִיט וְשָׂרִיד אֲשֶׁר־טִפַּחְתִּי וְרִבִּיתִי אֹיְבִי כִלָּם׃
א ב אֲנִי הַגֶּבֶר רָאָה עֳנִי בְּשֵׁבֶט עֶבְרָתוֹ׃ אוֹתִי נָהַג וַיֹּלַךְ חֹשֶׁךְ וְלֹא־אוֹר׃

DISCUSSION

2:16–17| **All your enemies opened their mouths…The Lord accomplished that which He devised:** Although this lamentation, like the other lamentations, is written in alphabetical order, verses 16 and 17 begin with *peh* and *ayin*, respectively, which is contrary to the common order. This change to the alphabetical order appears in the third and fourth lamentations as well (3:46–51; 4:16–17). There are various interpretive explanations for this phenomenon, but it is possible that in those days the order of the Hebrew alphabet was not entirely fixed (see also *Sanhedrin* 104b; *Eikha Rabba* 2:20).

3 **Indeed, against me He will again turn His hand all day.** God came back again and again to strike me relentlessly.

4 **He wore away my flesh and my skin, broke my bones.**

5 **He built against me** a wall of siege,[47] **and surrounded me with gall,**[B] a bitter and poisonous weed,[48] **and adversity.**

Gall, hemlock

6 **He settled me in darkness, like those long dead,** who dwell in eternal darkness.

7 **He fenced me in,** limited my movement, so **that I would not emerge;** He **made my fetters heavy,** so that they bind me down.[49]

Remains of fetters, Roman period

8 **Even as I cry and plead, He blocks my prayer,**[50] preventing it from reaching Him and being accepted.

9 **He fenced my ways with hewn stone,** stones for construction that block roads; He **distorted my paths.** Not only does He not redeem me from my troubles, but He gives me new ones.

10 **He,** God, **is like a bear in ambush to me, a lion in hiding.** Therefore, dangers appear in my life repeatedly.

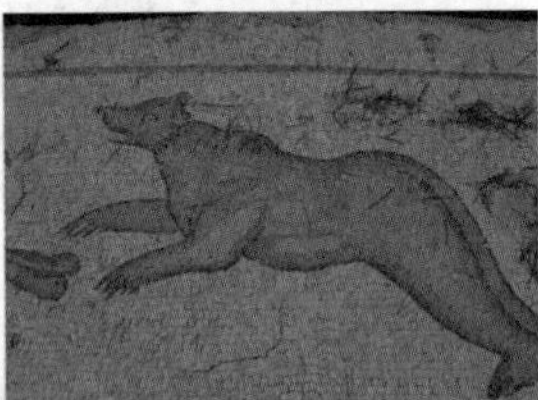

Bear, detail from the Birds Mosaic, Caesarea, Byzantine period

11 **He has twisted my ways,**[51] or, He has covered my ways with thorns,[52] **and mauled me,** torn me to pieces,[53] **rendered me desolate** and alone.

12 **He drew His bow and set me as the target for the arrow.**

13 **He** then **pierced my kidneys with** His arrows, **the contents of His quiver.**

14 **I have become a laughingstock to all my people, their song**[D] **all day.** I have become an object of mockery and satirical songs. The lamenter here is referring to himself, or alternatively, he is speaking of the people, in first person, as their representative.

15 **He,** God, **filled me with bitterness, sated me with** a solution of **wormwood,**[B] a bitter or poisonous drink.

16 Since God has withheld food from me, **He has ground my teeth with gravel,** forcing me to eat it, and He has **covered me in ashes.**[54]

17 **My soul has forsaken peace;** my soul has abandoned its hope for peace. **I have forgotten** the possibility of **goodness** because I am engulfed in distress.

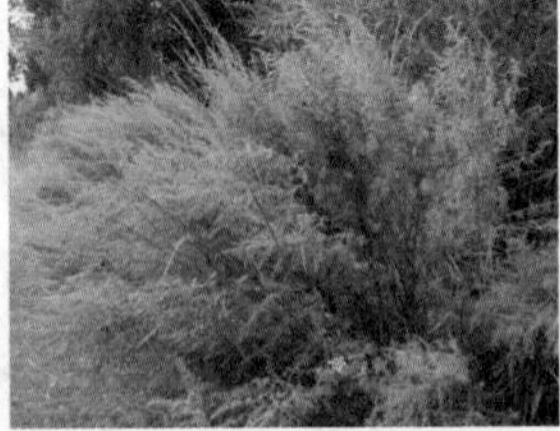

Wormwood

18 When I saw that God was ignoring me, **I said: My eternity,** my eternal soul, **and my expectation,** my hope, **have perished,** are lost, **from the Lord.**[55]

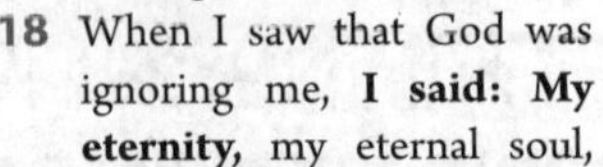

19 **Remember my affliction and my anguish,** my hardship, which is bitter like **wormwood and gall.**

20 In the future **You will remember, and** yet in the meantime, my soul **is bowed** down **within me** from the toil and suffering.[56]

21 Despite the pain and anguish that God has wrought upon me, almost leading me to despair, **this I will reply to my heart;** I constantly remind myself of the following principle, and **therefore I will await,** or I have hope.[57]

22 **It is** due to **the Lord's kindnesses that we have not ceased.** Thanks to the Lord's mercies we have not been utterly consumed; we still exist, despite all the troubles, **for His mercies have not ended.** This faith was expressed by the Jewish people in all of their exiles.[58]

23 **New every morning, great is the trust in You.**[D] Alternatively, every morning my faith in You strengthens anew.

24 **The Lord is my portion, says my soul,** choosing to be loyal to God.[59] **Therefore I will await Him.**

25 **The Lord is good to those who hope for Him, to the soul that seeks Him.**

26 **It is good** for a man **to await silently**[60] **the salvation of the Lord.**

27 The prophet further consoles himself: **It is good for a man that he bears a yoke in his youth.** Just as a young man can carry a heavy burden without getting injured, so too let him accept the challenge described in the next verse.

28 **Let him sit alone and be silent, because he took it upon himself;** he has accepted this life situation, despite its hardship.[61]

29 **Let him** subdue himself and **put his mouth in the dust,** so that he cannot speak;[62] **perhaps there is hope.**

30 Instead of striking back, **let him offer his cheek to one who strikes him; let him be filled with disgrace,** as he is smitten from every direction.

31 Nevertheless, there is still hope, **for the Lord will not forsake forever.**

32 **For,** even **if He torments,** ultimately **He will have compassion, according to His abundant kindness.**[63]

33 **For He does not afflict** people **willingly** for no reason, **and** He does not **torment the children of men** capriciously.[64]

ג ד ה אַךְ בִּי יָשֻׁב יַהֲפֹךְ יָדוֹ כָּל־הַיּוֹם: בִּלָּה בְשָׂרִי וְעוֹרִי שִׁבַּר עַצְמוֹתָי: בָּנָה עָלַי וַיַּקַּף
ו ז רֹאשׁ וּתְלָאָה: בְּמַחֲשַׁכִּים הוֹשִׁיבַנִי כְּמֵתֵי עוֹלָם: גָּדַר בַּעֲדִי וְלֹא אֵצֵא הִכְבִּיד
ח ט י נְחָשְׁתִּי: גַּם כִּי אֶזְעַק וַאֲשַׁוֵּעַ שָׂתַם תְּפִלָּתִי: גָּדַר דְּרָכַי בְּגָזִית נְתִיבֹתַי עִוָּה: דֹּב
יא יב אֹרֵב הוּא לִי אריה בְּמִסְתָּרִים: דְּרָכַי סוֹרֵר וַיְפַשְּׁחֵנִי שָׂמַנִי שֹׁמֵם: דָּרַךְ קַשְׁתּוֹ אֲרִי
יג יד וַיַּצִּיבֵנִי כַּמַּטָּרָא לַחֵץ: הֵבִיא בְּכִלְיוֹתָי בְּנֵי אַשְׁפָּתוֹ: הָיִיתִי שְּׂחֹק לְכָל־עַמִּי נְגִינָתָם
טו טז כָּל־הַיּוֹם: הִשְׂבִּיעַנִי בַמְּרוֹרִים הִרְוַנִי לַעֲנָה: וַיַּגְרֵס בֶּחָצָץ שִׁנָּי הִכְפִּישַׁנִי בָּאֵפֶר:
יז יח יט וַתִּזְנַח מִשָּׁלוֹם נַפְשִׁי נָשִׁיתִי טוֹבָה: וָאֹמַר אָבַד נִצְחִי וְתוֹחַלְתִּי מֵיהוה: זְכָר־עָנְיִי
כ כא וּמְרוּדִי לַעֲנָה וָרֹאשׁ: זָכוֹר תִּזְכּוֹר ותשיח עָלַי נַפְשִׁי: זֹאת אָשִׁיב אֶל־לִבִּי עַל־ וְתָשׁוֹחַ
כב כג כֵּן אוֹחִיל: חַסְדֵי יהוה כִּי לֹא־תָמְנוּ כִּי לֹא־כָלוּ רַחֲמָיו: חֲדָשִׁים לַבְּקָרִים רַבָּה
כד כה אֱמוּנָתֶךָ: חֶלְקִי יהוה אָמְרָה נַפְשִׁי עַל־כֵּן אוֹחִיל לוֹ: טוֹב יהוה לְקֹוָו לְנֶפֶשׁ
כו כז תִּדְרְשֶׁנּוּ: טוֹב וְיָחִיל וְדוּמָם לִתְשׁוּעַת יהוה: טוֹב לַגֶּבֶר כִּי־יִשָּׂא עֹל בִּנְעוּרָיו:
כח כט ל יֵשֵׁב בָּדָד וְיִדֹּם כִּי נָטַל עָלָיו: יִתֵּן בֶּעָפָר פִּיהוּ אוּלַי יֵשׁ תִּקְוָה: יִתֵּן לְמַכֵּהוּ לֶחִי
לא לב לג יִשְׂבַּע בְּחֶרְפָּה: כִּי לֹא יִזְנַח לְעוֹלָם אֲדֹנָי: כִּי אִם־הוֹגָה וְרִחַם כְּרֹב חֲסָדָו: כִּי לֹא

BACKGROUND

3:5| **Gall [*rosh*]:** *Rosh* is commonly identified as hemlock, *Conium maculatum*, an extremely poisonous plant that was used for the execution of criminals in ancient Greece. An herbaceous plant of the Apiaceae family that reaches a height of 1.5 m, hemlock has white flowers and its stalk is speckled with black spots; it grows wild, typically by the roadside or on the edges of cultivated fields. Others identify *rosh* as the opium poppy, *Papaver somniferum*. The fruit of the poppy resembles a head [*rosh*], and it is used to produce opium. Alternatively, *rosh* might be golden henbane, *Hyoscyamus aureus*, which also contains a strong poison.

3:15| **Wormwood [*la'ana*]:** *La'ana* is commonly identified with wormwood, *Artemisia absinthium*, which is common in Israel. The plant's flowers are yellow, and it reaches a height and width of 1.5 m. Alternatively, *la'ana* is a generic term for various bitter or poisonous plants.

DISCUSSION

3:14| **A laughingstock to all my people, their song:** This verse can be seen as a description of the suffering of the prophets due to the way they were perceived by the people, as demonstrated in the verse: "The prophet is a fool, the man of the spirit is mad" (Hosea 9:7). Unlike the metaphors used in the previous verses, this one relates to the actual reality of the prophet's life and his standing among his listeners. He was confined to a hopeless existence, where the people around him would shoot arrows of derision at him.

3:23| **New every morning, great is the trust in You:** Jews recite the following passage, based on this verse, every morning upon waking up: I offer thanks before You, living and eternal King, for You have mercifully restored my soul within me; Your faithfulness is great.

34 He does not want[65] **to subdue under His feet all the prisoners of the earth.**

"To subdue under his feet." Tiglat Pileser subduing his enemy under his feet, Nimrud, Iraq, 747–727 BCE

35 And it is not His habit[66] **to distort the judgment of man before the face of the Most High.** God does not pervert justice,

36 **to subvert a man in his quarrel,** his cause, **the Lord has deemed it unfit.**[67]

37 **Who is this,** what enemy could there be, **who said** that he would harm Israel **and it occurred,** whose declaration was fulfilled, **if the Lord did not command** it? If Israel suffers harm, it is certainly a divine decree.[68]

38 **From the mouth of the Most High, evil and good do not emerge.** God leaves the world in the hands of man's free will.[69]

39 When all is said and done, **what shall a living man complain?** His complaints about his difficulties and troubles are unjustified, as **each man for his sins.**[D] His dire situation is merely the result of his own evil deeds.[70]

40 Therefore, **let us search and examine our ways, and return to the Lord.**

41 **Let us lift up our heart with our hands, to God in the heavens.** Let us rip out our heart and give it, as it were, to God.[71]

42 Despite the call for appeasement and hope, notwithstanding the theodicy and logical explanations, the cry toward God reemerges: Although **we have transgressed and defied,** and we were therefore deserving of punishment, nevertheless, we would have expected You to pardon us, not only the way a master pardons his slaves, but as a father forgives his children.[72] However, **You have not forgiven.**

43 **You are covered with wrath,** or: You distanced yourself and hid behind a wall of wrath,[73] **and have pursued us; You killed; You did not have compassion.**

44 **You have covered Yourself,** as if **with a cloud, so that no prayer can pass** through, as though the gates of heaven are closed to our prayers.[74] The prophet speaks here in the name of all the people of Israel.

45 **You render us**[75] **filth and refuse in the midst of the peoples.**

46 **All our enemies have opened their mouth** wide **against us,** and we cannot respond.

47 **Terror and a trap,** or obstacles,[76] **came upon us, desolation and disaster.**[77]

48 The prophet returns to speaking in first person singular: When faced with our shameful state among the nations, **streams of water pour down from my eye,** crying **for the disaster of the daughter of my people.**

49 **My eye will flow** with tears **and will not cease,**[78] **from lack of respite.** The tears do not cease because there is no respite from our troubles.[79]

50 I cry continuously, **until the Lord looks out and sees** our misery **from the heavens,** and redeems us soon. Expressions of hope, loyalty, and faith in future salvation again come to the fore.

51 **My eye distressed my soul,**[80] or contaminated my soul,[81] **more than all the daughters of my city.** Alternatively: Jeremiah is lamenting over the fact that he has seen all of his neighbors and relatives going into exile or getting killed, while his own sobbing eyes are the only ones left to cry for all the rest, like an incompletely formed cluster of grapes [*olelet*] left on the vine during the harvest.

52 **My enemies hunted me like a bird** is hunted, **without cause.**

"My enemies hunted me like a bird." Hunting birds, relief, Tomb of Nebamun, Eighteenth Dynasty, Egypt

53 **They bound my life in the pit.**[82] **And** furthermore, they **cast stones at me.**

54 The pit was full of water; **waters rose over my head. I said: I am doomed.** My end has come.

55 **I called** upon **Your name,** I prayed to You, **Lord, from the depths of the pit.**[D]

56 **You heard my voice,** which is itself a minor salvation; please, **let Your ear not disregard my cry, for my comfort.** The prophet begs God not to ignore his plea, so that his conditions may improve.[83]

57 I had hope when **You approached on the day that I called You. You said** to me: **Do not fear.**

58 In the end, **Lord, You have fought the battles of my soul; You redeemed my life.**

59 **Lord, You have seen my wrongs,** the injustice that was done to me;[84] please **adjudicate my case.**

60 **You have seen all their,** the enemies', **vengeance, all their** evil **thoughts against me.**

לד לה עִנָּה מִלִּבּוֹ וַיַּגֶּה בְּנֵי־אִישׁ׃ לְדַכֵּא תַּחַת רַגְלָיו כֹּל אֲסִירֵי אָרֶץ׃ לְהַטּוֹת מִשְׁפַּט־
לו לז גָּבֶר נֶגֶד פְּנֵי עֶלְיוֹן׃ לְעַוֵּת אָדָם בְּרִיבוֹ אֲדֹנָי לֹא רָאָה׃ מִי זֶה אָמַר וַתֶּהִי אֲדֹנָי לֹא
לח לט צִוָּה׃ מִפִּי עֶלְיוֹן לֹא תֵצֵא הָרָעוֹת וְהַטּוֹב׃ מַה־יִּתְאוֹנֵן אָדָם חָי גֶּבֶר עַל־חֲטָאָו׃
מ מא נַחְפְּשָׂה דְרָכֵינוּ וְנַחְקֹרָה וְנָשׁוּבָה עַד־יְהוָה׃ נִשָּׂא לְבָבֵנוּ אֶל־כַּפָּיִם אֶל־אֵל
מב מג בַּשָּׁמָיִם׃ נַחְנוּ פָשַׁעְנוּ וּמָרִינוּ אַתָּה לֹא סָלָחְתָּ׃ סַכֹּתָה בָאַף וַתִּרְדְּפֵנוּ הָרַגְתָּ לֹא
מד מה חָמָלְתָּ׃ סַכּוֹתָה בֶעָנָן לָךְ מֵעֲבוֹר תְּפִלָּה׃ סְחִי וּמָאוֹס תְּשִׂימֵנוּ בְּקֶרֶב הָעַמִּים׃
מו מז מח פָּצוּ עָלֵינוּ פִּיהֶם כָּל־אֹיְבֵינוּ׃ פַּחַד וָפַחַת הָיָה לָנוּ הַשֵּׁאת וְהַשָּׁבֶר׃ פַּלְגֵי־מַיִם
מט נ תֵּרַד עֵינִי עַל־שֶׁבֶר בַּת־עַמִּי׃ עֵינִי נִגְּרָה וְלֹא תִדְמֶה מֵאֵין הֲפֻגוֹת׃ עַד־יַשְׁקִיף
נא נב וְיֵרֶא יְהוָה מִשָּׁמָיִם׃ עֵינִי עוֹלְלָה לְנַפְשִׁי מִכֹּל בְּנוֹת עִירִי׃ צוֹד צָדוּנִי כַּצִּפֹּר אֹיְבַי
נג נד נה חִנָּם׃ צָמְתוּ בַבּוֹר חַיָּי וַיַּדּוּ־אֶבֶן בִּי׃ צָפוּ־מַיִם עַל־רֹאשִׁי אָמַרְתִּי נִגְזָרְתִּי׃ קָרָאתִי
נו שִׁמְךָ יְהוָה מִבּוֹר תַּחְתִּיּוֹת׃ קוֹלִי שָׁמָעְתָּ אַל־תַּעְלֵם אָזְנְךָ לְרַוְחָתִי לְשַׁוְעָתִי׃
נז נח קָרַבְתָּ בְּיוֹם אֶקְרָאֶךָּ אָמַרְתָּ אַל־תִּירָא׃ רַבְתָּ אֲדֹנָי רִיבֵי נַפְשִׁי גָּאַלְתָּ חַיָּי׃
נט ס רָאִיתָה יְהוָה עַוָּתָתִי שָׁפְטָה מִשְׁפָּטִי׃ רָאִיתָה כָּל־נִקְמָתָם כָּל־מַחְשְׁבֹתָם לִי׃
סא סב שָׁמַעְתָּ חֶרְפָּתָם יְהוָה כָּל־מַחְשְׁבֹתָם עָלָי׃ שִׂפְתֵי קָמַי וְהֶגְיוֹנָם עָלַי כָּל־הַיּוֹם׃

61 You heard their taunt,[85] **Lord, all their thoughts about me.** When Jeremiah's harsh prophecies for the future did not materialize, his listeners would ridicule him and throw stones at him. When the prophecies were eventually fulfilled, the same people took revenge against him, as though he were to blame for the events, even though his statements had been meant merely to warn them.

62 The lips, the words, **of those who rise against me, and their thoughts, are against me all day.** In all their statements and thoughts, I am considered the sole guilty party.[86]

DISCUSSION

3:39| What shall a living man complain? Each man for his sins: King David said similarly: "Evil shall kill the wicked" (Psalms 34:22). Evil deeds are the cause of their author's misfortunes.

3:53–55| They bound my life in the pit… waters rose over my head…from the depths of the pit: These are not merely metaphoric expressions of confinement and humiliation; according to the book of Jeremiah (38:6), this actually happened to Jeremiah: "They took Jeremiah and they cast him into the pit of Malkiyahu the king's son, which was in the court of internment, and they lowered Jeremiah with ropes. And in the pit there was no water but only mud, and Jeremiah was drowning in the mud."

63 Look at their sitting and their rising, look at what they do constantly; **I am** the subject of **their song,** the object of their mockery and ridicule.
64 Pay them retribution, Lord, punish them, **according to their handiwork.**
65 May you give them hardness of heart, troubles that seal up the heart;[87] may **Your curse** be **upon them.**[88]
66 May you pursue them in wrath and destroy them from beneath the heavens of the Lord.

The Destruction of the Precious Sons of Zion

LAMENTATIONS 4:1–22

Due to its sins, Jerusalem was filled with victims, those dead of starvation and those killed by the sword. This lamentation describes the deterioration of the people of Jerusalem, from their previous stature as a refined population, to the lowest level it is possible to reach, through siege and war. The residents of Jerusalem had placed their trust in foreign aid and had also hoped that their king would save them, but their hopes were dashed. The lamentation ends with words of comfort: Edom, which rejoices in the misfortune of Israel, will be destroyed too, and Jerusalem's disaster will end.

4 1 **How can** shiny **gold tarnish?**[89] How can the appearance of **the fine gold change?**[90] **The sacred stones are spilled at the head of every street.** How is all that was beautiful and precious disgraced and gone to waste?
2 **The precious sons of Zion, who were valued as gold,**[91] **how are they** now **considered** as worthless as **earthenware jugs, the handiwork of the hands of the potter?**
3 **Even jackals take out a breast,**[B] **nurse their pups.** Even these animals, some of whom are predatory, are merciful in certain situations; but **the daughter of my people has become cruel.** The mothers of Jerusalem are malnourished; their breasts have shriveled, and their survival instincts prevent them from supplying the needs of their children.[92] They are **like ostriches,**[B] who abandon their offspring[93] **in the wilderness.** This is what has befallen Israel. Jerusalem has become like a wilderness, a place where people do not care for each other.

Female jackal and her offspring

"Nurse their pups." Female whale and her offspring

"Ostriches in the wilderness"

4 **The tongue of the suckling babe sticks to its palate from thirst,** because there is no milk for the nursing infants; **infants request bread, and no one breaks it for them,** because of the siege upon Jerusalem.
5 **The eaters of delicacies are** now **desolate** and penniless **in the streets; those reared**[94] **in** expensive **scarlet** garments now **embrace heaps of refuse,** as they are left with nothing.
6 **The iniquity of the daughter of my people** must have **exceeded the sin of Sodom,** as her punishment was more severe than that of Sodom, **which was overthrown in a moment, and no** enemy **hands seized it,** whereas in Jerusalem the suffering is continuous.[95]
7 In past times, **its,** Jerusalem's, **nazirites used to be purer than snow, whiter than milk; their appearance**[96] **was ruddier than gems,**[B] **their form a sapphire.**

Sapphire

Gems

8 The people of Jerusalem were clean, pure, refined, and beautiful. In better times, they engaged only in matters of holiness. Now, however, **their countenance is blacker than coal; they are not recognized in the streets. Their skin is shriveled on their bones;**[97] **it has become dry as wood.**
9 **Those killed by sword** in battle **were better off than those killed by hunger, for** from their **ruptured** bodies,[98] **they,** the victims of hunger, **leak with,** emit various liquids from, **the produce of the field.**[99] Alternatively, "these" refers to the victims of the sword, who were stabbed through while sated.[100]
10 **The hands of merciful women cooked their children; they,** the children, **were food for them,** their mothers,[101] **in the time** of **the disaster of the daughter of my people.**

סג סד שִׁבְתָּם וְקִימָתָם הַבִּיטָה אֲנִי מַנְגִּינָתָם׃ תָּשִׁיב לָהֶם גְּמוּל יְהוָה כְּמַעֲשֵׂה יְדֵיהֶם׃
סה סו תִּתֵּן לָהֶם מְגִנַּת־לֵב תַּאֲלָתְךָ לָהֶם׃ תִּרְדֹּף בְּאַף וְתַשְׁמִידֵם מִתַּחַת שְׁמֵי יְהוָה׃
א אֵיכָה יוּעַם זָהָב יִשְׁנֶא הַכֶּתֶם הַטּוֹב תִּשְׁתַּפֵּכְנָה אַבְנֵי־קֹדֶשׁ בְּרֹאשׁ כָּל־חוּצוֹת׃
ב בְּנֵי צִיּוֹן הַיְקָרִים הַמְסֻלָּאִים בַּפָּז אֵיכָה נֶחְשְׁבוּ לְנִבְלֵי־חֶרֶשׂ מַעֲשֵׂה יְדֵי יוֹצֵר׃
ג ד גַּם־תנין חָלְצוּ שַׁד הֵינִיקוּ גּוּרֵיהֶן בַּת־עַמִּי לְאַכְזָר כי ענים בַּמִּדְבָּר׃ דָּבַק לְשׁוֹן
ה יוֹנֵק אֶל־חִכּוֹ בַּצָּמָא עוֹלָלִים שָׁאֲלוּ לֶחֶם פֹּרֵשׂ אֵין לָהֶם׃ הָאֹכְלִים לְמַעֲדַנִּים נָשַׁמּוּ
ו בַּחוּצוֹת הָאֱמֻנִים עֲלֵי תוֹלָע חִבְּקוּ אַשְׁפַּתּוֹת׃ וַיִּגְדַּל עֲוֹן בַּת־עַמִּי מֵחַטַּאת סְדֹם
ז הַהֲפוּכָה כְמוֹ־רָגַע וְלֹא־חָלוּ בָהּ יָדָיִם׃ זַכּוּ נְזִירֶיהָ מִשֶּׁלֶג צַחוּ מֵחָלָב אָדְמוּ עֶצֶם
ח מִפְּנִינִים סַפִּיר גִּזְרָתָם׃ חָשַׁךְ מִשְּׁחוֹר תָּאֳרָם לֹא נִכְּרוּ בַּחוּצוֹת צָפַד עוֹרָם עַל־
ט עַצְמָם יָבֵשׁ הָיָה כָעֵץ׃ טוֹבִים הָיוּ חַלְלֵי־חֶרֶב מֵחַלְלֵי רָעָב שֶׁהֵם יָזוּבוּ מְדֻקָּרִים
י מִתְּנוּבֹת שָׂדָי׃ יְדֵי נָשִׁים רַחֲמָנִיּוֹת בִּשְּׁלוּ יַלְדֵיהֶן הָיוּ לְבָרוֹת לָמוֹ בְּשֶׁבֶר בַּת־

תַּנִּים
כַּיְעֵנִים

BACKGROUND

4:3| **Jackals [*tannim*] take out a breast:** According to the written text, the word is spelled *tannin*. This leads to the interpretation by some that the verse is referring to whales, which did exist in the Mediterranean Sea, though it is not their natural habitat. It may be suggested that the expression "take out a breast" supports this interpretation, as the nursing parts of the female whale are covered in pockets of skin and need to be drawn out for nursing. On the other hand, according to the traditional vocalization of the text, the word is *tannim*, the plural of *tan*, which is a jackal, an animal similar to a fox that feeds on various animals and carrion. The *tan* is mentioned in the Bible as a howling desert animal. This interpretation of the verse is supported by the comparison to the ostrich, another desert animal (see Isaiah 13:21–22, 34:13; 43:20). Alternatively, some identify the *tan* with the Pharaoh eagle-owl (*bubo ascalaphus*), a nocturnal bird of prey that dwells in ruins and crevices.

Like ostriches [*ye'enim*]: An ostrich does not have a nest; it leaves its eggs on the ground, without incubation. Perhaps for this reason it is described as cruel toward its offspring. A similar behavior is criticized in the book of Job (39:13–15): "The wing of the songbird beats joyously; are its pinions and its plumage of a stork? For it leaves its eggs on the earth and warms them on dust, and it forgets that a foot may crush it or a beast of the field trample it." There is an opinion that the term *ye'enim* refers not to a type of animal, but is the name of a tribe, based on one reading of Psalms 55:20 (*Tur Sinai*).

4:7| **Gems [*peninim*]:** In biblical Hebrew and in the Aramaic translations of the Bible, *peninim* are specific kinds of round precious stones, or alternatively, a generic word for all precious stones. In Ibn Ezra's commentary on Song of Songs (5:14), he interprets *peninim* to mean sapphires. However, others maintain that the term refers to pearls, which are formed in seashells from organic matter and are generally white, silver, or black. In ancient Egyptian, a similar word denotes a spherical marble, and in Akkadian, there is a similar word that refers to a precious stone that comes from the sea and perhaps means pearl or coral.

11 The Lord vented His fury, He poured out His enflamed wrath. He kindled a fire in Zion, and it consumed even **its foundations.**

12 The kings of the earth and all the inhabitants of the world did not believe that a besieger and enemy would enter the gates of Jerusalem,[B] which was such a central, fortified, and secure city.

"The gates of Jerusalem." Damascus Gate, 1910

13 It, this entire catastrophe, **was due to the sins of her** false **prophets,**[102] and because of **the iniquities of her priests, who shed the blood of the righteous in her midst,** in order to achieve wealth and honor.

14 The entire city was filled with the blood of the dead. **They wandered blind in the streets.** Alternatively, blind men wander in the streets without a guide, **having been sullied with blood,** as they could not see where the corpses were, **so that one could not touch their** filthy **garments.**

15 It was necessary to warn those approaching: **Turn away, impure, they called to them; turn away, turn away, do not touch, because they were begrimed,** had become dirty, **as well as wandering. They said among the nations: They will not continue to reside here,** in our land, or in Jerusalem.[103]

16 The attention of the Lord has divided them; God has scattered them in His anger.[104] **He will not continue to look at them,** as **they did not respect priests and were not gracious to elders.** They did not help the needy.[105]

17 Our eyes yet fail, seeking deliverance in vain; our hopes for help have turned out to be in vain. **In our waiting, we awaited** a foreign **nation that** we hoped would come to our aid, but it **cannot save** us.[106]

18 They, the enemies, **hunted our steps,** even preventing us[107] **from walking in our squares; our end approaches, our days are filled, as our end has come.**

19 Even those who did not stay in the city could not find refuge because **our pursuers were swifter than the eagles**[B] **of the heavens,** and they captured us. **They chased us on the mountains; they ambushed us in the wilderness.**

20 The breath of our nostrils, the anointed of the Lord,[D] a reference to the king of Judah, who was anointed with a special oil, **was captured in their traps.** This is the king **of whom we said: In his shade we will live among the nations.**

21 The lamenter expresses bitter scorn toward the people of Edom, who, during this period, enjoyed calm and bliss: **Be glad and rejoice, daughter of Edom,**[D] **who resides in the land of Utz.**[B] But not for long, as **the cup** of vengeance and destruction **will pass to you too; you will get drunk** from drinking it, **and you will be overturned,** ruined.[108]

Possible locations for the land of Utz

22 Your iniquity is completed, daughter of Zion; He, God, **will not continue to exile you.** You have received the entire punishment that you deserved and have consequently paid for all your sins. On the other hand, **He reckons your iniquity, daughter of Edom; He will expose your sins.** He will yet settle His account with you for your sins.

DISCUSSION

4:20 | **The anointed of the Lord:** The Sages identified this king as Yoshiya, the last great king of Judah, upon whom Israel placed their final hope for defense. This hope ended in disappointment when Yoshiya was shot dead by the Egyptian army (II Chronicles 35:23; *Tosefta, Ta'anit* 2:10; see introduction to this lamentation).

4:21 | **Edom:** The people of Edom supported Judah's enemies and mocked the inhabitants of Jerusalem during their destruction (see Obadiah 1:12–14). The final word of this verse is the rare verb *titari*, used by the prophet to prophesy the destruction of Edom. It literally means "you shall make yourself naked"; its implied meaning is that Israel will be overturned, torn down, and ruined. It paraphrases Edom's joyous exclamation when they celebrated Israel's defeat, encouraging their total destruction (Psalms 137:7): "Tear it down [*aru*], tear it down [*aru*], until its very foundation."

יא יב עַמִּי: כִּלָּה יהוה אֶת־חֲמָתוֹ שָׁפַךְ חֲרוֹן אַפּוֹ וַיַּצֶּת־אֵשׁ בְּצִיּוֹן וַתֹּאכַל יְסוֹדֹתֶיהָ: לֹא

יג הֶאֱמִינוּ מַלְכֵי־אֶרֶץ וכל יֹשְׁבֵי תֵבֵל כִּי יָבֹא צַר וְאוֹיֵב בְּשַׁעֲרֵי יְרוּשָׁלָםִ: מֵחַטֹּאת   כֹּל

יד נְבִיאֶיהָ עֲוֹנֹת כֹּהֲנֶיהָ הַשֹּׁפְכִים בְּקִרְבָּהּ דַּם צַדִּיקִים: נָעוּ עִוְרִים בַּחוּצוֹת נְגֹאֲלוּ

טו בַּדָּם בְּלֹא יוּכְלוּ יִגְּעוּ בִּלְבֻשֵׁיהֶם: סוּרוּ טָמֵא קָרְאוּ לָמוֹ סוּרוּ סוּרוּ אַל־תִּגָּעוּ כִּי

טז נָצוּ גַּם־נָעוּ אָמְרוּ בַּגּוֹיִם לֹא יוֹסִפוּ לָגוּר: פְּנֵי יהוה חִלְּקָם לֹא יוֹסִיף לְהַבִּיטָם

יז פְּנֵי כֹהֲנִים לֹא נָשָׂאוּ זקנים לֹא חָנָנוּ: עודינה תִּכְלֶינָה עֵינֵינוּ אֶל־עֶזְרָתֵנוּ הָבֶל   וּזְקֵנִים עוֹדֵינוּ

יח בְּצִפִּיָּתֵנוּ צִפִּינוּ אֶל־גּוֹי לֹא יוֹשִׁעַ: צָדוּ צְעָדֵינוּ מִלֶּכֶת בִּרְחֹבֹתֵינוּ קָרַב קִצֵּנוּ

יט מָלְאוּ יָמֵינוּ כִּי־בָא קִצֵּנוּ: קַלִּים הָיוּ רֹדְפֵינוּ מִנִּשְׁרֵי שָׁמָיִם עַל־הֶהָרִים דְּלָקֻנוּ

כ בַּמִּדְבָּר אָרְבוּ לָנוּ: רוּחַ אַפֵּינוּ מְשִׁיחַ יהוה נִלְכַּד בִּשְׁחִיתוֹתָם אֲשֶׁר אָמַרְנוּ בְּצִלּוֹ

כא נִחְיֶה בַגּוֹיִם: שִׂישִׂי וְשִׂמְחִי בַּת־אֱדוֹם יושבתי בְּאֶרֶץ עוּץ גַּם־עָלַיִךְ תַּעֲבָר־כּוֹס   יוֹשֶׁבֶת

כב תִּשְׁכְּרִי וְתִתְעָרִי: תַּם־עֲוֹנֵךְ בַּת־צִיּוֹן לֹא יוֹסִיף לְהַגְלוֹתֵךְ פָּקַד עֲוֹנֵךְ בַּת־אֱדוֹם

גִּלָּה עַל־חַטֹּאתָיִךְ:

BACKGROUND

4:12 | **That a besieger and enemy would enter the gates of Jerusalem:** Nebuchadnezzar's conquest of Jerusalem and his subsequent coronation of Tzidkiya are described in a Babylonian chronicle that was discovered during excavations of the city of Babylon: "In the seventh year of the month of Kislev, the king of Akkad [Nebuchadnezzar] gathered his soldiers and went to the land of the Hitites [Syria and Israel], and encamped by the city of Judah; and in the month of Adar, on the second day [of the month], he seized the city and captured the king, appointed in it a king whom he trusted, and took a heavy tax from it, and came to Babylon."

4:19 | **Eagle [*nesher*]:** Some explain that this is the griffon vulture, *Gyps fulvus*, a large bird that nests and soars at markedly high altitudes, which enables it to glide swiftly toward its food (see Jeremiah 48:40; Obadiah 1:4; Micah 1:16; Habakkuk 1:8; Job 39:27–28). This bird was a royal symbol in both Egypt and Assyria. Its wingspan stretches to 2.5 m and it weighs roughly 10 kg. Its head and neck are bare of feathers, as though they were plucked [*nashar*]; perhaps this accounts for the name. Some identify the *nesher* with the golden eagle, *Aquila chrysaetos*, which was an important Roman symbol, while yet others maintain that *nesher* is a general term that refers to several different types of birds of prey.

4:21 | **The land of Utz:** Apparently, there were several lands called Utz. In Genesis there is a son of Aram named Utz (10:23). In addition, the land of Utz appears as one of the lands of the Children of the East in the book of Job (1:3). Therefore, some place it somewhere in or near modern-day Syria. Ancient historians, e.g., Josephus Flavius, identified it as being in an area of the Bashan, now known as the Golan Heights. In addition, there was a grandson of Se'ir named Utz (Genesis 36:28), and that source and the verse here indicate that there was also a land called Utz in the Edomite region further south, in what is now Jordan.

Humiliation, Orphanhood, and Eternal Hope

LAMENTATIONS 5:1–22

This lamentation is different from the others in that it is not an alphabetical acrostic. But it is similar to most of them in that it has twenty-two verses, and in addition, like the previous lamentations, the suffering and troubles of the people of Jerusalem are described. Toward the end, the lamenter focuses his anguish on the destruction of Mount Zion, the source of his heartache. However, he emphasizes that although God's dwelling place in the world has been destroyed, He still remains. This provides hope for the restoration of the relationship and the covenant between God and His people.

5 1 **Remember, Lord, what befell us,** our terrible troubles. Alternatively, this means: Remember our glorious past, and on the other hand, **look and see our** current **disgrace.**[109]

2 **Our inheritance has been transferred to strangers,** after they invaded and plundered it, **our houses** have been given **to foreigners.**

3 **We have become orphans, fatherless; our mothers are like widows.**[110]

4 When the water reservoirs were full, there was no need to pay for water;[111] but during the siege, **our water we drank for money.** In better days, there was no shortage of wood that could be collected easily; now, **our wood comes at a price.**

5 Up **to our necks we were pursued; we are exhausted, and we have no respite.**

6 **We extended a hand to Egypt,** to receive financial aid from them. This may be referring to Tzidkiya's covenant with Egypt.[112] And we went to **Assyria, to be sated with bread;** but help came from neither kingdom.[113]

7 **Our fathers have sinned and are no more, and we have suffered** not only for our own sins, but for **their iniquities** as well.

8 **Servants rule over us.** The true kingdom has fallen, and as naturally happens when the government is weak, people from the bottom of society have risen to greatness. **There is none to deliver us from their hand.**

9 **We bring our bread at the peril of our lives due to the sword of the wilderness.** In order to obtain food, we must put our lives at risk by traveling through the desert, which is frequented by robbers.[114] Alternatively: In order to survive during the war we must bring food from faraway places, even from the wilderness.

10 **Our skin burns like an oven,**[115] or has shriveled as though it were baked in an oven,[116] **due to fear of famine.**

11 When the enemy soldiers invaded the city, **they raped women in Zion, virgins in the cities of Judah.**

12 **Princes were hanged by their hand.** The enemies would hang the dignitaries of Jerusalem by their hands as a punishment, for show, or in order to extract information from them. **The faces of elders were not shown deference.** No one honored the elders.

13 **The young,** strong **men carried the mill;** they were ordered to carry the mill on their shoulders so that this would wear them out.[117] **And the lads,** who were chained, **stumbled on the wood** to which they were chained.[118]

14 **The elders have ceased from** sitting at **the** city **gate,** as there is no longer anyone to listen to them. **The young men** have ceased **from their music** and parties.

"Princes were hanged by their hand." Men of Judah hanged, Lakhish reliefs, Nineveh, 701 BCE

15 **The gladness of our heart has ceased; our** joyous **dance has been transformed into mourning.**

16 **The crown has fallen from our head;** our honor is lost. Alternatively, this may refer to the crown and honor of the monarchy. **Woe to us, for we have sinned.**

17 **For this our heart suffers; for these our eyes are dim:**

18 **for Mount Zion,**[D] the Temple Mount, **which is desolate;** its past vitality is gone, and **foxes,** who commonly dwell in desolate areas, **walk on it.**

19 Despite the anguish, the book ends on a note of acceptance and hope: **You, Lord, are enthroned forever; Your throne is** secure **from generation to generation.** Although God's residency in this world is the mountain of Zion, which is now desolate, His heavenly throne is independent of worldly events, and it will stand forever.[119]

20 But as for us, **why do You forget us forever, forsake us for the length of our days?**

21 **Return us to You, Lord, and** if You do so, **we will return;** we will return to You, willingly and actively. **Renew our days as of old,** like the days when You loved us and honored us.

22 **For You have despised us,** or: You have indeed despised us. **You have been exceedingly angry with us.** We have suffered more than enough humiliation; our debt has been paid.

The penultimate verse is repeated in a communal recitation:

Return us to You, Lord, and we will return; renew our days as of old.[D]

א ב זְכֹ֤ר יְהוָה֙ מֶֽה־הָ֣יָה לָ֔נוּ הַבִּ֖יטָ וּרְאֵ֥ה אֶת־חֶרְפָּתֵֽנוּ׃ נַחֲלָתֵ֙נוּ֙ נֶֽהֶפְכָ֣ה לְזָרִ֔ים בָּתֵּ֖ינוּ
ג ד לְנָכְרִֽים׃ יְתוֹמִ֤ים הָיִ֙ינוּ֙ אֵ֣ין אָ֔ב אִמֹּתֵ֖ינוּ כְּאַלְמָנֽוֹת׃ מֵימֵ֙ינוּ֙ בְּכֶ֣סֶף שָׁתִ֔ינוּ עֵצֵ֖ינוּ [וְאֵ֣ין]
ה ו בִּמְחִ֥יר יָבֹֽאוּ׃ עַ֤ל צַוָּארֵ֙נוּ֙ נִרְדָּ֔פְנוּ יָגַ֖עְנוּ לֹ֥א הֽוּנַֽח־לָֽנוּ׃ מִצְרַ֙יִם֙ נָתַ֣נּוּ יָ֔ד אַשּׁ֖וּר [וְלֹ֥א]
ז ח לִשְׂבֹּ֥עַֽ לָֽחֶם׃ אֲבֹתֵ֤ינוּ חָֽטְאוּ֙ אֵינָ֔ם אֲנַ֖חְנוּ עֲוֺנֹתֵיהֶ֥ם סָבָֽלְנוּ׃ עֲבָדִים֙ מָ֣שְׁלוּ בָ֔נוּ [וְאֵינָ֔ם]
ט י פֹּרֵ֖ק אֵ֥ין מִיָּדָֽם׃ בְּנַפְשֵׁ֙נוּ֙ נָבִ֣יא לַחְמֵ֔נוּ מִפְּנֵ֖י חֶ֥רֶב הַמִּדְבָּֽר׃ עוֹרֵ֙נוּ֙ כְּתַנּ֣וּר נִכְמָ֔רוּ [וַאֲנַ֖חְנוּ]
יא יב מִפְּנֵ֖י זַלְעֲפ֥וֹת רָעָֽב׃ נָשִׁים֙ בְּצִיּ֣וֹן עִנּ֔וּ בְּתֻלֹ֖ת בְּעָרֵ֥י יְהוּדָֽה׃ שָׂרִים֙ בְּיָדָ֣ם נִתְל֔וּ
יג יד פְּנֵ֥י זְקֵנִ֖ים לֹ֥א נֶהְדָּֽרוּ׃ בַּחוּרִים֙ טְח֣וֹן נָשָׂ֔אוּ וּנְעָרִ֖ים בָּעֵ֥ץ כָּשָֽׁלוּ׃ זְקֵנִים֙ מִשַּׁ֣עַר
טו טז שָׁבָ֔תוּ בַּחוּרִ֖ים מִנְּגִינָתָֽם׃ שָׁבַת֙ מְשׂ֣וֹשׂ לִבֵּ֔נוּ נֶהְפַּ֥ךְ לְאֵ֖בֶל מְחוֹלֵֽנוּ׃ נָֽפְלָה֙ עֲטֶ֣רֶת
יז רֹאשֵׁ֔נוּ אוֹי־נָ֥א לָ֖נוּ כִּ֥י חָטָֽאנוּ׃ עַל־זֶ֗ה הָיָ֤ה דָוֶה֙ לִבֵּ֔נוּ עַל־אֵ֖לֶּה חָשְׁכ֥וּ עֵינֵֽינוּ׃
יח יט עַ֤ל הַר־צִיּוֹן֙ שֶׁשָּׁמֵ֔ם שׁוּעָלִ֖ים הִלְּכוּ־בֽוֹ׃ אַתָּ֤ה יְהוָה֙ לְעוֹלָ֣ם תֵּשֵׁ֔ב כִּסְאֲךָ֖ לְדֹ֥ר
כ כא וָדֽוֹר׃ לָ֤מָּה לָנֶ֙צַח֙ תִּשְׁכָּחֵ֔נוּ תַּעַזְבֵ֖נוּ לְאֹ֥רֶךְ יָמִֽים׃ הֲשִׁיבֵ֨נוּ יְהוָ֤ה ׀ אֵלֶ֙יךָ֙ וְנָשׁ֔וּבָה
כב חַדֵּ֥שׁ יָמֵ֖ינוּ כְּקֶֽדֶם׃ כִּ֚י אִם־מָאֹ֣ס מְאַסְתָּ֔נוּ קָצַ֥פְתָּ עָלֵ֖ינוּ עַד־מְאֹֽד׃

השיבנו יהוה אליך ונשובה חדש ימינו כקדם

DISCUSSION

5:18 | **Mount Zion:** In the book of Isaiah, the Temple Mount is commonly referred to as the mountain of Zion.

5:21 | **Renew our days as of old:** There are several books in the Bible that conclude on a negative note, and the custom is to repeat the second to last verse, which has a more optimistic tone, in order to finish the book with a positive message (see the final verses of Isaiah, Malachi, and Ecclesiastes). In the context of Lamentations, ending the book with this verse is an expression of the hope to renew Israel's relationship with God and restore it to its state at the beginning of the people's history. A similar aspiration appears in Malachi (3:4): "Then shall the offering of Judah and Jerusalem be pleasant to the Lord, as in the days of old, and as in ancient years." This verse is recited at the end of the *Amida* prayer.

Ecclesiastes

Ecclesiastes

INTRODUCTION TO ECCLESIASTES

Ecclesiastes is not a book of enthusiasm born of faith. Rather, the book of Ecclesiastes is based on human musings and insights. The speaker, Kohelet, critiques the state of affairs in the world in general and the way people conduct their lives in particular. Therefore, much negativity is expressed in it, and the decision to incorporate it into the biblical canon aroused opposition.[1]

Three books of the Bible are attributed to King Solomon: Proverbs, the Song of Songs, in which his authorship is explicitly mentioned, and Ecclesiastes, in which he appears by an alternative name. Although all three books share certain philosophical and linguistic features, overall they differ greatly from each other. It has therefore been suggested that they were composed at various stages of King Solomon's life. According to one opinion in the Midrash, Solomon wrote Song of Songs, which is a love song, in his youth; the book of Proverbs, which contains practical advice and guidance for appropriate behavior, in middle age; and after he had experienced all the adversities of life and grown old, he wrote Ecclesiastes, which deems all the toil and adventures of life, its ups and downs, as mere futility.[2]

This book articulates the thoughts of a wise, mature man who does not presume to offer a unified, coherent picture of reality beyond what he himself understands based on his rich experiences and the vicissitudes of his life. The central theme of the book is stripping the value and meaning from all matters of the world. The book provides some conventional words of wisdom and morality, but concurrently poses an unfathomable question with regard to the patterns of human existence, its significance and stability, and the congruence of visible reality with values of morality and justice. Positive faith in and of itself is not depicted in Ecclesiastes in a systematic, detailed manner, and those positive statements that occasionally surface are not easily reconcilable with its other statements.

Kohelet's recommendations are far more complex than the advice that appears in the book of Proverbs. There, King Solomon instructs the reader unambiguously to choose good and refrain from evil, while the book of Ecclesiastes describes the path of a man considering the world in which he lives and functions with considerable practical success; however, his attempt does not yield the results that he anticipated, and therefore he struggles to find purpose in life.

It is interesting to note that specifically in this book, in which human existence and the reality of this world are described as futile, there are several instances where the existence of the spirit independent of the body surfaces, a ray of optimism in the midst of the futility. Alone among the books of the Bible, Ecclesiastes speaks explicitly of a person's soul that returns to God after the body returns to dust (3:20). Ecclesiastes also mentions the existence of souls not yet born (see, e.g., 4:3).

The circular attempts to address all these topics, the recurring accounts of the author's search for new insights into the nature of human existence, and the frustrating return to the original point that all is futility are consistent with the content of the book. Both by means of the book's internal contradictions, as well as its tortuous structure, which resists any attempt to discover a consistent order or framework, Kohelet is saying that the world, in all its detail, is filled with trouble, confrontation, and pain. Kohelet also reveals that the world and human life are insipid. He repudiates accepted frameworks without suggesting alternatives. The reader, whom Kohelet has convinced that meaning cannot be found in this world, is left with two options: Holding on to that which is beyond this futile existence, that is, fear of God and the observance of His commandments, or living a life of delusion.

Ecclesiastes

Introduction and Summary

ECCLESIASTES 1:1–11

The opening verses of Ecclesiastes are also verses of summation. Its central themes are condensed into these verses: Everything is futile, everything passes, everything recurs, and there is no purpose.

1 1 **The words of Kohelet,** another name for Solomon,[3] whose
words of wisdom many people gathered [*nikhalu*] to hear, **son
of David,** who was **king in Jerusalem.**
2 **Futility of futilities,** the world is absolute futility, **says
Kohelet; futility of futilities, all is futility.**[D] Kohelet charac-
terizes all reality as lacking substance and significance.[4]
3 **What advantage is there for man in all his toil that he toils
under the sun**[D] in this world? Many events transpire here, but none of them is significant. Moreover, even when a matter of significance transpires, or a valuable item is discovered, it soon vanishes without a trace. At times, the one responsible for the event or the discovery ultimately realizes its futility himself, while at other times only future generations will arrive at that realization.[5]
4 **A generation goes and a generation comes, and the earth
stands forever.** Despite all the activity and the many apparent changes, the earth remains in place. The entire world is bound to a cyclicality that does not lead to any change.
5 **The sun rises and the sun sets and seeks** to continue uninter-
rupted to **its place; it rises there,** where it rose the previous day.[6] Faced with this fixed circular mechanism, one comes to question how one day differs from another.

"The sun rises"

"And the sun sets"

6 But the movements of the sun change slightly with the seasons:
It goes to the south of the sky during winter **and turns** more **to the north** in summer; **it turns and turns, goes in a** different **direction** [*ruaḥ*], **and in its circuit it returns to its** original **direction.**[7] Some commentaries hold that this verse refers not to the movements of the sun but to those of the wind [*ruaḥ*].[8] The wind was one of the four basic elements into which the world was thought to be divided in ancient times, earth, fire, wind, and water, and which are alluded to in these verses.
7 **All the streams go to the sea,** flowing continuously, **yet the
sea is** still **not full; to the place that the streams go, there they go again,** in the fixed water cycle.[9]

"The streams go to the sea"

8 **All matters are wearying.** People take action and take ac-
tion again, and exhaust themselves. **A man is unable to speak** everything that he would want to say, **the eye will not be satisfied to see** everything that it would want to see, **and the ear will not be filled from hearing** what it wants to hear.
9 In summary, **that which was is that which will be, and that
which was done is that which will be done; there is nothing new under the sun.** Events transpire over and over again in a recurring cycle.
10 **There is a matter of which one would say: See, this is new. It
has already been, in the ages that were before us.** Even when something appears to be novel, upon closer examination one realizes that it is the same old familiar object; perhaps there is a superficial change, but nothing more.
11 Kohelet returns to the subject with which he began:[10] Natural
existence is fixed and cyclical, and one's exertion under the sun is of no avail and leaves no trace, as one generation goes and another generation comes, and **there is no memory of the earlier ones,** who have already disappeared. One might then think that later generations will be remembered because their actions will be documented. In response, Kohelet declares:

קהלת

א ב דִּבְרֵי קֹהֶלֶת בֶּן־דָּוִד מֶלֶךְ בִּירוּשָׁלָם: הֲבֵל הֲבָלִים אָמַר קֹהֶלֶת הֲבֵל הֲבָלִים הַכֹּל א
ג ד הָבֶל: מַה־יִּתְרוֹן לָאָדָם בְּכָל־עֲמָלוֹ שֶׁיַּעֲמֹל תַּחַת הַשָּׁמֶשׁ: דּוֹר הֹלֵךְ וְדוֹר בָּא
ה וְהָאָרֶץ לְעוֹלָם עֹמָדֶת: וְזָרַח הַשֶּׁמֶשׁ וּבָא הַשָּׁמֶשׁ וְאֶל־מְקוֹמוֹ שׁוֹאֵף זוֹרֵחַ הוּא
ו שָׁם: הוֹלֵךְ אֶל־דָּרוֹם וְסוֹבֵב אֶל־צָפוֹן סוֹבֵב ׀ סֹבֵב הוֹלֵךְ הָרוּחַ וְעַל־סְבִיבֹתָיו
ז שָׁב הָרוּחַ: כָּל־הַנְּחָלִים הֹלְכִים אֶל־הַיָּם וְהַיָּם אֵינֶנּוּ מָלֵא אֶל־מְקוֹם שֶׁהַנְּחָלִים
ח הֹלְכִים שָׁם הֵם שָׁבִים לָלָכֶת: כָּל־הַדְּבָרִים יְגֵעִים לֹא־יוּכַל אִישׁ לְדַבֵּר לֹא־תִשְׂבַּע
ט עַיִן לִרְאוֹת וְלֹא־תִמָּלֵא אֹזֶן מִשְּׁמֹעַ: מַה־שֶּׁהָיָה הוּא שֶׁיִּהְיֶה וּמַה־שֶּׁנַּעֲשָׂה
י הוּא שֶׁיֵּעָשֶׂה וְאֵין כָּל־חָדָשׁ תַּחַת הַשָּׁמֶשׁ: יֵשׁ דָּבָר שֶׁיֹּאמַר רְאֵה־זֶה חָדָשׁ
יא הוּא כְּבָר הָיָה לְעֹלָמִים אֲשֶׁר הָיָה מִלְּפָנֵנוּ: אֵין זִכְרוֹן לָרִאשֹׁנִים וְגַם לָאַחֲרֹנִים
שֶׁיִּהְיוּ לֹא־יִהְיֶה לָהֶם זִכָּרוֹן עִם שֶׁיִּהְיוּ לָאַחֲרֹנָה:

DISCUSSION

1:2| **Futility [*havel*]:** Many abstract nouns in biblical Hebrew are based on metaphors. The simple meaning of this term is vapor or fumes. In Ecclesiastes and elsewhere, it is employed as a reference to futility and meaninglessness.

1:3| **Under the sun:** This expression appears numerous times in Ecclesiastes. Sometimes the parallel expression, "beneath the heavens," which appears elsewhere in the Bible as well (Genesis 6:17; Exodus 17:14; II Kings 14:27), is employed. These phrases, which appear in this context eleven times, refer to the actual world, which is essentially physical. In Ecclesiastes, this conveys the nihility of the world in and of itself, along with criticism of the actions and exertions of people inhabiting it. However, within these pointed statements about that which is performed under the sun, there is an allusion to a potential resolution. This resolution does not exist in this world under the sun or beneath the heavens; rather, it exists above the sun or above the heavens. Kohelet's critiques are directed exclusively at the physical world delineated by time and place, questioning its substance and undermining its pleasures, but does not address that which transcends it (Alsheikh; *Shabbat* 30b).

And also of the latter ones, who will be, there will be no memory among those who will be last, who will come after them, as they will be unaware of the other generations' earlier existence. All actions will ultimately disappear and be forgotten, as nothing lasts forever, not in reality and not in memory.

Personal Trials and Conclusions

ECCLESIASTES 1:12–2:26

The general abstract ideas that Kohelet outlined at the beginning of the book, he now goes on to illustrate by means of his life experiences and the insights that arose from them.

12 **I, Kohelet, was king over Israel in Jerusalem.** All opportunities were open to me.
13 **I directed my heart to seek and to search for wisdom about**
all that is performed beneath the heavens, and I reached the following conclusion about the deeds performed beneath the heavens: **It is an evil matter that God has given to the sons of man in which to be engaged,** since all of mankind's endeavors provide no benefit, joy, or fruits.[11]
14 **I have seen** and examined **all the actions that are performed**
under the sun, and behold, all is futility and herding [*re'ut*] wind. One who engages in futile actions of this kind is comparable to one who attempts to herd [*ro'eh*] the wind. Whereas one who herds sheep can produce milk, wool, or meat, one who attempts to herd wind will produce nothing from it. Indeed, the challenge of containing or directing the elusive wind is utterly ridiculous.[12]
15 Any action that is performed under the sun is considered **that**
which is warped that **cannot be mended and deficiency** that **cannot be restored.**
16 **I spoke with my heart,** I contemplated, **saying: Behold, I**
have increased and added wisdom, beyond all who were before me over Jerusalem.[D] **My heart has seen much wisdom and knowledge.**
17 **I directed my heart to know wisdom, and to know debauch-**
ery and folly. I knew that this too, analysis of these subjects and drawing novel conclusions, **is an empty notion,** a futile undertaking. There is no substance or benefit in either wisdom or foolishness.[13]
18 Wisdom does not console a person, nor is it beneficial, **for with**
great wisdom is great anger. As a person grows wiser and his powers of discernment become more sensitive, he discovers more truths that anger him. **And one who increases knowledge increases pain** for himself: The pain of life in the world, the pain of his disappointment with the world, and the pain associated with greater knowledge.
2 1 **I said in my heart:** Instead of contemplating abstract prob-
lems, **let us go now; I will pour** wine for you, or, alternatively, I will test you, my body, **with joy,**[14] **and** I will **see goodness.** I will live the good life. **But behold, it too,** enjoyment and sensual pleasure, **is futility.** It does nothing to resolve the questions of life, and it fails to calm the soul.
2 **Of laughter, I said: It is debauchery** and wildness; **and of joy,**
I said:[15] **What does it achieve,** and what is its purpose? The attempt to live a life of pleasure gradually loses its appeal. People can host a party or two, drink wine, and attempt to rejoice, but over time they begin to question the ultimate objective of their laughter and merriment. Jokes cease to be funny, and joy departs from the heart.
3 Once unbridled debauchery lost its excitement and ceased to
be attractive, **I searched in my heart** for another path, **to tempt my flesh with wine**[B] **and have my heart conduct itself with wisdom, and** yet still **grasp folly,** human pleasures, **until I could see what is best for the sons of man that they do beneath the heavens in the numbered,** limited, **days of their lives.** I would try to live a successful and beneficial life without sinking into the depths of wisdom or the shallowness of merriment.
4 Consequently, **I expanded**
my projects; I undertook a series of large-scale projects: **I built for myself houses, planted for myself vineyards.**
5 **I made for myself gardens**
and orchards and planted in them every fruit tree.
6 **I made for myself pools**
of water, to irrigate from them a forest of growing trees. I built a magnificent estate for myself.
7 **I purchased slaves and**
maidservants, and I had home-born servants; I also had much livestock of cattle and sheep, beyond, more than, **all who were before me in Jerusalem.**

Vineyards

Gardens and orchards

"Pools of water, to irrigate from them a forest of growing trees." Fresco, Tomb of Nebamun, Egypt, 1380 BCE

יב יג אֲנִי קֹהֶלֶת הָיִיתִי מֶלֶךְ עַל־יִשְׂרָאֵל בִּירוּשָׁלִָם׃ וְנָתַתִּי אֶת־לִבִּי לִדְרוֹשׁ וְלָתוּר
בַּחָכְמָה עַל כָּל־אֲשֶׁר נַעֲשָׂה תַּחַת הַשָּׁמָיִם הוּא ׀ עִנְיַן רָע נָתַן אֱלֹהִים לִבְנֵי
יד הָאָדָם לַעֲנוֹת בּוֹ׃ רָאִיתִי אֶת־כָּל־הַמַּעֲשִׂים שֶׁנַּעֲשׂוּ תַּחַת הַשָּׁמֶשׁ וְהִנֵּה הַכֹּל
טו טז הֶבֶל וּרְעוּת רוּחַ׃ מְעֻוָּת לֹא־יוּכַל לִתְקֹן וְחֶסְרוֹן לֹא־יוּכַל לְהִמָּנוֹת׃ דִּבַּרְתִּי אֲנִי
עִם־לִבִּי לֵאמֹר אֲנִי הִנֵּה הִגְדַּלְתִּי וְהוֹסַפְתִּי חָכְמָה עַל כָּל־אֲשֶׁר־הָיָה לְפָנַי עַל־
יז יְרוּשָׁלִָם וְלִבִּי רָאָה הַרְבֵּה חָכְמָה וָדָעַת׃ וָאֶתְּנָה לִבִּי לָדַעַת חָכְמָה וְדַעַת הֹלֵלוֹת
יח וְשִׂכְלוּת יָדַעְתִּי שֶׁגַּם־זֶה הוּא רַעְיוֹן רוּחַ׃ כִּי בְּרֹב חָכְמָה רָב־כָּעַס וְיוֹסִיף דַּעַת
א יוֹסִיף מַכְאוֹב׃ אָמַרְתִּי אֲנִי בְּלִבִּי לְכָה־נָּא אֲנַסְּכָה בְשִׂמְחָה וּרְאֵה בְטוֹב וְהִנֵּה
ב ג גַם־הוּא הָבֶל׃ לִשְׂחוֹק אָמַרְתִּי מְהוֹלָל וּלְשִׂמְחָה מַה־זֹּה עֹשָׂה׃ תַּרְתִּי בְלִבִּי
לִמְשׁוֹךְ בַּיַּיִן אֶת־בְּשָׂרִי וְלִבִּי נֹהֵג בַּחָכְמָה וְלֶאֱחֹז בְּסִכְלוּת עַד אֲשֶׁר־אֶרְאֶה
ד אֵי־זֶה טוֹב לִבְנֵי הָאָדָם אֲשֶׁר יַעֲשׂוּ תַּחַת הַשָּׁמַיִם מִסְפַּר יְמֵי חַיֵּיהֶם׃ הִגְדַּלְתִּי
ה מַעֲשָׂי בָּנִיתִי לִי בָּתִּים נָטַעְתִּי לִי כְּרָמִים׃ עָשִׂיתִי לִי גַּנּוֹת וּפַרְדֵּסִים וְנָטַעְתִּי
ו בָהֶם עֵץ כָּל־פֶּרִי׃ עָשִׂיתִי לִי בְּרֵכוֹת מָיִם לְהַשְׁקוֹת מֵהֶם יַעַר צוֹמֵחַ עֵצִים׃
ז קָנִיתִי עֲבָדִים וּשְׁפָחוֹת וּבְנֵי־בַיִת הָיָה לִי גַּם מִקְנֶה בָקָר וָצֹאן הַרְבֵּה הָיָה לִי

BACKGROUND

2:3| **To tempt [*limshokh*] my flesh with wine:** In the folk medicine of the ancient world, wine was utilized in various ways, among them for medicinal bathing and disinfection, presumably due to the alcohol it contains. In Sparta, they would immerse children in wine as a vaccination or to assess their strength. However, there are no extant records of wine used on the body for pleasure. Perhaps *limshokh* is a lyrical expression representing the flaunting of wealth, physical health, and abundance of wine. If so, it is reminiscent of Jacob's blessing of Judah: "He launders his garments in wine, and in the blood of grapes his clothes" (Genesis 49:11). Perhaps, though, unlike the root *mem-shin-ḥet*, the root *mem-shin-khaf* is not a reference to anointing; rather, it means tempting and enticing the body (see Rabbi Ovadya Bartenura, *Avot* 3:10).

DISCUSSION

1:16| **Behold, I have increased and added wisdom, beyond all who were before me over Jerusalem:** In the book of I Kings (3:9), God responds favorably to Solomon's request that he be given "an attentive heart to judge Your people, to discern between good and evil." He even promises Solomon: "Behold, I have granted you a wise and discerning heart, that there has not been anyone like you before you, and after you no one will arise like you" (I Kings 3:12). This promise indeed comes to fruition: "Solomon's wisdom exceeded the wisdom of all the people of the East and all the wisdom of Egypt" (I Kings 5:10). The identification of Kohelet with Solomon is partly based on this self-description.

8 **I also gathered for myself silver and gold and the** beautiful, unique, and rare **treasure of kings and countries,** the rare objects with which kings and the wealthy amuse themselves.[16] **I appointed for myself singers and songstresses** to sing before me, **and the pleasures of the sons of man, chests and wagons**[B] used for storing my collection of treasures.[17] I was constantly in action, living a life of restless luxury.

9 **I grew great, and I increased beyond all** those **who were before me in Jerusalem,**[D] not only because I am the son of a king, but because **my wisdom too stood by me,** so that I could invest my resources wisely.

10 **Everything that my eyes sought, I did not withhold from them;**[18] **I did not withhold my heart from any joy, for** rather **my heart rejoiced from all my toil, and that was my portion from all my toil.**

11 After I had invested so heavily in constructing and creating new entities, **I turned to** comprehend **all the actions that my hands had performed and the toil that I had toiled, and behold,** after a long reflection upon these matters, I discovered that **everything was futility and herding wind.** None of the houses, fields, songs, ornaments, or pleasures provided any real benefit or had any significance. **There was no advantage** to all these **under the sun.**

12 **I** therefore **turned** in a different direction: **To see** the distinction between **wisdom,**[D] **debauchery, and folly.** Following my unsuccessful attempts to investigate the entire range of activities performed under the sun and the potential to change events, I decided to analyze human wisdom philosophically and to understand the nature of foolishness without seeking to change the world. **For who is the man who would come after the** many acts of the **king to do** other than **that which he already did?**

13 Initially **I saw** and thought **that there is advantage to wisdom over folly, like the advantage of light over darkness.**

14 **The wise man's eyes are in his head,** and he sees everything clearly, **but the fool walks in darkness.** Foolishness prevents a person from ascertaining the details of reality and understanding the world. Therefore, the wise man, who accurately assesses the situation and resolves problems that present themselves, is superior to the fool, who habitually stumbles in the darkness. **But** on second thought, **I also knew that one fate will befall them all.** Both the wise man and the foolish one will ultimately perish. What, then, remains of all his wisdom?[19]

15 **I said in my heart: Like the fate of the fool, so will befall me,** I too will die; **why, then, did I become wiser?**[D] What use was my additional wisdom? **Then I said in my heart that this too,** the search for wisdom,[20] **is futility.**

16 **For there is no memory of the wise man with the fool forever.** The memory of the wisdom of one person or the foolishness of another will not remain forever. **After the passage of the coming days, everything is forgotten.** Future generations will shrug at the wise man who has already left the world. **How can the wise man die with the fool,** without any difference between them?[21]

17 **I hated life, for distressing to me was the deed that is performed under the sun, for everything is futility and herding wind.** Even if one can enjoy, act, and create in this world, nothing lasts forever, and there is no significance to these actions beyond the here and now.

18 **I hated all my toil that I have toiled under the sun,** seeing **that** after my death, **I will leave it to the man who will be after me.**

19 **Who knows: Will he** who inherits me **be a wise man or a fool?** I have no control over this matter. **He will control all my toil that I have toiled and that I have become wise under the sun.** Consequently, all of **that,** all my work **too, is futility.**

20 **I shifted** to a different path, **to cause my heart to despair of all the toil that I have toiled under the sun.** I decided not to invest any more effort in that toil.[22]

21 **For there is a man whose toil is in wisdom, in knowledge, and in skill,** and he achieves greatness, **but he will leave his portion to a man who did not toil in it.** Ultimately, the one who inherits the fruit of his labor might lack all wisdom, knowledge, or skill. **This too is futility and a great evil** [*ra'a*], an evil that is worse than herding [*re'ut*] wind (see 1:14).

BACKGROUND

2:8 | **Chests and wagons [*shidda veshiddot*]:** The Radak suggests an additional interpretation of this phrase: It is a reference to musical instruments. This suggestion is presumably based on the parallel terms in the preceding phrase, "singers and songstresses [*sharim vesharot*]," or on the phonetic similarity of these phrases. In Akkadian, the term *siddu* means metal utensil.

ח מִכֹּל שֶׁהָיוּ לְפָנַי בִּירוּשָׁלִָם׃ כָּנַסְתִּי לִי גַּם־כֶּסֶף וְזָהָב וּסְגֻלַּת מְלָכִים וְהַמְּדִינוֹת
ט עָשִׂיתִי לִי שָׁרִים וְשָׁרוֹת וְתַעֲנוּגֹת בְּנֵי הָאָדָם שִׁדָּה וְשִׁדּוֹת׃ וְגָדַלְתִּי וְהוֹסַפְתִּי
י מִכֹּל שֶׁהָיָה לְפָנַי בִּירוּשָׁלִָם אַף חָכְמָתִי עָמְדָה לִּי׃ וְכֹל אֲשֶׁר שָׁאֲלוּ עֵינַי לֹא
אָצַלְתִּי מֵהֶם לֹא־מָנַעְתִּי אֶת־לִבִּי מִכָּל־שִׂמְחָה כִּי־לִבִּי שָׂמֵחַ מִכָּל־עֲמָלִי וְזֶה־
יא הָיָה חֶלְקִי מִכָּל־עֲמָלִי׃ וּפָנִיתִי אֲנִי בְּכָל־מַעֲשַׂי שֶׁעָשׂוּ יָדַי וּבֶעָמָל שֶׁעָמַלְתִּי
יב לַעֲשׂוֹת וְהִנֵּה הַכֹּל הֶבֶל וּרְעוּת רוּחַ וְאֵין יִתְרוֹן תַּחַת הַשָּׁמֶשׁ׃ וּפָנִיתִי אֲנִי לִרְאוֹת
חָכְמָה וְהוֹלֵלוֹת וְסִכְלוּת כִּי ׀ מֶה הָאָדָם שֶׁיָּבוֹא אַחֲרֵי הַמֶּלֶךְ אֵת אֲשֶׁר־כְּבָר
יג עָשׂוּהוּ׃ וְרָאִיתִי אָנִי שֶׁיֵּשׁ יִתְרוֹן לַחָכְמָה מִן־הַסִּכְלוּת כִּיתְרוֹן הָאוֹר מִן־הַחֹשֶׁךְ׃
יד הֶחָכָם עֵינָיו בְּרֹאשׁוֹ וְהַכְּסִיל בַּחֹשֶׁךְ הוֹלֵךְ וְיָדַעְתִּי גַם־אָנִי שֶׁמִּקְרֶה אֶחָד יִקְרֶה
טו אֶת־כֻּלָּם׃ וְאָמַרְתִּי אֲנִי בְּלִבִּי כְּמִקְרֵה הַכְּסִיל גַּם־אֲנִי יִקְרֵנִי וְלָמָּה חָכַמְתִּי אֲנִי
טז אָז יֹתֵר וְדִבַּרְתִּי בְלִבִּי שֶׁגַּם־זֶה הָבֶל׃ כִּי אֵין זִכְרוֹן לֶחָכָם עִם־הַכְּסִיל לְעוֹלָם
יז בְּשֶׁכְּבָר הַיָּמִים הַבָּאִים הַכֹּל נִשְׁכָּח וְאֵיךְ יָמוּת הֶחָכָם עִם־הַכְּסִיל׃ וְשָׂנֵאתִי
אֶת־הַחַיִּים כִּי רַע עָלַי הַמַּעֲשֶׂה שֶׁנַּעֲשָׂה תַּחַת הַשָּׁמֶשׁ כִּי־הַכֹּל הֶבֶל וּרְעוּת
יח רוּחַ׃ וְשָׂנֵאתִי אֲנִי אֶת־כָּל־עֲמָלִי שֶׁאֲנִי עָמֵל תַּחַת הַשָּׁמֶשׁ שֶׁאַנִּיחֶנּוּ לָאָדָם
יט שֶׁיִּהְיֶה אַחֲרָי׃ וּמִי יוֹדֵעַ הֶחָכָם יִהְיֶה אוֹ סָכָל וְיִשְׁלַט בְּכָל־עֲמָלִי שֶׁעָמַלְתִּי
כ וְשֶׁחָכַמְתִּי תַּחַת הַשָּׁמֶשׁ גַּם־זֶה הָבֶל׃ וְסַבּוֹתִי אֲנִי לְיַאֵשׁ אֶת־לִבִּי עַל כָּל־הֶעָמָל
כא שֶׁעָמַלְתִּי תַּחַת הַשָּׁמֶשׁ׃ כִּי־יֵשׁ אָדָם שֶׁעֲמָלוֹ בְּחָכְמָה וּבְדַעַת וּבְכִשְׁרוֹן וּלְאָדָם

DISCUSSION

2:9| **I grew great, and I increased beyond all who were before me in Jerusalem:** This description is consistent with what is stated elsewhere about King Solomon. Since he was wise enough to prefer wisdom above other gifts, God promised him: "Also I have granted you that which you did not request, both riches and honor, that there has not been anyone like you among the kings, all your days" (I Kings 3:13). Indeed, Solomon was privileged to own massive amounts of property, to rule over a large kingdom, and to attain worldwide renown (see I Kings 5).

2:12| **I turned to see wisdom:** Kohelet's change of approach is similar to that of many modern philosophers, such as Descartes and Kant, who turned their attention away from concrete reality to abstract human thought, judgment, and philosophy.

2:15| **Why, then, did I become wiser:** Like many other issues raised in this book, the question of the value of wisdom is relevant only to the world that is under the sun. These existential questions lack a metaphysical basis. Man wonders what is the value of the philosophical expertise that he acquired, the broad knowledge that he amassed, or his delving into wisdom literature. In the final analysis, in the real world there is no difference between people who know more and people who know less, as wisdom is essentially valueless and ephemeral.

22 **For what is there**[23] **for a man in all his toil and in the contemplation of his heart that he labors under the sun?** Ultimately, what will he gain from all these deeds and thoughts?
23 **For all his days are pains, and anger is his concern; even at night his heart does not rest.** Even when the body rests, his heart is not at ease. On the contrary, it is specifically then that all the questions unresolved during the day arise. **This too,** his night worries and his day preoccupations,[24] **is futility.**
24 The obvious conclusion from this analysis is that one should refrain from exertion and amassing investments whose profits might never be realized, and simply enjoy the present. Accordingly, **there is nothing better for a man than that he should eat and drink, and indulge his soul through his toil. This too, I saw that it is** a gift **from the hand of God,** which is not dependent on man.
25 **For** after all, **who will eat** my food, **or who will** be quick to **enjoy,** or derive sensuous pleasure from my toil, **other than me?** My experiences are mine alone, and I gain no advantage or real benefit from them.
26 **For to the man who is good before Him,** whose honor God desires, **He gave wisdom, knowledge, and joy,** so that he will feel some satisfaction from his work and reap the benefit. **But to the sinner He gave the matter of gathering and amassing** possessions, in order **to** ultimately **give** them **to him who is good before God.** The property that the sinner has collected will not remain his but will be given to one who finds favor in the eyes of God. Both the righteous and the wicked could have heirs whose paths diverge from the path of their parents. Consequently, **this** matter of amassing possessions or squandering them[25] **too is futility and herding wind.**

The Order of the World

ECCLESIASTES 3:1–17

In the context of the fundamental uncertainties raised by Kohelet, the poem of the times appears. This is a rhythmic, ordered poem containing a series of sayings arranged in pairs of contrasting activities and life events. In this poem, Kohelet is saying that each of the listed matters has its own designated time. The various areas of human existence are organized in a fixed order, as arranged by Divine Providence.

The poem begins and ends with the phrase "a time for every purpose"; however, the knowledge that everything is conducted in accordance with a plan does not resolve the question of the purpose of man's existence. Even if one recognizes that all the events that transpire in the world are arranged and directed from above, he remains ignorant of God's design for the world, and he does not comprehend the meaning of all the events that unfold before his eyes. Nevertheless, certain conclusions do emerge from this poem: One must be aware of his limitations and his place in relation to God. The world is in God's hands, and the person who focuses on conducting his life joyfully and in the performance of good deeds will be privileged to receive His gifts. In addition, one must keep in mind that although the ways of the world might sometimes appear to be perversions of justice, ultimately divine justice will be revealed.

3 1 The section begins with a general statement: **For everything there is a season,** its appropriate time, **and** there is **a** suitable **time for every purpose,** action, desire, or wish, **beneath the heavens.**
2 The song lists the various events that man experiences in life: There is **a time to be born and a time to die; a time to plant and a time to uproot the planted.**

"A time to plant"

"And a time to uproot the planted"

3 There is **a time to kill** and destroy life **and a time to heal** and restore it; **a time to breach,** to demolish, **and a time to build;**
4 **a time to weep and a time to laugh; a time for lamenting and a time for dancing;**
5 **a time to cast stones and a time to gather stones**[B] together; **a time to embrace and a time to refrain from embracing.** In certain situations it is improper to embrace.
6 There is **a time to seek** or desire something **and a time to lose** it; **a time to keep and a time to discard;**
7 **a time to rend and a time to sew; a time to be silent and a time to speak;**
8 **a time to love and a time to hate; a time of war and a time of peace.**
9 In light of this perspective, that all worldly matters are arranged in an organized fashion, Kohelet reiterates his question on the benefit and purpose of the world: **What is the advantage of the doer in that he toils?**
10 **I have seen the concerns that God has given to the sons of man in which to engage,** to occupy themselves with.
11 **He made everything beautiful in its time; He put the world too in their heart,**[D] to think about and engage in its matters, **notwithstanding that man will not**[D] **discover,** understand, **from beginning to end** the significance of **the accomplishment that God has accomplished.**

כב שֶׁלֹּא עָמַל־בּוֹ יִתְּנֶנּוּ חֶלְקוֹ גַּם־זֶה הֶבֶל וְרָעָה רַבָּה: כִּי מֶה־הֹוֶה לָאָדָם בְּכָל־
כג עֲמָלוֹ וּבְרַעְיוֹן לִבּוֹ שֶׁהוּא עָמֵל תַּחַת הַשָּׁמֶשׁ: כִּי כָל־יָמָיו מַכְאֹבִים וָכַעַס עִנְיָנוֹ
כד גַּם־בַּלַּיְלָה לֹא־שָׁכַב לִבּוֹ גַּם־זֶה הֶבֶל הוּא: אֵין־טוֹב בָּאָדָם שֶׁיֹּאכַל וְשָׁתָה
כה וְהֶרְאָה אֶת־נַפְשׁוֹ טוֹב בַּעֲמָלוֹ גַּם־זֹה רָאִיתִי אָנִי כִּי מִיַּד הָאֱלֹהִים הִיא: כִּי מִי
כו יֹאכַל וּמִי יָחוּשׁ חוּץ מִמֶּנִּי: כִּי לְאָדָם שֶׁטּוֹב לְפָנָיו נָתַן חָכְמָה וְדַעַת וְשִׂמְחָה
וְלַחוֹטֶא נָתַן עִנְיָן לֶאֱסֹף וְלִכְנוֹס לָתֵת לְטוֹב לִפְנֵי הָאֱלֹהִים גַּם־זֶה הֶבֶל וּרְעוּת
א ב רוּחַ: לַכֹּל זְמָן וְעֵת לְכָל־חֵפֶץ תַּחַת הַשָּׁמָיִם: עֵת לָלֶדֶת וְעֵת לָמוּת
ג עֵת לָטַעַת וְעֵת לַעֲקוֹר נָטוּעַ: עֵת לַהֲרוֹג וְעֵת לִרְפּוֹא
ד עֵת לִפְרוֹץ וְעֵת לִבְנוֹת: עֵת לִבְכּוֹת וְעֵת לִשְׂחוֹק
ה עֵת סְפוֹד וְעֵת רְקוֹד: עֵת לְהַשְׁלִיךְ אֲבָנִים וְעֵת כְּנוֹס אֲבָנִים
ו עֵת לַחֲבוֹק וְעֵת לִרְחֹק מֵחַבֵּק: עֵת לְבַקֵּשׁ וְעֵת לְאַבֵּד
ז עֵת לִשְׁמוֹר וְעֵת לְהַשְׁלִיךְ: עֵת לִקְרוֹעַ וְעֵת לִתְפּוֹר
ח עֵת לַחֲשׁוֹת וְעֵת לְדַבֵּר: עֵת לֶאֱהֹב וְעֵת לִשְׂנֹא
ט עֵת מִלְחָמָה וְעֵת שָׁלוֹם: מַה־יִּתְרוֹן הָעוֹשֶׂה בַּאֲשֶׁר הוּא עָמֵל:
י יא רָאִיתִי אֶת־הָעִנְיָן אֲשֶׁר נָתַן אֱלֹהִים לִבְנֵי הָאָדָם לַעֲנוֹת בּוֹ: אֶת־הַכֹּל עָשָׂה
יָפֶה בְעִתּוֹ גַּם אֶת־הָעֹלָם נָתַן בְּלִבָּם מִבְּלִי אֲשֶׁר לֹא־יִמְצָא הָאָדָם אֶת־הַמַּעֲשֶׂה

BACKGROUND

3:5 | **To cast stones…to gather stones:** Casting and gathering stones were important agricultural activities in the mountains of the Land of Israel. One prepares its hilly slopes for seeding and planting by removing stones from the fields. The stones are subsequently gathered and used in the construction of terraces, for retention of rainwater, and for building watchmen's huts.

DISCUSSION

3:11 | **He put the world [*ha'olam*] too in their heart:** Obviously, a person is located in this world; however, the statement that the world is found within a person is also true. The Sages interpret this phrase in another manner as well: God also placed the ability to forget in their heart. This explanation is based on the linguistic similarity between the word *olam*, world, and *he'elem*, disappearance, and also on the way that *olam* is written here, without the *vav,* as well as the fact that in the Bible the word *olam* also refers to eternity (see *Midrash Tanḥuma, Kedoshim* 8).

Nothwithstanding that man will not [*mibli…lo*]: This expression should not be understood as a double negative; rather, it is a form of emphasis. This linguistic phenomenon is found elsewhere too, such as the rhetorical question "Is there no [*hamibli ein*] God in Israel that you send to inquire of Baal Zevuv, god of Ekron"? (II Kings 1:6).

12 Since no one is privy to God's actions or plans, **I know that there is nothing good for them,** the people,[26] **other than** for each **to rejoice** in his portion, **and to do good during his life.**
13 **Also, each man who eats and drinks and sees good in all his toil,** living a standard, reasonable life, **it is the gift of God.**
14 Regardless of all our actions, **I know that everything that God does, it will be forever; one cannot add to it and cannot subtract from it.** Since God is in charge of the world, man cannot alter it much. **God caused** the helplessness people experience because of the way He runs the world, so **that they would experience fear before Him.** This fear stems from the feeling of a lack of control over the world and all the vicissitudes that befall a person.[27]
15 **That which was already is** present now, **and that which will be** in the future **already was.** Nothing changes in the world. **And** in this state where nothing is under the control of man, it is **God** who **seeks the pursued** and assists him.
16 **Furthermore, I saw under the sun,** in this world: In **the place of judgment, there is the wickedness;** in **the place of justice, there is the wickedness.**[D] In contrast to expectations, the judicial system becomes institutionalized evil. In that case, there is no secure refuge from evil.
17 **I said in my heart: God will judge the righteous and the wicked, as there is a time for every purpose and** ultimately, the day will come when they will be held accountable **for every action** that was done **there,** even if it is not currently evident.[28]

Confrontations with Death

ECCLESIASTES 3:18–4:3

This section expresses in more extreme terms the transitory nature of human existence and the futility of human actions that were described at the beginning of the book. Death is decreed on man and animal alike, although Kohelet notes that in contrast to animals, the human spirit ascends to the heavens upon his death. However, Kohelet immediately proceeds to ignore this concept, preferring to focus on celebrating his actions and his lot in this world over contemplation that extends far beyond the horizon of human perspective.

At the end of this passage, Kohelet relates to death from a different perspective: He prefers the dead, who have already returned to dust, and those who never emerged from the dust of this world, over the world of the living, in light of the severe corruption of human society and the pain it causes.

18 **I said in my heart: It is by the speech of the sons of man that God has distinguished them** from other living creatures and elevated their status above the animal world,[29] **but** I **saw that** in truth, **they,** men, **are animals to themselves.** The difference between them and other life forms is not that significant.
19 **For the fate of the sons of man is the fate of the animal; there is one fate for them.** The demise of the animal awaits man as well. **Like the death of this, so is the death of that, and there is one spirit for all; the superiority of the man over the animal is nothing, as everything is futility.** The most impressive elements of human culture and achievement, e.g., the construction of the pyramids, the composition of brilliant music, and the development of higher-order mathematics, cannot remove the decree of death hovering over man's head as he is a member of the kingdom of the living.[30]
20 When one considers physical existence alone, it is clear that **everything goes to one place; everything was from the dust, and everything returns to the dust** upon death. All material objects begin as raw material and ultimately return to that state.
21 In contrast, with regard to the spirit, **who knows the spirit of the sons of man? Does it ascend upward, and the spirit of the animal, does it descend downward to the earth?** Most people do not consider the difference between the spirit of man and that of the animal.[31]
22 **I saw that there is nothing better,** at least as a temporary solution, a palliative, **than that a man should rejoice in his actions, as that is his portion, for who will bring him to see that which will be after him?** Since knowledge of what awaits him after death is unattainable, it is preferable to live a simple active life and rejoice in the portion that is presently his.

4 1 **I again** considered time after time the events of the world, and I **saw all the exploited,** the victims of corrupt deeds, **who are afflicted under the sun,** in the world. **Behold the tear of the exploited, but there is no comforter for them, and duress from their exploiters but there is no comforter for them.** The world is full of evil and pain.

"The exploited who are afflicted under the sun." Nubian slaves sold in the market, illustration based on sunken relief, Tomb of Horemheb, Egypt

2 **I praise** and prefer **the dead who are already dead,** or, alternatively, I favor them because they have already died, **more than the living who are still alive,** as the dead no longer suffer from the troubles of this world, whereas the living are surrounded by a life of iniquity.[32]

יב אֲשֶׁר־עָשָׂה הָאֱלֹהִים מֵרֹאשׁ וְעַד־סוֹף׃ יָדַעְתִּי כִּי אֵין טוֹב בָּם כִּי אִם־לִשְׂמוֹחַ
יג וְלַעֲשׂוֹת טוֹב בְּחַיָּיו׃ וְגַם כָּל־הָאָדָם שֶׁיֹּאכַל וְשָׁתָה וְרָאָה טוֹב בְּכָל־עֲמָלוֹ מַתַּת ב
יד אֱלֹהִים הִיא׃ יָדַעְתִּי כִּי כָּל־אֲשֶׁר יַעֲשֶׂה הָאֱלֹהִים הוּא יִהְיֶה לְעוֹלָם עָלָיו אֵין
טו לְהוֹסִיף וּמִמֶּנּוּ אֵין לִגְרֹעַ וְהָאֱלֹהִים עָשָׂה שֶׁיִּרְאוּ מִלְּפָנָיו׃ מַה־שֶּׁהָיָה כְּבָר הוּא
טז וַאֲשֶׁר לִהְיוֹת כְּבָר הָיָה וְהָאֱלֹהִים יְבַקֵּשׁ אֶת־נִרְדָּף׃ וְעוֹד רָאִיתִי תַּחַת הַשָּׁמֶשׁ
יז מְקוֹם הַמִּשְׁפָּט שָׁמָּה הָרֶשַׁע וּמְקוֹם הַצֶּדֶק שָׁמָּה הָרָשַׁע׃ אָמַרְתִּי אֲנִי בְּלִבִּי
אֶת־הַצַּדִּיק וְאֶת־הָרָשָׁע יִשְׁפֹּט הָאֱלֹהִים כִּי־עֵת לְכָל־חֵפֶץ וְעַל כָּל־הַמַּעֲשֶׂה
יח שָׁם׃ אָמַרְתִּי אֲנִי בְּלִבִּי עַל־דִּבְרַת בְּנֵי הָאָדָם לְבָרָם הָאֱלֹהִים וְלִרְאוֹת שְׁהֶם־
יט בְּהֵמָה הֵמָּה לָהֶם׃ כִּי מִקְרֶה בְנֵי־הָאָדָם וּמִקְרֶה הַבְּהֵמָה וּמִקְרֶה אֶחָד לָהֶם
כְּמוֹת זֶה כֵּן מוֹת זֶה וְרוּחַ אֶחָד לַכֹּל וּמוֹתַר הָאָדָם מִן־הַבְּהֵמָה אָיִן כִּי הַכֹּל
כ הָבֶל׃ הַכֹּל הוֹלֵךְ אֶל־מָקוֹם אֶחָד הַכֹּל הָיָה מִן־הֶעָפָר וְהַכֹּל שָׁב אֶל־הֶעָפָר׃
כא מִי יוֹדֵעַ רוּחַ בְּנֵי הָאָדָם הָעֹלָה הִיא לְמָעְלָה וְרוּחַ הַבְּהֵמָה הַיֹּרֶדֶת הִיא לְמַטָּה
כב לָאָרֶץ׃ וְרָאִיתִי כִּי אֵין טוֹב מֵאֲשֶׁר יִשְׂמַח הָאָדָם בְּמַעֲשָׂיו כִּי־הוּא חֶלְקוֹ כִּי מִי
א יְבִיאֶנּוּ לִרְאוֹת בְּמֶה שֶׁיִּהְיֶה אַחֲרָיו׃ וְשַׁבְתִּי אֲנִי וָאֶרְאֶה אֶת־כָּל־הָעֲשׁוּקִים
אֲשֶׁר נַעֲשִׂים תַּחַת הַשָּׁמֶשׁ וְהִנֵּה ׀ דִּמְעַת הָעֲשׁוּקִים וְאֵין לָהֶם מְנַחֵם וּמִיַּד
ב עֹשְׁקֵיהֶם כֹּחַ וְאֵין לָהֶם מְנַחֵם׃ וְשַׁבֵּחַ אֲנִי אֶת־הַמֵּתִים שֶׁכְּבָר מֵתוּ מִן־הַחַיִּים

DISCUSSION

3:16| **The place of judgment, there is the wickedness; the place of justice, there is the wickedness:** According to the greatest legal experts in Israel and the world, the purpose of the courts and the legal system is to uphold the law, not necessarily to uphold justice. Indeed, there are times when upholding the law undermines true justice.

3 **Better than both of them,** the living and the dead, **is he who has not yet been,** one who has not yet been born, **who has not seen the evil action that is performed under the sun.** The impression of evil remains upon the dead, and the living experience it, whereas evil has no effect on those not yet born.

Toil and Human Fervor

ECCLESIASTES 4:4–16

In this section, Kohelet emphasizes the costs of the worldview that prioritizes labor and success. He examines the two possible justifications for hard work, helping others and investing on behalf of future generations, and arrives at the conclusion that one who toils on behalf of his descendants is oblivious to the possibility that he will not be at all satisfied with his successors. Therefore, any laboring and stockpiling for the future at the expense of the present is futile.

4 **I saw all toil and all skilled action, that it is** motivated by **each man's envy of his counterpart.** One's talents and success often arouse jealousy among others, but **this too,** the envy of another's property and abilities,[33] **is futility and herding wind.**

5 On the one hand, **the fool folds his hands** in his lap, as he does not work and therefore lacks support and food, **and** ultimately **eats his own flesh.**[B] His flesh is consumed, and he dies of hunger.[34] Alternatively, he is ashamed due to frustration and inactivity.

6 On the other hand, **a handful of tranquility is better than two handfuls of toil and herding wind,** of hard yet futile labor.

7 I returned to contemplate the world, and **I again saw** that devotion to toil and diligence is **futility under the sun.**

8 For example, **there is one and no other** with him, or he chooses not to involve others in his activities, **without even a son or a brother. There is no end to all his toil, and his eye is not satisfied with riches,** as he constantly desires more. This person may well ask himself: **For whom** then **do I toil,** if I need not support anyone other than myself, **and** for what purpose do I **deny good from my soul** with my hard work? **This too is futility and a grave concern.**

9 In contrast, there are good reasons to engage in joint efforts: **Two are better than one,**[D] **because they have a good reward for their toil.** Two people who work together can earn a greater profit than the sum of their solitary efforts.[35]

10 The benefits to such a partnership go beyond the financial: **For if they fall, one will raise the other; and the one who falls, there is no other to raise him.**

11 **Also,** there is another advantage: **If two lie** together, at the very least **it is warm for them,** as they will provide each other with heat; **but for one** alone, **how will he be warm?** Who will warm him?

12 **If the one is attacked, both will stand against it.** If someone attacks one of two, neither will stand alone against the attacker. **And a threefold thread is not quickly severed.**[B] Intertwined threads are stronger than individual strands, and likewise a group of three is superior to a pair.[36]

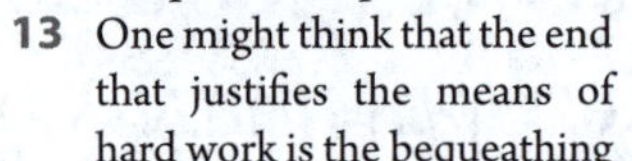

"And a threefold thread is not quickly severed"

13 One might think that the end that justifies the means of hard work is the bequeathing of the fruit of his toil to future generations. However, the future is not in his control, and the profit garnered from his labor guarantees nothing: **Better an impoverished but wise child** with nothing **than an old and foolish king** with everything but **who no longer knows to be cautious.** Wisdom involves caution and potential success, whereas a fool, even if he is a king, is liable to act impulsively and fail.

14 **For he,** a foolish king, is comparable to someone who was released and **emerged from prison to become king,** as he lacks the requisite tools to rule a kingdom. **For even in his reign he is revealed as poor,** as he is lacking in knowledge as well as leadership skills.

15 **I saw all the living** people, **who walk under the sun, with the child, the successor, who will stand in his stead.** Their hopes were placed in their children, as each generation invests great effort in the succeeding one, hoping that it will be more successful than its predecessor.

16 Indeed, **there is no end to the entire people, to all those,** all generations, **who were before them,** who lived in the past, **and also the later ones,** the generations that will come after; **they will not rejoice in him,** the child from whom the present generation have great expectations. **As this too,** the expectation and hope in the succession of the generations, **is futility and an empty notion.**[37]

ג אֲשֶׁר הֵמָּה חַיִּים עֲדֶנָה: וְטוֹב מִשְּׁנֵיהֶם אֵת אֲשֶׁר־עֲדֶן לֹא הָיָה אֲשֶׁר לֹא־רָאָה
ד אֶת־הַמַּעֲשֶׂה הָרָע אֲשֶׁר נַעֲשָׂה תַּחַת הַשָּׁמֶשׁ: וְרָאִיתִי אֲנִי אֶת־כָּל־עָמָל וְאֵת
ה כָּל־כִּשְׁרוֹן הַמַּעֲשֶׂה כִּי הִיא קִנְאַת־אִישׁ מֵרֵעֵהוּ גַּם־זֶה הֶבֶל וּרְעוּת רוּחַ: הַכְּסִיל
ו חֹבֵק אֶת־יָדָיו וְאֹכֵל אֶת־בְּשָׂרוֹ: טוֹב מְלֹא כַף נָחַת מִמְּלֹא חָפְנַיִם עָמָל וּרְעוּת
ז ח רוּחַ: וְשַׁבְתִּי אֲנִי וָאֶרְאֶה הֶבֶל תַּחַת הַשָּׁמֶשׁ: יֵשׁ אֶחָד וְאֵין שֵׁנִי גַּם בֵּן וָאָח
אֵין־לוֹ וְאֵין קֵץ לְכָל־עֲמָלוֹ גַּם־עֵינָיו לֹא־תִשְׂבַּע עֹשֶׁר וּלְמִי | אֲנִי עָמֵל וּמְחַסֵּר עֵינוֹ
ט אֶת־נַפְשִׁי מִטּוֹבָה גַּם־זֶה הֶבֶל וְעִנְיַן רָע הוּא: טוֹבִים הַשְּׁנַיִם מִן־הָאֶחָד אֲשֶׁר
י יֵשׁ־לָהֶם שָׂכָר טוֹב בַּעֲמָלָם: כִּי אִם־יִפֹּלוּ הָאֶחָד יָקִים אֶת־חֲבֵרוֹ וְאִילוֹ הָאֶחָד
יא שֶׁיִּפּוֹל וְאֵין שֵׁנִי לַהֲקִימוֹ: גַּם אִם־יִשְׁכְּבוּ שְׁנַיִם וְחַם לָהֶם וּלְאֶחָד אֵיךְ יֵחָם:
יב וְאִם־יִתְקְפוֹ הָאֶחָד הַשְּׁנַיִם יַעַמְדוּ נֶגְדּוֹ וְהַחוּט הַמְשֻׁלָּשׁ לֹא בִמְהֵרָה יִנָּתֵק:
יג יד טוֹב יֶלֶד מִסְכֵּן וְחָכָם מִמֶּלֶךְ זָקֵן וּכְסִיל אֲשֶׁר לֹא־יָדַע לְהִזָּהֵר עוֹד: כִּי־מִבֵּית
טו הָסוּרִים יָצָא לִמְלֹךְ כִּי גַּם בְּמַלְכוּתוֹ נוֹלַד רָשׁ: רָאִיתִי אֶת־כָּל־הַחַיִּים הַמְהַלְּכִים
טז תַּחַת הַשָּׁמֶשׁ עִם הַיֶּלֶד הַשֵּׁנִי אֲשֶׁר יַעֲמֹד תַּחְתָּיו: אֵין־קֵץ לְכָל־הָעָם לְכֹל
אֲשֶׁר־הָיָה לִפְנֵיהֶם גַּם הָאַחֲרוֹנִים לֹא יִשְׂמְחוּ־בוֹ כִּי־גַם־זֶה הֶבֶל וְרַעְיוֹן רוּחַ:

BACKGROUND

4:5| **Eats his flesh:** In the biological process known as catabolism, a body that fails to receive external sustenance breaks down its own fat and muscle tissue in order to sustain the brain and the nerves. Consequently, a person in that state can be described as eating his own flesh.

4:12| **And a threefold thread is not quickly severed:** Ropes with twisted fibers are made from a minimum of three strands, as the mutual friction of the threads enhances the strength of the rope. Likewise, ropes woven into a braid, like those used by mountain climbers, are entwined from at least three strands.

DISCUSSION

4:9| **Two are better than one:** This comment also constitutes social justification for marriage, as mutual assistance provides the couple with advantages in all realms of life.

Instructions concerning Man's Inferiority before God

ECCLESIASTES 4:17–5:7

In his awareness of man's lowliness before God, Kohelet calls on man to obey God rather than bring offerings without intent and purity of heart. His cautions against impulsive speech lacking requisite accompanying commitment are tied to the fear of God. Ultimately, he reminds man that the scope of his vision is limited; therefore, one must be restrained in judging that which he sees.

17 **Watching your step,** being cautious, **when you go to the House of God,** keeping in mind the purpose of your visit, **and listening attentively** to the Torah and its commandments, **is better than fools giving offerings, for** in their imprudence **they do not** even **know how to perform evil.**[38] Some explain that they know only to perform evil, or that they are unaware that what they have done is evil, or that fools bring offerings erroneously thinking that it can somehow exonerate them of their evil doings.

5 1 **Do not be rash with** the comments of **your mouth, and** also **let your heart,** your thoughts, **not be hasty to express a word before God, as God is in the heavens and you are on earth,** and consequently your knowledge is limited. **Therefore, your words** to God and about Him, and your statements in general,[39] **should be few.**

2 **For a dream comes with a multitude of** diverse **concerns, and** by the same token, **a fool's voice** comes **with a multitude of words.** A fool can invariably be identified by incessant prattle, like the meaningless portions of a dream.[40]

3 **When you take a vow to God, do not delay paying it.** Rather, bring the pledged offering at the proper time, **as He does not desire fools,** who vow indiscriminately and impulsively but do not fulfill their commitments.[41] **That which you vow, pay.**

4 In fact, **it is better that you not vow** at all **than that you vow and not pay.**

5 **Do not allow your mouth to cause your flesh to** let yourself **sin.** Imprecise and inappropriate statements can corrupt and endanger you. **And do not say before the messenger** who is responsible for collecting the money you vowed[42] **that it was a mistake. Why should God become angry at your voice and destroy your handiwork?**[43]

6 **So it is with a multitude of dreams, futilities, and many words.** Alternatively, it is because of the multitude of dreams and vanities and many words that troubles befall a person. **Rather, fear God.** One who fails to honor his word and commitments is likely to harm himself. In addition, it constitutes impertinence toward God.

7 **If you see exploitation of the poor, subversion of judgment and justice in the country, do not wonder at the purpose, for higher than high is watching, and** there are **high ones** who **are over them,** the events that you observe. The world contains many layers built upon other layers. You do not necessarily understand the reasons behind events, and they make you uneasy because you have a low vantage point and your perspective is limited. You are incapable of seeing the bigger picture.[44]

Kohelet Disparages the Accumulation of Money and Possessions for the Future

ECCLESIASTES 5:8–6:10

In this section, Kohelet criticizes the pursuit of money, as thereby the present, and life in general, is mortgaged for the sake of an undefined purpose. It is therefore preferable to celebrate one's accomplishments in the present. Even so, the section concludes with a critique of people who focus exclusively on their own lives, living a static existence with no possibility of effecting change in the world.

8 **The advantage of land is in every way.** Land is superior to all other property, as even **a king is subservient to a field.** The field is the source of life, and everyone is dependent on its cultivation.[45]

9 **A lover of silver will never be satisfied with silver.** One who desires money will never be satiated. **And he who loves abundance** of possessions **has no produce.** Alternatively, one who loves an abundance of possessions will not receive grain or sustenance from them;[46] **this** hoarding of excessive possessions **too is futility.**

10 **With the increase of goodness,** when plenty of food is brought home, **its consumers increase,** more people come to eat it; **and what use is it to its owner,** what does he gain from this abundance, **other than the sight of** his wealth before **his eyes?** He himself does not benefit from it in any other way. Alternatively, all he beholds with his eyes are others consuming his food.[47]

11 **Sweet is the sleep of the worker, whether he eats little or much** beforehand. **But the satiation of the wealthy does not allow him to sleep,** as he does not work hard enough to grow tired. Furthermore, due to

"Wealth kept for its owner." Collection of coins Carmel, first century BCE

יז שְׁמוֹר רגליך כַּאֲשֶׁר תֵּלֵךְ אֶל־בֵּית הָאֱלֹהִים וְקָרוֹב לִשְׁמֹעַ מִתֵּת הַכְּסִילִים זָבַח רַגְלְךָ
א כִּי־אֵינָם יוֹדְעִים לַעֲשׂוֹת רָע׃ אַל־תְּבַהֵל עַל־פִּיךָ וְלִבְּךָ אַל־יְמַהֵר לְהוֹצִיא דָבָר
לִפְנֵי הָאֱלֹהִים כִּי הָאֱלֹהִים בַּשָּׁמַיִם וְאַתָּה עַל־הָאָרֶץ עַל־כֵּן יִהְיוּ דְבָרֶיךָ מְעַטִּים׃
ב ג כִּי בָּא הַחֲלוֹם בְּרֹב עִנְיָן וְקוֹל כְּסִיל בְּרֹב דְּבָרִים׃ כַּאֲשֶׁר תִּדֹּר נֶדֶר לֵאלֹהִים
ד אַל־תְּאַחֵר לְשַׁלְּמוֹ כִּי אֵין חֵפֶץ בַּכְּסִילִים אֵת אֲשֶׁר־תִּדֹּר שַׁלֵּם׃ טוֹב אֲשֶׁר
ה לֹא־תִדֹּר מִשֶּׁתִּדּוֹר וְלֹא תְשַׁלֵּם׃ אַל־תִּתֵּן אֶת־פִּיךָ לַחֲטִיא אֶת־בְּשָׂרֶךָ וְאַל־
תֹּאמַר לִפְנֵי הַמַּלְאָךְ כִּי שְׁגָגָה הִיא לָמָּה יִקְצֹף הָאֱלֹהִים עַל־קוֹלֶךָ וְחִבֵּל אֶת־
ו מַעֲשֵׂה יָדֶיךָ׃ כִּי בְרֹב חֲלֹמוֹת וַהֲבָלִים וּדְבָרִים הַרְבֵּה כִּי אֶת־הָאֱלֹהִים יְרָא׃
ז אִם־עֹשֶׁק רָשׁ וְגֵזֶל מִשְׁפָּט וָצֶדֶק תִּרְאֶה בַמְּדִינָה אַל־תִּתְמַהּ עַל־הַחֵפֶץ כִּי גָבֹהַּ
ח מֵעַל גָּבֹהַּ שֹׁמֵר וּגְבֹהִים עֲלֵיהֶם׃ וְיִתְרוֹן אֶרֶץ בַּכֹּל היא מֶלֶךְ לְשָׂדֶה נֶעֱבָד׃ הוּא
ט י אֹהֵב כֶּסֶף לֹא־יִשְׂבַּע כֶּסֶף וּמִי־אֹהֵב בֶּהָמוֹן לֹא תְבוּאָה גַּם־זֶה הָבֶל׃ בִּרְבוֹת
יא הַטּוֹבָה רַבּוּ אוֹכְלֶיהָ וּמַה־כִּשְׁרוֹן לִבְעָלֶיהָ כִּי אִם־ראית עֵינָיו׃ מְתוּקָה שְׁנַת רְאוּת
יב הָעֹבֵד אִם־מְעַט וְאִם־הַרְבֵּה יֹאכֵל וְהַשָּׂבָע לֶעָשִׁיר אֵינֶנּוּ מַנִּיחַ לוֹ לִישׁוֹן׃ יֵשׁ
יג רָעָה חוֹלָה רָאִיתִי תַּחַת הַשָּׁמֶשׁ עֹשֶׁר שָׁמוּר לִבְעָלָיו לְרָעָתוֹ׃ וְאָבַד הָעֹשֶׁר
יד הַהוּא בְּעִנְיַן רָע וְהוֹלִיד בֵּן וְאֵין בְּיָדוֹ מְאוּמָה׃ כַּאֲשֶׁר יָצָא מִבֶּטֶן אִמּוֹ עָרוֹם
טו יָשׁוּב לָלֶכֶת כְּשֶׁבָּא וּמְאוּמָה לֹא־יִשָּׂא בַעֲמָלוֹ שֶׁיֹּלֵךְ בְּיָדוֹ׃ וְגַם־זֹה רָעָה חוֹלָה

his preoccupation with his concerns over his possessions, he cannot enjoy his abundance.[48]

12 **There is a grave evil,** or malady, **that I have seen under the sun: Wealth kept for its owner.** He does not enjoy his wealth at all, as he always anticipates greater profit. That wealth is **to his detriment,**

13 because when **that wealth is lost in an ill-fated concern,**[B] an unsuccessful business transaction, then **he,** that individual, **begets a son, and there is nothing** left **in his,** the son's, **hand.**

14 **As he emerged from his mother's womb,** with nothing, **so he will return naked, to go as he came** into the world, **and he will take nothing for his toil that he can carry in his hand.**

15 **This too is a grave evil; just as he came** to the world, **so will he go; and what is the advantage for he who toils for the wind,** for naught?

BACKGROUND

5:13 | **That wealth is lost in an ill-fated concern:** The field of economics involves recurring cycles consisting of peaks of capital growth and valleys of decline. There are recorded cycles of seven to eleven years, of fifteen to twenty-five years, and of forty-five to sixty years.

16 **Indeed,** not only does he derive no benefit from his wealth, but while preoccupied with his business he suffers, as **all his days he eats in darkness,** in the twilight hours, not during the day, as he must work all day, and not at night either, as he needs his sleep. Alternatively, the verse means that he eats in sorrow. **And he has much anger** throughout his life, **illness, and wrath.**[49]

17 Instead of dreaming of wealth, saving for an uncertain future and risking the loss of all one's money, **behold the good that I have seen: That it is fine to eat, and to drink, and to see benefit in all his toil that he toils under the sun,** throughout **the number of days of his life that God has given him,** rather than devising plans that are liable not to materialize,[50] **as that is his portion.**

18 **Also any man to whom God has given wealth and property, and to whom He has given control to eat from it, and to bear,** enjoy, **his portion, and to rejoice in his toil, that,** the possibility that one will actually enjoy his wealth, **is the gift of God.**

19 **Because he will not remember much of the days of his life; rather, it is God who is the solution** and who provides him with his needs, and He will grace a person **with the joy of his heart.** Therefore, it is preferable to enjoy one's state of serenity rather than get caught up in baseless plans for the future.

6 1 **There is an evil that I have seen under the sun,** in this world, **and it is widespread among men,** a pervasive phenomenon:[51]

2 **A man to whom God gives wealth, property, and honor, and he lacks nothing for himself from anything that he desires.** This person has unlimited potential to live a good life, **but God does not grant him the opportunity to consume it,** as he dies before he can fulfill his dreams and ambitions, and **rather, a stranger will consume it,** reaping the benefit of his achievements. **That is futility, and it is a grave illness.**

3 Kohelet presents another example of this same phenomenon: **If a man begets one hundred** children from many wives **and lives many years, and the days of his years are numerous,** more than average, **but** despite all of this goodness, **his soul is not sated from the goodness,** as he is unable to find satisfaction and enjoyment from his accomplishments and he continues to further pursuits, **and moreover, he** ultimately **has no burial,** since that person, despite his toil and achievements, might not receive a dignified burial, a fate common to many who traveled abroad in pursuit of greater wealth and then disappeared, **I say: A stillborn is better than he.** He would have been better off not being born.[52]

4 **For** like a stillborn, **he came in futility and will depart in darkness, and his name will be covered in darkness,** and nothing will remain of it.

5 This person comes into the world empty-handed, works hard, lives a long life, and fathers many offspring. Yet he ultimately dies in a foreign, distant land and leaves this world empty-handed, without benefiting from the fruit of his labor. In contrast, the non-viable newborn, **even the sun he did not see and** he **did not know** any hard toil or evil; therefore, **there is more gratification for that** non-viable newborn **than** for **this** wealthy person;[53]

6 and **even if he,** that rich individual, **had lived one thousand years twice, he would not have seen good,** as he was so obsessed with acquiring more possessions and expanding his options he never settled down to enjoy his possessions. **Doesn't it all go to one place,** the grave, and nothing remains from all that he amassed?[54]

7 **All the toil of man is for his mouth,** in order to eat and sustain himself,[55] **but** in actuality **his soul too is not filled.** In the majority of cases, one leaves this world without having satisfied even half his desires.

8 **For what advantage has the wise over the fool?** Neither of them is immune from the rat race during their lives, or from inevitable death. **Why should the knowing poor man,** who is aware that his spirit will not be sated, **go against life,** rather than take action in the world on behalf of the living?[56]

9 Everything stated until this point indicates that **better is the sight of the eyes,** real life itself, **than the pursuit of desire,** yearning after what has not yet been achieved. **That too,** the clear perception of reality, is preferable, even though reality **is futility and herding wind,**[57]

10 since **that which was, its name was already called.** Past events have already been imprinted upon the world, and they cannot be changed. **It is known that he is a man,** a mere mortal, **and he is unable to contend with that which is mightier than he.** Man cannot change reality, as it is more powerful than he.

What Is Good for Man in Life

ECCLESIASTES 6:11–7:29

The numerous matters and aspects of the world forcefully raise the question of what is good. At the margins of Kohelet's acknowledgment of the limitations of his intellect, he notes two phenomena that he has encountered in his ruminations: The danger posed by and the shortcomings of a seductive woman, and the distortion of the world generated by humanity. Were it not for these two factors, the world could be a simpler, better place.

11 **Since there are many matters,** large and small, in the world, **futility increases.** The richer a person grows, the more he becomes preoccupied with worthless matters, and one who lives confronted with an overabundance of worthless matters will inevitably encounter incalculably more vanity. **What remains for the person?** What will be left to man from all this?

טז כָּל־עֻמַּת שֶׁבָּא כֵּן יֵלֵךְ וּמַה־יִּתְרוֹן לוֹ שֶׁיַּעֲמֹל לָרוּחַ׃ גַּם כָּל־יָמָיו בַּחֹשֶׁךְ יֹאכֵל
יז וְכַעַס הַרְבֵּה וְחָלְיוֹ וָקָצֶף׃ הִנֵּה אֲשֶׁר־רָאִיתִי אָנִי טוֹב אֲשֶׁר־יָפֶה לֶאֱכוֹל וְלִשְׁתּוֹת
וְלִרְאוֹת טוֹבָה בְּכָל־עֲמָלוֹ ׀ שֶׁיַּעֲמֹל תַּחַת־הַשֶּׁמֶשׁ מִסְפַּר יְמֵי־חַיָּו אֲשֶׁר־נָתַן־
יח לוֹ הָאֱלֹהִים כִּי־הוּא חֶלְקוֹ׃ גַּם כָּל־הָאָדָם אֲשֶׁר נָתַן־לוֹ הָאֱלֹהִים עֹשֶׁר וּנְכָסִים
וְהִשְׁלִיטוֹ לֶאֱכֹל מִמֶּנּוּ וְלָשֵׂאת אֶת־חֶלְקוֹ וְלִשְׂמֹחַ בַּעֲמָלוֹ זֹה מַתַּת אֱלֹהִים
יט א הִיא׃ כִּי לֹא הַרְבֵּה יִזְכֹּר אֶת־יְמֵי חַיָּיו כִּי הָאֱלֹהִים מַעֲנֶה בְּשִׂמְחַת לִבּוֹ׃ יֵשׁ רָעָה
ב אֲשֶׁר רָאִיתִי תַּחַת הַשָּׁמֶשׁ וְרַבָּה הִיא עַל־הָאָדָם׃ אִישׁ אֲשֶׁר יִתֶּן־לוֹ הָאֱלֹהִים
עֹשֶׁר וּנְכָסִים וְכָבוֹד וְאֵינֶנּוּ חָסֵר לְנַפְשׁוֹ ׀ מִכֹּל אֲשֶׁר־יִתְאַוֶּה וְלֹא־יַשְׁלִיטֶנּוּ
ג הָאֱלֹהִים לֶאֱכֹל מִמֶּנּוּ כִּי אִישׁ נָכְרִי יֹאכְלֶנּוּ זֶה הֶבֶל וָחֳלִי רָע הוּא׃ אִם־יוֹלִיד
אִישׁ מֵאָה וְשָׁנִים רַבּוֹת יִחְיֶה וְרַב ׀ שֶׁיִּהְיוּ יְמֵי־שָׁנָיו וְנַפְשׁוֹ לֹא־תִשְׂבַּע מִן־הַטּוֹבָה
ד וְגַם־קְבוּרָה לֹא־הָיְתָה לּוֹ אָמַרְתִּי טוֹב מִמֶּנּוּ הַנָּפֶל׃ כִּי־בַהֶבֶל בָּא וּבַחֹשֶׁךְ יֵלֵךְ
ה ו וּבַחֹשֶׁךְ שְׁמוֹ יְכֻסֶּה׃ גַּם־שֶׁמֶשׁ לֹא־רָאָה וְלֹא יָדָע נַחַת לָזֶה מִזֶּה׃ וְאִלּוּ חָיָה
ז אֶלֶף שָׁנִים פַּעֲמַיִם וְטוֹבָה לֹא רָאָה הֲלֹא אֶל־מָקוֹם אֶחָד הַכֹּל הוֹלֵךְ׃ כָּל־עֲמַל
ח הָאָדָם לְפִיהוּ וְגַם־הַנֶּפֶשׁ לֹא תִמָּלֵא׃ כִּי מַה־יּוֹתֵר לֶחָכָם מִן־הַכְּסִיל מַה־
ט לֶּעָנִי יוֹדֵעַ לַהֲלֹךְ נֶגֶד הַחַיִּים׃ טוֹב מַרְאֵה עֵינַיִם מֵהֲלָךְ־נָפֶשׁ גַּם־זֶה הֶבֶל
י וּרְעוּת רוּחַ׃ מַה־שֶּׁהָיָה כְּבָר נִקְרָא שְׁמוֹ וְנוֹדָע אֲשֶׁר־הוּא אָדָם וְלֹא־יוּכַל לָדִין
יא עִם שהתקיף מִמֶּנּוּ׃ כִּי יֵשׁ־דְּבָרִים הַרְבֵּה מַרְבִּים הָבֶל מַה־יֹּתֵר לָאָדָם׃ שֶׁתַּקִּיף

12 **For who knows what is good for man in his life, the number of days of his life of futility that he renders** meaningless **like a shadow? For who can tell a man what will be after him under the sun?**[D] Since no one knows what will endure after his death, one cannot determine what endeavor is worth undertaking.

"The number of days of his life of futility that he renders like a shadow"

7 1 **A good name is better than fragrant oil.**[B] Whereas the fragrance of oil is appreciated only by those proximate to it, a good reputation spreads far and wide and remains in the consciousness of those who hear of it. **And the day of death** is better **than the day of one's birth,** as on the day of death it is clear how the person acquired his good name, whereas on the day of one's birth no one knows what will ultimately become of him.[58]

2 Kohelet elaborates on the advantages of death: **It is better to go to a house of mourning than to go to a house of feasting, as that,** death, **is the end of every man, and** therefore **the living,** one who goes to the house of mourning,[59] **will take it to his heart,** as he will say to himself: Since everything ends in death, I must utilize my life to do something worthwhile. One tends to repress those thoughts in the course one's daily routine, but when faced with the inevitability of death, one can transcend the mundane and choose to change his ways. Kohelet prefers unpleasant situations because they are likely to motivate a person to move forward.

3 Accordingly, Kohelet asserts that another person's **anger is better** and more productive **than laughter, for from a harsh visage the heart** of man **may benefit.** One's character can improve and become more refined in the wake of criticism from another.[60]

4 **The heart of the wise is in a house of mourning.** Wise people often reflect about death, and consequently they frequently contemplate the future and the destiny of man. **But the heart of fools is in a house of rejoicing,** where they can enjoy the present.[61]

"The heart of fools is in a house of rejoicing." Illustration based on Assyrian relief, seventh century BCE

5 **It is better to hear the rebuke of the wise,** unpleasant though it may be, as criticism has the potential to guide a person, **than to be a man who hears the song of fools.** The absurd and nonsensical songs of fools might be pleasant to the ear, but they teach nothing and do not present any challenge to the listener.[62]

6 **For like the sound of brambles**[B] that burn **under a pot, so is the laughter of the fool.** His laughter is insignificant and fleeting, like the momentary crackling of burning thorns. **That too,** the laughter of the fool,[63] **is futility.** Alternatively, Kohelet is referring back to the preference of the rebuke of the wise: Despite all his wisdom and advice, even this individual can lose his status with ease.[64]

Thorny burnet

7 **For exploitation discomfits a wise man,** as it causes even a wise person to lose his judgment,[65] **and destroys the gift of the** understanding **heart** that was given to man.[66]

8 Kohelet returns to addressing the matter of ethics and wisdom that he addressed earlier: His preference for matters that do not provide immediate gratification but whose benefits are longer term. **The end of a matter is better than its beginning.** Although the beginning may be impressive, it is what remains at the end that is genuinely significant. **One of patient spirit**[67] **is better than one of arrogant spirit.**[D]

9 This verse also praises the virtue of patience, and it too refers to the human spirit: **Do not precipitate your spirit to become angry.** Do not allow yourself to be annoyed easily, **as anger abides in the bosom of fools.** Outbursts of rage can provide instant emotional gratification, but hasty, thoughtless expressions of anger are characteristic of fools.

10 In contrast to the focus of the previous verses on the ultimate future, this verse addresses the past. **Do not say: How was it** in the past? And do not say **that the early days were better than these. For it is not from wisdom that you ask about this.** Do

יב כִּי מִי־יוֹדֵעַ מַה־טּוֹב לָאָדָם בַּחַיִּים מִסְפַּר יְמֵי־חַיֵּי הֶבְלוֹ וְיַעֲשֵׂם כַּצֵּל אֲשֶׁר
א מִי־יַגִּיד לָאָדָם מַה־יִּהְיֶה אַחֲרָיו תַּחַת הַשָּׁמֶשׁ׃ טוֹב שֵׁם מִשֶּׁמֶן טוֹב ג
ב וְיוֹם הַמָּוֶת מִיּוֹם הִוָּלְדוֹ׃ טוֹב לָלֶכֶת אֶל־בֵּית־אֵבֶל מִלֶּכֶת אֶל־בֵּית מִשְׁתֶּה
ג בַּאֲשֶׁר הוּא סוֹף כָּל־הָאָדָם וְהַחַי יִתֵּן אֶל־לִבּוֹ׃ טוֹב כַּעַס מִשְּׂחוֹק כִּי־בְרֹעַ פָּנִים
ד ה יִיטַב לֵב׃ לֵב חֲכָמִים בְּבֵית אֵבֶל וְלֵב כְּסִילִים בְּבֵית שִׂמְחָה׃ טוֹב לִשְׁמוֹעַ גַּעֲרַת
ו חָכָם מֵאִישׁ שֹׁמֵעַ שִׁיר כְּסִילִים׃ כִּי כְקוֹל הַסִּירִים תַּחַת הַסִּיר כֵּן שְׂחֹק הַכְּסִיל
ז ח וְגַם־זֶה הָבֶל׃ כִּי הָעֹשֶׁק יְהוֹלֵל חָכָם וִיאַבֵּד אֶת־לֵב מַתָּנָה׃ טוֹב אַחֲרִית דָּבָר
ט מֵרֵאשִׁיתוֹ טוֹב אֶרֶךְ־רוּחַ מִגְּבַהּ־רוּחַ׃ אַל־תְּבַהֵל בְּרוּחֲךָ לִכְעוֹס כִּי כַעַס בְּחֵיק
י כְּסִילִים יָנוּחַ׃ אַל־תֹּאמַר מֶה הָיָה שֶׁהַיָּמִים הָרִאשֹׁנִים הָיוּ טוֹבִים מֵאֵלֶּה כִּי לֹא

BACKGROUND

7:1 | **A good name is better than fragrant oil:** Fragrances dissolved in oil evaporate in the open air at normal room temperatures and quickly dissipate. These fragrances are typically organic compounds with a low boiling or evaporation point. They evaporate from their liquid state, become concentrated in a small space, and their scent is lost.

7:6 | **Brambles [*sirim*]:** These are generally identified as the thorny burnet, *Sarcopoterium spinosum*, from the rose family. This plant is a small, prickly bush typically found in mountainous regions of Israel. It reaches a height of 30 cm with a diameter of 50 cm. The thorny burnet spreads quickly and covers large tracts of uncultivated land and consequently has become a symbol for abandoned places (see Isaiah 34:13). It is also used as a hedgerow: In the hills of Judea and Samaria one sees vineyards surrounded by fences with thorny burnets on them. Likewise they were placed at the entrances of caves where sheep were tended (see Hosea 2:8). Since this plant is effective as kindling, it was also used for heating and cooking. When it burns, it crackles, as described in the verse.

DISCUSSION

6:12 | **That he renders like a shadow...under the sun:** The life of man passes like a shadow, and when it ends, nothing remains of it under the sun. When the midday sun shines, the shadow dissipates. When the position of the sun is to the east or to the west, a shadow appears in the opposite direction. Similarly, human life is ethereal, like a passing shadow that moves from place to place.

Kohelet wonders whether there is anyone who knows what is worthwhile for man in his life, wonderment intertwined with confusion in light of man's limitations in terms of foreseeing the future and understanding the meaning of existence in general. He seeks to answer this question, though it was initially presented as an unanswerable rhetorical question. In the context of addressing this question, the verses that follow contain statements relating to the relative good in human life from different perspectives.

7:8 | **One of patient spirit [*erekh ruaḥ*] is better than one of arrogant spirit [*gevah ruaḥ*]:** Literally, the verse addresses two dimensions: Length and height. The long-winded, patient person is preferable to the high-winded, arrogant person. One who is long-winded is receptive and will listen to the high-winded one, whereas the high-winded one is unwilling to learn from the long-winded one.

not cling to fond memories of the past, neither with regard to your personal life nor with regard to the broader historical context, as the days of yore were not actually better than present times.[68] Some interpret this statement in accordance with its prevalent meaning that the world deteriorates over the course of the generations: It is unwise to express the pointless wish for a reprisal of the past.[69] Either way, wistful, nostalgic remarks are unproductive; one should accept reality as it is.[70]

11 Kohelet now compiles a series of popular aphorisms, only to refute the accepted understanding of their wisdom: **Wisdom is good with an inheritance,** material possessions. The combination of spiritual assets together with material resources is beneficial for man, **and more so for those revealed to the sun.** A wise and wealthy person derives even greater benefit if the people surrounding him are aware of his riches.[71]

12 **For** one who is **in the shadow of wisdom** and **in the shadow of silver,** wealth, is doubly secure, and his influence on others is great. But **the advantage of knowledge** over wealth[72] **is that wisdom preserves the life of its possessors.** Wisdom and knowledge can bring life to their owner.[73]

13 **See the work of God,** reflect on the world and accept it as God made it, **for who can mend that which He has warped?** Even if you conclude that the world was created distorted, you cannot fix it.[74]

14 Therefore, **on a day of good, enjoy, and on a day of bad, see** what you can do to prevent matters from deteriorating. Alternatively, watch resignedly, accepting the situation.[75] **God made this,** good, **corresponding to that,** evil; **therefore, man cannot discover anything,** he is unable to achieve complete understanding, **about it.** Alternatively, man has no legitimate claim of bias and inequity[76] with regard to good and evil in the world.

15 **I have seen everything in the days of my futility,** my fleeting days. I have seen that **there is a righteous man who perishes in his righteousness,** even though he deserves to continue living, **and** in contrast, **there is a wicked person who endures in his wickedness,** despite the fact that he should perish.

16 Reality is complicated and twisted, and therefore one must be careful. The following recommendations contrast with each other and are juxtaposed in order to balance each other: **Do not be overly righteous,** do not be excessively virtuous, e.g., by being merciful in an exaggerated manner, overly ascetic, or extreme in distancing oneself from sin,[77] **and do not be exceedingly wise; why should you go insane?** One can grow mad or depressed through extreme behavior,[78] and excessive righteousness or wisdom can backfire.

17 Conversely, **do not be overly wicked,**[79] even if you have already performed some evil,[80] **and do not be foolish; why should you die before your time?** Evil and foolish people are more likely to die young.[81]

18 Therefore, **it is good that you grasp this, and from that also do not withdraw your hand.** Adopt the middle road; do not go to any extreme.[82] **For one who fears God,** he is the moderate person, and he **will emerge from them all,** the many problems destined to afflict those who tend toward the extremes.[83]

19 **Wisdom will fortify** and strengthen **the wise more than ten rulers,** a large number of powerful men,[84] **who were in a city.**[D]

20 It is advisable not to be overly righteous,[85] **for there is no righteous man upon the earth who does good and does not sin.** In this imperfect reality, there are no entirely righteous people. No matter how much a person exerts himself, he can never achieve the ideal.

21 **Also do not pay attention to all the matters that they speak** about you, **so that you will not hear your servant cursing you.** If you listen to everything, you will eventually hear comments that are not only insignificant but also unpleasant, e.g., your servant cursing you. It is therefore preferable not to listen to everything people say.[86]

22 Even if you hear speech of that kind, you should not grow angry, **for your heart also knows that many times you too have cursed others.** Just as at times you blurt out inappropriate speech, others do so as well.

23 With regard to the quest for greater wisdom,[87] **all this I attempted with wisdom; I said: I will become wise.** I sought to follow the path of the wise, **but** I discovered that **it,** wisdom, **is distant from me.** Even one who seeks to acquire wisdom cannot obtain it fully.[88]

24 I sought to understand everything, but I eventually realized that **that which was** in the past **is distant** and cannot be properly understood, **and** even that which is not in the past[89] is **exceedingly deep; who can find it?** It is beyond comprehension. I have learned from experience that human wisdom and knowledge are limited.

25 Although one who seeks knowledge and wisdom cannot realize his goal entirely, Kohelet notes that there are positive conclusions at which he arrived through wisdom. First, he warns one who yearns for wisdom and wishes to live a balanced life of the dangers of a seductive woman: **I and my heart went about to know and to search, to seek wisdom and cunning,** sophisticated thoughts, **to know that wickedness is stupidity and foolishness is debauchery.**

26 **I find more bitter than death the** seductive **woman, who, in her heart, is snares and nets, her hands, shackles.**[90] It is therefore fitting that **one who is good before God,** a good and honest man, **will escape from her, but the sinner will be captured by her** trap. Kohelet is not preaching celibacy, but rather is calling upon man to reflect soberly and cautiously upon his passions and the power of women over him, so that he does not get caught in the trap of a woman of that kind.[91]

יא יב מְחַכְמָה שָׁאַלְתָּ עַל־זֶה: טוֹבָה חָכְמָה עִם־נַחֲלָה וְיֹתֵר לְרֹאֵי הַשָּׁמֶשׁ: כִּי בְּצֵל
יג הַחָכְמָה בְּצֵל הַכָּסֶף וְיִתְרוֹן דַּעַת הַחָכְמָה תְּחַיֶּה בְעָלֶיהָ: רְאֵה אֶת־מַעֲשֵׂה
יד הָאֱלֹהִים כִּי מִי יוּכַל לְתַקֵּן אֵת אֲשֶׁר עִוְּתוֹ: בְּיוֹם טוֹבָה הֱיֵה בְטוֹב וּבְיוֹם רָעָה
רְאֵה גַּם אֶת־זֶה לְעֻמַּת־זֶה עָשָׂה הָאֱלֹהִים עַל־דִּבְרַת שֶׁלֹּא יִמְצָא הָאָדָם אַחֲרָיו
טו מְאוּמָה: אֶת־הַכֹּל רָאִיתִי בִּימֵי הֶבְלִי יֵשׁ צַדִּיק אֹבֵד בְּצִדְקוֹ וְיֵשׁ רָשָׁע מַאֲרִיךְ
טז יז בְּרָעָתוֹ: אַל־תְּהִי צַדִּיק הַרְבֵּה וְאַל־תִּתְחַכַּם יוֹתֵר לָמָּה תִּשּׁוֹמֵם: אַל־תִּרְשַׁע
יח הַרְבֵּה וְאַל־תְּהִי סָכָל לָמָּה תָמוּת בְּלֹא עִתֶּךָ: טוֹב אֲשֶׁר תֶּאֱחֹז בָּזֶה וְגַם־מִזֶּה
יט אַל־תַּנַּח אֶת־יָדֶךָ כִּי־יְרֵא אֱלֹהִים יֵצֵא אֶת־כֻּלָּם: הַחָכְמָה תָּעֹז לֶחָכָם מֵעֲשָׂרָה
כ שַׁלִּיטִים אֲשֶׁר הָיוּ בָּעִיר: כִּי אָדָם אֵין צַדִּיק בָּאָרֶץ אֲשֶׁר יַעֲשֶׂה־טּוֹב וְלֹא יֶחֱטָא:
כא גַּם לְכָל־הַדְּבָרִים אֲשֶׁר יְדַבֵּרוּ אַל־תִּתֵּן לִבֶּךָ אֲשֶׁר לֹא־תִשְׁמַע אֶת־עַבְדְּךָ
כב כג מְקַלְלֶךָ: כִּי גַּם־פְּעָמִים רַבּוֹת יָדַע לִבֶּךָ אֲשֶׁר גַּם־אַתָּ קִלַּלְתָּ אֲחֵרִים: כָּל־זֹה
כד נִסִּיתִי בַחָכְמָה אָמַרְתִּי אֶחְכָּמָה וְהִיא רְחוֹקָה מִמֶּנִּי: רָחוֹק מַה־שֶּׁהָיָה וְעָמֹק ׀
כה עָמֹק מִי יִמְצָאֶנּוּ: סַבּוֹתִי אֲנִי וְלִבִּי לָדַעַת וְלָתוּר וּבַקֵּשׁ חָכְמָה וְחֶשְׁבּוֹן וְלָדַעַת
כו רֶשַׁע כֶּסֶל וְהַסִּכְלוּת הוֹלֵלוֹת: וּמוֹצֶא אֲנִי מַר מִמָּוֶת אֶת־הָאִשָּׁה אֲשֶׁר־הִיא
מְצוֹדִים וַחֲרָמִים לִבָּהּ אֲסוּרִים יָדֶיהָ טוֹב לִפְנֵי הָאֱלֹהִים יִמָּלֵט מִמֶּנָּה וְחוֹטֵא

DISCUSSION

7:19| **Ten rulers who were in a city:** Several allegorical interpretations have been suggested for this phrase, as referring to a person's character traits, inclinations, or limbs. Wisdom is a force that can help one master all these elements (see *Pesikta Zutreta*; *Nedarim* 32b; *Kohelet Rabba* 7:19).

27 **See, this I have found, says** the wisdom of[92] **Kohelet.** I have
examined the details of the world, **one by one, to find a
scheme,** to reach a kind of statistically valid conclusion:[93]
28 **That,** those matters, **which my soul sought further** in my sur-
vey, **I did not find; one** perfect **man out of one thousand I
have found, but a** perfect **woman among all these I did not
find.** This assertion might be an allusion to Solomon's thousand wives and concubines.[94]
29 I sought many conclusions but emerged empty-handed; what I
have discovered is unimportant in my eyes. **However, see, this**
is the only insight that **I have found** and which deserves attention: **God made man straight, but they,** men, **have sought
out many schemes,** distortions and tricks. I have learned that
the world's troubles are caused by humanity. Were it not for the
commercial activities, gambling, tricks, and schemes of people,
the world could be a far better place.[95]

Obedience, Justice, and the Joy of Life

ECCLESIASTES 8:1–17

This section begins with sayings praising wisdom and the maintenance of the ruling order. Later, Kohelet also directs his attention to the problematic side of human rule and the helplessness of one confronted with what he considers a deviation from justice. However, the absence of just retribution is explained here as a temporary state, stemming from the limited perspective of man and his short life span. Nevertheless, in light of this situation, the wise man recommends that man focus on the simple joy of life, which renders his hard labor pleasant and eases the frustration engendered by the insoluble questions.

8 1 **Who is like the wise man, and who knows the meaning of
a matter?** Nobody understands the meaning of matters in the
world like a wise man. **The wisdom of a man illuminates his
face, and** in his wisdom, **his arrogance**[96] **is ameliorated.** In
other words, wisdom influences his character traits.[97]
2 **I keep the king's directive, and** I also observe **the word of an
oath to God,** the oath I took to God.[98]
3 **Do not flee; leave his,** the king's, **presence;**[99] go wherever he
sends you. **Do not stay in a bad situation, as he will do what
he wills.** If you disobey the king, misfortune will befall you,
4 **since governance is by the king's word,** as it is the instrument
of his reign, **and who will say to him: What are you doing?**
No one can challenge the king's decisions, and all the more so
the deeds of God.[100]
5 **One who follows a command** of the king **will not know an
evil matter, and a wise man's heart will know the time and
judgment.** A wise man remembers that the day of reckoning
will ultimately arrive, and he obeys the law in the present with
the future judgment in mind.[101] Alternatively, a wise man knows
the right time and framework for everything.
6 **For there is a time and a judgment for every purpose, as
the evil of man overwhelms him.** Great wisdom is required
in order to identify what is right and what is correct in every
situation.
7 A person sins because he chooses to overlook the consequences
of his deeds, **for he does not know what will be** in the future,
for whatever it, the consequences of his actions, **will be, who
will have told him** now?
8 **There is no man who rules the spirit,** his own living spirit, **to
retain the spirit,** to prevent it departing from the body when
his time comes;[102] **and there is no ruling** by man **over the day,**
the timing, **of** his **death. There is no sending a proxy in war,**
one cannot transfer his fate to others,[103] **and maneuvering,**
extensive efforts[104] or the amassing of wealth,[105] **will not rescue
its owner** from death.
9 **All this I have seen and taken to my heart, for every action
that is performed under the sun: Whenever man controlled
man, it was to his detriment.** Man's rule over another is detri-
mental to both the ruler and the ruled.[106] There is a fundamental
problem with the very concept of government.

"Whenever man controlled man, it was to his detriment." Pharaoh beating an Asian tribe member, ivory label, Den's tomb, Abydos, Egypt, ca. 3000 BCE

10 **So,** in this light, **I saw the wicked** who are now **buried and
gone,** who have vanished; **they went from a holy place** and
performed wickedness at will, **but they were forgotten** even
in the city where they acted like that.[107] **This too,** the fact that
the wicked are forgotten, **is futility.**

כז כח יִלָּכֶד בָּהּ׃ רְאֵה זֶה מָצָאתִי אָמְרָה קֹהֶלֶת אַחַת לְאַחַת לִמְצֹא חֶשְׁבּוֹן׃ אֲשֶׁר
עוֹד־בִּקְשָׁה נַפְשִׁי וְלֹא מָצָאתִי אָדָם אֶחָד מֵאֶלֶף מָצָאתִי וְאִשָּׁה בְכָל־אֵלֶּה לֹא
כט מָצָאתִי׃ לְבַד רְאֵה־זֶה מָצָאתִי אֲשֶׁר עָשָׂה הָאֱלֹהִים אֶת־הָאָדָם יָשָׁר וְהֵמָּה
א בִקְשׁוּ חִשְּׁבֹנוֹת רַבִּים׃ מִי כְּהֶחָכָם וּמִי יוֹדֵעַ פֵּשֶׁר דָּבָר חָכְמַת אָדָם תָּאִיר פָּנָיו
ב ג וְעֹז פָּנָיו יְשֻׁנֶּא׃ אֲנִי פִּי־מֶלֶךְ שְׁמוֹר וְעַל דִּבְרַת שְׁבוּעַת אֱלֹהִים׃ אַל־תִּבָּהֵל
ד מִפָּנָיו תֵּלֵךְ אַל־תַּעֲמֹד בְּדָבָר רָע כִּי כָּל־אֲשֶׁר יַחְפֹּץ יַעֲשֶׂה׃ בַּאֲשֶׁר דְּבַר־מֶלֶךְ
ה שִׁלְטוֹן וּמִי יֹאמַר־לוֹ מַה־תַּעֲשֶׂה׃ שׁוֹמֵר מִצְוָה לֹא יֵדַע דָּבָר רָע וְעֵת וּמִשְׁפָּט
ו ז יֵדַע לֵב חָכָם׃ כִּי לְכָל־חֵפֶץ יֵשׁ עֵת וּמִשְׁפָּט כִּי־רָעַת הָאָדָם רַבָּה עָלָיו׃ כִּי־אֵינֶנּוּ
ח יֹדֵעַ מַה־שֶּׁיִּהְיֶה כִּי כַּאֲשֶׁר יִהְיֶה מִי יַגִּיד לוֹ׃ אֵין אָדָם שַׁלִּיט בָּרוּחַ לִכְלוֹא אֶת־
הָרוּחַ וְאֵין שִׁלְטוֹן בְּיוֹם הַמָּוֶת וְאֵין מִשְׁלַחַת בַּמִּלְחָמָה וְלֹא־יְמַלֵּט רֶשַׁע אֶת־
ט בְּעָלָיו׃ אֶת־כָּל־זֶה רָאִיתִי וְנָתוֹן אֶת־לִבִּי לְכָל־מַעֲשֶׂה אֲשֶׁר נַעֲשָׂה תַּחַת
י הַשָּׁמֶשׁ עֵת אֲשֶׁר שָׁלַט הָאָדָם בְּאָדָם לְרַע לוֹ׃ וּבְכֵן רָאִיתִי רְשָׁעִים קְבֻרִים וָבָאוּ
יא וּמִמְּקוֹם קָדוֹשׁ יְהַלֵּכוּ וְיִשְׁתַּכְּחוּ בָעִיר אֲשֶׁר כֵּן־עָשׂוּ גַּם־זֶה הָבֶל׃ אֲשֶׁר אֵין־
נַעֲשָׂה פִתְגָם מַעֲשֵׂה הָרָעָה מְהֵרָה עַל־כֵּן מָלֵא לֵב בְּנֵי־הָאָדָם בָּהֶם לַעֲשׂוֹת
יב רָע׃ אֲשֶׁר חֹטֶא עֹשֶׂה רָע מְאַת וּמַאֲרִיךְ לוֹ כִּי גַּם־יוֹדֵעַ אָנִי אֲשֶׁר יִהְיֶה־טּוֹב
יג לְיִרְאֵי הָאֱלֹהִים אֲשֶׁר יִירְאוּ מִלְּפָנָיו׃ וְטוֹב לֹא־יִהְיֶה לָרָשָׁע וְלֹא־יַאֲרִיךְ יָמִים
יד כַּצֵּל אֲשֶׁר אֵינֶנּוּ יָרֵא מִלִּפְנֵי אֱלֹהִים׃ יֶשׁ־הֶבֶל אֲשֶׁר נַעֲשָׂה עַל־הָאָרֶץ אֲשֶׁר ׀
יֵשׁ צַדִּיקִים אֲשֶׁר מַגִּיעַ אֲלֵהֶם כְּמַעֲשֵׂה הָרְשָׁעִים וְיֵשׁ רְשָׁעִים שֶׁמַּגִּיעַ אֲלֵהֶם

11 Because justice for an evil act is not executed swiftly, therefore, as retribution is not immediate,[108] **the heart of the sons of man dares to perform evil.** They repress their knowledge of the calamity that will befall them in the distant future.

12 So a sinner performs one hundred evils,[109] **and** yet **He,** God, **prolongs for him.** He does not punish him immediately, in accordance with his evil. **For I indeed know that it will be well for the fearers of God, who fear before Him.**

13 Good will not be for the wicked, and he will not prolong his days, which are fleeting **like a shadow, since he does not fear before God.**

14 After asserting that retribution will eventually arrive, Kohelet once again reverses course: **There is futility that is done on the earth,** in our world, **in that there are righteous who receive in accordance with the action of the wicked and there are wicked who receive in accordance with the action of the righteous,** and nevertheless people expect to see justice and fairness. **I said that this too is futility,** as it is clear that the world does not operate as people think it should.[110]

15 I therefore **praised** simple **joy, as there is nothing better for a man under the sun than to eat, drink, and rejoice. That** joy **will accompany him**[111] **in his toil during the days of his life that God has given him under the sun.**

16 I reached this conclusion **when I applied my heart to know wisdom and to see,** understand, **the affairs that are carried out upon the earth. As** I discovered, **both during the day and during the night, he,** the one occupied with such matters, **does not see sleep in his eyes.** He finds no rest.

17 **I saw all the work of God, as man is not able to discover,** comprehend, **the work that is performed under the sun. Although man toils to seek,** to understand the meaning of existence, **he will not find; even if a wise man wishes to know, he will not be able to discover** that meaning. I therefore recommend natural, unsophisticated joy. It is good for man when this type of joy accompanies him in his toil, renders his life pleasant, and soothes his soul.

Life in the Face of Death and Danger

ECCLESIASTES 9:1–12

Death is the ultimate fate of both the righteous and the wicked; it consumes everything. Even if it seems better to repress death and instead focus on life in the present with its simple pleasures, this guarantees nothing. The ravages of the future may surprise even talented people. Although wisdom has greater power to protect an individual or his environment than other talents, attributes, and possessions, society does not always value wisdom as it should.

9 1 **For all this,** the present reality, **I have taken to my heart,** as I wish **to clarify all this,** to examine what is true, good, and important and what is false, evil, and inconsequential. I discovered **that the righteous, the wise, and their acolytes,**[112] or their deeds,[113] **are in the hand of God. Both love and hatred, man does not know.** People are not even fully aware of their own feelings, and this prevents them from finding their way in the world. **Everything is** potentially **before them.** All kinds of events over which they have no control can happen to them.

2 **Everything is as it is for everyone.** Anything can happen to any individual.[114] **There is one fate for the righteous and for the wicked, for the good, for the pure and for the impure, for one who sacrifices** offerings **and for one who does not sacrifice; like the good, so is the sinner; one who takes oaths,** and who therefore might occasionally take a false oath, **is like one who is leery of** taking **an oath.**

3 **This is evil among everything that is performed under the sun: That there is one fate for all,** the wicked and the righteous alike. The human eye cannot discern the link between people's deeds and the events of their lives, all their successes and failures, which is one reason man feels that life is meaningless. **Also,** due to the fact that people do not see any necessary connection between actions and consequences, **the heart of the son of man is full of evil, and debauchery** and drunkenness **is in their heart during their lives. And afterward, it,** the heart,[115] **is destined only to join the dead.**[116]

4 **For** only **whoever is joined to any of the** forms of the **living has hope; for** example, **a living dog is better than a dead lion.** Life, no matter how lowly, is better than death.[117]

5 **For** only **the living know** for a certainty **that they will die; but the dead do not know anything, and** what is more, **they no longer have a reward, as their memory is forgotten.**

6 **Even their love, even their hatred, and even their envy have already perished,** vanished and dissipated after their death; **they will never again have a portion in anything that is performed under the sun.** There is no trace of their history, exploits, and adventures in this world. The confidence gained in that very knowledge, slight or troubling though it may be, renders conscious, living people superior to the dead, who have no knowledge at all.

7 In conclusion, **go, eat your bread with joy, and drink your wine with a good heart.** Find satisfaction in your simple life, and avoid the upheavals of emotions like envy, animosity, and lust, **as** this lifestyle of simple joy will enable you to know that **God has already accepted your actions.**[118]

8 **At all times, may your garments be white.** Wear pleasant, simple, and clean clothes. **And may the oil on your head not be lacking.**[B] Anoint your hair with oil and thereby groom it.

9 **Appreciate life with a woman whom you love all the days of your futile life, which He has given you under the sun, all the days of your futility.** Even if you are not wise, and your life is meaningless, you should still find a way to enjoy your futile existence, **as that is your portion in life and in your toil that you toil under the sun.** This is your fate; be happy with it. Even if your life has no meaning to you, at least take comfort in a reasonable and unpretentious life.

10 **Everything that you are capable of doing with your strength,** whatever you are capable of doing, you should **do,** here and now, **as there is no action, scheme, knowledge, or wisdom in the grave where you are going.** After death, you cannot perform any more deeds,, and considerations of all kinds disappear. Therefore, it is advisable to live a life of comfort, and enjoy a happy marriage, while working in accordance with the possibilities open before you.

טו כְּמַעֲשֵׂה הַצַּדִּיקִים אָמַרְתִּי שֶׁגַּם־זֶה הָבֶל׃ וְשִׁבַּחְתִּי אֲנִי אֶת־הַשִּׂמְחָה אֲשֶׁר
אֵין־טוֹב לָאָדָם תַּחַת הַשֶּׁמֶשׁ כִּי אִם־לֶאֱכֹל וְלִשְׁתּוֹת וְלִשְׂמוֹחַ וְהוּא יִלְוֶנּוּ
טז בַעֲמָלוֹ יְמֵי חַיָּיו אֲשֶׁר־נָתַן־לוֹ הָאֱלֹהִים תַּחַת הַשָּׁמֶשׁ׃ כַּאֲשֶׁר נָתַתִּי אֶת־לִבִּי
לָדַעַת חָכְמָה וְלִרְאוֹת אֶת־הָעִנְיָן אֲשֶׁר נַעֲשָׂה עַל־הָאָרֶץ כִּי גַם בַּיּוֹם וּבַלַּיְלָה
יז שֵׁנָה בְּעֵינָיו אֵינֶנּוּ רֹאֶה׃ וְרָאִיתִי אֶת־כָּל־מַעֲשֵׂה הָאֱלֹהִים כִּי לֹא יוּכַל הָאָדָם
לִמְצוֹא אֶת־הַמַּעֲשֶׂה אֲשֶׁר נַעֲשָׂה תַחַת־הַשֶּׁמֶשׁ בְּשֶׁל אֲשֶׁר יַעֲמֹל הָאָדָם לְבַקֵּשׁ
א וְלֹא יִמְצָא וְגַם אִם־יֹאמַר הֶחָכָם לָדַעַת לֹא יוּכַל לִמְצֹא׃ כִּי אֶת־כָּל־זֶה נָתַתִּי
אֶל־לִבִּי וְלָבוּר אֶת־כָּל־זֶה אֲשֶׁר הַצַּדִּיקִים וְהַחֲכָמִים וַעֲבָדֵיהֶם בְּיַד הָאֱלֹהִים
ב גַּם־אַהֲבָה גַם־שִׂנְאָה אֵין יוֹדֵעַ הָאָדָם הַכֹּל לִפְנֵיהֶם׃ הַכֹּל כַּאֲשֶׁר לַכֹּל מִקְרֶה
אֶחָד לַצַּדִּיק וְלָרָשָׁע לַטּוֹב וְלַטָּהוֹר וְלַטָּמֵא וְלַזֹּבֵחַ וְלַאֲשֶׁר אֵינֶנּוּ זֹבֵחַ כַּטּוֹב
ג כַּחֹטֶא הַנִּשְׁבָּע כַּאֲשֶׁר שְׁבוּעָה יָרֵא׃ זֶה ׀ רָע בְּכֹל אֲשֶׁר־נַעֲשָׂה תַּחַת הַשֶּׁמֶשׁ
כִּי־מִקְרֶה אֶחָד לַכֹּל וְגַם לֵב בְּנֵי־הָאָדָם מָלֵא־רָע וְהוֹלֵלוֹת בִּלְבָבָם בְּחַיֵּיהֶם
ד וְאַחֲרָיו אֶל־הַמֵּתִים׃ כִּי־מִי אֲשֶׁר יבחר אֶל כָּל־הַחַיִּים יֵשׁ בִּטָּחוֹן כִּי־לְכֶלֶב חַי יְחֻבַּר
ה הוּא טוֹב מִן־הָאַרְיֵה הַמֵּת׃ כִּי הַחַיִּים יוֹדְעִים שֶׁיָּמֻתוּ וְהַמֵּתִים אֵינָם יוֹדְעִים
ו מְאוּמָה וְאֵין־עוֹד לָהֶם שָׂכָר כִּי נִשְׁכַּח זִכְרָם׃ גַּם אַהֲבָתָם גַּם־שִׂנְאָתָם גַּם־
קִנְאָתָם כְּבָר אָבָדָה וְחֵלֶק אֵין־לָהֶם עוֹד לְעוֹלָם בְּכֹל אֲשֶׁר־נַעֲשָׂה תַּחַת הַשָּׁמֶשׁ׃
ז לֵךְ אֱכֹל בְּשִׂמְחָה לַחְמֶךָ וּשְׁתֵה בְלֶב־טוֹב יֵינֶךָ כִּי כְבָר רָצָה הָאֱלֹהִים אֶת־ ד
ח ט מַעֲשֶׂיךָ׃ בְּכָל־עֵת יִהְיוּ בְגָדֶיךָ לְבָנִים וְשֶׁמֶן עַל־רֹאשְׁךָ אַל־יֶחְסָר׃ רְאֵה חַיִּים
עִם־אִשָּׁה אֲשֶׁר־אָהַבְתָּ כָּל־יְמֵי חַיֵּי הֶבְלֶךָ אֲשֶׁר נָתַן־לְךָ תַּחַת הַשֶּׁמֶשׁ כֹּל יְמֵי
י הֶבְלֶךָ כִּי הוּא חֶלְקְךָ בַּחַיִּים וּבַעֲמָלְךָ אֲשֶׁר־אַתָּה עָמֵל תַּחַת הַשָּׁמֶשׁ׃ כֹּל אֲשֶׁר
תִּמְצָא יָדְךָ לַעֲשׂוֹת בְּכֹחֲךָ עֲשֵׂה כִּי אֵין מַעֲשֶׂה וְחֶשְׁבּוֹן וְדַעַת וְחָכְמָה בִּשְׁאוֹל

BACKGROUND

9:8| **And may the oil on your head not be lacking:** In ancient times people would rub their heads with oil for hygienic purposes, in order to clean the head from parasites, such as lice. Certain oils repel nits and enable their quick removal with a comb. Applying oil to one's head and face was also an expression of goodwill, decency, and respect. Accordingly, kings and priests were typically anointed with oil.

11 Yet **I again saw under the sun** that even for one who lives a
simple life there is no guarantee of security and calm. I saw **that**
winning **the race is not** guaranteed **to the swift,** as one who
runs fast is not always able to escape or apprehend what he pur-
sues, **and** triumph in **the war is not** assured **to the valiant; also**
not to the wise is bread, a livelihood, guaranteed, **and also**
not to the clever is wealth, and also not to the knowledge-
able is favor. Although wisdom and knowledge are generally
beneficial, they are not always appreciated by others. **Rather,**
time and chance befalls all of them. The life of any one of
these talented people is liable to be destroyed.[119]
12 **For man also does not know his time,** the future that awaits
him. He does not know when he will experience failure and
from where it will come. Just **like the fish that are trapped,**
suffering, **in an evil net, and like the birds that are trapped**
in the snare, so are the sons of man snared at an evil time,
when it falls upon them suddenly. People can likewise find
themselves suddenly in a trap from which they cannot escape.
Even one who focuses on the present and represses all troubling
thoughts of death, while depending on his inherent or acquired
virtues, is not protected from life's trials and tribulations.

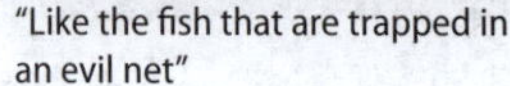

"Like the fish that are trapped in an evil net"

"Like the birds that are trapped in the snare"

Wisdom, Folly, and Their Consequences

ECCLESIASTES 9:13–10:20

In this section, Kohelet levels sharp criticism at a society that lacks proper esteem for wisdom. Alongside his discussion of the relationship between wisdom and folly, Kohelet addresses several related issues: speech in general, the respective statements of the wise man and the fool, the relationship between efforts and their consequences, and the power of money. Kohelet also dispenses various bits of practical advice.

13 **This** phenomenon **too I have I seen under the sun as wis-**
dom, and it is great to me:
14 **There was a small city, but**
few men in it, and a great
king came against it, and
surrounded it, and built
great siege works against
it,[B] ready to attack.
15 In this situation, it might
seem that the city has no
chance. But **a poor,**[120] or
wretched, **and wise man was**
found in it, and he saved
the city in his wisdom, but
after a while **nobody re-**
membered that poor man.[D] The leaders of the city took all the
credit and praise for themselves, and everyone forgot the poor
but wise man.

"And surrounded it, and built great siege works against it." City besieged with a battering ram on a siege ramp, relief, Nimrud, Iraq, 728 BCE

16 **I said** in conclusion that **wisdom is** still **better than courage,**
even **though the wisdom of the poor man is scorned, and**
his words are not heard, accepted and remembered, and his
deserved fame is taken by others.
17 Nevertheless, in other circumstances a wise man is accorded
recognition and people listen to him, thanks to his manner
of speech:[121] **The words of the wise, softly spoken, are bet-**
ter heard than the crying out of a ruler of fools. One who
imposes authority over fools often has to raise his voice, but
they take no notice of him
anyway.
18 Therefore, **wisdom is** ultimately **better than weapons**
of battle, and still, it does
not guarantee the wise man's
fate, as **one sinner** who fails
to recognize the benefit that
the wise man provides **de-**
stroys much good, since he causes it to be forgotten.
Alternatively, wisdom is better than weapons of war, and yet it
does not ensure military success, as even if the army follows the
wise man's advice, a single traitor can ruin the entire strategy.

"Weapons of battle." Assyrian army

10 1 Similarly,[122] **flies of death,** dead flies, or flies that accompany
rot, **putrefy and froth**[123] **the perfumed oil,**[B] an expensive fragrance oil. Although flies are
tiny insects, a single one can
impair the odor of a lot of
perfume. Likewise, **a little**
folly is weightier than wis-
dom, than honor. A small
measure of foolishness is sufficient to spoil a delicate and
refined environment. This is
similar to the statement of
the previous verse: One sinner is enough to spoil the works of
the wise man.[124]

"Flies of death putrefy and froth the perfumed oil"

יא אֲשֶׁר אַתָּה הֹלֵךְ שָׁמָּה׃ שַׁבְתִּי וְרָאֹה תַחַת־הַשֶּׁמֶשׁ כִּי לֹא֩ לַקַּלִּים הַמֵּרוֹץ וְלֹא

לַגִּבּוֹרִים הַמִּלְחָמָה וְ֠גַם לֹא לַחֲכָמִים לֶחֶם וְ֠גַם לֹא לַנְּבֹנִים עֹשֶׁר וְגַם לֹא לַיֹּדְעִים

יב חֵן כִּי־עֵת וָפֶגַע יִקְרֶה אֶת־כֻּלָּם׃ כִּ֡י גַּם֩ לֹא־יֵדַע הָאָדָם אֶת־עִתּוֹ כַּדָּגִים֙ שֶׁנֶּאֱחָזִים֙

בִּמְצוֹדָה רָעָה וְכַצִּפֳּרִים הָאֲחֻזוֹת בַּפָּח כָּהֵם יוּקָשִׁים֙ בְּנֵי הָאָדָם לְעֵת רָעָה

יג כְּשֶׁתִּפּוֹל עֲלֵיהֶם פִּתְאֹם׃ גַּם־זֹה רָאִיתִי חָכְמָה תַּחַת הַשָּׁמֶשׁ וּגְדוֹלָה הִיא אֵלָי׃

יד עִיר קְטַנָּה וַאֲנָשִׁים בָּהּ מְעָט וּבָא־אֵלֶיהָ מֶלֶךְ גָּדוֹל֙ וְסָבַב אֹתָהּ וּבָנָה עָלֶיהָ

טו מְצוֹדִים גְּדֹלִים׃ וּמָצָא בָהּ אִישׁ מִסְכֵּן חָכָם וּמִלַּט־הוּא אֶת־הָעִיר בְּחָכְמָתוֹ

טז וְאָדָם֙ לֹא זָכַר אֶת־הָאִישׁ הַמִּסְכֵּן הַהוּא׃ וְאָמַרְתִּי אָנִי טוֹבָה חָכְמָה מִגְּבוּרָה

יז וְחָכְמַת הַמִּסְכֵּן֙ בְּזוּיָה וּדְבָרָיו אֵינָם נִשְׁמָעִים׃ דִּבְרֵי חֲכָמִים בְּנַחַת נִשְׁמָעִים

יח מִזַּעֲקַת מוֹשֵׁל בַּכְּסִילִים׃ טוֹבָה חָכְמָה מִכְּלֵי קְרָב וְחוֹטֶא אֶחָד יְאַבֵּד טוֹבָה

א הַרְבֵּה׃ זְבוּבֵי מָוֶת יַבְאִישׁ יַבִּיעַ שֶׁמֶן רוֹקֵחַ יָקָר מֵחָכְמָה מִכָּבוֹד סִכְלוּת מְעָט׃

ב ג לֵב חָכָם֙ לִימִינוֹ וְלֵב כְּסִיל לִשְׂמֹאלוֹ׃ וְגַם־בַּדֶּרֶךְ כשהסכל הֹלֵךְ לִבּוֹ חָסֵר וְאָמַר כְּשֶׁסָּכָל

2 The heart of the wise inclines to his right, to his benefit, **and the heart of a fool inclines to his left,** the wrong side.[125]

3 Even while the fool walks on the way, his heart is lacking and says to everyone that he is a fool. His manner of walking and talking, and his behavior in general, attest to his foolishness.[126]

BACKGROUND

9:14| **And surrounded it, and built great siege works against it:** The laying of a siege has been a common war tactic throughout history. In order to subdue an enemy city or military camp, an army will surround it and prevent all access to and from the place. Historically, the army would often construct a dike, a wall surrounding the city that blocked all entrances. Sometimes fortifications were built around the besieged city to allow control of the access roads.

10:1| **Flies of death putrefy and froth the perfumed oil:** Drosophilidae are a family of flies that feed on liquids that emerge from fruits, some of which were used in ancient times to produce perfume. These flies spoil the fruit or their juices, causing them to sour or ferment, and their fine odor dissipates. These flies can be found all over the world. Even in ancient times, vessels containing perfumes would be tightly sealed in order to prevent both their evaporation and contact with flies or their larva. The term *zevuvei mavet*, flies of death, possibly stems from the fact that they hover over corpses in a manner similar to larger flies.

DISCUSSION

9:14–15| **There was a small city.... Nobody remembered that poor man:** The Sages interpret this story as a parable about man's situation in general: He is attacked by a great king, which is his evil inclination. The poor and wise man is one's good inclination, which saves him by encouraging repentance and good deeds, but when the evil inclination reigns, the individual fails to remember the good inclination (see Ralbag; *Nedarim* 32b; see also *Tanya, Likkutei Amarim* 9–17).

4 Kohelet offers a word to the wise: **If the spirit of the ruler shall be raised against you,** and he is angry with you, **do not abandon your place.** Stay put and do not depart from his presence because of his rebuke or in a state of shame, **for in its abating he will allow great sins.** Even great offenses can be forgiven over time, when the ruler's anger is assuaged, but if you abandon your position in embarrassment, you might lose everything.[127]

5 **There is an evil that I have seen under the sun, like an error that emerges from before the ruler.** One of the great evils in the world is the mistake of one in a position of power. When a person of authority errs, the harm that he is liable to cause is more severe than that of a commoner. Corruption and injustice inevitably follow:

6 Sometimes **folly is set on lofty heights,** as incompetent people can rise to prominence, **and** meanwhile **the wealthy** in spirit[128] **sit in lowliness.**

7 **I have seen servants** conducting themselves like masters, riding **upon horses, and princes walking on the ground like servants.**

8 Some people fail specifically due to their own actions, and against their best intentions:[129] **One who digs a pit, into it he will fall; and one who breaches a fence, a serpent,** hiding in the cracks between the stones of the fence, **will bite him.**[B]

Water pit, Tel Arad, early Bronze Age

9 It is never clear whether labor will yield a commensurate reward, as **one who transports stones** for a constructive purpose will not always achieve his objective, while he **will** certainly **be distressed by them,** as pain and suffering inevitably result from that grueling activity. **And** similarly, **one who splits wood will be endangered by them.**[130] He might be cut or wounded by the wood chips. Alternatively, his body may overheat from the hard labor.[131]

10 **If the iron** of an ax, or any other cutting tool, **is blunt, and one did not whet the edge** of the blade, even if **he intensifies his exertion** it will be to no avail. In that instance, **the advantage is in preparation with wisdom.** Wisdom is advantageous with respect to physical labor, as it enables one to prepare in advance and thus achieve one's objective with minimal effort.[132]

11 **If the serpent bites without a spell,**[D] since the charmer could not control it, **there is no advantage to the charmer [*ba'al halashon*].**[133] Alternatively, the term *ba'al halashon* refers to a person who speaks evil, likening him to a serpent that bites: Just as there are snakebites that no spell can heal, so too one who speaks evil can cause irrevocable harm.[134]

12 In contrast to one who speaks evil,[135] **the words of the mouth of a wise man are grace, but the lips of a fool,** his ill-advised comments, **will destroy him,** lead to his ruin, or cause him to lose the respect of others.

13 **The beginning of the words from his mouth is foolishness, and the end from his mouth is evil debauchery.** His statements are initially merely silly, but ultimately they will lead to insanity.

14 Unlike a wise person, who remains mostly quiet, mindful that silence is a safeguard for wisdom,[136] **the fool will proliferate words.** In his many comments he presumes to be able to foresee the future, but **man knows not what will be, and that which will be after him, who can tell him?**

15 **The toil of the fools will exhaust him, as he will not know how to go to a city.** Since a fool does not know how to reach his objective, he soon becomes weary and wastes his energy for nothing.[137]

16 One's wisdom or foolishness is manifest in his conduct. **Woe is you, land, that your king is a boy,** young and inexperienced, and ruins the land with his vanities, **and your princes dine in the morning,** instead of working on behalf of the country.

17 **Happy are you, land, that your king is a free man,** or the son of an esteemed family, a distinguished individual,[138] **and your princes dine at the proper time,** not immediately upon waking, but at the appropriate time, in accordance with the tasks ahead. If so, they will eat **in valor,** enough for them to be healthy and strong, **and not in drunkenness.**[139]

18 **With laziness,** due to idleness, **the ceiling sags,**[B] the roof collapses. When a roof is not properly maintained, it sags and may eventually collapse. **And with idleness of the hands, the house leaks.** Neglect of a house will lead to a leaky roof.

19 Kohelet lists the power of money alongside the value of wisdom and diligence: **For laughter,** entertainment, **one prepares bread,** a feast, and **wine cheers the living, and money answers everything,** provides a solution for all problems.

20 **Even in your thought do not curse a king,**[140] **and** even when you are alone **in your bedrooms do not curse the rich, as a bird of the heavens will carry the voice, and a winged creature will tell a matter.** Any spoken words will eventually become public, as even if they are not spread by people, they will be disseminated by birds or other airy, imperceptible airborne mediums.[141] Therefore, one must be careful even with regard to his thoughts, and all the more so with regard to his spoken words, which are liable to cause the speaker great trouble.

ד לַכֹּל סָכָל הוּא: אִם־רוּחַ הַמּוֹשֵׁל תַּעֲלֶה עָלֶיךָ מְקוֹמְךָ אַל־תַּנַּח כִּי מַרְפֵּא יַנִּיחַ
ה חֲטָאִים גְּדוֹלִים: יֵשׁ רָעָה רָאִיתִי תַּחַת הַשָּׁמֶשׁ כִּשְׁגָגָה שֶׁיֹּצָא מִלִּפְנֵי הַשַּׁלִּיט:
ו ז נִתַּן הַסֶּכֶל בַּמְּרוֹמִים רַבִּים וַעֲשִׁירִים בַּשֵּׁפֶל יֵשֵׁבוּ: רָאִיתִי עֲבָדִים עַל־סוּסִים
ח וְשָׂרִים הֹלְכִים כַּעֲבָדִים עַל־הָאָרֶץ: חֹפֵר גּוּמָּץ בּוֹ יִפּוֹל וּפֹרֵץ גָּדֵר יִשְּׁכֶנּוּ נָחָשׁ:
ט י מַסִּיעַ אֲבָנִים יֵעָצֵב בָּהֶם בּוֹקֵעַ עֵצִים יִסָּכֶן בָּם: אִם־קֵהָה הַבַּרְזֶל וְהוּא לֹא־פָנִים
יא קִלְקַל וַחֲיָלִים יְגַבֵּר וְיִתְרוֹן הַכְשֵׁיר חָכְמָה: אִם־יִשֹּׁךְ הַנָּחָשׁ בְּלוֹא־לָחַשׁ וְאֵין
יב יג יִתְרוֹן לְבַעַל הַלָּשׁוֹן: דִּבְרֵי פִי־חָכָם חֵן וְשִׂפְתוֹת כְּסִיל תְּבַלְּעֶנּוּ: תְּחִלַּת דִּבְרֵי־
יד פִיהוּ סִכְלוּת וְאַחֲרִית פִּיהוּ הוֹלֵלוּת רָעָה: וְהַסָּכָל יַרְבֶּה דְבָרִים לֹא־יֵדַע הָאָדָם
טו מַה־שֶׁיִּהְיֶה וַאֲשֶׁר יִהְיֶה מֵאַחֲרָיו מִי יַגִּיד לוֹ: עֲמַל הַכְּסִילִים תְּיַגְּעֶנּוּ אֲשֶׁר לֹא־
טז יז יָדַע לָלֶכֶת אֶל־עִיר: אִי־לָךְ אֶרֶץ שֶׁמַּלְכֵּךְ נָעַר וְשָׂרַיִךְ בַּבֹּקֶר יֹאכֵלוּ: אַשְׁרֵיךְ
יח אֶרֶץ שֶׁמַּלְכֵּךְ בֶּן־חוֹרִים וְשָׂרַיִךְ בָּעֵת יֹאכֵלוּ בִּגְבוּרָה וְלֹא בַשְּׁתִי: בַּעֲצַלְתַּיִם
יט יִמַּךְ הַמְּקָרֶה וּבְשִׁפְלוּת יָדַיִם יִדְלֹף הַבָּיִת: לִשְׂחוֹק עֹשִׂים לֶחֶם וְיַיִן יְשַׂמַּח חַיִּים
כ וְהַכֶּסֶף יַעֲנֶה אֶת־הַכֹּל: גַּם בְּמַדָּעֲךָ מֶלֶךְ אַל־תְּקַלֵּל וּבְחַדְרֵי מִשְׁכָּבְךָ אַל־תְּקַלֵּל

BACKGROUND

10:8 | **And one who breaches a fence, a serpent will bite him:** It was the practice to place dry construction between the boundaries of fields, e.g., stones without cement, as terraces of sorts. Various insects, lizards, and snakes would hide between the cracks and gaps of such fences. During the winter, snakes seek to slow their metabolism and enter a state of sluggishness similar to hibernation. The demolition of a fence in which a snake is hidden can provoke a defensive response from the creature, which might include biting the purported assailant, the one breaching the fence.

10:18 | **With laziness, the ceiling sags:** The roofs of houses in the ancient Land of Israel rested on wooden beams. For a reasonably sized house, the beams would consist of several sections. Therefore, regular inspection and reinforcement of the beams were essential for maintenance of structural integrity. If the beams were neglected, they could bend and break under the weight of the roof. Eventually, the roof was liable to collapse on the occupants of the house.

DISCUSSION

10:11 | **If the serpent bites without a spell:** Alternatively, this phrase means: If the serpent bites before it hisses. The hissing of a snake can result from the exhalation of air or the friction of its scales as it moves. These sounds alert those in proximity to the snake.

Dealing with the Future

ECCLESIASTES 11:1–12:8

This section begins with a series of statements addressing the manner in which people cope with their inability to know the future. Subsequently, Kohelet recommends that a person enjoy life while still young, but he also mentions that in old age there will be no recourse for a person to be taken to account for those uninhibited pleasures.

The section ends with a gradual and harsh description of old age, when God exacts a price for the desire of a person's childhood and the lust of his youth, in which he freely indulged. Through poetic, powerful images, Kohelet depicts the decline of the human body. His description of old age and inevitable death brings Kohelet back to his opening statement with regard to the futility of the world.

11 1 **Cast your bread upon the water,** perform acts of kindness and virtue, even if you receive no immediate remuneration, **for after many days,** at the appropriate time, **you will find it,** your reward.[142]

2 **Distribute a portion to seven, and even to eight;** divide your resources, **as you do not know what evil will be upon the earth,** and which of your possessions, or your land, will be harmed.

3 **If the clouds are filled with rain, they will** certainly **empty onto the earth,** but one cannot know where exactly the rain will fall. In contrast, **if a tree falls in the south or in the north, the place where the tree falls, there it will be.**[143] There are some occurrences whose consequences are predictable in all their details, whereas others are beyond man's grasp.

"If the clouds are filled with rain"

"The place where the tree falls, there it will be"

4 In these ambiguous conditions, the search for certainty and control can lead to paralysis: **One who awaits the wind,** postponing sowing his field until it calms, as it is difficult to sow in a strong wind, **will not** ever **sow, and** likewise, **one who gazes at the clouds,** calculating his steps to schedule his harvest at a time when he can be certain that it will not rain,[144] **will not** ever **reap.** One should act even when conditions are not ideal rather than endlessly delaying.

5 **Just as you do not know the conduct of the wind,** or one's inspiration or will power, **or**[145] **how the fetuses grow in a womb of the pregnant,** as the limbs of the fetus are hidden from the eye,[146] **so you will not know the work of God who does everything.**

6 Therefore, **in the morning sow your seed, and in the evening do not rest your hand.**[D] Do not be lazy, but rather sow again in the evening, even if you already sowed in the morning, **as you do not know which will succeed, this or that, or whether they both alike will be good.**

"Sow your seed"

"Do not rest your hand." Pioneer tossing seeds in a field, Kibbutz Rudgas, Petah Tikva, 1930–36

7 After recommending that one act even in conditions of uncertainty, Kohelet stresses that one should also enjoy the brightness of the world: **The light is sweet, and it is good for the eyes to see the sun.**[B]

8 **For if a man lives many years, let him rejoice in all of them, and** still, **let him remember the days of darkness,** old age, death, and bad times in general, **as they will be many.** He should remember that **everything that is coming is futility.**

9 Likewise, **rejoice, young man, in your childhood. Let your heart cheer you in the days of your youth. Follow the ways of your heart and the sight of your eyes, but** along with your enjoyment of the vast theater of action presented to you in your youth, **know that for all these, God will bring you to judgment.** The suggestion that you should do as you please is limited, as you cannot escape future judgment for your current choices.[147]

10 Therefore, despite the recommendation that one should do as he wishes, **remove anger from your heart,** thereby **purging evil from your flesh, as childhood and youth are futility.** The pleasures of youth will lose all meaning when you reflect upon them from a mature perspective and assess their consequences.

12 1 **Remember your Creator** even **in the days of your youth, before the evil days come, and the years arrive when you will say: I have no desire in them.** The evil days mentioned here do not necessarily feature devastating external events; rather, the verse is referring to a period when you will no longer be able to do as you wish, the period of old age.[148]

2 The following description of old age is detailed and poetic, with numerous images designed to arouse terror of this period

עָשִׁיר כִּי עוֹף הַשָּׁמַיִם יוֹלִיךְ אֶת־הַקּוֹל וּבַעַל הכנפים יַגִּיד דָּבָר: שַׁלַּח לַחְמְךָ כְּנָפַיִם
א עַל־פְּנֵי הַמָּיִם כִּי־בְרֹב הַיָּמִים תִּמְצָאֶנּוּ: תֶּן־חֵלֶק לְשִׁבְעָה וְגַם לִשְׁמוֹנָה כִּי לֹא
ב תֵדַע מַה־יִּהְיֶה רָעָה עַל־הָאָרֶץ: אִם־יִמָּלְאוּ הֶעָבִים גֶּשֶׁם עַל־הָאָרֶץ יָרִיקוּ
ג וְאִם־יִפּוֹל עֵץ בַּדָּרוֹם וְאִם בַּצָּפוֹן מְקוֹם שֶׁיִּפּוֹל הָעֵץ שָׁם יְהוּא: שֹׁמֵר רוּחַ לֹא
ד יִזְרָע וְרֹאֶה בֶעָבִים לֹא יִקְצוֹר: כַּאֲשֶׁר אֵינְךָ יוֹדֵעַ מַה־דֶּרֶךְ הָרוּחַ כַּעֲצָמִים בְּבֶטֶן
ה הַמְּלֵאָה כָּכָה לֹא תֵדַע אֶת־מַעֲשֵׂה הָאֱלֹהִים אֲשֶׁר יַעֲשֶׂה אֶת־הַכֹּל: בַּבֹּקֶר זְרַע
ו אֶת־זַרְעֶךָ וְלָעֶרֶב אַל־תַּנַּח יָדֶךָ כִּי אֵינְךָ יוֹדֵעַ אֵי זֶה יִכְשַׁר הֲזֶה אוֹ־זֶה וְאִם־
ז ח שְׁנֵיהֶם כְּאֶחָד טוֹבִים: וּמָתוֹק הָאוֹר וְטוֹב לַעֵינַיִם לִרְאוֹת אֶת־הַשָּׁמֶשׁ: כִּי
אִם־שָׁנִים הַרְבֵּה יִחְיֶה הָאָדָם בְּכֻלָּם יִשְׂמָח וְיִזְכֹּר אֶת־יְמֵי הַחֹשֶׁךְ כִּי־הַרְבֵּה יִהְיוּ
ט כָּל־שֶׁבָּא הָבֶל: שְׂמַח בָּחוּר בְּיַלְדוּתֶךָ וִיטִיבְךָ לִבְּךָ בִּימֵי בְחוּרוֹתֶךָ וְהַלֵּךְ בְּדַרְכֵי
י לִבְּךָ ובמראי עֵינֶיךָ וְדָע כִּי עַל־כָּל־אֵלֶּה יְבִיאֲךָ הָאֱלֹהִים בַּמִּשְׁפָּט: וְהָסֵר כַּעַס וּבְמַרְאֵה
א מִלִּבֶּךָ וְהַעֲבֵר רָעָה מִבְּשָׂרֶךָ כִּי־הַיַּלְדוּת וְהַשַּׁחֲרוּת הָבֶל: וּזְכֹר אֶת־בּוֹרְאֶיךָ
בִּימֵי בְּחוּרֹתֶיךָ עַד אֲשֶׁר לֹא־יָבֹאוּ יְמֵי הָרָעָה וְהִגִּיעוּ שָׁנִים אֲשֶׁר תֹּאמַר אֵין־לִי
ב בָהֶם חֵפֶץ: עַד אֲשֶׁר לֹא־תֶחְשַׁךְ הַשֶּׁמֶשׁ וְהָאוֹר וְהַיָּרֵחַ וְהַכּוֹכָבִים וְשָׁבוּ הֶעָבִים

BACKGROUND

11:7| **The light is sweet, and it is good for the eyes to see the sun:** When the eyes absorb sunlight, they signal to the pineal gland in the brain to delay the secretion of melatonin. This hormone causes fatigue, drowsiness, and sleep. Melatonin is an important component of the biological clock, because its secretion induces sleep, whereas its reduction or absence enables one to stay alert.

DISCUSSION

11:6| **In the morning sow your seed, and in the evening do not rest your hand:** The Sages apply this proverb to having children. They state that if one is capable of fathering children in his old age, he should do so, since there is no way of knowing what will become of his offspring, which of them will be righteous (*Yevamot* 62b).

of human life: **Before the sun, the light, the moon, and the stars darken,**[B] since an aging person, whose eyesight is dimming, feels as though the sun does not shine as brightly as it did during his youth, and that the moon and stars are dull, **and** as though **the clouds return** to cast shade,[149] darkening the sunlight, even **after the rain** has stopped;

3 **on the day that the guards of the house tremble,** the hands shake and malfunction, **and the infantry men**[150] **are distorted, and the grinders,** the teeth,[151] **cease because they have dwindled,** as most of them have fallen out, **and it is dark for the gazers,** the eyes, **through the windows,** as their vision is impaired;[152]

4 **and the doors to the street are shut,** as the elderly person feels as though the gates of the marketplace are locked to him,[153] **with the fading of the noise of the mill,** since he is no longer active in the world, or because he does not eat much and he sees no reason to run to the marketplace, or alternatively, the doors to the street are the person's orifices,[154] or his lips,[155] and in that case, the grinders (verse 3) refer to the digestive organs; **and one,** the aging person, **arises,** wakes up, even **at the sound of the bird,** as his sleep is not deep, and he has trouble going back to sleep after he has woken up, and **yet,** although he awakens even at the sound of a bird,[156] **all the sources of music are muted,** as he cannot hear music clearly, either because he is hard of hearing, or because he no longer has any interest in listening to music,[157] or, alternatively, the voice of the old person itself is muted, because he is no longer capable of singing loudly;[158]

5 **when they,** the elderly, **will also be fearful of heights** and look for ways to circumvent any hill or mound,[159] **and obstacles will be on the way.** When they were young, they did not even notice obstacles in the road but simply passed over them; however, in old age, when every step requires effort, it becomes clear that the road is not smooth. **The almond tree will blossom,** certain bones begin to bulge,[160] **but the grasshopper will be burdened,** other parts of the body grow heavy and feel like a burden,[161] and **the caper berry will fail,** sexual desire wanes and disappears.[162] **For the man goes to his eternal home,** his death, **and the mourners will circle in the street.**[B] These are the people who announce a death and conduct a public eulogy.

6 **Before the silver cord,** human will and strength to live, **is severed,**[163] **and the golden skull is shattered, and the pitcher is broken at the spring,** an allusion to the stomach, which holds food as a spring holds water,[164] **and the wheel** used for drawing water **is smashed into the cistern** and the body falls into the grave,[165]

Wheel for drawing water from a well

7 **and the dust returns to the earth as it was, and the spirit returns to God who provided it.**

8 Since every human life flows toward its end, and very few of a person's accomplishments survive him, **futility of futilities, says Kohelet;**[D] **all is futility.**

The Conclusion of the Book

ECCLESIASTES 12:9–14

Kohelet's concluding remarks begin with a description of his works of wisdom in the third person. At the end of his book, Kohelet emphasizes the single source of the many and diverse sayings of the Sages and warns against too many literary projects.

Although the book analyzes the various human life experiences and the fluctuations of the mind that seeks meaning in man's world, it ends with an unequivocal statement about the value of the fear of God and the observance of His commandments.

9 **Beyond that Kohelet was wise** himself, **he moreover taught the people knowledge, considered,**[166] or preached, **and investigated, composed many proverbs,** both orally and in writing, e.g., in the book of Proverbs, which contains many sayings and wise maxims.[167]

10 **Kohelet sought to find matters of value, and** to find **that which was written with integrity, matters of truth** that have already been written.

11 **The words of the wise are** strong **like prods,** sticks with nails at their ends, which are used for striking and piercing animals in order to urge them along,[168] **and like well-fastened**[169] **nails are the collectors of wisdom,** statements of the Sages, whose words of wisdom appear to have been collected from many sources, but in reality **they were given from one shepherd,** God.[170]

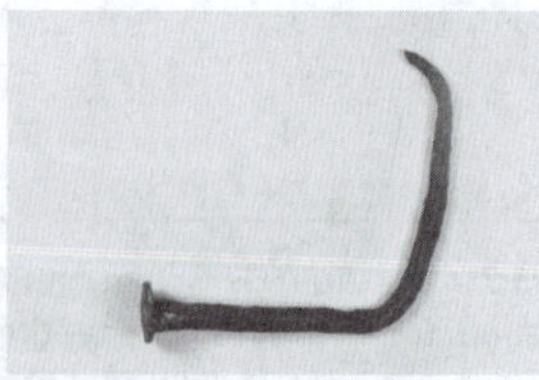
Nail from the Persian period, Nahal Tut, Israel

12 At the end of the book, Kohelet advises his reader: **More than**

ג אַחַ֥ר הַגָּֽשֶׁם׃ בַּיּ֗וֹם שֶׁיָּזֻ֙עוּ֙ שֹׁמְרֵ֣י הַבַּ֔יִת וְהִֽתְעַוְּת֖וּ אַנְשֵׁ֣י הֶחָ֑יִל וּבָטְל֤וּ הַטֹּֽחֲנוֹת֙

ד כִּ֣י מִעֵ֔טוּ וְחָשְׁכ֖וּ הָרֹא֥וֹת בָּאֲרֻבּֽוֹת׃ וְסֻגְּר֤וּ דְלָתַ֙יִם֙ בַּשּׁ֔וּק בִּשְׁפַ֖ל ק֣וֹל הַטַּחֲנָ֑ה

ה וְיָקוּם֙ לְק֣וֹל הַצִּפּ֔וֹר וְיִשַּׁ֖חוּ כׇּל־בְּנ֥וֹת הַשִּֽׁיר׃ גַּ֣ם מִגָּבֹ֤הַּ יִרָ֙אוּ֙ וְחַתְחַתִּ֣ים בַּדֶּ֔רֶךְ

וְיָנֵ֤אץ הַשָּׁקֵד֙ וְיִסְתַּבֵּ֣ל הֶֽחָגָ֔ב וְתָפֵ֖ר הָֽאֲבִיּוֹנָ֑ה כִּֽי־הֹלֵ֤ךְ הָאָדָם֙ אֶל־בֵּ֣ית עוֹלָמ֔וֹ

ו וְסָבְב֥וּ בַשּׁ֖וּק הַסֹּפְדִֽים׃ עַ֣ד אֲשֶׁ֤ר לֹֽא־ירחק חֶ֣בֶל הַכֶּ֔סֶף וְתָרֻ֖ץ גֻּלַּ֣ת הַזָּהָ֑ב יֵרָתֵק

ז וְתִשָּׁ֤בֶר כַּד֙ עַל־הַמַּבּ֔וּעַ וְנָרֹ֥ץ הַגַּלְגַּ֖ל אֶל־הַבּֽוֹר׃ וְיָשֹׁ֧ב הֶעָפָ֛ר עַל־הָאָ֖רֶץ כְּשֶׁהָיָ֑ה

ח וְהָר֣וּחַ תָּשׁ֔וּב אֶל־הָאֱלֹהִ֖ים אֲשֶׁ֥ר נְתָנָֽהּ׃ הֲבֵ֧ל הֲבָלִ֛ים אָמַ֥ר הַקּוֹהֶ֖לֶת הַכֹּ֥ל הָֽבֶל׃

ט וְיֹתֵ֕ר שֶֽׁהָיָ֥ה קֹהֶ֖לֶת חָכָ֑ם ע֗וֹד לִמַּֽד־דַּ֙עַת֙ אֶת־הָעָ֔ם וְאִזֵּ֣ן וְחִקֵּ֔ר תִּקֵּ֖ן מְשָׁלִ֥ים

י יא הַרְבֵּֽה׃ בִּקֵּ֣שׁ קֹהֶ֔לֶת לִמְצֹ֖א דִּבְרֵי־חֵ֑פֶץ וְכָת֥וּב יֹ֖שֶׁר דִּבְרֵ֥י אֱמֶֽת׃ דִּבְרֵ֤י חֲכָמִים֙

יב כַּדׇּ֣רְבֹנ֔וֹת וּֽכְמַשְׂמְר֥וֹת נְטוּעִ֖ים בַּעֲלֵ֣י אֲסֻפּ֑וֹת נִתְּנ֖וּ מֵרֹעֶ֥ה אֶחָֽד׃ וְיֹתֵ֥ר מֵהֵ֖מָּה

BACKGROUND

12:2| **Before the sun, the light, the moon, and the stars darken:** One of the characteristics of an aging body is visual impairment. The aging of the lens leads to a decrease in focus and in the flexibility of vision at various distances, turbidity of the lens, cataracts, and a gradual degradation of vision. Glaucoma, which affects the optic nerve, can reduce the nerve's activity to the point of blindness. In the absence of focus, the stars disappear first, then the moon blurs, and finally vision itself, sunlight, entirely vanishes.

12:5| **And the mourners [*sofedim*] will circle in the street:** A *hesped*, eulogy, or *sipittu* in Akkadian, is a system of ceremonies held around a person's death. In ancient times, professional eulogizers would come to enhance the honor of the deceased by spreading the news of his death in public. They would issue sounds of mourning, wear mourning garments, e.g., sackcloth, spread ashes on their heads, and participate in the funeral and eulogies (see also Esther 4:3).

DISCUSSION

12:8| **Kohelet [*hakohelet*]:** The word *hakohelet* literally means *the* Kohelet, which indicates that Kohelet was not the name of an individual but a term for a preacher or sage who delivers lectures to the public. This is how the word has been translated into other languages as well (see Rashi; Ibn Ezra).

that, my son, be careful. Alternatively, do not go further than
the books that have already been written, with their words of
truth:[171] Refrain from **making many books,** as it **is without**
end, and in them there is **much prattle** or drivel, and it **is wea-**
riness of the flesh. Reading those books provides little benefit.
13 **The end of the matter, everything,** all I have to say, **has**
been heard, and after having established that childhood and
adolescence are vanity, old age is terrifying, and everything
else is herding wind, only one value remains: **Fear God and**
observe His commandments, for that is all of man.[D]
14 **For every action** of man[172] **God will bring to judgment, for**
every unknown. You cannot hide or escape. This judgment
will encompass even actions that you have forgotten, **whether**
good or evil.[D]

The penultimate verse is repeated in a communal recitation:

The end of the matter, everything has been heard: Fear God and observe His commandments, for that is all of man.

DISCUSSION

12:13 | **Fear God and observe His commandments, for that is all of man:** This verse is not a superficial addition designed to end this pessimistic book positively. Rather, it presents the conclusion that emerges from Kohelet's previous observations. The entire book has addressed human life, people's downfalls, and the futility and hope of life under the sun. In his ongoing journey of the mind, many ideas have been voiced that may negatively affect one's attitude toward human reality as such, but they do not refer to, or intend to harm, man's relationship with God. Therefore, Kohelet concludes with the declaration that the fear of God and the observance of His commandments are the only matters of value that remain.

12:14 | **The last verse:** In the public reading of Ecclesiastes, it is customary to repeat this, the penultimate verse of the book, as the last verse ends on a negative note. This is the custom with regard to the books of Isaiah, Malachi, and Lamentations as well.

יג בְּנִ֣י הִזָּהֵ֑ר עֲשׂ֨וֹת סְפָרִ֤ים הַרְבֵּה֙ אֵ֣ין קֵ֔ץ וְלַ֥הַג הַרְבֵּ֖ה יְגִעַ֥ת בָּשָֽׂר׃ ס֥וֹף דָּבָ֖ר הַכֹּ֣ל
יד נִשְׁמָ֑ע אֶת־הָאֱלֹהִ֤ים יְרָא֙ וְאֶת־מִצְוֺתָ֣יו שְׁמ֔וֹר כִּי־זֶ֖ה כָּל־הָאָדָֽם׃ כִּ֣י אֶת־כָּל־
מַעֲשֶׂ֔ה הָאֱלֹהִ֛ים יָבִ֥א בְמִשְׁפָּ֖ט עַ֣ל כָּל־נֶעְלָ֑ם אִם־ט֖וֹב וְאִם־רָֽע׃

סוף דבר הכל נשמע את האלהים ירא
ואת מצותיו שמור כי זה כל האדם

Esther

Esther

INTRODUCTION TO ESTHER

The book of Esther relates an attempt to destroy the entire Jewish people, and its failure due to the interference of Queen Esther. Haman's motivation for his evil plan seems to be a combination of his contempt for Jewish separateness and the Jews' unique lifestyle and religion (3:8) with his personal rivalry with and hatred of Mordekhai and, by extension, of his people (3:4–5). However the motivation is understood, the Jewish people are treated as a single entity with a single fate, despite their exiled state, in which they are "scattered and dispersed among the peoples in all the provinces" (3:8). It is therefore fitting that their salvation is celebrated with a national holiday, Purim, as described at the end of the book (9:20–28). The Sages instituted that the book of Esther be read on Purim in the evening and in the morning.[1]

The book of Esther states that it was written by Mordekhai and Esther as an epistle to the Jewish people throughout the Persian Empire.[2] It is possible that it was composed with the assistance of various sages and advisors as a semi-official document of the Persian Empire.[3] This status accounts for the book's gentle treatment of King Ahashverosh despite his role as one of the central figures in the attempted annihilation of the Jews. Although it is possible to detect unflattering undercurrents with regard to the king, there is not one word of direct criticism of Ahashverosh explicitly stated in the text.

The absence of any direct reference to God is perhaps also a reflection of the book of Esther's status as a Persian imperial document, to be read by all Persia's subjects.[4] Although the Septuagint and the Aramaic translations insert a passage depicting Esther praying to God, it does not appear in the original. In fact, God's name does not appear in the book at all. Nevertheless, there are not-very-subtle allusions to the hidden hand of Divine Providence that pulls the strings in the story: The sequence of events, described so fully and dramatically, contains no peripheral incidents. Each detail is linked to another aspect of the plot, until the complex chain of events directed from on High reaches its inevitable conclusion and is revealed to all. Faith in God is undoubtedly at the heart of the book.

Chronology of Events in the Book of Esther according to the Sages[5]

Kings	Year BCE	Major events	Prophets of the era
Nebuchadnezzar	422	Destruction of the First Temple	Jeremiah, Ezekiel, Daniel
Cyrus the Great and Darius the Mede	370	Conquest of Babylon by Cyrus the Persian and Darius the Mede Founding of the Persian Empire	
Cyrus the Great (3 years)	370	Edict of Cyrus Return of Zerubavel (Sheshbatzar) and Yehoshua the High Priest to the Land of Israel Rebuilding of the altar and laying of the foundations of the Second Temple (Ezra 3:10)	
Ahashverosh son of Darius the Mede (14 years)	367	Death of Cyrus Temporary cessation of work on the Second Temple due to political interference by Israel's enemies (Ezra 4)	
	363	Crowning of Esther as queen of Ahashverosh, in the third year of his reign	
	354	Haman's plot and downfall	
Darius the Persian (Artahshasta, 36 years)	353	Suppression of a revolt in the city of Babylon	Haggai, Zechariah
	348	Completion of work on the Second Temple (Ezra 6:15)	
	347	Return of Ezra to the Land of Israel (Ezra 7)	Malachi
	334	Appointment of Nehemiah as governor Rebuilding of the walls of Jerusalem and renewal of the covenant (Nehemiah 10:1)	
	318	Conquests of Alexander the Great	

Chronology of Events in the Book of Esther according to the Standard Chronology

Kings	Year BCE	Major events	Prophets of the era
Nebuchadnezzar	586	Destruction of the First Temple	Jeremiah, Ezekiel, Daniel
Cyrus the Great	550	Founding of the Persian Empire	
	539	Conquest of Babylon by Cyrus	
	538	Edict of Cyrus Return of Zerubavel (Sheshbatzar) and Yehoshua the High Priest to the Land of Israel	
	537	Rebuilding of the altar and laying of the foundations of the Second Temple (Ezra 3:10) Temporary cessation of work on the Second Temple due to interference by Judah's enemies (Ezra 4)	
Cambyses	530	Succession as emperor after Cyrus	
	525	Conquest of Egypt	
Darius the Great	522	Beginning of reign with the suppression of a revolt in the city of Babylon and in Persia	
	520	Resumption of work on the Second Temple (Ezra 4:24–6:14)	Haggai, Zechariah
	516	Completion of work on the Second Temple (Ezra 6:15)	
Xerxes (Ahashverosh)	486	Accusations against the inhabitants of Judah and Jerusalem (Ezra 4:6)	Malachi
	483	Crowning of Esther as queen of Ahashverosh, in the third year of his reign	
	474	Haman's plot and downfall	
Artaxerxes (Artahshasta)	458	Arrival of Ezra in the Land of Israel (Ezra 7)	
	445	Appointment of Nehemiah as governor Rebuilding of the walls of Jerusalem and renewal of the covenant (Nehemiah 10:1)	
Alexander the Great	331	Conquest of the Persian Empire by Alexander	

Esther

The Feasts and the End of Vashti's Reign

ESTHER 1:1–22

As a backdrop to the main story, this prelude vividly represents the hedonistic culture that was prevalent in the kingdom of Persia and Media by detailing a series of ostentatious banquets held for the masses, featuring an abundance of wine and extravagant displays of wealth. However, affairs take a turn for the worse when the queen refuses to obey the king, thereby undermining the self-image of a ruler who was accustomed to being obeyed without question.

1 1 **It was in the days of Ahashverosh,**[D] **that Ahashverosh who reigned from India to Kush,**[B] southern Egypt. The Persian kingdom, which was at its zenith at the time, was divided into **one hundred and twenty-seven provinces.**[B] The empire was divided into large regions that were under the control of governors, called satraps, while a subordinate governor was appointed over each state or province.

Xerxes I, identified as Ahashverosh, stone relief, 560–331 BCE

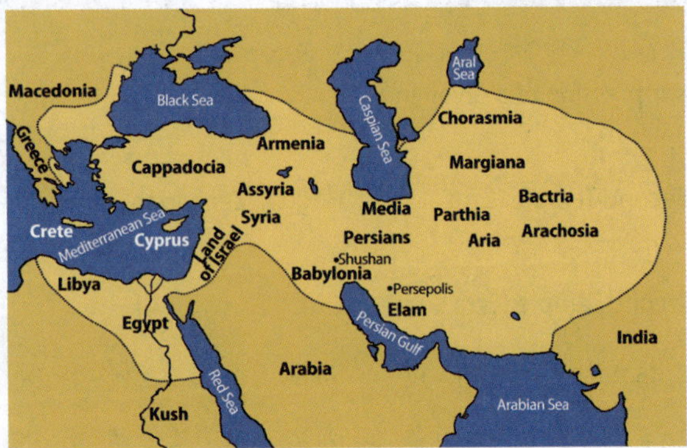

Map of the Persian Empire

2 It happened that **in those days, when King Ahashverosh sat on the royal throne that was in the Shushan citadel** [***habira***].[B] Shushan, also known as Susa, was a city in Elam, whose ruins are still extant.[6] Inside the city was a royal fortress, or citadel [*bira*], where both the central government and Ahashverosh's palace were located.[7]

3 **In the third year of his reign,** after he had crushed all those who stood in his way,[8] **he made a** large public **banquet for all his princes and his servants.** He did not hold his coronation celebrations immediately upon ascending the throne, possibly because he was preoccupied with settling internal disputes.[9] Once he had firmly established his reign, he invited **the elite of**

King of Persia on his throne receiving a royal audience, stone relief, Persepolis, 560–331 BCE

Persia and Media,[B] two separate states that were partly unified; **the nobles**[B] **and princes** who were appointed to be in charge **of the provinces before him,**

4 **with his showing the riches of his glorious kingdom, and the honor of his splendid majesty, for many days.** The feast, which was designed to publicly display the king's riches and might, lasted **one hundred and eighty days.**

Persian soldiers in flat hats, and Medes in rounded hats, relief, Persepolis, sixth century BCE

5 **Upon the completion of those days,** during which a banquet was held for people who came from afar, **the king made a**

אסתר

א וַֽיְהִי בִּימֵי אֲחַשְׁוֵרוֹשׁ הוּא אֲחַשְׁוֵרוֹשׁ הַמֹּלֵךְ מֵהֹדּוּ וְעַד־כּוּשׁ שֶׁבַע וְעֶשְׂרִים א
ב וּמֵאָה מְדִינָה: בַּיָּמִים הָהֵם כְּשֶׁבֶת ׀ הַמֶּלֶךְ אֲחַשְׁוֵרוֹשׁ עַל כִּסֵּא מַלְכוּתוֹ אֲשֶׁר
ג בְּשׁוּשַׁן הַבִּירָה: בִּשְׁנַת שָׁלוֹשׁ לְמָלְכוֹ עָשָׂה מִשְׁתֶּה לְכָל־שָׂרָיו וַעֲבָדָיו חֵיל ׀
ד פָּרַס וּמָדַי הַפַּרְתְּמִים וְשָׂרֵי הַמְּדִינוֹת לְפָנָיו: בְּהַרְאֹתוֹ אֶת־עֹשֶׁר כְּבוֹד מַלְכוּתוֹ
ה וְאֶת־יְקָר תִּפְאֶרֶת גְּדוּלָּתוֹ יָמִים רַבִּים שְׁמוֹנִים וּמְאַת יוֹם: וּבִמְלוֹאת ׀ הַיָּמִים

BACKGROUND

1:1 | **From India to Kush:** The conquests of Darius, the first king of Persia, also known as Darius the Great (550–486 BCE), stretched from the banks of the Indus in the east, to the kingdom of Ethiopia-Nubia in the south. He also conquered parts of Greece and the Balkans.

One hundred and twenty-seven provinces: The Persian Empire was divided into provinces, each headed by a satrap [*aḥashdarpan*]. In Old Persian, the word *aḥashdarpan* means shield of the kingdom (see 3:12). External sources indicate that the number of provinces established by the Persian government was far fewer than one hundred and twenty-seven, but such provinces were often divided into smaller units ruled by subordinate governors. Taking this into account, one may arrive at 127 provinces.

1:2 | **The Shushan citadel:** In Old Persian this city was called Susha, Susa in Greek and Latin, and Shush in modern Persian. It was the oldest and most important city of the Proto-Elamite kingdom in southwest Persia, in the vicinity of the Karkheh River, at the foot of the Zagros Mountains. Cambyses II (died 521 BCE), the son of Cyrus II, also known as Cyrus the Great, established Shushan as his capital, and during the reign of Darius I, Shushan was the political and administrative capital of Persia and one of its four capital cities, together with Persepolis, Ecbatana, and Babylon. The city lost its prominence after the Alexandrian conquests at the end of the fourth century BCE.

1:3 | **Persia and Media:** Media was an ancient kingdom in the northeast of Persia, south of the Caspian Sea. From the ninth century BCE it was involved in unremitting conflict with Assyria. After Media entered into a pact with Babylon toward the end of the seventh century, the two nations defeated Assyria. In 550 BCE, Cyrus the Great conquered Media and unified it with Persia. Some attribute the difference in the order of the two names, "Persia and Media" or "Media and Persia" (e.g., 10:2; Daniel 5:28, 6:9), to the change of kings from Persian to Median, and vice versa. Others claim that the interchangeability of the order reflects the equality of the two states in the unified kingdom.

The nobles [*partemim*]: From the Old Persian *partema*, meaning the first, those that are closest to the king.

DISCUSSION

1:1 | **Ahashverosh:** Since the Persian name of the king was not Ahashverosh, it is difficult to identify this figure. It is most likely that he is the king known in Greek literature as Xerxes I, or Khshayarsha in Persian. Much of the information about Xerxes I comes from Greek historians, who documented the wars the Greeks fought against the Persians. Their accounts indicate that Xerxes I ascended the throne after the Persian kingdom had suffered civil wars, conspiracies, and betrayals. This may explain why some of Ahashverosh's behavior as related in the book makes him appear paranoid. Even when the king was sitting "on the royal throne" (verse 2), nothing could be taken for granted.

banquet for all the people who were present in the Shushan citadel, from great to small, seven days. He may have treated them to this feast in an attempt to win the trust of the citadel's residents, many of whom were government officials.[10] This banquet took place **in the court of the garden of the king's audience hall,**[B] a courtyard with a garden or orchard, adjacent to the audience hall.

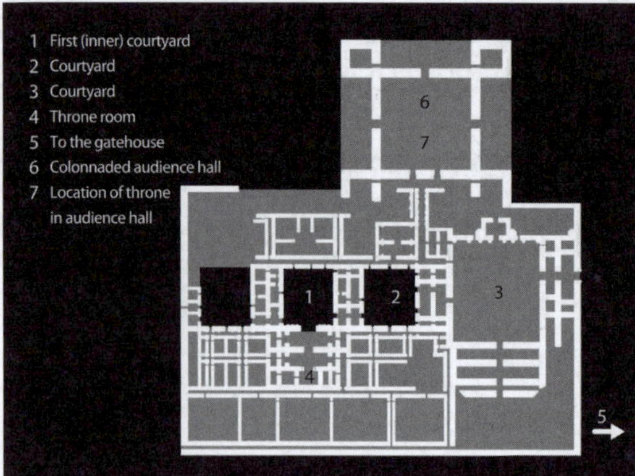

Plan of the ancient palace, Shushan

6 The place was decorated with expensive fabrics: **White linen,**[B] **green cotton [*karpas*],**[B] **and sky-blue wool,** all **bound with**

Remains of pillars from the palace of the kings of Persia, Persepolis, fifth century BCE

cords of fine **linen**[B] **and purple**[B] **wool.** All these fabrics and cords were hung **on silver rods**[B] **and marble pillars,**[B] and there were **couches of gold and silver on a floor of alabaster, marble, mother-of-pearl, and precious stone.**[B]

7 **Serving drink in vessels of gold,** as befitted a royal feast, **and vessels of diverse kinds;** the guests were offered vessels of various shapes and colors, in accordance with their status and needs. **And abundant royal wine** was provided at the king's expense, **in accordance with the king's bounty,** offered freely and without concern for the cost.

Excavated vessels, Shushan

8 **The drinking was as customary,** following the accepted rules of etiquette, and **without constraint.** Since the king wanted the people to feel part of the royal feast, they were free to drink as they pleased. **For so did the king establish,** command,[11] **for all the officials of his palace, to act in accordance with the wishes of each and every man.** The Persian policy was not to try to impose conformity within the multicultural empire, but to grant each nation the freedom to preserve their identity, language, and customs.

9 **Also Vashti**[D] **the queen made a banquet for the women,** in parallel to the great feast for the men, **in** another wing of **the royal palace of King Ahashverosh.** The feast for the women was held separately from that of the men to avoid the undesirable consequences of mixed festivities.[12] Unlike the king's wild feast, the women's banquet was a more dignified affair.

10 **On the seventh day** of the feast, **when the king was merry with wine;** he was in good spirits after much drinking. It is hard to tell whether he was actually drunk, partly due to the rather formal tone of the description here. In any case, **he,** Ahashverosh, **said to Mehuman, Bizeta, Harbona, Bigta, Avagta, Zetar, and Karkas, the seven** special **chamberlains [*sarisim*]**[B] **who attended to King Ahashverosh,** and who were closest to him. The word *sarisim* can also mean eunuchs and it can be assumed that these were actual eunuchs, as their job required them to pass between the men and the women.[13] In the raucous atmosphere of debauchery at the party, the king

DISCUSSION

1:9| **Vashti:** This sounds like a Persian name (see Ibn Ezra, second commentary), and in a collection of Zoroastrian texts from the tenth century BCE there are two words that are possibly the source of the name: *vashita*, the best, and *ushiti*, the beloved. However, there is no certainty that Vashti was Persian. It is clear from the story that she was more than merely one of the king's many wives and concubines, and that she was well aware of her superior status. According to a tradition of the Sages, Vashti was originally a Babylonian princess (see, e.g., *Megilla* 10b). There are other instances in the Bible where a foreigner who was brought into a royal house was given a new name upon entering the royal household (see Genesis 41:45; Daniel 1:7).

הָאֵלֶּה עָשָׂה הַמֶּלֶךְ לְכָל־הָעָם הַנִּמְצְאִים בְּשׁוּשַׁן הַבִּירָה לְמִגָּדוֹל וְעַד־קָטָן
ו מִשְׁתֶּה שִׁבְעַת יָמִים בַּחֲצַר גִּנַּת בִּיתַן הַמֶּלֶךְ׃ חוּר ׀ כַּרְפַּס וּתְכֵלֶת אָחוּז בְּחַבְלֵי־
בוּץ וְאַרְגָּמָן עַל־גְּלִילֵי כֶסֶף וְעַמּוּדֵי שֵׁשׁ מִטּוֹת ׀ זָהָב וָכֶסֶף עַל רִצְפַת בַּהַט־וָשֵׁשׁ
ז וְדַר וְסֹחָרֶת׃ וְהַשְׁקוֹת בִּכְלֵי זָהָב וְכֵלִים מִכֵּלִים שׁוֹנִים וְיֵין מַלְכוּת רָב כְּיַד הַמֶּלֶךְ׃
ח וְהַשְּׁתִיָּה כַדָּת אֵין אֹנֵס כִּי־כֵן ׀ יִסַּד הַמֶּלֶךְ עַל כָּל־רַב בֵּיתוֹ לַעֲשׂוֹת כִּרְצוֹן
ט אִישׁ־וָאִישׁ׃ גַּם וַשְׁתִּי הַמַּלְכָּה עָשְׂתָה מִשְׁתֵּה נָשִׁים בֵּית הַמַּלְכוּת
י אֲשֶׁר לַמֶּלֶךְ אֲחַשְׁוֵרוֹשׁ׃ בַּיּוֹם הַשְּׁבִיעִי כְּטוֹב לֵב־הַמֶּלֶךְ בַּיָּיִן אָמַר לִמְהוּמָן
בִּזְּתָא חַרְבוֹנָא בִּגְתָא וַאֲבַגְתָא זֵתַר וְכַרְכַּס שִׁבְעַת הַסָּרִיסִים הַמְשָׁרְתִים אֶת־

BACKGROUND

1:5 | **The court of the garden of the king's audience hall [*bitan*]:** The royal palace in Shushan, which has been unearthed in archaeological excavations, was built in the Syrian-western style. It included four inner garden courtyards, while its northern section contained the *bitan*, the audience hall. The word *bitan* is from the Akkadian *bitanu*, meaning an inner part or inner structure of a palace or temple. It has been surmised that this term developed from the Persian word *apadana*, an audience hall with columns. Sometimes tents or canopies were erected for guests in this hall or in an adjoining courtyard. During the excavations of the palace at Shushan, a tablet with cuneiform script was discovered. The text on this tablet describes the glories of the palace, specifically the cost and rarity of the building materials, and the expertise of its builders.

1:6 | **White linen [*ḥur*]:** A brilliant-white woven linen fabric, from *ḥiver*, meaning pale. Alternatively, this is a perforated [*meḥurar*] woven material, similar to netting (see Genesis 40:16; Isaiah 19:9).

Green cotton [*karpas*]: Apparently a woven cotton fabric, which was brought to the region from India in the time of Sennacherib. It is called *karpasa* in Sanskrit and *kirpas* in Persian.

Sky-blue [*tekhelet*] wool...purple [*argaman*] wool: These are wool fabrics colored with dyes extracted from snails that live in the Mediterranean Sea. *Tekhelet* is a shade of deep blue, extracted from the banded dye-murex, *Murex trunculus*, while *argaman* is the general name for a dark reddish-purple or deep purple dye produced from the spiny dye-murex, *Murex brandaris*. The liquid used for preparing these dyes was extracted from a protective secretion of the snails found in minute quantities in their hypobranchial glands. Many thousands of snails were required in order to dye a fabric or item of clothing and therefore these dyes were very expensive and the fabric dyed with them was used mainly by nobles and kings.

These two dyes were used for coloring the cloth tent-coverings of the Tabernacle (Exodus 26, 36–38) and the cloths with which the vessels of the Tabernacle were covered during journeys (Exodus 39), as well as the vestments of the High Priest (Exodus 28, 39). *Tekhelet* was also the dye used in ritual fringes (Numbers 15:38–39). In the affluent Persian kingdom, the king would have curtains and clothes that were made entirely of *tekhelet*-dyed wool.

Bound with cords of linen [*butz*]: Linen is made from flax, *Linum usitatissimum*, in Akkadian, *busu* (see Onkelos, Leviticus 16). The Sages likewise called the linen of the vestments of the High Priest *butz* (Mishna *Yoma* 3:4). These cords were used to spread the fabrics above the garden of the king's palace, where the feast was held, and to tie them to the silver and marble pillars. Linen cords are particularly strong and therefore well suited for this purpose. It seems that the cords of the Tent of Meeting were also made of linen.

Silver rods: These were poles of silver or a shiny white metal that supported the curtains which were hung to provide shade and decoration in the garden courtyard of the palace.

Marble pillars [*shesh*]: In ancient times, palace courtyards were often surrounded by a colonnade of pillars. These pillars often supported roofs, providing the courtyard with a shaded area. *Shesh* is white marble, which was preferred for monolithic, cylindrical pillars because it can be smoothed or engraved. Possibly, some of the pillars mentioned here did not have a roof over them and instead curtains were hung over them.

A floor of alabaster [*bahat*], marble, mother-of-pearl [*dar*], and precious stone [*soḥaret*]: The palaces and royal gardens of the kings of Persia and Media were paved with ceramic tiles or colorful flagstones, which were both decorative and durable. *Bahat* may not be alabaster, but rather *purfir*, a hard, red stone. *Dar* is mother-of-pearl, a substance produced by mollusks as an inner shell layer. Alternatively, *dar* may mean gold, from the Old Persian *darniya*. *Soḥaret* is probably a light-bluish precious stone, *sikhru* in Akkadian and *saharet* in ancient Egyptian. The Persians were experts in the production of ceramic tiles, in many different colors, including gold with a metallic sheen. It is possible that this list refers to different kinds of tiles in a colorful array.

1:10 | **Chamberlains [*sarisim*]:** While not all chamberlains would have been eunuchs, eunuchs did hold positions of authority in the royal courts of Assyria and Babylon, as well as in the

bragged about his power, wealth, wisdom, and success. He also boasted of his beautiful wife.

11 The king, not satisfied with mere boasts, commanded his officials **to bring Queen Vashti before the king with the royal crown,** in order **to display her beauty to** all **the peoples and the princes,**[D] **as she was of fair appearance.**

12 **Queen Vashti refused to come at the king's word,**[B] delivered **by means of the chamberlains.** Her refusal to obey the command of the king, whose authority was absolutely unlimited, is indicative of her high status. She was unwilling to humiliate herself by parading her body before an audience. **The king was very angry, and his fury burned within him.** His rage was provoked by his wife's audacity in rejecting his demand, which was not issued privately but by an official delegation. His sensitivity to any slight to his honor was undoubtedly heightened by his inebriated state. Under the circumstances, he had anticipated that his request would be obeyed immediately and in full. Perhaps Vashti also alluded to his drunkenness, or mocked him, further enflaming his anger.[14] This is possibly the meaning of the phrase in verse 17, "for the matter [*devar*] of the queen," which can also mean the statement of the queen.

13 **The king communicated with the wise men, knowledgeable of the portents,** the astrologers, or his advisors in charge of managing the affairs of the kingdom,[15] **for so was the practice of the king before those learned in custom and law,**[BD] to present his problems before his legal counselors.[16]

14 The verse notes that **those** advisors who were **close to him,** the king, **were Karshena, Shetar, Admata, Tarshish, Meres, Marsena, and Memukhan, the seven princes of Persia and Media, who viewed the king's face,** who would meet with him. The king did not ordinarily appear in public and only his closest courtiers would regularly encounter him face-to-face.[17] It was these advisors **who were seated first in the kingdom,** as the chief ministers of his government.

15 The legal question under discussion was as follows: **As to the policy: What to do to Queen Vashti, in that she did not follow the order of King Ahashverosh by means of the chamberlains?** What is to be done in light of the queen's public refusal to obey the king's command, which was delivered to her by an official delegation?

16 **Memukhan said before the king and the princes** that the queen's sin was even worse than might have been thought: **It is not the king alone that Queen Vashti has wronged,** by failing to obey his instruction; **rather, it is all the princes, and all the peoples, who are in all the provinces of King Ahashverosh.** Since she publicly rebelled against the king, her decision will have ramifications that will spread throughout the entire Persian Empire.

17 **For the matter of the queen will get out to all the women, rendering their husbands contemptible in their eyes.** Although the queen did not issue an explicit declaration to this effect, and did not preach this type of conduct, her personal example here is likely to become the norm, **in their saying,** by women who seek to copy her: **King Ahashverosh said to bring Queen Vashti before him, but she did not come.** The queen has created a dangerous precedent.

18 From **this day** onward, **the princesses of Persia and Media,** the wives of the officials and nobles, **who have heard of the matter of the queen, will recount it to all the king's princes,** they will issue similar statements, and perhaps the wives of commoners will follow suit as well. Vashti's refusal will embolden these women when they quarrel with their husbands, **and** through this incident **there will be no end of contempt and wrath,** or contempt that should arouse our anger. This is not merely a personal slight, which the king could potentially overlook; rather, the broader consequences of the queen's refusal will be severe, as her scandalous behavior, even if not repeated, is likely to serve as a model that will be imitated throughout the kingdom.

19 Therefore, **if it pleases the king, let the royal edict be issued before him.** The decision should be published as a formal decree, **and** furthermore, **let it be written in** the book of **the decrees of Persia and Media,**[B] **not to be repealed,** as despite the king's power and position, he is considered to be

BACKGROUND

Persian court, and were always used in positions which involved the women of the royal court, and the royal harem. In Persia, such officials could achieve the status of senior advisors to the king, or be awarded other governmental posts, including that of generals who commanded military campaigns. The Persian kings relied on eunuchs for the most sensitive roles, such as the king's personal bodyguard, or his cupbearer.

1:12 | **Queen Vashti refused to come at the king's word:** The principal wife of the king of Persia enjoyed a lofty status in the court. She was typically an educated woman in control of her own daily routine who could even be involved in religious matters. Ahashverosh's request that Vashti be summoned in the middle of a feast was in defiance of the accepted practice, whereby only women from the harem were present at drinking parties; the queen would depart at the conclusion of the official meal. In fact, the queen had the right to choose whether or not to be seen by the king. Despite Zoroastrian beliefs according the king significant religious status as the agent of Ahura Mazda, even the king was not permitted to diverge from these ancient rules of the court unless they were changed by consent.

1:13 | **For so was the practice of the king before those learned in custom and law:** Since the rights of the Persian queen were based on ancient law, the discussion about her refusal required the presence of legal scholars.

יא פְּנֵי הַמֶּלֶךְ אֲחַשְׁוֵרוֹשׁ׃ לְהָבִיא אֶת־וַשְׁתִּי הַמַּלְכָּה לִפְנֵי הַמֶּלֶךְ בְּכֶתֶר מַלְכוּת
יב לְהַרְאוֹת הָעַמִּים וְהַשָּׂרִים אֶת־יָפְיָהּ כִּי־טוֹבַת מַרְאֶה הִיא׃ וַתְּמָאֵן הַמַּלְכָּה
וַשְׁתִּי לָבוֹא בִּדְבַר הַמֶּלֶךְ אֲשֶׁר בְּיַד הַסָּרִיסִים וַיִּקְצֹף הַמֶּלֶךְ מְאֹד וַחֲמָתוֹ בָּעֲרָה
יג בוֹ׃ וַיֹּאמֶר הַמֶּלֶךְ לַחֲכָמִים יֹדְעֵי הָעִתִּים כִּי־כֵן דְּבַר הַמֶּלֶךְ לִפְנֵי
יד כָּל־יֹדְעֵי דָּת וָדִין׃ וְהַקָּרֹב אֵלָיו כַּרְשְׁנָא שֵׁתָר אַדְמָתָא תַרְשִׁישׁ מֶרֶס מַרְסְנָא
טו מְמוּכָן שִׁבְעַת שָׂרֵי ׀ פָּרַס וּמָדַי רֹאֵי פְּנֵי הַמֶּלֶךְ הַיֹּשְׁבִים רִאשֹׁנָה בַּמַּלְכוּת׃ כְּדָת
מַה־לַּעֲשׂוֹת בַּמַּלְכָּה וַשְׁתִּי עַל ׀ אֲשֶׁר לֹא־עָשְׂתָה אֶת־מַאֲמַר הַמֶּלֶךְ אֲחַשְׁוֵרוֹשׁ
טז בְּיַד הַסָּרִיסִים׃ וַיֹּאמֶר מומכן לִפְנֵי הַמֶּלֶךְ וְהַשָּׂרִים לֹא עַל־הַמֶּלֶךְ מְמוּכָן
לְבַדּוֹ עָוְתָה וַשְׁתִּי הַמַּלְכָּה כִּי עַל־כָּל־הַשָּׂרִים וְעַל־כָּל־הָעַמִּים אֲשֶׁר בְּכָל־
יז מְדִינוֹת הַמֶּלֶךְ אֲחַשְׁוֵרוֹשׁ׃ כִּי־יֵצֵא דְבַר־הַמַּלְכָּה עַל־כָּל־הַנָּשִׁים לְהַבְזוֹת
בַּעְלֵיהֶן בְּעֵינֵיהֶן בְּאָמְרָם הַמֶּלֶךְ אֲחַשְׁוֵרוֹשׁ אָמַר לְהָבִיא אֶת־וַשְׁתִּי הַמַּלְכָּה
יח לְפָנָיו וְלֹא־בָאָה׃ וְהַיּוֹם הַזֶּה תֹּאמַרְנָה ׀ שָׂרוֹת פָּרַס־וּמָדַי אֲשֶׁר שָׁמְעוּ אֶת־דְּבַר
יט הַמַּלְכָּה לְכֹל שָׂרֵי הַמֶּלֶךְ וּכְדַי בִּזָּיוֹן וָקָצֶף׃ אִם־עַל־הַמֶּלֶךְ טוֹב יֵצֵא דְבַר־
מַלְכוּת מִלְּפָנָיו וְיִכָּתֵב בְּדָתֵי פָרַס־וּמָדַי וְלֹא יַעֲבוֹר אֲשֶׁר לֹא־תָבוֹא וַשְׁתִּי

DISCUSSION

1:11 | **To display her beauty to the peoples and the princes:** Although the book of Esther does not offer any explicit criticism of this command, the Persian king's demand to display the queen was clearly in poor taste. The Sages suggest that the order was in even worse taste than is obvious here, and that when Ahashverosh ordered Vashti to appear with the royal crown, he was actually commanding that she wear nothing *but* the crown, expecting her to display her nakedness before all (see *Megilla* 12b).

1:13 | **The practice of the king before those learned in custom and law:** There is a measure of irony here: Later in the story, the king alone, and apparently without any hesitation, makes decisions that will have dramatic moral and political ramifications. In this situation, by contrast, when he is drunk and angry, he assembles an entire legal team in order to discuss the fate of his wife. His behavior is similar to that of various dictators over the course of history who sought to preserve the image of a law-abiding ruler, and who were careful that everything be documented and performed in a very formal manner.

It should be noted that Ahashverosh's consultation with his ministers is nothing more than a matter of etiquette through which he expresses his respect for the legal establishment; in practice, they are at his mercy: He appointed them, and he can remove them from their posts and have them executed. Therefore, his legal advisors were naturally careful to tailor their comments to fit what they assumed the king would want to hear, as ultimately the law depended upon his whim.

BACKGROUND

1:19 | **And let it be written in the decrees of [*datei*] Persia and Media:** *Data* is the Old Persian word for law. The Persians were committed to preserving their legal records. Persian legal codes were written in cuneiform on clay tablets, as well as on parchment. Their archives were placed in the most fortified sections of the palace walls, as has been discovered by archaeologists at Persepolis.

bound by the laws and proclamations of the kingdom, at least technically (see 8:8), **that Vashti will not come before King Ahashverosh.** Memukhan did not specify her fate; whether she was to be killed, permanently exiled, or simply deposed from her position as queen. **And** it should also be decreed that **the king will give her queenship,** her official status as queen, **to her counterpart who is worthier than she.** The king should dispense with her and choose a more suitable woman to replace her.

20 **The king's edict**[B] **that he will enact will be heard throughout his entire kingdom, although it,** the kingdom, **is vast, and all the wives,** following the dissemination of the royal precedent, **will confer honor on their husbands,** and will not disobey their commands, **from great to small.**

21 **The matter was pleasing in the eyes of the king and the princes.** Memukhan's appraisal of the fundamental problem, with its potentially serious consequences, was greeted with approval. In his speech, Memukhan presented his solution not as a royal whim, but rather as an important precedent in the management of the country. The angry, drunken king was delighted at the opportunity to inflate the incident into an event of imperial importance. **And** therefore **the king acted in accordance with the word of Memukhan.** As noted in the introduction, the book of Esther, with its formal style, does not criticize the king overtly. However, reading between the lines, Ahashverosh emerges as a ridiculous, easily manipulated figure.

22 **He,** Ahashverosh, **sent scrolls** containing the official order **to all the provinces of the king, to each and every province in its script, and to each and every people in its language: Every man shall be ruler in his house.** The king did not mention Vashti by name, but simply declared that each man should be in charge of his house, **and** that he should **speak the language of his people.** People of different nationalities in his kingdom had intermarried, thereby mixing their languages.[18] Consequently, the king took this opportunity to issue a decree that from this point forward the language of the husband should be the one spoken by all members of his household.[19]

"To each and every province in its script." Trilingual inscription of Xerxes I, Van Fortress, Turkey, 485–465 BCE

Esther Is Crowned Queen

ESTHER 2:1–20

This section starts by relating the consequences of the incident described in the previous section, as a search is undertaken to find a queen to replace Vashti. Esther is then introduced, and these two narrative strands intertwine into a single plotline.

2 1 **After these matters, when the fury of king Ahashverosh had abated, he remembered Vashti, and what she had done, and what was decreed against her.** Since it is not explicitly stated that she was executed, and imposition of the death penalty for the nobility was rare, except for the most serious crimes, it can be assumed that she was not put to death. Perhaps Vashti had been exiled, and Ahashverosh missed her.[20]

2 The king's ministers did not merely carry out his commands; they also paid attention to his moods and tried to anticipate his wishes. **The king's lads, his attendants, said:** We can find a replacement for Vashti. **Let there be sought for the king virgin young women who are of fair appearance,** as befits the honor of a king.

3 In keeping with the king's status, this was to be a large and organized project, ensuring that only suitable candidates would be sent: **Have the king appoint officials in all the provinces of his kingdom** to perform an initial selection, **and they will gather every virgin young woman of fair appearance to the Shushan citadel, to the harem, to the custody of Hegai, the king's chamberlain, guardian of the women** in the palace; **and** to complement and enhance their natural beauty, **their** perfumes and **cosmetics will be provided.**

4 **The young woman who will be pleasing in the eyes of the king** at the end of this process **will be crowned queen in place of Vashti. The proposal was pleasing in the eyes of the king and he did so.**

5 **There was a Judean [*Yehudi*] man,**[B] from the land of Judah,[21] the small independent province which the Persians called Yehud, who was **in the Shushan citadel.** It is not clear whether he actually lived there or simply worked there as a court official. **And his name was Mordekhai, son of Ya'ir, son of Shimi, son of Kish, a Benjamite,**[D] from the tribe of Benjamin. Although he came from the land of Judah, he was from the tribe of Benjamin. This was Mordekhai,

כ לִפְנֵי הַמֶּלֶךְ אֲחַשְׁוֵרוֹשׁ וּמַלְכוּתָהּ יִתֵּן הַמֶּלֶךְ לִרְעוּתָהּ הַטּוֹבָה מִמֶּנָּה: וְנִשְׁמַע
פִּתְגָם הַמֶּלֶךְ אֲשֶׁר־יַעֲשֶׂה בְּכָל־מַלְכוּתוֹ כִּי רַבָּה הִיא וְכָל־הַנָּשִׁים יִתְּנוּ יְקָר
כא לְבַעְלֵיהֶן לְמִגָּדוֹל וְעַד־קָטָן: וַיִּיטַב הַדָּבָר בְּעֵינֵי הַמֶּלֶךְ וְהַשָּׂרִים וַיַּעַשׂ
כב הַמֶּלֶךְ כִּדְבַר מְמוּכָן: וַיִּשְׁלַח סְפָרִים אֶל־כָּל־מְדִינוֹת הַמֶּלֶךְ אֶל־מְדִינָה וּמְדִינָה
כִּכְתָבָהּ וְאֶל־עַם וָעָם כִּלְשׁוֹנוֹ לִהְיוֹת כָּל־אִישׁ שֹׂרֵר בְּבֵיתוֹ וּמְדַבֵּר כִּלְשׁוֹן
א עַמּוֹ: אַחַר הַדְּבָרִים הָאֵלֶּה כְּשֹׁךְ חֲמַת הַמֶּלֶךְ אֲחַשְׁוֵרוֹשׁ זָכַר אֶת־
ב וַשְׁתִּי וְאֵת אֲשֶׁר־עָשָׂתָה וְאֵת אֲשֶׁר־נִגְזַר עָלֶיהָ: וַיֹּאמְרוּ נַעֲרֵי־הַמֶּלֶךְ מְשָׁרְתָיו
ג יְבַקְשׁוּ לַמֶּלֶךְ נְעָרוֹת בְּתוּלוֹת טוֹבוֹת מַרְאֶה: וְיַפְקֵד הַמֶּלֶךְ פְּקִידִים בְּכָל־מְדִינוֹת
מַלְכוּתוֹ וְיִקְבְּצוּ אֶת־כָּל־נַעֲרָה־בְתוּלָה טוֹבַת מַרְאֶה אֶל־שׁוּשַׁן הַבִּירָה אֶל־
ד בֵּית הַנָּשִׁים אֶל־יַד הֵגֶא סְרִיס הַמֶּלֶךְ שֹׁמֵר הַנָּשִׁים וְנָתוֹן תַּמְרוּקֵיהֶן: וְהַנַּעֲרָה
אֲשֶׁר תִּיטַב בְּעֵינֵי הַמֶּלֶךְ תִּמְלֹךְ תַּחַת וַשְׁתִּי וַיִּיטַב הַדָּבָר בְּעֵינֵי הַמֶּלֶךְ וַיַּעַשׂ
ה כֵּן: אִישׁ יְהוּדִי הָיָה בְּשׁוּשַׁן הַבִּירָה וּשְׁמוֹ מָרְדֳּכַי בֶּן יָאִיר בֶּן־שִׁמְעִי ב

BACKGROUND

1:20| **Edict [*pitgam*]:** In Old Persian, *pratigama* denotes something which goes out to meet something else. In this instance, this is a message from the king to the people. This is the source for the Aramaic term *pitgama*, meaning a publicized command or decree.

2:5| **A Judean man:** This refers to one who came from the land of Judah, or the Persian province of Yehud. Judah became a Persian province when Cyrus defeated Babylon and took over its empire. He subsequently issued an edict authorizing and encouraging the Judean exiles to return to Judah and rebuild the Temple (see Ezra 1:1–4). The province of Yehud was a sub-province of Avar Nahara, literally "beyond the river," which was the area of the Persian Empire west of the Euphrates River. It was semi-independent, as is clear from the unsuccessful attempts of its governor to suppress rebuilding of the Temple and the successful appeals to the Persian kings made by the leaders of Judah (see Ezra 4–6). The province of Yehud was governed by a satrap appointed from the ranks of the returning exiles. It was divided into administrative areas, centered around five cities: Jerusalem; Beit HaKerem, possibly modern-day Bethlehem; Mitzpa, in the region of Benjamin; Beit Tzur, in modern-day Gush Etzion; and Ke'ila, near modern-day Beit Guvrin (see Nehemiah 3).

DISCUSSION

2:5| **A Judean man…a Benjamite:** The tribes of Judah and Benjamin inhabited adjacent areas of the Land of Israel. They were both exiled to Babylon, and members of both tribes later returned to the Land of Israel (see Nehemiah 11:7, 25–36). Mordekhai's lineage, specified in this verse, indicates that he was descended from the royal line of King Saul (see *Pirkei deRabbi Eliezer* 48; *Megilla* 16a).

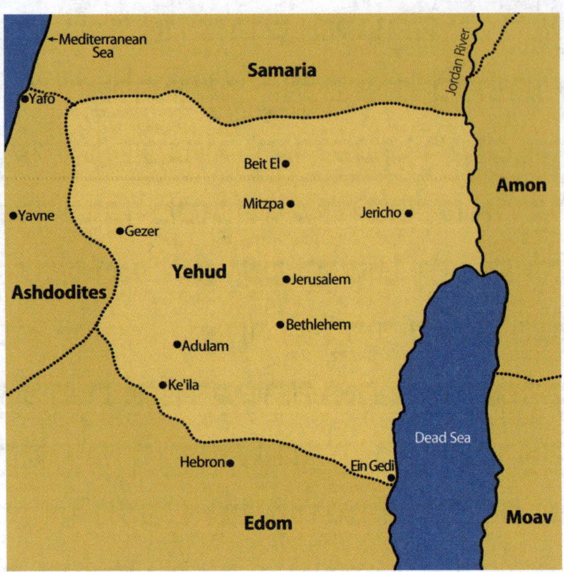

Province of Yehud

6 **who had been exiled from Jerusalem** in his youth, together **with the** first **exile, that was exiled with Yekhonya king of Judah, whom Nebuchadnezzar king of Babylon exiled.**

7 **He was rearing Hadassa** as her guardian, **she was Esther.**[B] Hadassa was her Hebrew name, while Esther was her Persian or Babylonian name. She was **his uncle's daughter** and was much younger than he. Mordekhai had become her guardian **as she had no father or mother. The young woman was of fine form and fair appearance, and with the death of her father and her mother, Mordekhai had adopted her as his own daughter.**

8 **It was when the edict of the king and his** new **decree was heard, and when** there was **the gathering of many young women to the Shushan citadel, to the custody of Hegai, that Esther was taken** against her will[22] **to the king's palace, to the custody of Hegai, guardian of the women.** Presumably, most of the young women were delighted to come from their lands to the capital city and excited at the opportunity the search for the queen provided. The young woman who was chosen would become the queen of the empire. Esther, in contrast, was taken against her will.

9 **The young woman was pleasing in his eyes.** Hegai, who was in charge of the women of the royal household, and was familiar with the king's tastes, considered Esther a serious candidate for the role of queen.[23] **She exhibited grace before him.** In addition to her beauty, he was charmed by her, **and** therefore he took special care of her needs: **He hastened to provide her** with a supply of **cosmetics, and her portions** of food to which she was entitled, **and the seven young women it was requisite to provide her from the king's palace.** It was unbecoming for a candidate for queen of Persia to venture forth by herself, and therefore she was given seven maidservants. **And** he elevated her status, as **he promoted her and her young women to the best** place **of the harem.**

10 Throughout this entire period **Esther did not disclose her people or her birthplace.** She had hidden her ethnic origin and her place of birth, **because Mordekhai had commanded her that she should not disclose it,**[D] her identity. Even after she left his house, and when she later rose to a position of greatness, she remained obedient to Mordekhai.

11 **On each and every day, Mordekhai would walk before the courtyard of the harem, to know Esther's well-being, and what would be done with her.** As her guardian, Mordekhai had both personal affection for Esther and was responsible for her welfare.

12 The young women's preparation for their encounters with the king followed a clearly defined process: **When each and every maiden's turn arrived to come to King Ahashverosh, at the end of her having twelve months, according to the custom of the women,** when she had been readied for the king by completing the standard beauty regimen as instructed, a process lasting twelve months, **for so were prescribed the days for their treatment: Six months** she was anointed **with myrrh oil,** which, among other things, was a depilatory,[24] **and six months with** various **perfumes, and with women's cosmetics,**

Ivory perfume bottle, Persepolis, 560–331 BCE

13 **and with that the young woman would come to the king,** after she had completed all of the treatments. One of the rules of her arrival was that **whatever she would say,** or request, in order to enhance her beauty **would be given to her, to come with her from the harem to the king's palace.** She was entitled to ask for a special ornament, or escort, or even an entire retinue, and her every wish would be granted.

14 **She would come in the evening** to the king and stay the night, **and return in the morning to the second harem,**[D] **to the custody of Shaashgaz, the king's chamberlain, guardian of the concubines.**[25] She would not go back to the compound where

ו בֶּן־קִישׁ אִישׁ יְמִינִי: אֲשֶׁר הָגְלָה מִירוּשָׁלַיִם עִם־הַגֹּלָה אֲשֶׁר הָגְלְתָה עִם יְכָנְיָה

ז מֶלֶךְ־יְהוּדָה אֲשֶׁר הֶגְלָה נְבוּכַדְנֶצַּר מֶלֶךְ בָּבֶל: וַיְהִי אֹמֵן אֶת־הֲדַסָּה הִיא אֶסְתֵּר

בַּת־דֹּדוֹ כִּי אֵין לָהּ אָב וָאֵם וְהַנַּעֲרָה יְפַת־תֹּאַר וְטוֹבַת מַרְאֶה וּבְמוֹת אָבִיהָ

ח וְאִמָּהּ לְקָחָהּ מָרְדֳּכַי לוֹ לְבַת: וַיְהִי בְּהִשָּׁמַע דְּבַר־הַמֶּלֶךְ וְדָתוֹ וּבְהִקָּבֵץ נְעָרוֹת

רַבּוֹת אֶל־שׁוּשַׁן הַבִּירָה אֶל־יַד הֵגָי וַתִּלָּקַח אֶסְתֵּר אֶל־בֵּית הַמֶּלֶךְ אֶל־יַד הֵגַי

ט שֹׁמֵר הַנָּשִׁים: וַתִּיטַב הַנַּעֲרָה בְעֵינָיו וַתִּשָּׂא חֶסֶד לְפָנָיו וַיְבַהֵל אֶת־תַּמְרוּקֶיהָ

וְאֶת־מָנוֹתֶהָ לָתֵת לָהּ וְאֵת שֶׁבַע הַנְּעָרוֹת הָרְאֻיוֹת לָתֶת־לָהּ מִבֵּית הַמֶּלֶךְ

י וַיְשַׁנֶּהָ וְאֶת־נַעֲרוֹתֶיהָ לְטוֹב בֵּית הַנָּשִׁים: לֹא־הִגִּידָה אֶסְתֵּר אֶת־עַמָּהּ וְאֶת־

יא מוֹלַדְתָּהּ כִּי מָרְדֳּכַי צִוָּה עָלֶיהָ אֲשֶׁר לֹא־תַגִּיד: וּבְכָל־יוֹם וָיוֹם מָרְדֳּכַי מִתְהַלֵּךְ

יב לִפְנֵי חֲצַר בֵּית־הַנָּשִׁים לָדַעַת אֶת־שְׁלוֹם אֶסְתֵּר וּמַה־יֵּעָשֶׂה בָּהּ: וּבְהַגִּיעַ תֹּר

נַעֲרָה וְנַעֲרָה לָבוֹא ׀ אֶל־הַמֶּלֶךְ אֲחַשְׁוֵרוֹשׁ מִקֵּץ הֱיוֹת לָהּ כְּדָת הַנָּשִׁים שְׁנֵים

עָשָׂר חֹדֶשׁ כִּי כֵּן יִמְלְאוּ יְמֵי מְרוּקֵיהֶן שִׁשָּׁה חֳדָשִׁים בְּשֶׁמֶן הַמֹּר וְשִׁשָּׁה חֳדָשִׁים

יג בַּבְּשָׂמִים וּבְתַמְרוּקֵי הַנָּשִׁים: וּבָזֶה הַנַּעֲרָה בָּאָה אֶל־הַמֶּלֶךְ אֵת כָּל־אֲשֶׁר תֹּאמַר

יד יִנָּתֵן לָהּ לָבוֹא עִמָּהּ מִבֵּית הַנָּשִׁים עַד־בֵּית הַמֶּלֶךְ: בָּעֶרֶב ׀ הִיא בָאָה וּבַבֹּקֶר

הִיא שָׁבָה אֶל־בֵּית הַנָּשִׁים שֵׁנִי אֶל־יַד שַׁעַשְׁגַז סְרִיס הַמֶּלֶךְ שֹׁמֵר הַפִּילַגְשִׁים

BACKGROUND

2:7 | **Esther:** Esther is a Persian name, from *astra*, which means a star in Indo-European languages (see *Megilla* 13a), perhaps referring to the planet Venus (see *Targum*, 10:13), whereas her Hebrew name was Hadassa, from *hadas*, meaning myrtle. It should be noted that the flowers of the myrtle, with their many stamens, resemble ancient drawings of stars. Some suggest that the name Esther is derived from that of the Babylonian goddess Ishtar, while the name Mordekhai is based on the Babylonian god Marduk. In this context, it is interesting to note that documents from ancient Shushan dating back to the reign of Xerxes I, who died in 465 BCE and whom some identify with Ahashverosh, mention a royal treasurer called Marduka.

DISCUSSION

2:10 | **Because Mordekhai had commanded her that she should not disclose it:** The text does not explain Mordekhai's motives, but presumably he thought that Esther could potentially be a secret agent. It can be safely assumed that Mordekhai would have preferred her to marry a Judean man, but that when she was forcibly taken to the house of the king, he quickly adapted to the new situation (see Rashi; Rav Yosef Kara). As one who held a position in the royal court (see 2:19), Mordekhai wanted to keep Esther's identity secret in case he should need to reveal it at an opportune moment, although of course he did not know how necessary that would ultimately be. He realized that it was in his interests to have a sleeper agent in the palace, who would be ready to act in a time of need.

2:14 | **To the second harem:** After a woman had spent the night with the king, she was considered his property, and she was therefore transferred to a special residence for his concubines. It would be disrespectful to the monarch if she were given to another man (Ibn Ezra). An example of this from elsewhere in the Bible is the case of Avishag the Shunamite, King David's companion. After David's death, his son Adoniyahu requested Avishag from King Solomon as a wife for himself, and it can be inferred from Solomon's incensed reaction that a woman who had shared the king's bed was forbidden to any other man, including a member of the royal family (I Kings 1:1–4, 2:13–25; see commentary on II Samuel 20:3).

the candidates were being groomed, but rather to the harem of the concubines, where all the young women went after they had been with the king.[26] **She would not come to the king anymore, unless the king desired her, and she was called by name.** If the king remembered her, he would instruct his minister to call her again, and if not, she would remain with the other concubines in the harem.

15 **With the arrival of the turn of Esther, daughter of Avihayil,** who had been the **uncle of Mordekhai, who had taken her as a daughter for him, to come to the king, she did not request anything except that which Hegai, the king's chamberlain, guardian of the women, said.** The other young women made an effort to impress the king, whereas Esther refrained from taking such measures on her own initiative and merely accepted the recommendations of the expert, Hegai. **And Esther found favor in the eyes of everyone who saw her.**

16 **Esther was taken to King Ahashverosh to his royal palace, in the tenth month, which is the month of Tevet, in the seventh year of his reign.** This was four years after Ahashverosh had dismissed Vashti. During this period the young women had been gathered and had undergone meticulous preparation before presentation to the king.

17 **The king loved Esther more than all the** other **women, and she found favor and grace in his eyes more than all the** other **virgins. He placed the royal crown on her head, and he crowned her queen in place of Vashti.** It is surprising that in Persia and Media a woman who was not of royal blood would be selected as queen. As stated above,[27] it seems likely that although Esther concealed her origins, she was believed to come from a noble family.

18 **The king made a great banquet for all his princes and his servants, the banquet of Esther.** A private celebration to mark the appointment of the new queen did not suffice; rather, he issued an announcement to all the nations. Since everyone had heard about the removal of Vashti, the king decided to declare publicly that her replacement had been found. **He awarded an abatement for the provinces;** he lowered the taxes so his subjects would participate in his joy. **And** furthermore, **he gave gifts in accordance with the king's bounty,** in order to improve the general welfare of his subjects and encourage their devotion.

19 **With the gathering of the virgins a second time;** it seems that some of the candidates who had been gathered had not yet had been presented to the king, and therefore the process continued in some form even after Esther had been chosen,[28] **Mordekhai was sitting at the king's gate,**[BD] that is, he held a position in the royal court, from which he was able to follow the events at the palace.[29]

Gates of the palace of the kings of Persia, Persepolis, fifth century BCE

20 It had been some time since she had entered the house of the king, and still **Esther did not disclose her birthplace or her people, as Mordekhai had commanded her; Esther would perform the directive of Mordekhai, as it was when she was reared by him,** in her childhood.

BACKGROUND

2:19 | **The king's gate:** There was a special structure for the king's gate in the palace in Shushan (see image below 1:5). Those who sought the king or his counselors were permitted to approach no further than the gatehouse, where they would wait to be received, or to hear an answer to their request.

2:23 | **And the two of them were hanged on a gibbet:** Researchers maintain that the practice of public hanging as a method of execution originated in ancient Persia. This manner of killing is a simple procedure that does not require an expert hangman and does not involve the actual shedding of blood. However, some claim that the hanging referred to in the book of Esther is actually impalement, in which a sharp wood pole is inserted into the chest or between the legs of the condemned until it emerges on the other side of the body. The Persians inherited this method of execution from the Assyrians and Babylonians.

DISCUSSION

2:19 | **Mordekhai was sitting at the king's gate:** The name Mordekhai appears in the list of those who initially immigrated to the Land of Israel from Babylonia (see Ezra 2:2; *Megilla* 16b). It is possible that after he arrived in the Land of Israel, Mordekhai was sent back to Shushan to serve in a kind of diplomatic role, representing the interests of the province of Judah in the king's court.

טו לֹא־תָבוֹא עוֹד אֶל־הַמֶּלֶךְ כִּי אִם־חָפֵץ בָּהּ הַמֶּלֶךְ וְנִקְרְאָה בְשֵׁם׃ וּבְהַגִּיעַ תֹּר־
אֶסְתֵּר בַּת־אֲבִיחַיִל ׀ דֹּד מׇרְדֳּכַי אֲשֶׁר לָקַח־לוֹ לְבַת לָבוֹא אֶל־הַמֶּלֶךְ לֹא בִקְשָׁה
דָּבָר כִּי אִם אֶת־אֲשֶׁר יֹאמַר הֵגַי סְרִיס־הַמֶּלֶךְ שֹׁמֵר הַנָּשִׁים וַתְּהִי אֶסְתֵּר נֹשֵׂאת
טז חֵן בְּעֵינֵי כׇּל־רֹאֶיהָ׃ וַתִּלָּקַח אֶסְתֵּר אֶל־הַמֶּלֶךְ אֲחַשְׁוֵרוֹשׁ אֶל־בֵּית מַלְכוּתוֹ
יז בַּחֹדֶשׁ הָעֲשִׂירִי הוּא־חֹדֶשׁ טֵבֵת בִּשְׁנַת־שֶׁבַע לְמַלְכוּתוֹ׃ וַיֶּאֱהַב הַמֶּלֶךְ אֶת־
אֶסְתֵּר מִכׇּל־הַנָּשִׁים וַתִּשָּׂא־חֵן וָחֶסֶד לְפָנָיו מִכׇּל־הַבְּתוּלֹת וַיָּשֶׂם כֶּתֶר־מַלְכוּת
יח בְּרֹאשָׁהּ וַיַּמְלִיכֶהָ תַּחַת וַשְׁתִּי׃ וַיַּעַשׂ הַמֶּלֶךְ מִשְׁתֶּה גָדוֹל לְכׇל־שָׂרָיו וַעֲבָדָיו
יט אֵת מִשְׁתֵּה אֶסְתֵּר וַהֲנָחָה לַמְּדִינוֹת עָשָׂה וַיִּתֵּן מַשְׂאֵת כְּיַד הַמֶּלֶךְ׃ וּבְהִקָּבֵץ
כ בְּתוּלוֹת שֵׁנִית וּמׇרְדֳּכַי יֹשֵׁב בְּשַׁעַר־הַמֶּלֶךְ׃ אֵין אֶסְתֵּר מַגֶּדֶת מוֹלַדְתָּהּ וְאֶת־
עַמָּהּ כַּאֲשֶׁר צִוָּה עָלֶיהָ מׇרְדֳּכָי וְאֶת־מַאֲמַר מׇרְדֳּכַי אֶסְתֵּר עֹשָׂה כַּאֲשֶׁר הָיְתָה
כא בְאׇמְנָה אִתּוֹ׃ בַּיָּמִים הָהֵם וּמׇרְדֳּכַי יֹשֵׁב בְּשַׁעַר־הַמֶּלֶךְ קָצַף
בִּגְתָן וָתֶרֶשׁ שְׁנֵי־סָרִיסֵי הַמֶּלֶךְ מִשֹּׁמְרֵי הַסַּף וַיְבַקְשׁוּ לִשְׁלֹחַ יָד בַּמֶּלֶךְ אֲחַשְׁוֵרֹשׁ׃
כב וַיִּוָּדַע הַדָּבָר לְמׇרְדֳּכַי וַיַּגֵּד לְאֶסְתֵּר הַמַּלְכָּה וַתֹּאמֶר אֶסְתֵּר לַמֶּלֶךְ בְּשֵׁם מׇרְדֳּכָי׃
כג וַיְבֻקַּשׁ הַדָּבָר וַיִּמָּצֵא וַיִּתָּלוּ שְׁנֵיהֶם עַל־עֵץ וַיִּכָּתֵב בְּסֵפֶר דִּבְרֵי הַיָּמִים לִפְנֵי

Discovery of an Assassination Plot against the King

ESTHER 2:21–23

At this stage, an apparently random incident of marginal importance is presented. However, it later becomes clear that this incident is a pivotal link in the chain of events.

21 **In those days, as Mordekhai was sitting at the king's gate, two of the king's chamberlains, Bigtan and Teresh, among the guardians of the threshold, became angry and sought to do violence to King Ahashverosh,** to assassinate him. The royal court in Persia was rife with intrigue, plots, and conspiracies at that time. In some cases it is hard to know whether a particular Persian king took the throne by virtue of his lineage, or essentially successfully performed a coup d'etat.

22 **The matter,** the plot that was being hatched, **became known to Mordekhai.** One suggestion is that Mordekhai discovered the plot because the men conversed in a language they thought no one knew, but which Mordekhai could understand.[30] **And he,** Mordekhai, **told Queen Esther** about it, in order that she pass the message on to Ahashverosh, since Mordekhai himself did not have direct contact with the king, as he was a mere official or representative of the Judeans in the royal court. **And Esther reported** the plot **to the king in the name of Mordekhai,** with whom the king was unfamiliar.

23 **The matter was investigated, and it was revealed** that Bigtan and Teresh were indeed involved in the plot, **and the two of them were hanged on a gibbet.**[B] It seems that hanging was the preferred method of execution by the Persian monarchy, as it served to display publicly the offenders' dishonorable end. **It,** the two men's attempt to assassinate King Ahashverosh on that date, as well as how he was saved, **was recorded in the book of the chronicles before the king.**

Haman and the Plot to Destroy the Jews

ESTHER 3:1–15

In this section Mordekhai refuses to accept the authority of Haman, who has become the most distinguished minister in Persia. Haman, affronted at this personal slight, convinces the king to permit the systematic annihilation of all of Mordekhai's nation, the Jews, in his empire. The word for the members of Mordekhai's nation, *Yehudim*, can be translated as either Judeans or Jews. Elsewhere in the Bible this translation has used Judeans, but in this context it makes use of the term Jews. It is in the book of Esther that the Jewish people's identity is first conceived as not necessarily a function of their origins in Judah. Most of Haman's potential victims did not live in Judah, and their families had not lived there for several generations. They nevertheless maintained a unique religious, ethnic, and cultural identity wherever they were found in the vast Persian Empire.

3 1 **After these matters,** the appointment of Esther and the foiled plot of Bigtan and Teresh, **King Ahashverosh promoted** from among his ministers **Haman son of Hamedata the Agagite,**[BD] **and he elevated him,** raised his status, **and he placed his seat above all the princes who were with him.** Advancing one particular minister to the status of a close confidant of the king was not unheard of, as attested in other documents of the period.[31]
2 **All the king's servants,** his ministers and attendants, **who were at the king's gate, were bowing and prostrating themselves to Haman, for so had the king commanded concerning him; but Mordekhai would not bow and would not prostrate himself,**[D] for an undetermined reason.[32]
3 **The king's servants, who were at the king's gate, said to Mordekhai: Why are you violating the king's commandment** that all must bow before Haman?
4 **It was, when they spoke to him day after day, and he did not listen to them, that they told** this to **Haman.** Perhaps Haman had not noticed Mordekhai's refusal up to that point, as a large crowd would pass before him, all bowing,[33] but those present, seeking to stir up trouble, informed Haman of the situation in order **to see whether Mordekhai's words would prevail,** whether he would remain firm in his decision not to bow to Haman, **for he had told them that he was a Jew** and perhaps for that reason he would not prostrate himself to Haman.[34]
5 **Haman saw that Mordekhai was not bowing and not prostrating himself to him, and Haman was filled with fury** over what he considered a public insult.
6 Haman could have punished Mordekhai for his behavior, or tried to do away with him, but **he disdained to do violence to Mordekhai alone;** merely harming Mordekhai himself was not enough for him, **for he had been told of Mordekhai's people.** This indicates that in those times there was no external sign that made it easy to differentiate between Jews and gentiles. **Haman sought to destroy all the Jews**[D] **in the entire kingdom of Ahashverosh, the people of Mordekhai.** Despite Haman's many duties as senior minister of a massive empire, he developed an obsession with the Jews, because they were Mordekhai's nation, and he sought a way to eliminate them all.
7 Haman was determined to destroy all the Jews, and he plotted how to bring this idea to fruition. **In the first month, which is the month of Nisan, during the twelfth year of King Ahashverosh, he had cast a pur,** a Persian word,[35] **which is the lot** [*goral*] in Hebrew. This was a means of divination through which one would determine the best course of action to take, and the ideal time to take it.[36] The lot was cast **before Haman.** Haman wanted to find the right date, and to that end cast lots **for each day and for each month, to the twelfth month, which is the month of Adar.** He came to the conclusion that the best time to bring about the downfall of the Jews was the month of Adar, presumably in the upcoming year.

Lot of Yahalu, illustration based on stone die, Assyria, ninth century BCE

8 Since Haman had no independent authority, he needed to incite Ahashverosh to approve his initiative. **Haman said to King Ahashverosh: There is one people**[D] **that is scattered and**

BACKGROUND

3:1 | **Haman son of Hamedata the Agagite:** It is possible that the name Haman is derived from the name of the Elamite sky god, Humban or Humman. Alternatively, it relates to a sacred bird in Persian mythology, *homa* or *huma*, whose supposed characteristics were similar to those of the phoenix, specifically long life and resistance to fire. There is also mention in Persian manuscripts of a Persian officer called Humadat, which is similar to Hamedata. The Sages understood Agagite to refer to the fact that Haman was a descendant of Agag king of Amalek (see I Samuel 15:8–9), but the name Agaga also exists in the Elamite language.

א הַמֶּלֶךְ׃ אַחַר ׀ הַדְּבָרִים הָאֵלֶּה גִּדַּל הַמֶּלֶךְ אֲחַשְׁוֵרוֹשׁ אֶת־הָמָן
בֶּן־הַמְּדָתָא הָאֲגָגִי וַיְנַשְּׂאֵהוּ וַיָּשֶׂם אֶת־כִּסְאוֹ מֵעַל כָּל־הַשָּׂרִים אֲשֶׁר אִתּוֹ׃
ב וְכָל־עַבְדֵי הַמֶּלֶךְ אֲשֶׁר־בְּשַׁעַר הַמֶּלֶךְ כֹּרְעִים וּמִשְׁתַּחֲוִים לְהָמָן כִּי־כֵן צִוָּה־
ג לוֹ הַמֶּלֶךְ וּמָרְדֳּכַי לֹא יִכְרַע וְלֹא יִשְׁתַּחֲוֶה׃ וַיֹּאמְרוּ עַבְדֵי הַמֶּלֶךְ אֲשֶׁר־בְּשַׁעַר
ד הַמֶּלֶךְ לְמָרְדֳּכָי מַדּוּעַ אַתָּה עוֹבֵר אֵת מִצְוַת הַמֶּלֶךְ׃ וַיְהִי באמרם אֵלָיו יוֹם וָיוֹם כְּאָמְרָם
וְלֹא שָׁמַע אֲלֵיהֶם וַיַּגִּידוּ לְהָמָן לִרְאוֹת הֲיַעַמְדוּ דִּבְרֵי מָרְדֳּכַי כִּי־הִגִּיד לָהֶם
ה אֲשֶׁר־הוּא יְהוּדִי׃ וַיַּרְא הָמָן כִּי־אֵין מָרְדֳּכַי כֹּרֵעַ וּמִשְׁתַּחֲוֶה לוֹ וַיִּמָּלֵא הָמָן חֵמָה׃
ו וַיִּבֶז בְּעֵינָיו לִשְׁלֹחַ יָד בְּמָרְדֳּכַי לְבַדּוֹ כִּי־הִגִּידוּ לוֹ אֶת־עַם מָרְדֳּכָי וַיְבַקֵּשׁ הָמָן
ז לְהַשְׁמִיד אֶת־כָּל־הַיְּהוּדִים אֲשֶׁר בְּכָל־מַלְכוּת אֲחַשְׁוֵרוֹשׁ עַם מָרְדֳּכָי׃ בַּחֹדֶשׁ
הָרִאשׁוֹן הוּא־חֹדֶשׁ נִיסָן בִּשְׁנַת שְׁתֵּים עֶשְׂרֵה לַמֶּלֶךְ אֲחַשְׁוֵרוֹשׁ הִפִּיל פּוּר
הוּא הַגּוֹרָל לִפְנֵי הָמָן מִיּוֹם ׀ לְיוֹם וּמֵחֹדֶשׁ לְחֹדֶשׁ שְׁנֵים־עָשָׂר הוּא־חֹדֶשׁ
ח אֲדָר׃ וַיֹּאמֶר הָמָן לַמֶּלֶךְ אֲחַשְׁוֵרוֹשׁ יֶשְׁנוֹ עַם־אֶחָד מְפֻזָּר וּמְפֹרָד ג
בֵּין הָעַמִּים בְּכֹל מְדִינוֹת מַלְכוּתֶךָ וְדָתֵיהֶם שֹׁנוֹת מִכָּל־עָם וְאֶת־דָּתֵי הַמֶּלֶךְ

DISCUSSION

3:1 | **The Agagite:** This probably means that he was a descendant of Agag the Amalekite king (see the Aramaic translations of the Bible; *Masekhet Soferim* 13; *Aggadat Esther* 3). The Agag mentioned in the Bible lived during the period of Saul (see I Samuel 15:8–9). It is possible, however, that Agag was the standard royal name for all kings of the Amalekites (see Rashbam, and Ramban, Numbers 24:7; see also Jerusalem Talmud, *Yevamot* 2:6). Haman might have changed his original Amalekite name to one that sounded more Persian.

3:2 | **But Mordekhai would not bow and would not prostrate himself:** It would seem that Mordekhai's refusal to bow before Haman was not motivated by religious concerns. After all, it is related about other righteous figures that they bowed down and prostrated themselves before ministers and kings, and this was not considered a sin (see Genesis 42:6; Exodus 18:7; I Samuel 24:8; I Kings 1:23). Perhaps Mordekhai, who was from Judean nobility, considered the idea of bowing down to Haman an act of humiliation for all Jews (see also *Yalkut Shimoni* 954). It is also possible that his refusal to lower himself before Haman was due to the personal enmity between the men. According to tradition, they had a prior acquaintance, and Mordekhai despised Haman personally (see *Megillat Setarim*; *Megilla* 15a–16a). Some say that he refused to bow down because Haman presented himself as a god, or because he hung an idol from his clothing (see Ibn Ezra; Ralbag; *Megilla* 10b, 19a; *Sanhedrin* 61b).

3:6 | **Haman sought to destroy all the Jews:** This phenomenon of a personal hatred that expands into hatred of an entire people is unusual and puzzling. The background of this enmity is related to Haman's Amalekite roots. Although not a large nation, Amalek hated the nation of Israel from the beginning of its history as a people (see Exodus 17:8–16). Haman's confrontation with Mordekhai was not the only reason for his extreme reaction; it awakened a primeval enmity that he and his people had nurtured against Israel from time immemorial.

3:8 | **There is one people:** The fact that Haman had to tell Ahashverosh about the Jews indicates that the king knew very little about them. Although the Jews were his subjects, and they even had a small state of their own in the area surrounding Jerusalem, it is doubtful whether Ahashverosh had ever thought about this tiny nation. The 127 provinces over which he reigned, some of which were very large and important, contained many peoples and tribes. Even if Ahashverosh had been a conscientious and organized ruler, he would not have been intimately familiar with the Jewish people. However, it is known that he received a letter from Samaritans libeling the exiles who had returned to the Land of Israel (see Ezra 4:6), and therefore it is likely that Haman's comments evoked his existing negative associations, making him receptive to the idea of their destruction.

dispersed[B] **among the peoples in all the provinces of your kingdom;** they are not concentrated in one country;[37] and **their laws,** their practices, their ways of life, **are different from every people's.** A significant proportion of the commandments of the Torah serve to keep Jews apart from gentiles and prevent them from engaging in idolatry. **And** while the Jews observe their own laws, **they do not follow the king's laws,** and therefore **it is not worthwhile for the king to tolerate them.** They are a small nation of no importance, and an annoyance that disrupts the harmony of your kingdom.

9 **If it pleases the king** to accept my proposal, **let it be written** as an official order **to eliminate them,**[D] **and I will weigh ten thousand talents of silver**[D] **into the hands of the king's craftsmen.** I volunteer to give ten thousand silver talents of my own to those who can turn it into silver bullion, **to bring to the king's treasuries.**[B] The donation to the king's treasuries would compensate Ahashverosh for any possible financial costs incurred by the course of action suggested by Haman, as the king might fear the loss of so many taxpayers.

10 Apathetic as he was to the fate of the Jews, Ahashverosh was apparently enthused by the generous gift of his chief minister. Therefore, **the king removed his ring** with the royal seal **from his hand,**[D] **and he gave it to Haman son of Hamedata the Agagite, the adversary of the Jews.** This was not merely a verbal agreement; by giving him his seal, Ahashverosh granted Haman practical permission and authority to sign in the king's name.[38]

Ring seal, Shushan, third century BCE

11 **The king said to Haman: The silver** that you offered to donate **is given to you;** it shall remain in your possession, as the kingdom will bear the cost, **and the people** are also given to you, **to do with them as it is pleasing in your eyes,** in accordance with your wishes.

12 Haman acted with great haste. He cast the lots at the beginning of Nisan, and by the thirteenth of the month everything was ready for the next stage of his plan: **The king's scribes were summoned in the first month, on the thirteenth day of it, and it was written in accordance with everything that Haman commanded to the king's satraps,**[B] who presided over the larger regions, **and to the governors**[B] **who were over each and every province,** the smaller areas, **and to the princes of each and every people, to each and every province in its script, and to each and every people in its language.**[B] **In the name of King Ahashverosh, it,** the missive with the decree, **was written, and it was sealed with the king's ring.**

Assyrian scribes, illustration based on stone relief, Nimrud, Iraq, eighth century BCE

13 **The scrolls were sent in the hand of the couriers to all the king's provinces,** in which it was written that the king permitted his subjects **to destroy, to kill, and to eliminate all the Jews, from lad to elder, children and women, in one day, on the thirteenth of the twelfth month, which is the month of Adar, and to plunder their spoils,** their property. The instructions were sent almost a year in advance, perhaps in order to establish the facts on the ground as soon as possible, and so that the missives would reach the farthest corners of the empire in time. Due to Haman's trust in his divination, he was resolute in keeping the determined date, at which point the Jews would be deemed legitimate targets. There does not seem to have been any need to enforce this decree. It simply stated that on such and such a date the Jews would no longer enjoy the protection of the law. Haman assumed that that was sufficient, and that the members of the various nations of the empire would take the opportunity to annihilate the Jews.

DISCUSSION

3:9 | **Let it be written to eliminate them:** Haman's proposal and his conduct toward Mordekhai is the first case of anti-Semitism in the sense of Jew-hatred. In previous generations various nations had fought against the kingdoms of Israel, but those were not anti-Semitic wars that sought to exterminate the nation, but struggles for power due to conflicts of interest. Similarly, the Israelites suffered in Egypt because they were strangers, and perhaps because the ruling authorities felt threatened by their presence. Most of these wars were not etched in the collective national memory. The attack recorded here is of a different kind entirely. Haman's speech is an ancient model for anti-Semitic propaganda, which has been used, with minor variations, by many anti-Semites in subsequent generations. It is possible to see signs of anti-Semitism in the struggle against the exiles returning to Judah on the part of Sanbalat the Horonite, the leader of the Samaritans, which occurred at roughly the same time as the events described in this book. He and his men sought to sabotage the rebuilding of Jerusalem and the Temple through mockery, the weakening of the Jews' resolve, and scaremongering and informing on them to the authorities, as well general abuse and threats of destruction (see Nehemiah 2–6).

ט אֵינָ֥ם עֹשִׂ֖ים וְלַמֶּ֥לֶךְ אֵין־שֹׁוֶ֖ה לְהַנִּיחָֽם׃ אִם־עַל־הַמֶּ֣לֶךְ ט֔וֹב יִכָּתֵ֖ב לְאַבְּדָ֑ם
וַעֲשֶׂרֶת֩ אֲלָפִ֨ים כִּכַּר־כֶּ֜סֶף אֶשְׁקוֹל֙ עַל־יְדֵי֙ עֹשֵׂ֣י הַמְּלָאכָ֔ה לְהָבִ֖יא אֶל־גִּנְזֵ֥י
י הַמֶּֽלֶךְ׃ וַיָּ֧סַר הַמֶּ֛לֶךְ אֶת־טַבַּעְתּ֖וֹ מֵעַ֣ל יָד֑וֹ וַֽיִּתְּנָ֗הּ לְהָמָ֧ן בֶּֽן־הַמְּדָ֛תָא הָאֲגָגִ֖י צֹרֵ֥ר
יא הַיְּהוּדִֽים׃ וַיֹּ֤אמֶר הַמֶּ֙לֶךְ֙ לְהָמָ֔ן הַכֶּ֖סֶף נָת֣וּן לָ֑ךְ וְהָעָ֕ם לַעֲשׂ֥וֹת בּ֖וֹ כַּטּ֥וֹב בְּעֵינֶֽיךָ׃
יב וַיִּקָּרְא֞וּ סֹפְרֵ֣י הַמֶּ֗לֶךְ בַּחֹ֣דֶשׁ הָרִאשׁ֮וֹן בִּשְׁלוֹשָׁ֨ה עָשָׂ֣ר יוֹם֮ בּוֹ֒ וַיִּכָּתֵ֣ב כְּכָל־אֲשֶׁר־
צִוָּ֣ה הָמָ֡ן אֶ֣ל אֲחַשְׁדַּרְפְּנֵֽי־הַ֠מֶּלֶךְ וְאֶל־הַפַּחוֹת֩ אֲשֶׁ֨ר ׀ עַל־מְדִינָ֜ה וּמְדִינָ֗ה וְאֶל־
שָׂרֵ֤י עַם֙ וָעָ֔ם מְדִינָ֤ה וּמְדִינָה֙ כִּכְתָבָ֔הּ וְעַ֥ם וָעָ֖ם כִּלְשׁוֹנ֑וֹ בְּשֵׁ֨ם הַמֶּ֤לֶךְ אֲחַשְׁוֵרֹשׁ֙
יג נִכְתָּ֔ב וְנֶחְתָּ֖ם בְּטַבַּ֥עַת הַמֶּֽלֶךְ׃ וְנִשְׁלוֹחַ֩ סְפָרִ֨ים בְּיַ֣ד הָרָצִים֮ אֶל־כָּל־מְדִינ֣וֹת
הַמֶּלֶךְ֒ לְהַשְׁמִ֡יד לַהֲרֹ֣ג וּלְאַבֵּ֣ד אֶת־כָּל־הַ֠יְּהוּדִים מִנַּ֨עַר וְעַד־זָקֵ֜ן טַ֣ף וְנָשִׁ֗ים
בְּי֣וֹם אֶחָ֔ד בִּשְׁלוֹשָׁ֥ה עָשָׂ֛ר לְחֹ֥דֶשׁ שְׁנֵים־עָשָׂ֖ר הוּא־חֹ֣דֶשׁ אֲדָ֑ר וּשְׁלָלָ֖ם לָבֽוֹז׃

BACKGROUND

3:8 | **Scattered and dispersed:** The Assyrian kings first exiled the ten tribes of Israel to northwest Mesopotamia, after which Nebuchadnezzar exiled the leading Judeans to central and southern Mesopotamia. In some cases, these exiles achieved high social and political status, and they also dealt in international trade. In this manner they spread across the Persian Empire, from Afghanistan and India to Libya, southern Egypt, and western Anatolia. Judeans apparently served on Phoenician ships and conducted business with Sidonian merchants, and they may have even reached distant trading stations in northern Africa and Spain.

3:9 | **The king's treasuries [*ginzei*]:** In Old Persian, *ganzaka* is a small treasure chamber. This word is also the source of the Hebrew terms *ganzakh*, archive, and *gizbar*, treasurer.

3:10 | **The king removed his ring from his hand:** Royal commands were generally etched in cuneiform script on clay tablets which were authorized with the impression of a seal. Some seals were attached to a ring, while others were hung on a chain around the neck. It is possible that the king did not need to be literate, as all his orders were written by scribes, who would read out the texts to him when necessary (see 6:1).

3:12 | **The king's satraps [*aḥashdarpenei*]:** The Persian word originally denoted a shield of the kingdom, but this meaning was broadened to include the rulers of administrative units of the Persian Empire.

The governors [*hapaḥot*]: *Peḥa*, or *pihatu* in Akkadian, was an official of a lower status than a satrap. A *paḥavva*, which was ruled by a *peḥa*, was part of a larger unit.

To each and every province in its script, and to each and every people in its language: According to the standard procedure of the Persian monarchy, the king would dictate his order in Persian, while the Aramean scribes would write it in Aramaic. The missives were sent to the local scribes of each province, who would read the Aramaic and translate it into the local language while reading them aloud. In this instance the missives were sent in different languages due to the importance of their content.

DISCUSSION

Ten thousand talents of silver: If this is referring to sacred talents mentioned in the book of Exodus, then a silver talent weighed roughly 30 kg. According to this calculation, Haman proposed to give the king some 300 metric tons of silver. It is unusual for such a large sum to be in the possession of a private individual. Haman was clearly an immensely wealthy man with the powerful position of the chief minister of the empire (see 5:11; *Bemidbar Rabba* 22:6).

14 **A copy**[39] **of the document**[B] **went out to issue the decree in each and every province, publicizing it to all the peoples: To be ready for that day.** Although it is unlikely that Jews were to be found in every remote corner of the Persian Empire, for bureaucratic reasons the announcement was sent to each province; a general decree of the king had to reach the entire kingdom.

15 **The couriers went out urgently by the word of the king, and the decree was issued in the Shushan citadel. The king and Haman sat to drink** and toast the success of their plan. Ahashverosh and Haman were so delighted that the plan had been put into motion that they held a small feast; **and** meanwhile **the city of Shushan,** mainly its Jewish community, of which Mordekhai[40] was a prominent member, **was confounded** by the sudden harsh decree.

Mordekhai and Esther React to the Decree

ESTHER 4:1–17

Mordekhai's refusal to bow before Haman is the pretext for the decree to destroy the Jews. When the decree is publicized, he reacts without delay, calling upon Esther, his secret representative in the king's palace, to thwart it. The conversation between Mordekhai and Esther reveals both their profound concerns about the king's decree, and their faith and trust in God. At the start of this section, Mordekhai cries out in distress, and at its conclusion, Esther asks for all the Jews to gather together and fast. Even if they are uncertain as to whether their prayers will be accepted, they both believe that their fervent supplications and their fasting will influence the unfolding events.

4 1 **Mordekhai,** who was a court official, **knew everything that was done,** as he was presumably one of the first to read a copy of the decree that had been distributed throughout the kingdom. He understood the severity of the situation and its implications for the future of the Jews, even before the rest of the Jews living in Shushan knew what had transpired. He was deeply concerned by the likely effectiveness of Haman's propaganda, as well as Haman's growing influence in the royal court. **And** consequently, **Mordekhai rent his garments and donned sackcloth, and** placed **ashes** upon his head, all signs of mourning. **He went out in the midst of the city and cried a loud and bitter cry,** a cry of prayer and entreaty to God,[41] and a cry of protest against the authorities.

2 **He came up to before the king's gate;** although he was generally authorized to enter, he did not approach further, **as** in accordance with the royal dress code,[42] **one may not come to the king's gate in a sackcloth garment.**

3 **And in each and every province, any place where the word of the king and his decree reached, there was great mourning among the Jews, fasting, weeping, and keening; sackcloth and ashes were draped by the multitudes;** alternatively, sackcloth and ashes were laid out in the streets for public use.

4 **Esther's young women and her chamberlains came and told her** of Mordekhai's actions. Those who were close to Esther knew about her relationship with him, as Mordekhai would inquire about her welfare every day, and it was she who had passed on Mordekhai's warning about the plot on the king's life (2:11, 22). **And the queen was greatly shocked,** as she had not heard anything about what was going on. The king's decree had not been disclosed to the women, as they were presumed to not be interested in political matters. **And** as Esther wanted to hear from Mordekhai what was happening, and since she knew that he could not enter while wearing sackcloth, **she sent garments to clothe Mordekhai and to remove from upon him his sackcloth, but he would not accept them,** refusing to take off his sackcloth.

5 **Esther called Ḥatakh, one of the king's chamberlains, whom he had set before her.** Hatakh was no ordinary servant; he had been granted explicit authority to help the queen with whatever she might need. **And** she **commanded him concerning Mordekhai,** in order **to know what this is, and why this is.** She wanted to know the reason for his behavior, and what he wanted.[43]

6 **Hatakh went out to Mordekhai, to the city square that was before the king's gate.** Since Mordekhai did not approach the king's gate, Hatakh came out to the square outside it, where he asked Mordekhai to explain his conduct.

7 **Mordekhai told him everything that had happened to him.** This did not necessarily include his refusal to bow down to Haman, as Mordekhai might have considered Haman's decree no more than his manifestation of a tradition of hatred for Jews he had inherited from his ancestors, the tribe of Amalek. **And** he informed Hatakh of **the matter of the silver that Haman had said to weigh out for the king's treasuries concerning the Jews,** in order **to destroy them.** In addition to the decree

BACKGROUND

3:14 | **A copy [*patshegen*] of the document:** In Old Persian, this means a faithful copy of the source of the law, signed with the seal of the king's ring.

יד פַּתְשֶׁגֶן הַכְּתָב לְהִנָּתֵן דָּת בְּכָל־מְדִינָה וּמְדִינָה גָּלוּי לְכָל־הָעַמִּים לִהְיוֹת עֲתִדִים
טו לַיּוֹם הַזֶּה: הָרָצִים יָצְאוּ דְחוּפִים בִּדְבַר הַמֶּלֶךְ וְהַדָּת נִתְּנָה בְּשׁוּשַׁן הַבִּירָה
א וְהַמֶּלֶךְ וְהָמָן יָשְׁבוּ לִשְׁתּוֹת וְהָעִיר שׁוּשָׁן נָבוֹכָה: וּמָרְדֳּכַי יָדַע אֶת־
כָּל־אֲשֶׁר נַעֲשָׂה וַיִּקְרַע מָרְדֳּכַי אֶת־בְּגָדָיו וַיִּלְבַּשׁ שַׂק וָאֵפֶר וַיֵּצֵא בְּתוֹךְ הָעִיר
ב וַיִּזְעַק זְעָקָה גְדֹלָה וּמָרָה: וַיָּבוֹא עַד לִפְנֵי שַׁעַר־הַמֶּלֶךְ כִּי אֵין לָבוֹא אֶל־שַׁעַר
ג הַמֶּלֶךְ בִּלְבוּשׁ שָׂק: וּבְכָל־מְדִינָה וּמְדִינָה מְקוֹם אֲשֶׁר דְּבַר־הַמֶּלֶךְ וְדָתוֹ מַגִּיעַ
ד אֵבֶל גָּדוֹל לַיְּהוּדִים וְצוֹם וּבְכִי וּמִסְפֵּד שַׂק וָאֵפֶר יֻצַּע לָרַבִּים: ותבואינה נַעֲרוֹת   וַתָּבוֹאנָה
אֶסְתֵּר וְסָרִיסֶיהָ וַיַּגִּידוּ לָהּ וַתִּתְחַלְחַל הַמַּלְכָּה מְאֹד וַתִּשְׁלַח בְּגָדִים לְהַלְבִּישׁ
ה אֶת־מָרְדֳּכַי וּלְהָסִיר שַׂקּוֹ מֵעָלָיו וְלֹא קִבֵּל: וַתִּקְרָא אֶסְתֵּר לַהֲתָךְ מִסָּרִיסֵי הַמֶּלֶךְ
ו אֲשֶׁר הֶעֱמִיד לְפָנֶיהָ וַתְּצַוֵּהוּ עַל־מָרְדֳּכָי לָדַעַת מַה־זֶּה וְעַל־מַה־זֶּה: וַיֵּצֵא
ז הֲתָךְ אֶל־מָרְדֳּכָי אֶל־רְחוֹב הָעִיר אֲשֶׁר לִפְנֵי שַׁעַר־הַמֶּלֶךְ: וַיַּגֶּד־לוֹ מָרְדֳּכַי אֵת
כָּל־אֲשֶׁר קָרָהוּ וְאֵת ׀ פָּרָשַׁת הַכֶּסֶף אֲשֶׁר אָמַר הָמָן לִשְׁקוֹל עַל־גִּנְזֵי הַמֶּלֶךְ
ח ביהודיים לְאַבְּדָם: וְאֶת־פַּתְשֶׁגֶן כְּתָב־הַדָּת אֲשֶׁר־נִתַּן בְּשׁוּשָׁן לְהַשְׁמִידָם נָתַן   בַּיְּהוּדִים
לוֹ לְהַרְאוֹת אֶת־אֶסְתֵּר וּלְהַגִּיד לָהּ וּלְצַוּוֹת עָלֶיהָ לָבוֹא אֶל־הַמֶּלֶךְ לְהִתְחַנֶּן־לוֹ
ט י וּלְבַקֵּשׁ מִלְּפָנָיו עַל־עַמָּהּ: וַיָּבוֹא הֲתָךְ וַיַּגֵּד לְאֶסְתֵּר אֵת דִּבְרֵי מָרְדֳּכָי: וַתֹּאמֶר
יא אֶסְתֵּר לַהֲתָךְ וַתְּצַוֵּהוּ אֶל־מָרְדֳּכָי: כָּל־עַבְדֵי הַמֶּלֶךְ וְעַם־מְדִינוֹת הַמֶּלֶךְ יֹדְעִים

itself, word had spread of the enormous sum that Haman had proposed to give to the king in his determination to annihilate the Jews.

8 **He** also **gave him,** Hatakh, **a copy of the written decree to destroy them,** the Jews, **that was issued in Shushan** in order **to show it,** the decree, **to Esther, to inform her** of the situation, **and** furthermore **to command her** in his name **to go to the king, to plead with him, and to request before him on behalf of her people.** Only she could stop Haman, who enjoyed such privileged status in the kingdom. Mordekhai himself was not close to the king, whereas Esther lived in the palace and was beloved by Ahashverosh. Since the decree was essentially motivated by emotion, Mordekhai hoped that she had the power to annul it through her entreaties.

9 **Hatakh came and told Esther the words of Mordekhai.**

10 **Esther said to Hatakh, and commanded him** to take back the following message **for Mordekhai:**

11 The rules of entering to see the king are well known: **All the king's servants** in the court, **and the people of the king's provinces, know that for any man or woman who comes to the king to the inner courtyard who has not been summoned** and has not been granted permission, **there is but one rule for him: To be put to death.** It was forbidden to enter without special invitation, as the king had quasi-divine status.

Esther continued: This fate is the rule, **except for one to whom the king will extend the golden scepter,**[B] **who lives.** If the king does not want a person who has entered without permission to be executed, he stretches forth his golden scepter to the person. Esther concludes: And **I have not been summoned to come to the king these thirty days.** Although I am the king's beloved queen, he has thousands of wives and concubines. I do not know his current mood, but the fact that he has not invited me for a month does not bode well. If I simply march in to see him, I will be endangering my life.

12 **They told Mordekhai Esther's words.**

13 **Mordekhai said to respond to Esther:** You feel protected in the palace, and you suppose that you will be spared any harm from Haman's order. However, you are wrong; **do not imagine escaping** because you are **in the king's palace,** that **out of all the Jews** you will be safe.

14 **For if you are silent** and do nothing **at this time,** I trust that **relief and deliverance will arise for the Jews from another place.** The decree does not go into effect for another eleven months, and I have faith in God that He will deliver us before then, **but** I am sure that **you and your father's house will perish,** as you did not act at the opportune time to save the Jews. Destruction will be visited upon you and your family, including myself.[44] **Who knows whether you have attained royalty for a time like this?** You came to a position of power without planning to do so, and now you find yourself in a situation where you can act to change the course of events and thereby save your people. Don't you think that this apparent coincidence is significant? Can't you see that it is a sign from Heaven?

15 Esther, as usual, accepted Mordekhai's instructions. **Esther said to respond to Mordekhai:**

16 **Go, assemble all the Jews who are present in Shushan, and** pray[45] and **fast on my behalf; do not eat and do not drink for three days, night and day,** an unusually severe fast. **Also I and my young women will fast in this manner,** as we must all pray for my success; **and then I will go to the king, against the rule, and if I perish, I perish.** Perhaps the day when I approach the king will be the last of my life.

17 **Mordekhai went on** his way, **and acted in accordance with everything that Esther had commanded him.** He gathered together all the Jews, informed them of the evil decree and of Esther's situation, and instructed them to pray and fast. The Jews' high regard for Mordekhai inspired them to rally behind him and follow his instructions.

Esther Risks Her Life

ESTHER 5:1–14

In dramatic contrast to Vashti, who violated the law by refusing to appear before Ahashverosh when he called her, Esther dares to transgress the law by approaching the king without having been called, thereby putting her life at risk. The feast for the public described at the beginning of the book likewise stands in contrast to the intimate feasts orchestrated by Esther for the king and Haman. As the story continues, the pace of events increases, and all the main characters are placed under stress: Ahashverosh does not understand why Esther risked her life in approaching him, nor why she keeps inviting him and Haman to parties; Haman enjoys the great honor granted to him by the queen and concurrently suffers humiliation in his dealings with Mordekhai; Esther does not know whether her plans and efforts will help her save her brethren, or whether they will bring disaster upon her; meanwhile, a death sentence hovers over Mordekhai's head.

5 1 **It was on the third day;**[D] **Esther donned royalty,**[46] royal apparel, **and stood in the inner courtyard of the king's palace, facing the king's palace; the king was sitting on his royal throne in the royal palace, facing the entrance of the palace,**[B] where he could see who was present in the court.[47]

2 **It was as the king saw Queen Esther standing in the courtyard that she found favor in his eyes;** the affection that he had initially felt toward her when he chose her was rekindled, **and** consequently **the king extended the golden scepter that was in his hand to Esther,** thereby granting her official permission to enter. **Esther approached and touched the top of the scepter,** which was apparently the accepted ceremonial response to receiving royal permission to approach.

Darius seated on throne, holding his scepter, Persepolis, fifth century BCE

3 **The king said to her: What is it with you, Queen Esther, and what is your request?** You clearly want something. In my love for you I will grant it, **up to half of the kingdom, and it will be granted to you.**[B] The king expresses in exaggerated terms his willingness to act for her sake.

4 **Esther said,** in the same formal manner: **If it pleases the king, let the king and Haman,** the most important man in the kingdom and the one closest to the king, **come**[D] **today to the banquet that I have prepared for him,** the king.

אֲשֶׁר כָּל־אִישׁ וְאִשָּׁה אֲשֶׁר־יָבוֹא אֶל־הַמֶּלֶךְ אֶל־הֶחָצֵר הַפְּנִימִית אֲשֶׁר לֹא־
יִקָּרֵא אַחַת דָּתוֹ לְהָמִית לְבַד מֵאֲשֶׁר יוֹשִׁיט־לוֹ הַמֶּלֶךְ אֶת־שַׁרְבִיט הַזָּהָב
יב וְחָיָה וַאֲנִי לֹא נִקְרֵאתִי לָבוֹא אֶל־הַמֶּלֶךְ זֶה שְׁלוֹשִׁים יוֹם׃ וַיַּגִּידוּ לְמָרְדֳּכָי אֵת
יג דִּבְרֵי אֶסְתֵּר׃ וַיֹּאמֶר מָרְדֳּכַי לְהָשִׁיב אֶל־אֶסְתֵּר אַל־תְּדַמִּי בְנַפְשֵׁךְ לְהִמָּלֵט
יד בֵּית־הַמֶּלֶךְ מִכָּל־הַיְּהוּדִים׃ כִּי אִם־הַחֲרֵשׁ תַּחֲרִישִׁי בָּעֵת הַזֹּאת רֶוַח וְהַצָּלָה
יַעֲמוֹד לַיְּהוּדִים מִמָּקוֹם אַחֵר וְאַתְּ וּבֵית־אָבִיךְ תֹּאבֵדוּ וּמִי יוֹדֵעַ אִם־לְעֵת
טו טז כָּזֹאת הִגַּעַתְּ לַמַּלְכוּת׃ וַתֹּאמֶר אֶסְתֵּר לְהָשִׁיב אֶל־מָרְדֳּכָי׃ לֵךְ כְּנוֹס אֶת־כָּל־
הַיְּהוּדִים הַנִּמְצְאִים בְּשׁוּשָׁן וְצוּמוּ עָלַי וְאַל־תֹּאכְלוּ וְאַל־תִּשְׁתּוּ שְׁלֹשֶׁת יָמִים
לַיְלָה וָיוֹם גַּם־אֲנִי וְנַעֲרֹתַי אָצוּם כֵּן וּבְכֵן אָבוֹא אֶל־הַמֶּלֶךְ אֲשֶׁר לֹא־כַדָּת
יז וְכַאֲשֶׁר אָבַדְתִּי אָבָדְתִּי׃ וַיַּעֲבֹר מָרְדֳּכָי וַיַּעַשׂ כְּכֹל אֲשֶׁר־צִוְּתָה עָלָיו אֶסְתֵּר׃
א וַיְהִי ׀ בַּיּוֹם הַשְּׁלִישִׁי וַתִּלְבַּשׁ אֶסְתֵּר מַלְכוּת וַתַּעֲמֹד בַּחֲצַר בֵּית־הַמֶּלֶךְ הַפְּנִימִית
נֹכַח בֵּית הַמֶּלֶךְ וְהַמֶּלֶךְ יוֹשֵׁב עַל־כִּסֵּא מַלְכוּתוֹ בְּבֵית הַמַּלְכוּת נֹכַח פֶּתַח
ב הַבָּיִת׃ וַיְהִי כִרְאוֹת הַמֶּלֶךְ אֶת־אֶסְתֵּר הַמַּלְכָּה עֹמֶדֶת בֶּחָצֵר נָשְׂאָה חֵן בְּעֵינָיו
וַיּוֹשֶׁט הַמֶּלֶךְ לְאֶסְתֵּר אֶת־שַׁרְבִיט הַזָּהָב אֲשֶׁר בְּיָדוֹ וַתִּקְרַב אֶסְתֵּר וַתִּגַּע בְּרֹאשׁ
ג הַשַּׁרְבִיט׃ וַיֹּאמֶר לָהּ הַמֶּלֶךְ מַה־לָּךְ אֶסְתֵּר הַמַּלְכָּה וּמַה־בַּקָּשָׁתֵךְ עַד־חֲצִי
ד הַמַּלְכוּת וְיִנָּתֵן לָךְ׃ וַתֹּאמֶר אֶסְתֵּר אִם־עַל־הַמֶּלֶךְ טוֹב יָבוֹא הַמֶּלֶךְ וְהָמָן הַיּוֹם

BACKGROUND

4:11 | **Scepter [*sharvit*]:** The Akkadian source of *sharvit* is *sabbitu*, a rod, branch, or staff that symbolizes the authority of the bearer. The parallel Hebrew term, *shevet*, is a metonym, as the physical staff represents the monarchy (see Genesis 49:10; II Samuel 7:7; Rashi, I Chronicles 18:5). Throughout history, various kings developed a custom of holding a gold or gold-plated ceremonial scepter, and this is practiced to this day by the monarchs of Britain and Scandinavia.

5:1 | **His royal throne in the royal palace, facing the entrance of the palace:** According to the map of the palace (see image alongside 1:5), the throne room was open, and from there the king could see who was standing in the inner courtyard.

5:3 | **Up to half of the kingdom, and it will be granted to you:** The queen of Persia, the foremost wife of the king, enjoyed a privileged status and great authority. This is supported by the account of Herodotus, who portrayed Atossa, Darius' wife and the mother of Xerxes I, in such terms. She ensured that her son would become king despite the fact that he was not the heir apparent (*The Histories* VII:2).

DISCUSSION

5:1 | **On the third day:** That is, the third day of the fast the Jews had taken upon themselves. This may also have been the third day since Haman's decree had been issued, which was the first day of the festival of Passover, or one or two days later (see Rav Yeshaya of Trani; *Seder Olam Rabba* 29; *Pirkei deRabbi Eliezer* 49; *Esther Rabba* 8; see also the *piyyut*: "Your Mighty Strength You Displayed on Passover," from the Passover Haggadah; *Targum*; Rashi, Esther 4:17; *Megilla* 15a).

5:4 | **Let the king and Haman come:** It seems that Esther's plan was to display personal affection for, and bestow particular honor upon, Haman, in order to sow discord and engender the king's suspicion

5 **The king said: Hasten Haman to do Esther's bidding.** The tone of this order is somewhat dismissive of Haman, as the king is treating him like a servant who must instantly obey any desire of the queen.[48] **The king and Haman,** who was very pleased at this honor, **came to the banquet that Esther had prepared.**

6 Ahashverosh understood that this feast was not a celebration for its own sake, but rather was designed to create a favorable opportunity for the queen to state her request. Therefore **the king said to Esther at the wine banquet: What is your wish? It will be granted to you. What is your request? Up to half of the kingdom, and it will be done.**

7 **Esther answered and she said: My wish and my request** is as follows:

8 **If I have found favor in the eyes of the king, and if it pleases the king to grant my wish and to perform my request, let the king and Haman come to the banquet that I will** again **prepare for them, and tomorrow I will do the king's bidding.** Despite the expressions of affection that she had heard from Ahashverosh, Esther still hesitated; she was not yet ready to present her request. She was unsure of her ability to take a drastic step immediately, and she knew that were she to fail, she would also place herself in danger.

9 Ahashverosh left the feast in a state of intense curiosity. Esther had approached him the previous day, against the rules. In light of her repeated deferrals, he realized that she was preparing herself to request something important. In contrast, **Haman emerged on that day joyful and glad of heart.** He felt that he had reached the pinnacle of his success, as he was now not only a confidant of the king, but the queen had also shown him special favor, and he considered this a clear sign of his exalted status. **But upon Haman's seeing Mordekhai at the king's gate,** where Mordekhai had returned in his usual apparel after the end of the fast, **and he did not stand, and he did not move on his account,** but ignored Haman completely, Haman's mood changed for the worse; **Haman became filled with fury against Mordekhai.** The loftier his position in the kingdom, the more uncontrollable his anger over this act of disrespect.

10 Nevertheless **Haman restrained himself,** as he could do nothing at that time,[49] **and** he **entered his house and brought,** gathered, **his supporters, and Zeresh, his** influential **wife.**

11 **Haman** arranged a celebratory gathering of his supporters in order to tell them that he had been invited to the queen's feast, and he **related to them the honor of his wealth, and the multitude of his children, and all** the ways **that the king had promoted him, and that he had elevated him over the princes and servants of the king.** It is mentioned later (9:7–10) that ten sons of Haman were hanged, and he might have had even more children from other wives.[50]

12 **Haman said: Indeed, Queen Esther did not bring anyone but me with the king to the banquet that she prepared; tomorrow too, I am invited to her with the king.** This is the crowning glory. Not only am I the chief minister of the kingdom, but I have become the favorite in the royal household.

13 **But all this is not worthwhile for me**[D] **whenever I see Mordekhai the Jew sitting at the king's gate.** Yes, I have honor, wealth, and a bright future, but Mordekhai treats me with disrespect.

14 **Zeresh his wife and all his supporters said to him,** all in agreement with each other: **Let a gibbet be prepared, fifty cubits high; in the morning say to the king that they should hang Mordekhai upon it.** Do not wait until the feast. Go to the king in the morning and tell him that there is someone who aggravates you and refuses to accept your authority. Request that that person be hanged even before the rest of the Jews are killed. **And** then, in the evening, you can **come joyfully, with the king to the banquet. The matter,** this idea, **was pleasing to Haman, and he prepared the gibbet.** He gave an order that a gibbet of this kind be built in preparation for Mordekhai's hanging, paving the way for Haman's ultimate triumph.

DISCUSSION

that perhaps his chief minister was becoming too powerful. Furthermore, in light of Haman's prominent position, his deviousness, and his influence over the king, it is reasonable to assume that he had enemies in the royal court. Esther's maids and officials would certainly have informed the queen of the goings-on in the court, and she likely assumed that if Haman were to receive preferential treatment from his queen as well, it would inspire suspicion and mistrust in the court. This course of action was a gamble, as the success of Esther's plan depended on the reaction of Ahashverosh, who was not the most stable of men.

There were constant intrigues, conspiracies, and plots at work in the Persian court, and Ahashverosh, who apparently had seized the throne in a not entirely legal manner (see *Yalkut Shimoni* 954; *Megilla* 14a), was well aware of this state of affairs. Upon seeing Esther showing such favoritism to Haman, he might well have thought that a plot of some sort was being hatched against him, and that the queen was signaling to the protagonist her willingness to assist him. Even if an idea of this kind had not entered Haman's mind, Esther hoped to play on the king's fears, so that he would come to view Haman as someone who had gained too much power and who posed a threat to his reign (see *Megilla* 15b).

5:13 | **But all this is not worthwhile for me:** According to some commentaries, Mordekhai and Haman had known each other even before Haman rose to greatness (see *Megilla* 16a). For Haman, the encounter with someone who remembered him from when he was a lowly commoner, and who refused to honor him, would have been especially galling.

אֶל־הַמִּשְׁתֶּה אֲשֶׁר־עָשִׂיתִי לוֹ: וַיֹּאמֶר הַמֶּלֶךְ מַהֲרוּ אֶת־הָמָן לַעֲשׂוֹת אֶת־דְּבַר ה
אֶסְתֵּר וַיָּבֹא הַמֶּלֶךְ וְהָמָן אֶל־הַמִּשְׁתֶּה אֲשֶׁר־עָשְׂתָה אֶסְתֵּר: וַיֹּאמֶר הַמֶּלֶךְ ו
לְאֶסְתֵּר בְּמִשְׁתֵּה הַיַּיִן מַה־שְּׁאֵלָתֵךְ וְיִנָּתֵן לָךְ וּמַה־בַּקָּשָׁתֵךְ עַד־חֲצִי הַמַּלְכוּת
וְתֵעָשׂ: וַתַּעַן אֶסְתֵּר וַתֹּאמַר שְׁאֵלָתִי וּבַקָּשָׁתִי: אִם־מָצָאתִי חֵן בְּעֵינֵי הַמֶּלֶךְ ז ח
וְאִם־עַל־הַמֶּלֶךְ טוֹב לָתֵת אֶת־שְׁאֵלָתִי וְלַעֲשׂוֹת אֶת־בַּקָּשָׁתִי יָבוֹא הַמֶּלֶךְ וְהָמָן
אֶל־הַמִּשְׁתֶּה אֲשֶׁר אֶעֱשֶׂה לָהֶם וּמָחָר אֶעֱשֶׂה כִּדְבַר הַמֶּלֶךְ: וַיֵּצֵא הָמָן בַּיּוֹם ט
הַהוּא שָׂמֵחַ וְטוֹב לֵב וְכִרְאוֹת הָמָן אֶת־מָרְדֳּכַי בְּשַׁעַר הַמֶּלֶךְ וְלֹא־קָם וְלֹא־
זָע מִמֶּנּוּ וַיִּמָּלֵא הָמָן עַל־מָרְדֳּכַי חֵמָה: וַיִּתְאַפַּק הָמָן וַיָּבוֹא אֶל־בֵּיתוֹ וַיִּשְׁלַח י
וַיָּבֵא אֶת־אֹהֲבָיו וְאֶת־זֶרֶשׁ אִשְׁתּוֹ: וַיְסַפֵּר לָהֶם הָמָן אֶת־כְּבוֹד עָשְׁרוֹ וְרֹב בָּנָיו יא
וְאֵת כָּל־אֲשֶׁר גִּדְּלוֹ הַמֶּלֶךְ וְאֵת אֲשֶׁר נִשְּׂאוֹ עַל־הַשָּׂרִים וְעַבְדֵי הַמֶּלֶךְ: וַיֹּאמֶר יב
הָמָן אַף לֹא־הֵבִיאָה אֶסְתֵּר הַמַּלְכָּה עִם־הַמֶּלֶךְ אֶל־הַמִּשְׁתֶּה אֲשֶׁר־עָשָׂתָה
כִּי אִם־אוֹתִי וְגַם־לְמָחָר אֲנִי קָרוּא־לָהּ עִם־הַמֶּלֶךְ: וְכָל־זֶה אֵינֶנּוּ שֹׁוֶה לִי בְּכָל־ יג
עֵת אֲשֶׁר אֲנִי רֹאֶה אֶת־מָרְדֳּכַי הַיְּהוּדִי יוֹשֵׁב בְּשַׁעַר הַמֶּלֶךְ: וַתֹּאמֶר לוֹ זֶרֶשׁ יד
אִשְׁתּוֹ וְכָל־אֹהֲבָיו יַעֲשׂוּ־עֵץ גָּבֹהַּ חֲמִשִּׁים אַמָּה וּבַבֹּקֶר | אֱמֹר לַמֶּלֶךְ וְיִתְלוּ
אֶת־מָרְדֳּכַי עָלָיו וּבֹא עִם־הַמֶּלֶךְ אֶל־הַמִּשְׁתֶּה שָׂמֵחַ וַיִּיטַב הַדָּבָר לִפְנֵי הָמָן
וַיַּעַשׂ הָעֵץ: בַּלַּיְלָה הַהוּא נָדְדָה שְׁנַת הַמֶּלֶךְ וַיֹּאמֶר לְהָבִיא א
אֶת־סֵפֶר הַזִּכְרֹנוֹת דִּבְרֵי הַיָּמִים וַיִּהְיוּ נִקְרָאִים לִפְנֵי הַמֶּלֶךְ: וַיִּמָּצֵא כָתוּב אֲשֶׁר ב

The Night between the Two Feasts

ESTHER 6:1–14

The previous section ended at the lowest ebb of the story. Haman, who has been called for the second time to join the queen and king, is overjoyed; Mordekhai is to be hanged; and the decree of destruction still hovers over the Jews. There appears to be no hope on the horizon. However, in this next section the power relations between Mordekhai and Haman begin to reverse themselves. Haman arrives at the king's courtyard in order to request that Mordekhai be hanged on the gibbet that he has prepared at the precise moment when the king is inquiring as to how he can repay Mordekhai for his good deed. Haman is betrayed by his own lust for honor.

6 1 **On that night,** after Esther's feast, **the king's sleep was disturbed,** for no evident reason; **and he said to bring the book of records, the chronicles,** the book of royal history, **and they,** sections of the book, **would be read before the king,** in order to divert his mind with memories of past events.

2 **It was found written,** among the various events that had transpired in the kingdom, **that Mordekhai had reported of Bigtana,** Bigtan, **and Teresh, two of the king's chamberlains, among the guardians of the threshold,** who were very close to the king, **who had sought to do violence to King**

Ahashverosh. Their assassination attempt, the disclosure of the plot, and the fact that they had been hanged, were all recorded in the book.

3 **The king said: What honor or greatness has been bestowed upon Mordekhai[D] for this?** Perhaps he had received some form of reward, but as the details did not involve the king, they were not recorded in the book. **The king's lads, his servants, said to him: Nothing was done with him** to reward him.

4 **The king said: Who is in the courtyard?** These events likely occurred in the wee hours of the morning, and the king sought someone with whom he could converse and receive counsel about the matters that were disturbing his rest.[51] Now just at that moment **Haman had come to the outer courtyard of the king's palace,[B] to say to the king** his request **to hang Mordekhai on the gibbet that he had prepared for him,** in accordance with the advice he had received from his wife and friends. Although Mordekhai and the Jewish people were associated in his mind, since it was Mordekhai's presence that bothered Haman on a daily basis, he wished to dispose of him without delay.

5 **The king's lads said to him: Behold, Haman is standing in the courtyard. The king said: Let him enter.**

6 **Haman came, and the king said to him: What is to be done to the man whose honoring the king desires,** whom he wishes to honor in public? **Haman said in his heart: Upon whom would the king desire to bestow honor more than I?** Under the circumstances, Haman interpreted the king's question as though it were directed to him personally: How would you wish to be honored?

7 **Haman said to the king:** My advice is, **for the man whose honoring the king desires,**

8 **let them bring royal garments that the king** himself **has worn, and a horse upon which the king has ridden[B] while a royal crown was set on his,** the king's, **head,** while he rode the horse.[52] Alternatively, a royal crown was set upon the horse's head, demonstrating that it was the king's horse.

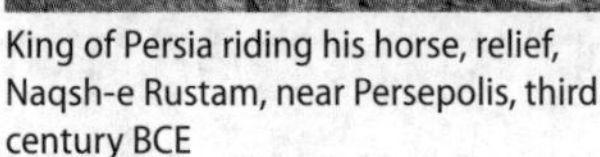

King of Persia riding his horse, relief, Naqsh-e Rustam, near Persepolis, third century BCE

Persian royal crown, relief

9 **And** once all these have been assembled, have them **put the garments and the horse in the hand of one of the king's princes, of the nobles,** a senior minister rather than a lowly servant; **they will dress the man whose honoring the king desires, and they will lead him riding on the horse in the city square, and they,** the nobles who lead him, **will proclaim before him: So shall be done to the man whose honoring the king desires.** Haman had no difficulty imagining himself riding on the horse, wearing royal clothing, after selecting one of the other ministers who would run before him.

10 **The king said to Haman:** This is indeed a good idea. Hurry, **quickly take the garments and the horse, as you have spoken, and do so to Mordekhai the Jew,[D] who sits at the king's gate.** Perhaps the king was not greatly familiar with Mordekhai, but he was not an anonymous figure either. His status and position in the royal court were well known. **Do not omit anything[D] from all that you have spoken.**

11 The king's order left Haman no choice. **Haman took the garments and the horse, dressed Mordekhai, led him riding through the city square, and proclaimed before him: So shall be done to the man whose honoring the king desires.**

BACKGROUND

6:4 | **Haman had come to the outer courtyard of the king's palace:** Even important ministers might soon find themselves on the gibbet if they entered from the outer courtyard without invitation or permission (see commentary on 5:1). However, it is clear from the next verse that when the king sought an advisor at night and was told that Haman was in the outer courtyard, he gave him explicit permission to enter unharmed.

6:8 | **And a horse upon which the king has ridden:** According to Herodotus, horses were highly esteemed creatures in Persia and were even considered sacred. Only kings and nobles were permitted what was considered the best breed, called by Herodotus the Nisean, due to its origins in the plains of Nisa in Media. Riding the king's horse was therefore a great honor. The horses' heads were sometimes adorned with a sort of crown. In Old Persian, the word for horse was *aspa*, or *asp*, a word that appears in names of people at the time of the book of Esther, e.g., Aspata, one of Haman's sons (9:7), as well as in contemporary Persian names (see also Song of Songs 1:9, and commentary ad loc.).

הִגִּיד מָרְדֳּכַי עַל־בִּגְתָנָא וָתֶרֶשׁ שְׁנֵי סָרִיסֵי הַמֶּלֶךְ מִשֹּׁמְרֵי הַסַּף אֲשֶׁר בִּקְשׁוּ
ג לִשְׁלֹחַ יָד בַּמֶּלֶךְ אֲחַשְׁוֵרוֹשׁ: וַיֹּאמֶר הַמֶּלֶךְ מַה־נַּעֲשָׂה יְקָר וּגְדוּלָּה לְמָרְדֳּכַי
ד עַל־זֶה וַיֹּאמְרוּ נַעֲרֵי הַמֶּלֶךְ מְשָׁרְתָיו לֹא־נַעֲשָׂה עִמּוֹ דָּבָר: וַיֹּאמֶר הַמֶּלֶךְ מִי
בֶחָצֵר וְהָמָן בָּא לַחֲצַר בֵּית־הַמֶּלֶךְ הַחִיצוֹנָה לֵאמֹר לַמֶּלֶךְ לִתְלוֹת אֶת־מָרְדֳּכַי
ה עַל־הָעֵץ אֲשֶׁר־הֵכִין לוֹ: וַיֹּאמְרוּ נַעֲרֵי הַמֶּלֶךְ אֵלָיו הִנֵּה הָמָן עֹמֵד בֶּחָצֵר וַיֹּאמֶר
ו הַמֶּלֶךְ יָבוֹא: וַיָּבוֹא הָמָן וַיֹּאמֶר לוֹ הַמֶּלֶךְ מַה־לַּעֲשׂוֹת בָּאִישׁ אֲשֶׁר הַמֶּלֶךְ
חָפֵץ בִּיקָרוֹ וַיֹּאמֶר הָמָן בְּלִבּוֹ לְמִי יַחְפֹּץ הַמֶּלֶךְ לַעֲשׂוֹת יְקָר יוֹתֵר מִמֶּנִּי:
ז ח וַיֹּאמֶר הָמָן אֶל־הַמֶּלֶךְ אִישׁ אֲשֶׁר הַמֶּלֶךְ חָפֵץ בִּיקָרוֹ: יָבִיאוּ לְבוּשׁ מַלְכוּת
אֲשֶׁר לָבַשׁ־בּוֹ הַמֶּלֶךְ וְסוּס אֲשֶׁר רָכַב עָלָיו הַמֶּלֶךְ וַאֲשֶׁר נִתַּן כֶּתֶר מַלְכוּת
ט בְּרֹאשׁוֹ: וְנָתוֹן הַלְּבוּשׁ וְהַסּוּס עַל־יַד־אִישׁ מִשָּׂרֵי הַמֶּלֶךְ הַפַּרְתְּמִים וְהִלְבִּישׁוּ
אֶת־הָאִישׁ אֲשֶׁר הַמֶּלֶךְ חָפֵץ בִּיקָרוֹ וְהִרְכִּיבֻהוּ עַל־הַסּוּס בִּרְחוֹב הָעִיר וְקָרְאוּ
י לְפָנָיו כָּכָה יֵעָשֶׂה לָאִישׁ אֲשֶׁר הַמֶּלֶךְ חָפֵץ בִּיקָרוֹ: וַיֹּאמֶר הַמֶּלֶךְ לְהָמָן
מַהֵר קַח אֶת־הַלְּבוּשׁ וְאֶת־הַסּוּס כַּאֲשֶׁר דִּבַּרְתָּ וַעֲשֵׂה־כֵן לְמָרְדֳּכַי הַיְּהוּדִי
יא הַיּוֹשֵׁב בְּשַׁעַר הַמֶּלֶךְ אַל־תַּפֵּל דָּבָר מִכֹּל אֲשֶׁר דִּבַּרְתָּ: וַיִּקַּח הָמָן אֶת־הַלְּבוּשׁ ד
וְאֶת־הַסּוּס וַיַּלְבֵּשׁ אֶת־מָרְדֳּכָי וַיַּרְכִּיבֵהוּ בִּרְחוֹב הָעִיר וַיִּקְרָא לְפָנָיו כָּכָה יֵעָשֶׂה

DISCUSSION

6:3 | **What honor or greatness has been bestowed upon Mordekhai:** It can be assumed that when the king was reminded of this earlier effort to assassinate him, he began to wonder: Since there are people in the kingdom who oppose me to such an extent that they will attempt to assassinate me, have I properly rewarded those who protect me? Esther's mysterious invitation to another feast, to which once again the chief minister had been invited, further aroused his suspicions. The king might have reasoned that if he failed to repay those who saved his life, it was no wonder that people concealed their plans from him (Rashi, verse 1; *Megilla* 15b).

6:10 | **And do so to Mordekhai the Jew:** In addition to the great honor that the king sought to bestow upon Mordekhai by having him led by his chief minister, there is no doubt that he also wanted to humiliate Haman. It can be presumed that word of the animosity between Mordekhai and Haman had spread beyond mere servants' gossip to the royal court itself. Although the king had no special connection to Mordekhai, now that he had been reminded of how Mordekhai had helped him, Ahashverosh took advantage of this opportunity to reinforce in his subjects the awareness that all power and status are derived from the crown. From the fact that Haman wished to be displayed in the city square in the manner of the king on the day of his coronation, Ahashverosh came to the conclusion that his chief minister had been granted too much power, and that his megalomaniacal ambitions might undermine the king's own regime. By insisting that Haman be the one to lead Mordekhai, the king thereby publicized his own authority over Haman (see Malbim 10).

Do not omit anything: Some infer from here that Haman tried to persuade the king to exchange this parade for a monetary gift or some other type of honor. Therefore, the king gave him explicit instructions to carry out his suggestion to the letter, without any changes (*Megilla* 16a).

12 **Mordekhai returned to the king's gate.** Even if Mordekhai was pleased at Haman's humiliation, this did not ease the terror in his heart over the fate of the Jews.[53] **And Haman hastened to his house, mourning and with covered head,** as he was humiliated and wanted to hide his shame.

13 **Haman related to Zeresh his wife and to all his supporters everything that had befallen him.** He told them that he had followed their advice, but that he had arrived at the king's courtyard at the wrong moment and had suffered a terrible humiliation. **His wise men** who, perhaps significantly, are no longer described as his supporters, **and Zeresh his wife, said to him** dispassionately: **If Mordekhai, before whom you have begun to fall, is of the progeny of the Jews, you will not prevail against him; rather, you will fall before him.** There is no middle ground in our relations with the Jews. One who fights against them will either crush them or be utterly defeated by them.

14 These comments certainly did not improve Haman's mood. **They were still talking with him, and the king's chamberlains arrived, and they hastened to bring Haman to the banquet that Esther had prepared,** despite the fact that feasts were generally held in the evening hours. As part of the royal formalities, officials were sent to Haman informing him that his presence was requested at the feast immediately.

Haman's Downfall and Mordekhai's Rise to Power

ESTHER 7:1–8:2

Although the humiliation Haman has suffered does not necessarily cause him to change his plans, it can be assumed that he comes to Esther's second party dispirited and discouraged. This second party is also an intimate affair. Esther wants only Ahashverosh, Haman, and herself to be present, so that Haman will suddenly discover that both the king and the queen are against him, and that there is no one to defend him.

Subsequently, Esther lobbies the king to promote Mordekhai in Haman's place, and so the turnabout is complete. Haman is hanged on the gibbet that he had prepared for Mordekhai, and Mordekhai, who had refused to bend his knee to Haman, takes his place.

7 1 **The king and Haman came to** attend the **banquet with Queen Esther.**

2 **The king said to Esther also on the second day at the wine banquet: What is your wish, Queen Esther, and it will be granted to you. What is your request? Up to half the kingdom and it will be done.** The king repeated his earlier question because he knew that Esther wanted something, which she was to reveal at this second feast.

3 **Queen Esther answered** with the customary etiquette **and said: If I have found favor in your eyes, the king, and if it pleases the king, let my life be given me with my wish, and my people with my request.** You have agreed, in principle, to grant me half the kingdom, but all I want is that my life and my people be spared. This dramatic opening statement was designed to have maximum effect upon the king.

4 The queen clarifies her meaning: **For we have been sold, my people and I,** for our enemies **to destroy, to kill, and to eliminate** us. **If we had** only **been sold as slaves and as maidservants, I would have been silent** and would not ask for anything, **as** in that case **the trouble,** such an unfortunate event, **would not have been worth the distress to the king.** It would not be worth upsetting the king if we were only to be enslaved.[54]

5 **King Ahashverosh,** who was caught by surprise, as Esther had not told him that she was a Jew, **said, he said to Queen Esther:**[D] **Who is he, and where is he, who was so presumptuous to do so?** What kind of person would dare seek to destroy you and your people?

6 **Esther said: A man who is an adversary and an enemy, this evil Haman.** Haman advised you to destroy us because he is an enemy of the Jews. Moreover, he is an evil man, and his intentions are far from pure; you should not trust him. Although Haman had been discouraged by his experience with Mordekhai, he was still under the impression that Esther had invited him because she held him in high regard and was entirely unprepared for the queen's accusation. Therefore, **Haman was terrified in the presence of the king and the queen.**

7 **The king rose in his fury**[D] **from the wine banquet and went to the garden of the house.** He had forgotten his own involvement in the decree, and the fact that he had granted permission for Haman's plan. At this point, all he could see was Haman trying to destroy Esther and her people. In order to calm himself, he got up and went to take some air in the garden. **And Haman remained to plead for his life from Queen Esther.** Although by now Haman realized that she did not seek his favor, he hoped that she might have mercy upon him, as he had not yet harmed her in any way. He might also have sought to arouse her innate feminine compassion,[55] **for he saw that harm was resolved against him by the king.**

8 **The king returned from the garden of the house to the chamber of the wine banquet, and** he saw that **Haman was falling upon the couch on which Esther was** lying. According to Persian and Greek custom, wealthy and noble individuals would not sit on chairs during a feast; rather, they would recline on couches.[56] Haman was bending over Esther's couch in supplication but the king interpreted it in the worst way possible. **The king said: Is it also** part of your plan **to conquer**

יב לָאִישׁ אֲשֶׁר הַמֶּלֶךְ חָפֵץ בִּיקָרוֹ: וַיָּשָׁב מָרְדֳּכַי אֶל־שַׁעַר הַמֶּלֶךְ וְהָמָן נִדְחַף
יג אֶל־בֵּיתוֹ אָבֵל וַחֲפוּי רֹאשׁ: וַיְסַפֵּר הָמָן לְזֶרֶשׁ אִשְׁתּוֹ וּלְכָל־אֹהֲבָיו אֵת כָּל־
אֲשֶׁר קָרָהוּ וַיֹּאמְרוּ לוֹ חֲכָמָיו וְזֶרֶשׁ אִשְׁתּוֹ אִם מִזֶּרַע הַיְּהוּדִים מָרְדֳּכַי אֲשֶׁר
יד הַחִלּוֹתָ לִנְפֹּל לְפָנָיו לֹא־תוּכַל לוֹ כִּי־נָפוֹל תִּפּוֹל לְפָנָיו: עוֹדָם מְדַבְּרִים עִמּוֹ
וְסָרִיסֵי הַמֶּלֶךְ הִגִּיעוּ וַיַּבְהִלוּ לְהָבִיא אֶת־הָמָן אֶל־הַמִּשְׁתֶּה אֲשֶׁר־עָשְׂתָה
ז א ב אֶסְתֵּר: וַיָּבֹא הַמֶּלֶךְ וְהָמָן לִשְׁתּוֹת עִם־אֶסְתֵּר הַמַּלְכָּה: וַיֹּאמֶר הַמֶּלֶךְ לְאֶסְתֵּר
גַּם בַּיּוֹם הַשֵּׁנִי בְּמִשְׁתֵּה הַיַּיִן מַה־שְּׁאֵלָתֵךְ אֶסְתֵּר הַמַּלְכָּה וְתִנָּתֵן לָךְ וּמַה־
ג בַּקָּשָׁתֵךְ עַד־חֲצִי הַמַּלְכוּת וְתֵעָשׂ: וַתַּעַן אֶסְתֵּר הַמַּלְכָּה וַתֹּאמַר אִם־מָצָאתִי
חֵן בְּעֵינֶיךָ הַמֶּלֶךְ וְאִם־עַל־הַמֶּלֶךְ טוֹב תִּנָּתֶן־לִי נַפְשִׁי בִּשְׁאֵלָתִי וְעַמִּי בְּבַקָּשָׁתִי:
ד כִּי נִמְכַּרְנוּ אֲנִי וְעַמִּי לְהַשְׁמִיד לַהֲרוֹג וּלְאַבֵּד וְאִלּוּ לַעֲבָדִים וְלִשְׁפָחוֹת נִמְכַּרְנוּ
ה הֶחֱרַשְׁתִּי כִּי אֵין הַצָּר שֹׁוֶה בְּנֵזֶק הַמֶּלֶךְ: וַיֹּאמֶר הַמֶּלֶךְ אֲחַשְׁוֵרוֹשׁ
וַיֹּאמֶר לְאֶסְתֵּר הַמַּלְכָּה מִי הוּא זֶה וְאֵי־זֶה הוּא אֲשֶׁר־מְלָאוֹ לִבּוֹ לַעֲשׂוֹת כֵּן:
ו וַתֹּאמֶר אֶסְתֵּר אִישׁ צַר וְאוֹיֵב הָמָן הָרָע הַזֶּה וְהָמָן נִבְעַת מִלִּפְנֵי הַמֶּלֶךְ וְהַמַּלְכָּה:
ז וְהַמֶּלֶךְ קָם בַּחֲמָתוֹ מִמִּשְׁתֵּה הַיַּיִן אֶל־גִּנַּת הַבִּיתָן וְהָמָן עָמַד לְבַקֵּשׁ עַל־נַפְשׁוֹ
ח מֵאֶסְתֵּר הַמַּלְכָּה כִּי רָאָה כִּי־כָלְתָה אֵלָיו הָרָעָה מֵאֵת הַמֶּלֶךְ: וְהַמֶּלֶךְ שָׁב מִגִּנַּת
הַבִּיתָן אֶל־בֵּית ׀ מִשְׁתֵּה הַיַּיִן וְהָמָן נֹפֵל עַל־הַמִּטָּה אֲשֶׁר אֶסְתֵּר עָלֶיהָ וַיֹּאמֶר

DISCUSSION

7:5 | **He said to Queen Esther:** As long as Esther kept her origins secret, her personal status was suspect. It would naturally be assumed that a woman who refused to reveal her ethnicity and background was in fact a maidservant of indeterminate birth, perhaps the daughter of a slave. Even among slaves and maidservants, a slave born to a slave lacked any social standing, and was considered inferior to a freeman who was captured in war. Ahashverosh had no particular familiarity with, or affection for, the Jewish people, but the Sages explain that Esther revealed at this point that she was descended from a royal line. She was no maidservant whom the king had raised up from misery, but a woman of noble descent (*Megilla* 16a).

7:7 | **The king rose in his fury:** The conversation between Ahashverosh and Haman the previous night had changed the image of Haman in the king's eyes. He realized that Haman was power hungry and would attempt to advance his status in the kingdom at any price. This impression that Haman had left upon the king the night before was reinforced by Esther's accusations. The king was therefore filled with great rage.

It should be noted that in royal courts of this kind, the chief minister is accorded great honor, but is also highly exposed. The king will always be wary of the person filling this role becoming too powerful. It is no coincidence that neither Haman nor Mordekhai, the two men whom Ahashverosh appointed to this position, came from the Persian nobility, and in fact were both foreigners. Such individuals could be removed from their posts with relative ease when the need arose. This might well have been one of Pharaoh's motivations for appointing Joseph (Genesis 41:39–44).

the queen with me in the house, to rape the queen in my own presence? **The words emerged from the king's mouth, and Haman's face fell.** He turned pale as he realized that he was facing his demise. Apologizing was futile, as in these circumstances nothing he could say would save him.

9 The feast was served by waiters who were not considered to be attendees. However, when the king revealed his opinion about Haman, one of them dared to interject in support of that sentiment. **Harvona,** who was **one of the chamberlains who was before the king, said: Indeed, behold, the gibbet that Haman prepared for Mordekhai,** who is someone **who spoke beneficially for the king.** This is the true nature of Haman; he is a man who prepares a gibbet for one who helps the king. The gibbet **is standing in the house of Haman,** and is **fifty cubits high.** Perhaps Harvona disliked Haman for reasons of his own, and he now saw the chance to retaliate. **The king said: Hang him on it.** If the gibbet is already prepared, Haman's sentence can be carried out without delay.

10 **They hanged Haman on the gibbet that he had prepared for Mordekhai, and the king's fury abated.**

8 1 Once Haman had been hanged, the king decided to bestow further favors upon Esther. **On that day, King Ahashverosh gave the house of Haman, adversary of the Jews, to Queen Esther.** This gift included the enormous amount of wealth that Haman had accumulated.[57] **And Mordekhai came** for a personal audience **before the king, as Esther had related what he was to her.** She presented him as her cousin, who had adopted, raised, and educated her. Ahashverosh was in good spirits now that Haman was gone, and for her part Esther treated him with affection and gratitude. Furthermore, if Ahashverosh was not yet personally familiar with Mordekhai, he was now given the opportunity to meet this loyal subject who had been instrumental in uncovering the assassination plot against him.

2 **The king removed his ring that he had taken from Haman, and he gave it to Mordekhai,** as a sign of trust. **Esther appointed Mordekhai over the house of Haman.** She appointed him to be in charge of Haman's estate.

The Order against Haman's Decree

ESTHER 8:3–17

Although the problem of Haman himself had been resolved, the decree permitting the annihilation of the Jews still stood. Esther seeks to take advantage of her favor with the king and annul the evil decree that threatens her people.

3 **Esther spoke again before the king, fell before his feet, cried, and besought him to repeal the evil of Haman the Agagite and his plot that he had devised against the Jews.**

4 **The king extended to Esther the golden scepter,** to signal to the queen, who was lying on the floor at his feet, that she was permitted to rise and speak her mind. **And Esther rose and stood before the king.**

5 **She said,** choosing her words carefully in order to arouse all the king's love and affection for her: **If it pleases the king, and if I have found favor before him, and the matter is proper before the king, and I am pleasing in his eyes, let it be written to return the scrolls** that were sent as part of **the plot of Haman son of Hamedata the Agagite that he wrote, to eliminate the Jews who are in all the king's provinces,** and to annul the decree they contain;

6 **for how can I bear and see the harm that will find my people;**[D] **and how can I bear and see the elimination of my birthplace?** By this stage, Esther no longer had any concerns for herself. She knew that she would be left untouched, but she implored the king not to let her people be harmed as a result of the decree.

7 **King Ahashverosh said to Queen Esther and to Mordekhai the Jew,** who was present: **Behold, I gave the house of Haman to Esther,** as a gesture of goodwill, **and they hanged him on the gibbet because he sought to do violence to the Jews.** Once again the king places the blame entirely on Haman while conveniently disregarding his own involvement in the plot against the Jews.

8 **As for you, write concerning the Jews** a different missive **as is pleasing in your eyes, in the king's name, and seal it with the king's ring,** so that the two orders cancel each other out; **for a document that is written in the name of the king, and sealed with the ring of the king, may not be revoked.** According to the laws of the kingdom, not even the king could nullify his own orders, as once written they were considered to be absolute, divine commands. Consequently, another royal communiqué, formulated in such a manner that it bypasses the previous command and limits its significance, must be written.

9 Indeed, **the king's scribes were summoned at that time, in the third month, which is the month of Sivan, on the twenty-third day of it,**[B] roughly three months after Haman was hanged; **it was written according to everything that Mordekhai commanded concerning the Jews.** The missives

הַמֶּלֶךְ הֲגַם לִכְבּוֹשׁ אֶת־הַמַּלְכָּה עִמִּי בַּבָּיִת הַדָּבָר יָצָא מִפִּי הַמֶּלֶךְ וּפְנֵי הָמָן
ט חָפוּ׃ וַיֹּאמֶר חַרְבוֹנָה אֶחָד מִן־הַסָּרִיסִים לִפְנֵי הַמֶּלֶךְ גַּם הִנֵּה־הָעֵץ אֲשֶׁר־עָשָׂה
הָמָן לְמָרְדֳּכַי אֲשֶׁר דִּבֶּר־טוֹב עַל־הַמֶּלֶךְ עֹמֵד בְּבֵית הָמָן גָּבֹהַּ חֲמִשִּׁים אַמָּה
י וַיֹּאמֶר הַמֶּלֶךְ תְּלֻהוּ עָלָיו׃ וַיִּתְלוּ אֶת־הָמָן עַל־הָעֵץ אֲשֶׁר־הֵכִין לְמָרְדֳּכָי וַחֲמַת
ח א הַמֶּלֶךְ שָׁכָכָה׃ בַּיּוֹם הַהוּא נָתַן הַמֶּלֶךְ אֲחַשְׁוֵרוֹשׁ לְאֶסְתֵּר הַמַּלְכָּה
אֶת־בֵּית הָמָן צֹרֵר היהודיים וּמָרְדֳּכַי בָּא לִפְנֵי הַמֶּלֶךְ כִּי־הִגִּידָה אֶסְתֵּר מַה הַיְּהוּדִים
ב הוּא־לָהּ׃ וַיָּסַר הַמֶּלֶךְ אֶת־טַבַּעְתּוֹ אֲשֶׁר הֶעֱבִיר מֵהָמָן וַיִּתְּנָהּ לְמָרְדֳּכָי וַתָּשֶׂם
ג אֶסְתֵּר אֶת־מָרְדֳּכַי עַל־בֵּית הָמָן׃ וַתּוֹסֶף אֶסְתֵּר וַתְּדַבֵּר לִפְנֵי
הַמֶּלֶךְ וַתִּפֹּל לִפְנֵי רַגְלָיו וַתֵּבְךְּ וַתִּתְחַנֶּן־לוֹ לְהַעֲבִיר אֶת־רָעַת הָמָן הָאֲגָגִי וְאֵת
ד מַחֲשַׁבְתּוֹ אֲשֶׁר חָשַׁב עַל־הַיְּהוּדִים׃ וַיּוֹשֶׁט הַמֶּלֶךְ לְאֶסְתֵּר אֵת שַׁרְבִט הַזָּהָב
ה וַתָּקָם אֶסְתֵּר וַתַּעֲמֹד לִפְנֵי הַמֶּלֶךְ׃ וַתֹּאמֶר אִם־עַל־הַמֶּלֶךְ טוֹב וְאִם־מָצָאתִי
חֵן לְפָנָיו וְכָשֵׁר הַדָּבָר לִפְנֵי הַמֶּלֶךְ וְטוֹבָה אֲנִי בְּעֵינָיו יִכָּתֵב לְהָשִׁיב אֶת־הַסְּפָרִים
מַחֲשֶׁבֶת הָמָן בֶּן־הַמְּדָתָא הָאֲגָגִי אֲשֶׁר כָּתַב לְאַבֵּד אֶת־הַיְּהוּדִים אֲשֶׁר בְּכָל־
ו מְדִינוֹת הַמֶּלֶךְ׃ כִּי אֵיכָכָה אוּכַל וְרָאִיתִי בָּרָעָה אֲשֶׁר־יִמְצָא אֶת־עַמִּי וְאֵיכָכָה
ז אוּכַל וְרָאִיתִי בְּאָבְדַן מוֹלַדְתִּי׃ וַיֹּאמֶר הַמֶּלֶךְ אֲחַשְׁוֵרֹשׁ לְאֶסְתֵּר
הַמַּלְכָּה וּלְמָרְדֳּכַי הַיְּהוּדִי הִנֵּה בֵית־הָמָן נָתַתִּי לְאֶסְתֵּר וְאֹתוֹ תָּלוּ עַל־הָעֵץ
ח עַל אֲשֶׁר־שָׁלַח יָדוֹ ביהודיים׃ וְאַתֶּם כִּתְבוּ עַל־הַיְּהוּדִים כַּטּוֹב בְּעֵינֵיכֶם בְּשֵׁם בַּיְּהוּדִים
הַמֶּלֶךְ וְחִתְמוּ בְּטַבַּעַת הַמֶּלֶךְ כִּי־כְתָב אֲשֶׁר־נִכְתָּב בְּשֵׁם־הַמֶּלֶךְ וְנַחְתּוֹם
ט בְּטַבַּעַת הַמֶּלֶךְ אֵין לְהָשִׁיב׃ וַיִּקָּרְאוּ סֹפְרֵי־הַמֶּלֶךְ בָּעֵת־הַהִיא בַּחֹדֶשׁ הַשְּׁלִישִׁי

DISCUSSION

8:6 | **For how can I bear and see the harm that will find my people:** A person's concern for his people or family, even when it does not accord with the interests of the kingdom, would not be considered a betrayal, but rather a respectable, appropriate reaction. This is also seen in the response of King Artahshasta to Nehemiah's misery (Nehemiah 2:1–9).

BACKGROUND

8:9 | **In the third month, which is the month of Sivan, on the twenty-third day of it:** One explanation for the long delay between the hanging of Haman and the sending of the missives negating his decree is that they waited for the original messengers to return in order to send them back again, as the return of the very same messengers would reinforce the credibility of the new command (see Vilna Gaon, *Seder Olam Rabba* 29).

were sent **to the satraps, the governors, and princes of the provinces, which are from India to Kush, one hundred and twenty-seven provinces, each and every province according to its script, and each and every people according to its language, and** on this occasion even **to the Jews according to their script, and according to their language.** Since this time Jews were not merely the passive targets of the order but active participants in its implementation, they too received the missives.[58]

10 **He,** Mordekhai, **wrote in the name of King Ahashverosh, and he sealed** the missives **with the ring of the king** that he had received. **He sent scrolls in the hand of the couriers on horses, riders on the finest steeds** owned by the king,[59] **the mules born to mares.**[B]

Horseman, stone relief, Nineveh, 645–635 BCE

11 The missives stated **that the king had authorized the Jews who were in each and every city to assemble and to defend themselves.** Whereas the previous order allowed all those who wished to do so to attack the Jews, under the assumption that the Jews were forbidden to retaliate, here the king permitted them to defend themselves, and even **to destroy, to kill, and to eliminate the forces of people and provinces that are hostile to them, children and women, and to plunder their spoils.** The Jews were granted royal consent to wage total war against any enemy.

12 This order would come into effect **on one day, in all the provinces of King Ahashverosh, on the thirteenth** day **of the twelfth month, which is the month of Adar,** the same date that was previously fixed for their destruction.

13 **A copy of the document went out to issue the decree in each and every province, publicizing it to all the peoples: For the Jews to be ready for that day, to avenge themselves on their enemies.** The same day that had been designated for their destruction would be the day of their salvation.

14 **The couriers, riders on the finest steeds, went out** again **urgently and hastily, by edict of the king,** in order to disseminate the new order as quickly as possible throughout the kingdom, **and the decree was** also **issued in the Shushan citadel** itself.

15 **Mordekhai,** who had recently been appointed the chief minister, **came out from before the king** dressed **in royal garments** made **of sky-blue and white** woven material, **with a great golden crown** upon his head, **and** wrapped in **a cloak**[60] **of fine linen and purple wool,**[B] **and** the Jewish population of **the city of Shushan reveled and rejoiced** upon seeing that their representative had become the most influential man in the kingdom.

16 **For the Jews there was light, and joy, and gladness, and honor,** as instead of the bloody pogrom that had been planned, in which they were not meant to have any right to self-defense whatsoever, they were now legally permitted to protect themselves and fight their enemies.

17 **In each and every province and in each and every city, any place where the king's edict and his decree reached, there was joy and gladness for the Jews, a banquet and a holiday, and many from the peoples of the land pretended to be Jews,**[61] or professed to favor the Jews but without internal conviction, **as the fear of the Jews had fallen upon them.** The missives alone produced such a great impression that even before the decree was put into practice, the Jews began rejoicing and others became fearful.

The Jews' Victory and Its Commemoration

ESTHER 9:1–32

In this section, the order issued by the king together with Esther and Mordekhai is carried out. It is implemented to an even greater extent than Ahashverosh has already authorized. As the book of Esther nears its conclusion, it relates how this miraculous deliverance is to be memorialized in the Jewish national consciousness. This is achieved in two ways: First, the initially spontaneous days of rejoicing over the salvation and the victory are established as permanent dates of feasting and joy for the nation, throughout the generations. Second, Esther and Mordekhai write a record of the events, which is this book.

9 1 **In the twelfth month, which is the month Adar, on the thirteenth day of it,** the date that Haman had set for the destruction of the Jews, **when the time arrived for the king's edict and his decree to be implemented, on the day that the enemies of the Jews had hoped to rule over them, it was** in fact **reversed, so that it was the Jews who ruled over those who hated them.**

הוא־חדש סיון בשלושה ועשרים בו ויכתב ככל־אשר־צוה מרדכי אל־
היהודים ואל האחשדרפנים והפחות ושרי המדינות אשר ׀ מהדו ועד־כוש
שבע ועשרים ומאה מדינה מדינה ומדינה ככתבה ועם ועם כלשנו ואל־
י היהודים ככתבם וכלשונם: ויכתב בשם המלך אחשורש ויחתם בטבעת
המלך וישלח ספרים ביד הרצים בסוסים רכבי הרכש האחשתרנים בני
יא הרמכים: אשר נתן המלך ליהודים ׀ אשר ׀ בכל־עיר ועיר להקהל ולעמד
על־נפשם להשמיד ולהרג ולאבד את־כל־חיל עם ומדינה הצרים אתם טף
יב ונשים ושללם לבוז: ביום אחד בכל־מדינות המלך אחשורוש בשלושה עשר
יג לחדש שנים־עשר הוא־חדש אדר: פתשגן הכתב להנתן דת בכל־מדינה
ומדינה גלוי לכל־העמים ולהיות היהודיים עתודים ליום הזה להנקם מאיביהם: היהודים עתידים
יד הרצים רכבי הרכש האחשתרנים יצאו מבהלים ודחופים בדבר המלך והדת
טו נתנה בשושן הבירה: ומרדכי יצא ׀ מלפני המלך בלבוש מלכות
תכלת וחור ועטרת זהב גדולה ותכריך בוץ וארגמן והעיר שושן צהלה
טז יז ושמחה: ליהודים היתה אורה ושמחה וששן ויקר: ובכל־מדינה ומדינה ה
ובכל־עיר ועיר מקום אשר דבר־המלך ודתו מגיע שמחה וששון ליהודים
משתה ויום טוב ורבים מעמי הארץ מתיהדים כי־נפל פחד־היהודים עליהם:
ט א ובשנים עשר חדש הוא־חדש אדר בשלושה עשר יום בו אשר הגיע דבר־
המלך ודתו להעשות ביום אשר שברו איבי היהודים לשלוט בהם ונהפוך

BACKGROUND

8:10 | **The couriers on horses, riders on the finest steeds [*rekhesh*], the mules born to mares:** These royal messengers were part of a remarkable system of communication and road networks created by Darius I. In order to increase their speed across the flat terrain of Mesopotamia, the king's messengers would change their horses at waystations. *Rekhesh* is the name for a famously swift breed of horse. The last part of the verse is probably referring to riders of fast mules, the offspring of a select breed of mares, as these could ride through the mountainous regions of central and northern Persia, as well as Anatolia. Perhaps the three different types of messengers specified in this verse, those on "horses," "riders on the finest steeds," and on "mules born to mares," performed different missions, for short, medium, and long distances. Only those messengers sent to the far corners of the kingdom required mules that could cope with mountainous terrain.

8:15 | **In royal garments of sky blue and white, with a great golden crown, and a cloak of fine linen and purple wool:** See commentary on 1:6; see also the image of the king with his second-in-command standing behind him, dressed in similar attire, above 1:4.

2 **The Jews assembled in their cities in all the provinces of King Ahashverosh** where there were Jewish communities, **to do violence to those who sought their harm, and no man could withstand them, as fear of them had fallen upon all the peoples.**
3 **All the princes of the provinces, the satraps, the governors, and the king's administrators elevated** or honored **the Jews, because the fear of Mordekhai had fallen upon them.** When the first missives were sent, Haman was chief minister to Ahashverosh. By this point, however, Mordekhai was the foremost of the king's ministers, and therefore everyone granted the Jews the freedom of action they required.
4 **For Mordekhai was great** in status **in the king's palace, and his renown** had **spread in all the provinces, for the man Mordekhai was growing more and more powerful.**
5 **The Jews smote all their enemies a blow of the sword, killing, and destruction, and they did to their enemies as they willed.** Presumably this also took place in the province of Judah, which is not explicitly mentioned here, but whose Jewish residents were experiencing harassment during this time.[62]

Sword, Persepolis, 560–331 BCE

6 **In the Shushan citadel the Jews killed and eliminated five hundred men,** their enemies who had planned to attack the Jews on that day, and who had perhaps taunted the Jews earlier and boasted of their heinous plans.
7 **And Parshandata, Dalfon, Aspata,**
8 **Porata, Adalya, Aridata,**
9 **Parmashta, Arisai, Aridai, and Vayzata,**
10 **the ten sons of Haman the son of Hamedata, the adversary of the Jews, they killed; but they did not extend their hands to the spoils.** The Jews did not consider this conflict a war, but an act of self-defense, and since they wished to avoid provoking hatred against themselves they did not touch their enemies' property, despite the fact that in his missive the king had granted the Jews permission to loot their enemies' possessions.[63]
11 **On that day, the number of those killed in the Shushan citadel came before the king,** through his extensive intelligence network.
12 **The king said to Queen Esther: The Jews have killed and eliminated five hundred men in the Shushan citadel, along with the ten sons of Haman; in the rest of the king's provinces they** presumably **have done likewise.** It can be assumed that the results are comparable in the other provinces, even though the numbers are not yet known. Your people have avenged themselves upon their enemies, as you wished. **What is your wish and it will be granted to you. What else do you request? It will be done.**
13 **Esther said,** realizing that the king wanted to make her happy and to fulfill her every desire: **If it pleases the king, let tomorrow, too, be granted to the Jews who are in Shushan to do in accordance with today's decree.** Although this was not written in the original missives, I would like you to issue a verbal instruction permitting the Jews in Shushan, which was likely the center of Haman's support,[64] to complete the task, **and have them hang Haman's ten sons,** who have already been killed,[65] **upon the gibbet,** as a public display that the king and the authorities support the action that has been taken, and that they consider these men criminals, rather than random victims of indiscriminate rioting.
14 **The king said to do so, and a decree was issued** permitting another day of vengeance **in Shushan, and they hanged Haman's ten sons.**
15 **The Jews who were in Shushan assembled on the fourteenth day of the month of Adar as well, and killed** another **three hundred men in Shushan, but** also in this instance **they did not extend their hand to the spoils.**
16 **The rest of the Jews who were in the king's provinces assembled and defended themselves, and rested from their enemies.** By the end of the day, **they** had **killed seventy-five thousand of those who hated them,** throughout the kingdom, **but** they **did not extend their hand to the spoils.**
17 **It,** all this, **was on the thirteenth day of the month of Adar, and the rest** after the fighting **was on the fourteenth of it, and it was made a day of banqueting and joy,** in honor of the victory.
18 **But the Jews who were in Shushan assembled** together to avenge themselves upon their enemies **on the thirteenth of it and on the fourteenth of it, and rested** after the fighting **on the fifteenth of it, and it was made a day of banqueting and joy.** They celebrated the victory one day later than the rest of the empire.

ב הוּא אֲשֶׁר יִשְׁלְטוּ הַיְּהוּדִים הֵמָּה בְּשֹׂנְאֵיהֶם: נִקְהֲלוּ הַיְּהוּדִים בְּעָרֵיהֶם בְּכָל־
מְדִינוֹת הַמֶּלֶךְ אֲחַשְׁוֵרוֹשׁ לִשְׁלֹחַ יָד בִּמְבַקְשֵׁי רָעָתָם וְאִישׁ לֹא־עָמַד לִפְנֵיהֶם
ג כִּי־נָפַל פַּחְדָּם עַל־כָּל־הָעַמִּים: וְכָל־שָׂרֵי הַמְּדִינוֹת וְהָאֲחַשְׁדַּרְפְּנִים וְהַפַּחוֹת
וְעֹשֵׂי הַמְּלָאכָה אֲשֶׁר לַמֶּלֶךְ מְנַשְּׂאִים אֶת־הַיְּהוּדִים כִּי־נָפַל פַּחַד־מָרְדֳּכַי עֲלֵיהֶם:
ד כִּי־גָדוֹל מָרְדֳּכַי בְּבֵית הַמֶּלֶךְ וְשָׁמְעוֹ הוֹלֵךְ בְּכָל־הַמְּדִינוֹת כִּי־הָאִישׁ מָרְדֳּכַי
ה הוֹלֵךְ וְגָדוֹל: וַיַּכּוּ הַיְּהוּדִים בְּכָל־אֹיְבֵיהֶם מַכַּת־חֶרֶב וְהֶרֶג וְאַבְדָן וַיַּעֲשׂוּ
ו בְשֹׂנְאֵיהֶם כִּרְצוֹנָם: וּבְשׁוּשַׁן הַבִּירָה הָרְגוּ הַיְּהוּדִים וְאַבֵּד חֲמֵשׁ מֵאוֹת
ז אִישׁ: וְאֵת ׀ פַּרְשַׁנְדָּתָא וְאֵת ׀
ח דַּלְפוֹן וְאֵת ׀ אַסְפָּתָא: וְאֵת ׀
פּוֹרָתָא וְאֵת ׀ אֲדַלְיָא וְאֵת ׀
ט אֲרִידָתָא: וְאֵת ׀ פַּרְמַשְׁתָּא וְאֵת ׀
אֲרִיסַי וְאֵת ׀ אֲרִדַי וְאֵת ׀
י וַיְזָתָא: עֲשֶׂרֶת בְּנֵי הָמָן בֶּן־הַמְּדָתָא צֹרֵר הַיְּהוּדִים
יא הָרָגוּ וּבַבִּזָּה לֹא שָׁלְחוּ אֶת־יָדָם: בַּיּוֹם הַהוּא בָּא מִסְפַּר הַהֲרוּגִים בְּשׁוּשַׁן הַבִּירָה
יב לִפְנֵי הַמֶּלֶךְ: וַיֹּאמֶר הַמֶּלֶךְ לְאֶסְתֵּר הַמַּלְכָּה בְּשׁוּשַׁן הַבִּירָה הָרְגוּ הַיְּהוּדִים
וְאַבֵּד חֲמֵשׁ מֵאוֹת אִישׁ וְאֵת עֲשֶׂרֶת בְּנֵי־הָמָן בִּשְׁאָר מְדִינוֹת הַמֶּלֶךְ מֶה עָשׂוּ
יג וּמַה־שְּׁאֵלָתֵךְ וְיִנָּתֵן לָךְ וּמַה־בַּקָּשָׁתֵךְ עוֹד וְתֵעָשׂ: וַתֹּאמֶר אֶסְתֵּר אִם־עַל־
הַמֶּלֶךְ טוֹב יִנָּתֵן גַּם־מָחָר לַיְּהוּדִים אֲשֶׁר בְּשׁוּשָׁן לַעֲשׂוֹת כְּדָת הַיּוֹם וְאֵת עֲשֶׂרֶת
יד בְּנֵי־הָמָן יִתְלוּ עַל־הָעֵץ: וַיֹּאמֶר הַמֶּלֶךְ לְהֵעָשׂוֹת כֵּן וַתִּנָּתֵן דָּת בְּשׁוּשָׁן וְאֵת
טו עֲשֶׂרֶת בְּנֵי־הָמָן תָּלוּ: וַיִּקָּהֲלוּ הַיְּהוּדִיים אֲשֶׁר־בְּשׁוּשָׁן גַּם בְּיוֹם אַרְבָּעָה עָשָׂר הַיְּהוּדִים
טז לְחֹדֶשׁ אֲדָר וַיַּהַרְגוּ בְשׁוּשָׁן שְׁלֹשׁ מֵאוֹת אִישׁ וּבַבִּזָּה לֹא שָׁלְחוּ אֶת־יָדָם: וּשְׁאָר
הַיְּהוּדִים אֲשֶׁר בִּמְדִינוֹת הַמֶּלֶךְ נִקְהֲלוּ ׀ וְעָמֹד עַל־נַפְשָׁם וְנוֹחַ מֵאֹיְבֵיהֶם וְהָרוֹג
יז בְּשֹׂנְאֵיהֶם חֲמִשָּׁה וְשִׁבְעִים אָלֶף וּבַבִּזָּה לֹא שָׁלְחוּ אֶת־יָדָם: בְּיוֹם־שְׁלוֹשָׁה עָשָׂר
יח לְחֹדֶשׁ אֲדָר וְנוֹחַ בְּאַרְבָּעָה עָשָׂר בּוֹ וְעָשֹׂה אֹתוֹ יוֹם מִשְׁתֶּה וְשִׂמְחָה: וְהַיְּהוּדִיים וְהַיְּהוּדִים

19 **Therefore, the unwalled Jews,** that is, those **who live in the**
unwalled cities,[B] whose residents were exposed to great danger, **observe the fourteenth day of the month** of **Adar as a**
day of joy, banqueting, and a holiday, and furthermore, a day
of sending portions of food **one to another,** in order to increase joy and publicly express happiness. The date on which
they spontaneously celebrated at that time was established as a
day of rejoicing in the following years.[66]
20 It was Mordekhai who established the conversion of the spontaneous celebration into a permanent holiday: **Mordekhai**
wrote these matters, the events that occurred, **and he sent**
scrolls to all the Jews who were in all the provinces of King
Ahashverosh, near and far, instructing them
21 **to establish for themselves to observe** the victory celebrations of **the fourteenth day of the month Adar, and the**
fifteenth day of it, in each and every year, as permanent days
of merriment and feasting:
22 **In accordance with** the dates of **the days that the Jews** of that
generation had **rested from their enemies, and the month**
that was transformed for them from sorrow to joy, and
from mourning to holiday, to observe them as days of ban-
quet and joy, and of sending portions one to another, and
gifts to the indigent, so that the poor should also participate in
the festivities.
23 **The Jews** as a people **undertook,**[67] or committed to continu-
ing, **that which they had begun to practice** at the time, **and**
that which Mordekhai wrote to them.
24 Mordekhai's brief summary of the events, as he wrote to the
Jews, went as follows: **Because Haman son of Hamedata**
the Agagite, adversary of all the Jews, not only the enemy of
Mordekhai alone,[68] **had plotted against the Jews to eliminate**
them, and he cast the pur, that is the lot, in order to determine a date on which **to crush them, and eliminate them.**
25 **But when she,** Esther,[69] **came before the king;** alternatively,
when it, Haman's intention, came before the king, **he said: By**
means of the scroll, may his evil plot that he had devised
against the Jews return upon his head. When he summa-
rized what happened, Mordekhai was careful not to mention
that Ahashverosh had initially signed Haman's decree. Rather,
he described the events in such a manner that it seemed that
when the missives appeared, the king was surprised to discover
that his minister had used his authority for reprehensible ends,
and as a result he commanded that Haman be punished.[70]
Subsequently, **they hanged him and his sons on the gibbet.**
26 **Therefore, they called these days Purim, after the lot [*pur*]**
cast by Haman. **Therefore, for all the matters of this epistle**
of Mordekhai's, **and what they saw about that matter,** that is,
what led them to establish these days: Haman's **pur, and what**
befell them, how they ultimately achieved victory and rest,
27 **the Jews established and accepted upon themselves, and**
upon their descendants, and as these days of Purim were established for the entire people throughout the generations, they
were also accepted **upon everyone associated with them,**
converts,[71] despite the fact that their biological ancestors were
not affected. **And** it was agreed that **it will not be neglected,**
to observe these two days as they are written, and on their
dates, each and every year.
28 **These days are remembered and observed in each and**
every generation, each and every family, each and every
province, and each and every city. Celebration of the holiday spread through all Jewish communities. Therefore, **these**
days of Purim will not pass from among the Jews, and their
memory will not perish from their descendants; they will be
commemorated forever. Often, national days of celebration are
temporary, and forgotten over the passage of time. By contrast,
because this episode involved a plot to destroy the entire nation, it must be commemorated by the entire people through
all its generations.
29 **Queen Esther daughter of Avihayil, and Mordekhai the**
Jew, wrote of all the significant events,[72] alternatively, they
wrote with all their authority, **confirming this second letter**
of Purim. The first one, which contained a summary of the
events, was sent by Mordekhai. Later they together wrote a re-
vised epistle, signed by the queen.[73]
30 **He,** Mordekhai, **sent scrolls to all the Jews, to one hun-**
dred and twenty-seven provinces of the kingdom of
Ahashverosh, matters of peace and truth. These epistles were
not binding orders, but inspirational instruction from the spiritual leader of the Jews.

BACKGROUND

9:19 | **The unwalled [*haperazim*] Jews, who live in the unwalled cities:** The authors of the book of Esther may have felt it was necessary to elaborate and precisely define the term *perazim* because of the similar Persian word *perazona*, which means people from diverse origins, similar to the Hebrew term *pezura*, diaspora. It is therefore emphasized that this term denotes specifically Jews who lived outside the fortified capital or other fortified cities, which were protected by soldiers of the Persian kingdom (Tamar Eilam Gindin, *The Book of Esther Unmasked*. Zeresh Publications, 2016 [Hebrew], pp. 144–145).

אֲשֶׁר־בְּשׁוּשָׁ֗ן נִקְהֲלוּ֙ בִּשְׁלוֹשָׁ֤ה עָשָׂר֙ בּ֔וֹ וּבְאַרְבָּעָ֥ה עָשָׂ֖ר בּ֑וֹ וְנ֗וֹחַ בַּחֲמִשָּׁ֤ה עָשָׂר֙
יט בּ֔וֹ וְעָשֹׂ֣ה אֹת֔וֹ י֖וֹם מִשְׁתֶּ֥ה וְשִׂמְחָֽה׃ עַל־כֵּ֞ן הַיְּהוּדִ֣ים הַפְּרוֹזִ֗ים הַיֹּשְׁבִים֮ בְּעָרֵ֣י הַפְּרָזִים
הַפְּרָזוֹת֒ עֹשִׂ֗ים אֵ֠ת י֣וֹם אַרְבָּעָ֤ה עָשָׂר֙ לְחֹ֣דֶשׁ אֲדָ֔ר שִׂמְחָ֥ה וּמִשְׁתֶּ֖ה וְי֣וֹם ט֑וֹב
כ וּמִשְׁלֹ֥חַ מָנ֖וֹת אִ֥ישׁ לְרֵעֵֽהוּ׃ וַיִּכְתֹּ֣ב מָרְדֳּכַ֔י אֶת־הַדְּבָרִ֖ים הָאֵ֑לֶּה וַיִּשְׁלַ֨ח סְפָרִ֜ים
אֶל־כָּל־הַיְּהוּדִ֗ים אֲשֶׁר֙ בְּכָל־מְדִינוֹת֙ הַמֶּ֣לֶךְ אֲחַשְׁוֵר֔וֹשׁ הַקְּרוֹבִ֖ים וְהָרְחוֹקִֽים׃
כא לְקַיֵּם֮ עֲלֵיהֶם֒ לִהְי֣וֹת עֹשִׂ֗ים אֵ֠ת י֣וֹם אַרְבָּעָ֤ה עָשָׂר֙ לְחֹ֣דֶשׁ אֲדָ֔ר וְאֵ֛ת יוֹם־חֲמִשָּׁ֥ה
כב עָשָׂ֖ר בּ֑וֹ בְּכָל־שָׁנָ֖ה וְשָׁנָֽה׃ כַּיָּמִ֗ים אֲשֶׁר־נָ֨חוּ בָהֶ֤ם הַיְּהוּדִים֙ מֵאֹ֣יְבֵיהֶ֔ם וְהַחֹ֗דֶשׁ
אֲשֶׁר֩ נֶהְפַּ֨ךְ לָהֶ֤ם מִיָּגוֹן֙ לְשִׂמְחָ֔ה וּמֵאֵ֖בֶל לְי֣וֹם ט֑וֹב לַעֲשׂ֣וֹת אוֹתָ֗ם יְמֵי֙ מִשְׁתֶּ֣ה
כג וְשִׂמְחָ֔ה וּמִשְׁלֹ֤חַ מָנוֹת֙ אִ֣ישׁ לְרֵעֵ֔הוּ וּמַתָּנ֖וֹת לָאֶבְיֹנִֽים׃ וְקִבֵּל֙ הַיְּהוּדִ֔ים אֵ֥ת
כד אֲשֶׁר־הֵחֵ֖לּוּ לַעֲשׂ֑וֹת וְאֵ֛ת אֲשֶׁר־כָּתַ֥ב מָרְדֳּכַ֖י אֲלֵיהֶֽם׃ כִּי֩ הָמָ֨ן בֶּֽן־הַמְּדָ֜תָא
הָאֲגָגִ֗י צֹרֵר֙ כָּל־הַיְּהוּדִ֔ים חָשַׁ֥ב עַל־הַיְּהוּדִ֖ים לְאַבְּדָ֑ם וְהִפִּ֨ל פּוּר֙ ה֣וּא הַגּוֹרָ֔ל
כה לְהֻמָּ֖ם וּֽלְאַבְּדָֽם׃ וּבְבֹאָהּ֮ לִפְנֵ֣י הַמֶּלֶךְ֒ אָמַ֣ר עִם־הַסֵּ֔פֶר יָשׁ֞וּב מַחֲשַׁבְתּ֧וֹ הָרָעָ֛ה
כו אֲשֶׁר־חָשַׁ֥ב עַל־הַיְּהוּדִ֖ים עַל־רֹאשׁ֑וֹ וְתָל֥וּ אֹת֛וֹ וְאֶת־בָּנָ֖יו עַל־הָעֵֽץ׃ עַל־כֵּ֡ן קָֽרְאוּ֩
לַיָּמִ֨ים הָאֵ֤לֶּה פוּרִים֙ עַל־שֵׁ֣ם הַפּ֔וּר עַל־כֵּ֕ן עַל־כָּל־דִּבְרֵ֖י הָאִגֶּ֣רֶת הַזֹּ֑את וּמָֽה־
כז רָא֣וּ עַל־כָּ֔כָה וּמָ֥ה הִגִּ֖יעַ אֲלֵיהֶֽם׃ קִיְּמ֣וּ וְקִבְּל֣ הַיְּהוּדִים֩ ׀ עֲלֵיהֶ֣ם ׀ וְעַל־זַרְעָ֡ם
וְעַ֨ל כָּל־הַנִּלְוִ֤ים עֲלֵיהֶם֙ וְלֹ֣א יַעֲב֔וֹר לִהְי֣וֹת עֹשִׂ֗ים אֵ֚ת שְׁנֵ֣י הַיָּמִ֣ים הָאֵ֔לֶּה כִּכְתָבָ֖ם
כח וְכִזְמַנָּ֑ם בְּכָל־שָׁנָ֖ה וְשָׁנָֽה׃ וְהַיָּמִ֣ים הָ֠אֵלֶּה נִזְכָּרִ֨ים וְנַעֲשִׂ֜ים בְּכָל־דּ֣וֹר וָד֗וֹר מִשְׁפָּחָה֙
וּמִשְׁפָּחָ֔ה מְדִינָ֥ה וּמְדִינָ֖ה וְעִ֣יר וָעִ֑יר וִימֵ֞י הַפּוּרִ֣ים הָאֵ֗לֶּה לֹ֤א יַֽעַבְרוּ֙ מִתּ֣וֹךְ
כט הַיְּהוּדִ֔ים וְזִכְרָ֖ם לֹא־יָס֥וּף מִזַּרְעָֽם׃ וַ֠תִּכְתֹּב אֶסְתֵּ֨ר הַמַּלְכָּ֧ה בַת־
אֲבִיחַ֛יִל וּמָרְדֳּכַ֥י הַיְּהוּדִ֖י אֶת־כָּל־תֹּ֑קֶף לְקַיֵּ֗ם אֵ֣ת אִגֶּ֧רֶת הַפֻּרִ֛ים הַזֹּ֖את הַשֵּׁנִֽית׃
ל וַיִּשְׁלַ֨ח סְפָרִ֜ים אֶל־כָּל־הַיְּהוּדִ֗ים אֶל־שֶׁ֨בַע וְעֶשְׂרִ֤ים וּמֵאָה֙ מְדִינָ֔ה מַלְכ֖וּת

31 The epistle was sent **to establish these days of Purim on their dates, as Mordekhai the Jew and Queen Esther had established for them, and as they established the matters of the fasts and their lamentations**[D] **for themselves and for their descendants.** Just as all the Jews throughout the kingdom of Ahashverosh had taken part in the communal fast and prayers when the evil decree was issued, it was fitting that the entire people likewise share in the commemoration of the events.
32 **The edict of Esther established these matters of Purim, and it was written in the scroll.** As queen, Esther's affirmation of the holiday by writing and signing the account of these events, i.e., this book, gave great force to the establishment of the holiday.[74]

Scroll of Esther, Fez, Morocco, thirteenth to fourteenth century CE

The Greatness of Ahashverosh and Mordekhai

ESTHER 10:1–3

This short section, which concludes the book of Esther, parallels its opening verses. The book began with a description of the kingdom of Ahashverosh and his lavish feasts; it ends here with a historical record of his reign, conveyed in a formal style.

10 1 **King Ahashverosh imposed a tax on the land, and on the lands of the sea,**[B] as under his rule the kingdom of Persia reached the pinnacle of its greatness and power.
2 **All** the details of **the acts of his,** Ahashverosh's, **authority, and his might, and the episode of the greatness of Mordekhai, that the king promoted him** to the chief minister of the kingdom; **are they not written in the book of the chronicles of the kings of Media and Persia?** These historical matters are not relevant to this book; further descriptions may be found in the chronicles of the kings of Persia and Media. Similar statements directing the reader to the royal chronicles appear elsewhere in the Bible.[75]
3 The book concludes by returning to the matter at hand: **For Mordekhai the Jew** had achieved the high status of a man who **was viceroy to King Ahashverosh, and** as such, he was also **prominent** as a great leader **among the Jews,** and **accepted by most of his brethren.**[D] Mordekhai was **a** constant **seeker of good for his people,** as he tried to help the Jewish population with all the means at his disposal, **and** an unwavering **spokesman of peace for all his descendants.** All his children and grandchildren benefited from his position of greatness.

Alleged tomb of Mordekhai and Esther, Hamadan, western Iran

לא אֲחַשְׁוֵר֖וֹשׁ דִּבְרֵ֥י שָׁל֖וֹם וֶאֱמֶֽת׃ לְקַיֵּ֡ם אֶת־יְמֵי֩ הַפֻּרִ֨ים הָאֵ֜לֶּה בִּזְמַנֵּיהֶ֗ם כַּאֲשֶׁר֩
קִיַּ֨ם עֲלֵיהֶ֜ם מָרְדֳּכַ֣י הַיְּהוּדִי֮ וְאֶסְתֵּ֣ר הַמַּלְכָּה֒ וְכַאֲשֶׁ֛ר קִיְּמ֥וּ עַל־נַפְשָׁ֖ם וְעַל־זַרְעָ֑ם
לב דִּבְרֵ֥י הַצּוֹמ֖וֹת וְזַעֲקָתָֽם׃ וּמַאֲמַ֣ר אֶסְתֵּ֔ר קִיַּ֕ם דִּבְרֵ֥י הַפֻּרִ֖ים הָאֵ֑לֶּה וְנִכְתָּ֖ב
א ב בַּסֵּֽפֶר׃ וַיָּ֩שֶׂם֩ הַמֶּ֨לֶךְ אחשרש ׀ מַ֛ס עַל־הָאָ֖רֶץ וְאִיֵּ֥י הַיָּֽם׃ וְכָל־ אֲחַשְׁוֵר֖וֹשׁ
מַעֲשֵׂ֤ה תָקְפּוֹ֙ וּגְב֣וּרָת֔וֹ וּפָרָשַׁת֙ גְּדֻלַּ֣ת מָרְדֳּכַ֔י אֲשֶׁ֥ר גִּדְּל֖וֹ הַמֶּ֑לֶךְ הֲלוֹא־הֵ֣ם
ג כְּתוּבִ֗ים עַל־סֵ֙פֶר֙ דִּבְרֵ֣י הַיָּמִ֔ים לְמַלְכֵ֖י מָדַ֥י וּפָרָֽס׃ כִּ֣י ׀ מָרְדֳּכַ֣י הַיְּהוּדִ֗י מִשְׁנֶה֙
לַמֶּ֣לֶךְ אֲחַשְׁוֵר֔וֹשׁ וְגָדוֹל֙ לַיְּהוּדִ֔ים וְרָצ֖וּי לְרֹ֣ב אֶחָ֑יו דֹּרֵ֥שׁ טוֹב֙ לְעַמּ֔וֹ וְדֹבֵ֥ר שָׁל֖וֹם
לְכָל־זַרְעֽוֹ׃

DISCUSSION

9:31 | **The matters of the fasts and their lamentations:** Some explain that this is the Fast of Esther, which the Jews accepted upon themselves as a day of prayer and supplication forever (Ra'avad). Many other commentaries disagree, maintaining that the verse is referring to the fast days observed in memory of the destruction of the Temple, which are mentioned in Zechariah 8:19 (see Malbim; Ran, *Ta'anit* 18b).

10:3 | **Accepted by most of his brethren:** The Sages expound that Mordekhai was accepted by most, but not all, of his brethren, as some members of the Sanhedrin parted ways with him, perhaps because he had taken on such a senior position of authority (see Rashi; *Megilla* 16b). Alternatively, there were some who objected to him because the building of Jerusalem and the Temple were not renewed during his tenure. On the other hand, this period of calm may have been a contributing factor that allowed the Jews to later petition the king of Persia and request that the Temple in Jerusalem be rebuilt.

BACKGROUND

10:1 | **The lands of the sea:** At its height, the Persian Empire controlled the Anatolian coast and many of the Greek islands in the Aegean Sea, as well as the island of Cyprus. This was achieved thanks to the powerful Persian navy, which was manned by Phoenician mercenaries.

Notes

The Song of Songs

1. See *Shevuot* 35b; *Shir HaShirim Rabba* 1:11.
2. See, e.g., Isaiah 50:1, 54:4–12; Jeremiah 2:2; Ezekiel 16.
3. See *Soferim* 14.
4. See I Kings 5:12, and commentary ad loc.
5. See Rashi; Ibn Ezra.
6. See Rashbam here and 3:7.
7. See I Samuel 6:19.
8. See Ibn Ezra.
9. See Genesis 29:2–11.
10. See, e.g., Judges 8:21; Ibn Ezra, Esther 6:8, and commentary ad loc.
11. See Ralbag; Radak, I Chronicles 17:20.
12. See Ibn Ezra.
13. See *Shir HaShirim Rabba*.
14. See *Lekaḥ Tov*.
15. See Malbim.
16. See commentary on II Samuel 6:19.
17. See Rashi.
18. See Alsheikh.
19. See Rashi; Onkelos, Genesis 8:22; *Targum*, Jeremiah 36:22.
20. See commentary on Genesis 8:22.
21. See Rav Yeshaya of Trani.
22. See *Metzudat David*; *Metzudat Tzion*.
23. See Joshua 15:19.
24. See Ibn Ezra; Rav Yosef Kara.
25. See Rashbam, Exodus 30:23.
26. See Alsheikh.
27. Jeremiah 2:2.
28. See Ibn Ezra.
29. See Rashi; Rav Yosef Kara; Rav Yeshaya of Trani.
30. See Psalms 22:15; Ruth 1:11.
31. See Rashi.
32. See Daniel 5:10, and the commentaries ad loc.
33. See Leviticus 13:31.
34. See Mishna *Para* 9:3.
35. See Rashi.
36. See Alsheikh.
37. See Ibn Ezra.
38. See Ibn Ezra; Ralbag; I Kings 15:33.
39. See, e.g., Psalms 48:3; Lamentations 2:15; *Kiddushin* 49b.
40. See Rashbam; Ibn Ezra.
41. See Rashi; Rashbam; Rav Yeshaya of Trani.
42. See Rashbam.
43. See Rashi; Alsheikh; *Shir HaShirim Rabba*.
44. See Rav Yeshaya of Trani.
45. See Ramban, Job 8:12.
46. See Ibn Ezra; Rashbam, Exodus 12:13.
47. Rashbam; Ramban, Exodus 25:12.
48. Rav Yeshaya of Trani.
49. See Rashi; Ibn Ezra.
50. See Rashbam.
51. See Rashi.
52. See Rashi; Ibn Ezra.
53. See Rashi; Malbim; *Da'at Mikra*.
54. See Rav Yosef Kara, 1:2.
55. See Rashi; Ibn Ezra.
56. See Ramban, Leviticus 19:20.
57. See Ibn Ezra.
58. See Rashi.
59. See Rashi.

Ruth

1. Psalms 118:22.
2. Rashi; see also Rashi, Ezra 2:2; *Midrash Tanḥuma, Shemini 9*.
3. See Joshua 19:15.
4. See Rashi's second interpretation; commentary on I Samuel 17:12.
5. I Chronicles 4:4.
6. See commentary on Song of Songs 5:4.
7. See *Ruth Rabba 2:15*.
8. Rashi; Ibn Ezra.
9. See Rashi; *Ruth Rabba 3:6*.
10. Ibn Ezra.
11. Rashi.
12. Rashi.
13. Rashi; Ibn Ezra.
14. See Rashi.
15. Rav Yosef Kara.
16. See Ibn Ezra; Gra; Malbim.
17. See Malbim.
18. See II Samuel 16:4.
19. See Rashi; Ibn Ezra.
20. See Rav Yosef Kara; Ralbag; Malbim.
21. See Rashi; Rashbam, Exodus 3:5.
22. See Gra; Malbim.
23. See Ibn Ezra.
24. See Leviticus 25:25; *Kiddushin 21a*.
25. See Rambam, *Hilkhot Shemitta 11:18; Rashi and* Rav Yeshaya of Trani on 3:9.
26. Exodus 34:22.
27. *Ruth Rabba 5:11*.
28. See *Ketubot 7a*.
29. See Ibn Ezra; Malbim.
30. See Alshekh; Malbim.
31. See Ibn Ezra; Ralbag.
32. Rashi.
33. See Rashi.
34. See Malbim; *Ruth Rabba 6:2*.
35. See Alshekh.
36. See Proverbs 12:4; 31:10.
37. See *Kiddushin 21a*.
38. Ibn Ezra; *Bekhor Shor*.
39. *Ruth Rabba 6:4*.
40. See Rashi; Ralbag; Malbim; *Ruth Rabba 6:4*.
41. See Rashi.
42. See *Pesikta Zutreta;* Rav Yeshaya of Trani; Malbim.
43. See *Pesikta Zutreta; Malbim*.
44. See Malbim.
45. Rashi; Rabbi Yosef Caspi; see commentary on Ruth 3:13.
46. See Malbim; Ramban, Leviticus 25:33.
47. See *Targum; Rav Yeshaya of Trani, 3:9; Ramban, Genesis 38:9*.
48. Rashi.
49. See Ibn Ezra; Rav Yeshaya of Trani.
50. See Rashi; Ibn Ezra; *Bava Metzia 47a*.
51. See Deuteronomy 25:5–6.
52. See Rashi; *Bekhor Shor; Ralbag on I Chronicles 10:13; Deuteronomy 25:6, and Ramban ad loc.*
53. Rav Yosef Kara; see Alshekh.
54. See Rashi.
55. See Alshekh.
56. See *Sanhedrin 19b*.
57. See Numbers 1:7.

Lamentations

1. *Bava Batra* 15a.
2. See *Moed Katan* 26a; *Menaḥot* 30a and Rashi ad loc.; Abravanel, Jeremiah 36:4; *Da'at Mikra* on Daniel, summary to chapter 1.
3. II Chronicles 35:25.
4. See Rashi, Lamentations 1:1; *Moed Katan* 26a; *Eikha Rabba* 1:53; Abravanel, Jeremiah 36:2; commentary on 4:20.
5. Ibn Ezra.
6. See Rashi.
7. See Rashi; Ibn Ezra.
8. See Rashi.
9. Rashi.
10. See *Targum Yonatan*; Rashi.
11. *Targum Yonatan*.
12. Rashi.
13. Deuteronomy 23:4.
14. *Targum Yonatan*; Rashi; *Yevamot* 16b.
15. *Targum Yonatan*.
16. *Pesikta Zutreta*; Rav Yosef Kara.
17. *Targum Yonatan*; Ibn Ezra.
18. Rashi.
19. Rashi; Ibn Ezra.
20. See *Targum Yonatan*; Leviticus 20:18.
21. See Rashi.
22. Rashi; Ibn Ezra.
23. See Ibn Ezra.
24. Rashi.
25. Bekhor Shor.
26. Rashi.
27. See *Targum Yonatan*; Rashi.
28. See Ibn Ezra, Job 16:16.
29. Rashi; Ibn Ezra.
30. *Targum Yonatan*; Rashi; see Psalms 132:7; I Chronicles 28:2; commentary on Exodus 24:9.
31. *Targum Yonatan*; Rashi.
32. *Targum Yonatan*; Rashi.
33. See Rashi.
34. *Targum Yonatan*.
35. Rashi; see Rav Yosef Kara, Ezekiel 22:26.
36. Rashi.
37. See Psalms 42:5.
38. *Targum Yonatan*.
39. See Ibn Ezra, Job 16:16.
40. See Rashi; *Pesikta Zutreta*.
41. Ibn Ezra.
42. See *Pesikta Zutreta*.
43. *Targum Yonatan*.
44. *Pesikta Zutreta*.
45. See Rashi.
46. Rashi.
47. Bekhor Shor.
48. See Rashi.
49. *Targum Yonatan*; Rashi.
50. Rashi.
51. Rav Yosef Caspi.
52. Rashi.
53. *Targum Yonatan*.
54. See *Targum Yonatan*; Rashi.
55. Alsheikh.
56. See *Pesikta Zutreta*; Rashi.
57. See Rashi; Ibn Ezra.
58. See *Pesikta Zutreta*.
59. *Pesikta Zutreta*.
60. *Targum Yonatan*; Rashi.
61. See Ibn Ezra.
62. See *Targum Yonatan*; Ibn Ezra.
63. *Targum Yonatan*.
64. See *Pesikta Zutreta*; Rashi.
65. Rashi.
66. *Pesikta Zutreta*.
67. See Rashi.
68. See *Pesikta Zutreta*.
69. See Rashi.
70. See *Eikha Rabba* 3:13.
71. See Rashi.
72. Rashi.
73. *Targum Yonatan*; Rashi.
74. *Targum Yonatan*.
75. Rashi.
76. Rashi.
77. Ibn Ezra.
78. *Targum Yonatan*.
79. Alsheikh.
80. Ibn Ezra; Rav Yosef Caspi.
81. See Rashi.
82. Rashi.
83. See Ibn Ezra.
84. Ibn Ezra.
85. See *Pesikta Zutreta*.
86. Alsheikh.
87. Rashi.
88. Ibn Ezra.
89. *Targum Yonatan*; Rashi.
90. *Targum Yonatan*; Rashi.
91. Rashi; Rav Yeshaya of Trani.
92. Rashi.
93. Rav Yosef Kara; Bekhor Shor.
94. *Pesikta Zutreta*; Rashi.
95. See Rashi.
96. Rashi.
97. See *Targum Yonatan*; *Pesikta Zutreta*.
98. Rashi.
99. See *Pesikta Zutreta*; Rashi.
100. Ibn Ezra.
101. Rashi.
102. Rashi.
103. See Rashi; *Pesikta Zutreta*; Rav Yosef Caspi.
104. *Targum Yonatan*; Rashi.
105. See Rashi; *Pesikta Zutreta*.
106. See Rashi.
107. Rashi.
108. See *Pesikta Zutreta*.
109. Alsheikh.
110. See commentary on 1:1.
111. See Isaiah 55:1.
112. See Ezekiel 17:18.
113. See *Targum Yonatan*; Rashi.
114. *Targum Yonatan*; Rashi.
115. Rashi.
116. See *Pesikta Zutreta*.
117. Rashi.
118. See *Pesikta Zutreta*.
119. See *Targum Yonatan*; Bekhor Shor.

Ecclesiastes

1. See Mishna *Yadayim* 3:5; *Vayikra Rabba* 28:1; *Kohelet Rabba* 1:4.
2. See *Shir HaShirim Rabba* 1:10; *Ramban's Sermon on Ecclesiastes*.
3. Rashi; *Kohelet Rabba* 1:1.
4. See Rashi; *Kohelet Rabba* 1:2.
5. See Alsheikh.
6. See Rashi.
7. See *Targum*; Rashi; *Bava Batra* 25b.
8. Ibn Ezra.
9. See Ibn Ezra.
10. See Rashbam here and Deuteronomy 20:5.
11. See Ibn Ezra.
12. See Ibn Ezra.
13. See Ibn Ezra.
14. Rashi.
15. See Ibn Ezra.
16. Rashi.
17. See Rashi; Mishna *Kelim* 18:1.
18. See *Pesikta Zutreta*.
19. See Rashi; Ibn Ezra.
20. Ibn Ezra.
21. See Ibn Ezra.
22. Rashi; Ibn Ezra.
23. Ibn Ezra.
24. See Ibn Ezra; *Pesikta Zutreta*.
25. Ibn Ezra.
26. Rashi.
27. See Rashi; Ibn Ezra.
28. See Rashi.
29. See Rashi; Ibn Ezra.
30. See Rashi.
31. See Alsheikh.
32. See Ibn Ezra.
33. See *Pesikta Zutreta*.
34. See Ibn Ezra.
35. See Rashi.
36. Rashi.
37. See Ibn Ezra.
38. See Ibn Ezra.
39. See Rambam, *Guide of the Perplexed* 1:59, 3:52.
40. Ibn Ezra.
41. See *Pesikta Zutreta*.
42. Rashi.
43. Ibn Ezra.
44. See Ibn Ezra.
45. Ibn Ezra.
46. See Ibn Ezra.
47. See Ibn Ezra.
48. See Rashi.
49. See Ibn Ezra.
50. Ibn Ezra.
51. See Rashi.
52. See *Pesikta Zutreta*; Rashi.
53. See Ibn Ezra.
54. See Rashi.
55. See Ibn Ezra.
56. See Ibn Ezra.
57. See Ibn Ezra.
58. *Pesikta Zutreta*; Rashi.
59. See Ibn Ezra.
60. See *Pesikta Zutreta*.
61. Rashi; see Ibn Ezra.
62. Ibn Ezra.
63. Rashi; Ibn Ezra.
64. Rav Yeshaya of Trani.
65. See Ibn Ezra.
66. See Rashi.
67. Rashi.
68. See Ibn Ezra; Ralbag.
69. See Rashi; Rashbam.
70. See Rav Yosef Kara.
71. Ibn Ezra.
72. Ibn Ezra.
73. See Rashbam.
74. See Ibn Ezra; Rashbam; Rav Yeshaya of Trani.
75. Rashbam; Rav Yosef Kara.
76. See Ibn Ezra.
77. See Rashi; Ibn Ezra; Rav Yeshaya of Trani.
78. See *Pesikta Zutreta*; Ibn Ezra; Rambam, *Guide of the Perplexed* 1:32.
79. See Ibn Ezra; Rav Yeshaya of Trani; Ralbag.
80. Rashi; Rav Yosef Kara.
81. See Ibn Ezra.
82. See Rambam, *Sefer HaMadda*, *Hilkhot Deot* 1:1; Rambam's introduction to *Avot* 4.
83. See Rashi; Ibn Ezra.
84. See Ibn Ezra here and Daniel 1:20.
85. Ibn Ezra.
86. See Ibn Ezra.
87. Ibn Ezra.
88. See Alsheikh.
89. See Rashi; Ibn Ezra.
90. Rashi.
91. See Ibn Ezra.
92. Ibn Ezra.
93. See Ibn Ezra.
94. Ibn Ezra; I Kings 11:3.
95. See Alsheikh.
96. Ibn Ezra.
97. See Ibn Ezra.
98. See Ibn Ezra.
99. See Rashi.
100. Ibn Ezra.
101. See Rashi.
102. Rashi.
103. Rashi.
104. See, e.g., Job 34:29.
105. See Ibn Ezra; Rashbam.
106. *Kohelet Rabba* 8:9.
107. See Rashi.
108. Rashi; Ibn Ezra.
109. Ibn Ezra.
110. See Rashi.
111. Ibn Ezra.
112. See Rashi.
113. Ibn Ezra; Ralbag; see Job 34:25.
114. See Ibn Ezra; *Pesikta Zutreta*.
115. Ibn Ezra.
116. See *Pesikta Zutreta*.
117. Ibn Ezra.
118. Rav Yosef Kara.
119. Ibn Ezra.
120. See Ibn Ezra; Deuteronomy 8:9.
121. Ibn Ezra.
122. See Rashi; Rashbam; *Emunot VeDeot* 5:3.
123. Rashi.
124. See Ibn Ezra.
125. Rashbam; see Rashi.
126. Rashi; Ibn Ezra.
127. See *Pesikta Zutreta*.
128. See Rashi.
129. See Rashi.
130. Ibn Ezra.
131. Rashi.
132. See Ibn Ezra.
133. Rashbam.
134. See *Pesikta Zutreta*; Ibn Ezra.
135. See Ibn Ezra.
136. *Avot* 3:13.
137. See *Pesikta Zutreta*; Rashi.
138. See, e.g., I Kings 21:8.
139. See Ibn Ezra.
140. Rashi.
141. See Rambam, *Guide of the Perplexed* 2:47.
142. See Rashi.
143. See Ibn Ezra.
144. See Rashi.
145. Rashi.
146. Ibn Ezra.
147. See Rashi; Ibn Ezra.
148. See Ibn Ezra; *Pesikta Zutreta*; *Kohelet Rabba* 12:1.
149. See Ibn Ezra.
150. See *Shabbat* 152a.
151. Rashi.
152. Rashi.
153. *Pesikta Rabbati*; see Rav Yeshaya of Trani.
154. Rashi; *Shabbat* 152a.
155. Ibn Ezra.
156. *Shabbat* 152a.
157. See *Shabbat* 152a.
158. Ibn Ezra; *Pesikta Rabbati*.
159. *Shabbat* 152a.
160. See *Shabbat* 152a.
161. See *Shabbat* 152a.
162. *Shabbat* 152a.
163. See Rashi.
164. *Shabbat* 151b.
165. *Pesikta Rabbati*.
166. See Ibn Ezra.
167. *Targum Kohelet*.
168. See Isaiah 41:7; Jeremiah 10:4.
169. See *Pesikta Zutreta*.
170. Ibn Ezra.
171. See Rashi.
172. Rashi.

Esther

1. *Megilla* 20a.
2. 9:26,29. There seem to have been two epistles out of which the book was assembled.
3. See *Megilla* 7a.
4. See Ibn Ezra's introduction to the book of Esther and his commentary on 5:13, citing Rav Se'adya Gaon.
5. *Seder Olam Rabba*.
6. See Daniel 8:2.
7. Ibn Ezra; Rav Yeshaya of Trani; Vilna Gaon.
8. See, e.g., Rashi; Rashbam; Ibn Ezra.
9. See Ibn Ezra, second commentary.
10. See *Megilla* 12a.
11. Rashi.
12. Based on Rashbam; Bekhor Shor; Ralbag; see also Daniel 5:10.
13. See Ralbag.
14. See *Megilla* 12b.
15. See Ibn Ezra, second commentary; Rav Yosef Kara; Rav Yeshaya of Trani; Ralbag.
16. *Esther Rabba* 1:15; Rashi.
17. Ibn Ezra.
18. See Nehemiah 13:23–24.
19. See, e.g., Rashi.
20. See Rashbam; Ibn Ezra; Rav Yosef Kara; Rav Yeshaya of Trani.
21. Rav Yosef Naḥmias.
22. See *Megilla* 15a; *Targum*; Ibn Ezra.
23. See Malbim.
24. *Targum*; *Megilla* 13a; see Ramban, Exodus 30:23.
25. See Ibn Ezra; Rashbam; Ibn Ezra, second commentary.
26. See, e.g., Rashbam.
27. See discussion on verse 5.
28. See *Megilla* 13a.
29. Ibn Ezra, second commentary; Malbim; see Ruth 4:1; Daniel 2:49.
30. *Megilla* 13a; see *Menaḥot* 65a.
31. See II Kings 25:28; Daniel 5:29.
32. See Rav Yosef Caspi; *Megillat Setarim*.
33. Rav Yosef Kara, verse 5.
34. See the Aramaic translations of the Bible; *Sanhedrin* 61b; *Megilla* 13a.
35. Ibn Ezra.
36. See Ibn Ezra; Ralbag. See also Ezekiel 21:26–27; commentary on Isaiah 36:10.
37. See *Megilla* 13b.
38. See Rashi.
39. Rashbam and Ralbag, 4:8; Ibn Ezra, second commentary, 8:13.
40. See Rashi; Ibn Ezra; Ibn Ezra, 1:2.
41. *Targum*.
42. See Malbim.
43. See Nehemiah 2:4.
44. Ibn Ezra.
45. *Targum*; Ralbag.
46. See Rashi; Ibn Ezra.
47. Ibn Ezra.
48. See Malbim.
49. See Rashi.
50. See *Megilla* 15b.
51. See Rashbam; Rav Yosef Kara.
52. See Malbim.
53. See *Targum*; *Megilla* 16a.
54. See Ibn Ezra; Rav Yosef Kara.
55. Ibn Ezra.
56. See 1:6; Ezekiel 23:41, and Radak ad loc.
57. See *Targum*.
58. See also 3:12.
59. Ibn Ezra.
60. Ibn Ezra.
61. See Ibn Ezra; Rav Yeshaya of Trani.
62. See Ezra 4:6.
63. See Rav Yosef Kara; Esther 8:11.
64. See Ralbag.
65. Rashi; Rashbam.
66. Rambam, *Megilla* 2a, Ibn Ezra.
67. See *Targum*.
68. Malbim.
69. *Targum*; Rashi; Rashbam; Ibn Ezra; see *Megilla* 16b.
70. See Ibn Ezra, 8:8.
71. Rashi.
72. See Rashi.
73. See Ibn Ezra, second commentary.
74. *Targum*; Rashi; Malbim.
75. I Kings 14:29, 15:23; II Kings 14:15; II Chronicles 25:26.

Credits

All images are copyright © Koren Publishers Jerusalem Ltd., except:

THE SONG OF SONGS

p4 © Etan J. Tal; **p6** left image © Myrabella / Wikimedia Commons / CC BY-SA 3.0; **p6** right image © Ippolito Rosellini, Bodleian Libraries, Oxford University; **p7** left and right images © public domain; **p8** lavender image © Veronique Pagnier; **p8** pendant image © public domain; **p8** myrrh image © Vladimir Melnik https://www.shutterstock.com; **p8** henna image © Tu7uh; **p8** date flower image © Корниенко Виктор; **p8** daffodil image © Zeynel Cebeci; **p8** lily image © Habib M'henni / Wikimedia Commons; **p8** apple tree image © public domain; **p10** upper left image © Ettore Balocchi; **p10** upper right image © Umberto Nicoletti; **p10** lower image © public domain; **p12** nightingale image © Frebeck; **p12** turtledove image © Paco Gómez; **p12** fig tress image © Steve Slater; **p12** dove image © public domain; **p12** jackal image © Shubhamjaincan; **p12** fox image © I, Malene; **p12** mountain image © Bukvoed; **p14** frankincense image © Peter Presslein, modified by Meco; **p14** altar © HaRav Menachem Makover, courtesy of Harenu Bevinyano; **p14** crown image © I, Sailko; **p16** dove image © public domain; **p16** goats image © public domain; **p16** pomegranate image © Noa Fisher Pikiwiki Israel; **p16** pendant image © Fabien Dany - www.fabiendany.com / www.datka.kg; **p16** fawn image © public domain; **p18** hermon image © mykaul; **p18** lebanon image © rabiem22; **p18** sealed spring image © Deror Avi; **p18** pomegranate image © public domain; **p18** saffron image © Serpico; **p18** cinnamon image © Simon A. Eugster; **p18** frankincense tree image © Mauro Raffaelli; **p18** aloe tree © public domain; **p20** upper left image © Luc Viatour / Lucnix.be; **p20** lower left image © public domain; **p20** right image © Waugsberg; **p22** dove image © public domain; **p22** aquamarine image © Kopytin Georgy https://www.shutterstock.com; **p22** ivory image © Dominik Matus; **p22** peridot image © Erik Lernestål; **p22** sapphire image © thisisbossi; **p22** field-bed image © Laslovarga; **p23** © Tamara from Hebrew Wikipedia, modified; **p24** dawn image © public domain; **p24** fruits image © Victor Korniyenko; **p24** dates image © משה רענן; **p24** pomegranate image © public domain; **p24** necklace image © public domain; **p24** pile image © Dûrzan cîrano; **p26** carmel image © ד"ר אבישי טייכר; **p26** headdress image © I, Sailko; **p26** date palms trees image © public domain; **p26** date palm branches © Shijan Kaakkara; **p26** clusters image © Roberto Vertzo; **p26** grape bud image © Stojanoski Slave; **p26** mandrakes image © tato grasso; **p28** left image © Christopher, Tania and Isabelle Luna; **p28** upper right image © Museo nazionale di Ravenna; **p28** lower right image © Ovedc; **p28** © Tomascastelazo

RUTH

p36 lower left image © DavidB; **p40** upper image © Yann Forget / Wikimedia Commons / CC-BY-SA-3.0; **p40** lower right image © weegiboy; **p41** © Xtuv Photography https://www.shutterstock.com; **p42** upper right image © Yohanan Ben Yaakov; **p42** lower right image © Yohanan Ben Yaakov; **p44** upper left image © Tarish Khan; **p44** upper center image © Mark Robinson; **p44** upper right image © public domain - congerdesign; **p44** lower left image © Yohanan Ben Yaakov; **p45** © A. Davey from Where I Live Now: Pacific Northwest; **p48** © public domain - Daderot; **p50** © Neil Ward

LAMENTATIONS

p56 left image © Osama Shukir Muhammed Amin FRCP(Glasg); **p56** © Matt Neale from UK; **p58** left image © Steerpike; **p58** upper right image © Luke; **p58** lower right image © Mike Peel (www.mikepeel.net); **p60** upper image © public domain; **p60** lower left image © Carole Raddato from Frankfurt, Germany; **p60** lower right image © public domain; **p64** upper left image © Mick Talbot from Lincoln (U.K.), England; **p64** center left image © Portable Antiquities Scheme; **p64** lower left image © public domain; **p64** right image © Matt Lavin from Bozeman, Montana, USA; **p66** right image © public domain; **p68** left jackal image © Alastair Rae; **p68** left whale image © Gabriel Barathieu; **p68** lower left ostrich image © Peter Dowley from Dubai, United Arab Emirates; **p68** right sapphire image © Sapphiredge; **p68** right gem image © Mauro Cateb; **p70** left image © public domain, colorized; **p72** © kevincellis36109

ECCLESIASTES

p78 left image © public domain; **p78** center image © public domain; **p78** right image © Steve (Sids1); **p80** upper image © Shuhrataxmedov; **p80** middle image © Leonard Bentley; **p80** lower image © public domain; **p84** left image © Pacific Southwest Region 5; **p84** right image © Armando Frazao https://www.shutterstock.com; **p88** © Quinn Dombrowski; **p90** © Hanay; **p94** left image © Ann W; **p94** lower right image © Zeynel Cebeci; **p98** © CaptMondo; **p102** left seige image © public domain; **p102** upper left fish image © Conor Ashleigh, AusAID; **p102** upper right bird image © public domain; **p102** center right chariot image © public domain; **p102** lower right fly image © Sanjay Acharya; **p104** © Sarashany1234; **p106** left cloud image © public domain; **p106** left tree image © Daniel Gonzalez; **p106** right sowing image © Center for Bayanihan Economics; **p106** right pioneer image © public domain; **p108** upper image © Darren Wickham; **p108** lower image © Clara Amit, Yoram Lehmann, Yael Yolovitch, Miki Koren, and Mariana Salzberger, courtesy of the Israel Antiquities Authority

ESTHER

p118 Xerxes image © Jona Lendering, site: www.livius.org; **p118** King of Persia image © alisamii; **p118** Persian soldier image © peteropaliu; **p120** lower left image © Hansueli Krapf; **p120** right image © Siren-Com; **p124** © Philippe Chavin; **p126** right image © public domain; **p128** © Elnaz Sarbar; **p132** left image © Fabien Dany - www.fabiendany.com / www.datka.kg; **p132** right image © public domain; **p136** © public domain; **p140** left image © George Dickie; **p140** right image © public domain; **p146** © Benjamín Núñez González; **p148** © درفش کاویانی; **p152** upper image © Deror avi; **p152** © Philippe Chavin (Simorg)

KOREN

Steinsaltz Center